AF801721

Trends and Challenges of Electronic Finance

"This edited book is an intuitive guide full of discussions on recent technological advancements and their impact on emerging markets. The editors of this book have ensured a comprehensive coverage of the latest developments in the field of electronic finance. The chapters contribute to the argument that digital finance transforms lives and economic prospects at the individual and country levels, thus boosting the GDP and ensuring financial inclusivity in emerging markets. I strongly recommend this book for a comprehensive discussion on the effect of electronic finance, FinTech, and alternative investments."

—Dr. Sowmya Vivek, *Director, Institutional Effectiveness and Quality Assurance, EM Normandie Business School—Dubai Campus, Dubai Knowledge Park, Dubai, UAE*

Ananda S. · Tamanna Dalwai ·
Dharmendra Singh
Editors

Trends and Challenges of Electronic Finance

Perspectives from Emerging Markets

palgrave
macmillan

Editors
Ananda S.
College of Banking and Financial Studies
Muscat, Oman

Tamanna Dalwai
Nottingham Business School
Nottingham Trent University
Nottingham, UK

Dharmendra Singh
Faculty of Business and Economics
Modern College of Business and Science
Muscat, Oman

ISBN 978-981-96-3303-6 ISBN 978-981-96-3304-3 (eBook)
https://doi.org/10.1007/978-981-96-3304-3

© The Editor(s) (if applicable) and The Author(s), under exclusive licence to Springer Nature Singapore Pte. Ltd 2025

This work is subject to copyright. All rights are solely and exclusively licensed by the Publisher, whether the whole or part of the material is concerned, specifically the rights of translation, reprinting, reuse of illustrations, recitation, broadcasting, reproduction on microfilms or in any other physical way, and transmission or information storage and retrieval, electronic adaptation, computer software, or by similar or dissimilar methodology now known or hereafter developed.
The use of general descriptive names, registered names, trademarks, service marks, etc. in this publication does not imply, even in the absence of a specific statement, that such names are exempt from the relevant protective laws and regulations and therefore free for general use.
The publisher, the authors and the editors are safe to assume that the advice and information in this book are believed to be true and accurate at the date of publication. Neither the publisher nor the authors or the editors give a warranty, expressed or implied, with respect to the material contained herein or for any errors or omissions that may have been made. The publisher remains neutral with regard to jurisdictional claims in published maps and institutional affiliations.

This Palgrave Macmillan imprint is published by the registered company Springer Nature Singapore Pte Ltd.
The registered company address is: 152 Beach Road, #21-01/04 Gateway East, Singapore 189721, Singapore

If disposing of this product, please recycle the paper.

Foreword

It is an honor to write the foreword for "Trends and challenges of electronic finance: Perspectives from emerging markets", a book that makes a significant contribution to the field of electronic finance by providing insightful perspectives on its latest developments. Having spent time in FPSB India office, I have witnessed firsthand the rapidly evolving landscape of finance, where technological advancements continually reshape the ways we understand and engage with financial systems and therefore the financial planning.

The importance of financial inclusivity has never been more apparent, as governments and development agencies such as the World Bank and International Monetary Fund strive to overcome the barriers of racial, religious, and geographic limitations to socioeconomic progress. Financial inclusion, sustainability, and stability are critical goals for all nations, and the development and adoption of financial technologies have become essential in achieving these objectives. Research has consistently shown that digital financial transformation supports the attainment of multiple Sustainable Development Goals (SDGs), underscoring the need to develop regional ecosystems that foster digital innovations to address both national and international challenges.

"Trends and challenges of electronic finance: Perspectives from emerging markets" is thoughtfully organized into three main sub-themes: electronic finance and sustainability, fintech and, alternative finance, which encompass emerging areas like cryptocurrency, blockchain, and artificial intelligence. The chapters delve deeply into the drivers of e-finance, such as technology, globalization, regulation, entrepreneurship, capital, competition, and the recent impacts of the pandemic. They articulate the numerous advantages of e-finance, including enhanced user and service experiences, reduced financial transaction costs, increased alternative investments, minimized information asymmetry, and overall growth in the real economy.

I extend my heartfelt appreciation to the editors for charting an innovative course to support the progress of modern financial systems. I also commend the diverse contributions from the authors, whose expertise in various technological advancements and alternative finance mechanisms make this book an essential read for anyone interested in the future of finance.

I am confident that this book will captivate regulators, decision-makers, academics, researchers, and students, providing them with a comprehensive understanding of the growth and challenges in the digitization of finance. I wish "Trends and challenges of electronic finance: Perspectives from emerging markets" great success and look forward to future editions that continue to explore and illuminate the evolving advancements in finance.

Krishan Mishra
Chief Executive Officer
FPSB Institute India Pvt Ltd
kmishra@fpsb.in

Preface

Economic development has always been the priority of all countries but the side effects of the increase in GDP activities are an increase in carbon emissions and environmental pollution. The financial sector including the banking sector can contribute to the sustainable growth of the economy by adopting paperless banking methods. The emerging payment methods like mobile payment apps and e-banking have been helpful in this direction, as e-bank statements, green pins, and all sorts of other e-payments have helped in minimizing the use of paper which was used in printing currency notes and other bank documents. The other aspects of sustainability are improving quality of life and financial inclusivity. Financial technologies like blockchain, payment apps, mobile banking, and crowdfunding have been highly useful in improving the level of financial inclusion and quality of life in general. The economy can have sustainable growth if the maximum number of individuals participate in economic activities, and various e-finance channels are supporting this sustainability drive. With this background the critical role of e-finance in the overall sustainable development of the economy is evident. The usage and availability of e-finance lead to instant and hassle-free payments, better individual participation in crowdfunding campaigns, and more financing options. Overall, the development and usage of e-finance channels ensure the quality of life, financial inclusion, and sustainability of the economy. Hence, there is a strong need for useful literature for the stakeholders on e-finance in framing policies, guidelines, strategic planning, and designing initiatives and activities to set future directions. This book seeks to bring global experiences and findings of the researchers in the form of chapters for providing useful insights on e-finance to minimize the hurdles in the path of awareness, adoption, and usage.

The book aims to explore the various strategic issues and ideas about e-finance through the lens of theoretical, practical, and empirical research. This book focuses on key developments in e-finance, as well as its contributions to the sustainable economic development of emerging economies. The book consists of fourteen informative scientific papers and essays under three sub-themes. These papers were selected after a double-blind peer review process. The chapters are authored by thirty-two researchers and practitioners across the globe. In this book, we have tried to capture a comprehensive picture of the various e-finance channels, their adoption, issues, and challenges in emerging markets. The book is representing the scenario of e-finance from various parts of the world; MENA and GCC region, USA, Serbia, and India. The key areas captured in the book are the challenges related to the adoption and usage of financial technologies, the impact of financial technologies on the various sectors of the economy, and the role of artificial intelligence and blockchain in different industries especially the banking and insurance sector. We hope the book fills the gap in the academic and policy literature on e-finance by sharing the original ideas covering the theoretical and empirical issues related to this domain in emerging economies.

We recognize the sincere efforts and time devoted by the authors in sharing their invaluable thoughts by way of chapters in this edited book. We express our deepest sense of gratitude to all the authors for their efforts in transferring their knowledge through this book. We are thankful to all the reviewers for their constructive feedback in bringing improvement to the overall quality of this book. We also thank Ms. Geetha Chockalingam and Aparajita Singh, Associate Editor of Palgrave Macmillan for their continuous support and guidance in publishing this book. We certainly hope that the insightful ideas of this book will receive widespread acceptance in the community.

Ananda S.
Director, Postgraduate Studies
Research & Innovation Department
College of Banking and Financial Studies
Sultanate of Oman

Tamanna Dalwai
Senior Lecturer (Assistant Professor)
Nottingham Trent University, UK

Dharmendra Singh
Associate Professor
Modern College of Business and Science
Sultanate of Oman

Contents

Editors and Contributors

About the Editors

Dr. Ananda S. is the Director of the Postgraduate Studies, Research, and Innovation Department at the College of Banking and Financial Studies, Muscat, Sultanate of Oman. He has a Ph.D. in Finance, with over thirty years of expertise in management education, consulting, and the financial services industry. He has also been a visiting professor at leading B-schools in Dubai, Germany, and India. He has published around 55 articles in peer-reviewed journals indexed by Scopus, Web of Sciences and ABDC ranking list, and presented 45 research papers in national and international conferences. Recently, the Institute of Chartered Accountants of India (ICAI) has selected his research paper for "ICAI International Research Awards 2020" as Second-Best Research Paper under the Economics category. He has written books on Mutual Funds, Mergers & Acquisitions and Financial System & Commercial Banking. He has also edited five books on Banking, Financial Sector, Economic Diversification, Fourth Industrial Revolution and Financial Inclusion. He is an associate editor in Sage Publication international journal titled 'Business Perspective and Research'. He is also Guest Editor, member of the Editorial Board, and Reviewer for refereed International Research Journals. He has been a member of the subject expert committee to review the master and undergraduate curriculum in universities in India and Oman. He has also conducted training courses for leading corporates in India and Oman and delivered keynote address in various international conferences, seminars and forums.

Dr. Tamanna Dalwai is a Senior Lecturer (Assistant Professor) at the Nottingham Business School of Nottingham Trent University, UK. She has been working in the higher education sector for more than 15 years. From 2008 to 2023, she was employed with Muscat College and served a spectrum of roles that included the position of Deputy Director of Quality Assurance, supporting the institution for the development and continuance of quality management. She has a PhD in accounting from Universiti Teknologi Malaysia, MBA (finance and accounting) from California State University, East Bay and is a Fellow of Advance HE UK. On completion of her PhD, she was awarded the Best Student Award for International Business School UTM. Dr. Tamanna has conducted several seminars and workshops for national and international higher education institutions. She is an external reviewer for Ministry of Higher Education, Research and Innovation (MoHERI) externally funded research grants and ad-hoc reviewer for various Scopus-indexed journals. She has been awarded four MoHERI externally funded research grants until 2025. She is an avid researcher in the fields of intellectual capital, bank stability, capital structure, accounting education, corporate governance, corporate social responsibility, financial theories, international accounting standards, cost of capital, quality assurance and Islamic Finance. Her edited book titled, "Handbook of banking and finance in MENA region" was published by World Scientific Publishing in 2024. She has 40 Scopus indexed journal articles and chapters until June 2025.

Dr. Dharmendra Singh is an Associate Professor (Finance) at Modern College of Business and Science, Muscat (Oman). He possesses rich professional experience of over 24 years in the field of finance. He holds a Ph.D. (Finance), professional certifications like Certified Financial Planner (CFP), an associate diploma (life insurance) from the Insurance Institute of India, and a CFA from ICFAI. He has published several articles & research papers in ABDC, CABS, and Scopus Q1-ranked international and refereed journals. He has authored and published five edited books on contemporary subjects in finance with renowned publishers and these publications have been included in the Scopus index. His research areas include banking, corporate finance, entrepreneurial finance, and financial markets. He has conducted training programs in collaboration with CMA,

Oman, as well as in multiple universities as well as outside Oman. He also serves as a reviewer for high rank journals. He is a member of the Financial Planning Standard Board (FPSB), the Indian Econometric Society, and the Insurance Institute of India.

Contributors

Dr. Liaqat Ali is a Senior Assistant Professor at School of Management Studies, Punjabi University, Patiala (Punjab), India. With more than 15 years of teaching experience, Dr. Ali has published his research articles in reputed international journals and conferences in the areas namely financial inclusion, accounting, banking, sustainable marketing, digitalization, and sustainability. He is actively reviewing for several high-quality journals. His teaching interests include finance and accounting, cost accounting, management control systems, international financial management, and related courses.

Dr. Seraj Bahrawe is Assistant Professor of Accounting at Albaha University, Saudi Arabia. Having taught and done research for more than 10 years, Dr. Behrawe has grown personally as a dedicated academician in the field of financial accounting. Reflecting his strong commitment to advancing knowledge in these disciplines, his expertise spans relevant financial topics and International Financial Reporting Standards (IFRs). Dr. Behrawe has enhanced the academic community and underlined his status as a thought leader in his field by writing in reputable indexed publications. His efforts not only improve the intellectual debate but also direct accounting profession best practices.

Dr. Souvik Banerjee is an Assistant Professor of Finance at Management Development Institute (MDI) Murshidabad. His research interests include Corporate Finance, Corporate Governance, Behavioral Finance, and Financial Economics. His work has been published in Scopus-indexed and ABDC-listed journals. At present, he is the Editor of the MDIM Journal of Management Review and Practice (Sage). He has developed several business cases for MBA and executive education. He has trained executives from Fortune 500 companies in Corporate Finance and Corporate Valuation.

Dr. Arindam Banerjee is an Associate Professor of Finance and Assistant Dean for the full-time MBA programs at SP Jain School of Global

Management's Dubai Campus. He also serves as a strategic advisory board member at Department of Finance, College of Business Administration at Ajman University and member Board of Governors, Delhi Private School, Dubai and Sharjah. Dr. Banerjee have travelled across the globe and lectured in more than twenty countries across Asia, Africa and Australia. In India, he has been a guest faculty at various leading institutions. As an academic, he has edited/authored more than a dozen books in Finance. In 2019, Dr. Banerjee was recognized among the top 100 leaders in education by the Global Forum for Education and Leadership, US for his continuous research contributions in higher education. In 2021, Dr. Banerjee was awarded SP Jain's professor of the year for the period 2020–2021 amongst all professors from its five global campuses that included Dubai, Singapore, Australia and India.

Dr. Savitha Basri, MA (Economics), MBA, HGDip (UK), MPhil, PhD PGDHE is a Professor at Department of Commerce, Manipal Academy of Higher Education, Manipal, India and Coordinator, Centre for Advanced Research in Financial Inclusion, Manipal. The centre has carried out various research projects on financial inclusion and FinTech. She has published more than 30 research articles in national and international journals and several research papers as book chapters. Her main areas of research interests include financial inclusion, banking and insurance and FinTech. Her area of expertise includes financial services, portfolio management, financial markets, and insurance.

Fadwa Betane is a PhD student in applied economics, Mohammed V University in Rabat, Morrocco, Faculty of Law, Economics, & Social Sciences, Salé. Affiliated with the "Money, Banking & Finance" research structure. She holds a Master's degree in Financial Markets & Applied Economics at Hassan II University of Casablanca in 2023. Her research interests include financial inclusion, Fintechs and financial innovation in Africa.

Deepak Bhatia is currently working as Assistant Professor in Department of Management Studies at JIET group of institutions Jodhpur. He has over 5 years of academic experience with specialisation in Finance and Marketing. Currently pursing PhD from Jai Narain Vyas University, Jodhpur.

Sudha Bishnoi is currently working as Research Scholar at the Department of Management Studies at Jai Narain Vyas University in Jodhpur.

She has completed her MBA at Banasthali Vidyapith University in Jaipur, Rajasthan. She has a master's degree with a dual major in finance and marketing. She holds several qualifications from the Coursera learning platform, including a six-sigma green belt in lean technique. Her research interests include finance, trade, FinTech, artificial intelligence, and foreign direct investment.

Dr. Elizabeth Chacko is currently working with Christ (Deemed to be) University, Bangalore, Karnataka, India. She has completed her PhD (Management) from Banasthali University, Rajasthan on Ergonomics. She has 14 years of rich experience in academics with specialization in HR. Research areas includes Ergonomics, HR analytics, Fintech, Artificial Intelligence, Work Stress, Work Life Balance.

Dr. K. S. Chandrasekar currently working as Campus Director, Professor and Head of the Institute of Management in Kerala (IMK). He is the Chairman of the Board of Studies in Business Management of University of Kerala and Mahatma Gandhi University, Kerala. He was the Vice-Chairman of the Centre for Management Development, Kerala. He has written ten leading books and published 213 research articles in various reputed journals and newspapers. He presented 259 research papers in International and National seminars. He is the editorial board member of 18 reputed international and national journals. He won around 16 Awards for his academic excellence, He is currently the National council member of AIMA and ISTD, New Delhi.

Dr. Kavitha Desai holds an M. Com, MBA, and a PhD in Commerce, with a specialization in Finance. With over 24 years of experience in teaching, research, and administration, she has significantly contributed to academia. She has published 16 research papers in Scopus Indexed journals and has presented her work at various national and international conferences. As an approved PhD guide at multiple universities, she has successfully guided seven PhD scholars. Dr. Desai has also been involved in several research and consultancy projects in Management and serves on the boards of reputed academic institutions. She has held significant academic leadership roles and her academic contributions extend to chairing boards of studies, serving on academic councils, and organizing conferences that focus on business education and accreditation processes. Her work spans across various domains including financial literacy, derivatives and digital financial inclusion.

Rachida El Yamani is a professor of economics and econometrics at Faculty of law, Economic and Social Sciences—Mohammedia City, (Hassan II University, Casablanca. Her current research focuses on the factors that influence economic growth, financial inclusion, financial innovation and financial development. She is a finance, macro, and microeconomics teacher of applied econometrics. Her fundamental knowledge in econometrics was provided by her research master's degree in Economic Modelling Techniques and Econometrics from Hassan II University of Casablanca (2015). She has published numerous research articles in applied economics and finance journals that are indexed by Scopus. She reviews articles for publications that are indexed by Scopus.

Dr. Krishn A. Goyal, Director (IES) & Professor, Business Finance and Economics, Jai Narain Vyas (State) University, Jodhpur, India. He holds MBA, M.Com, M.Phil., (Economic Administration & Financial Management), and Ph.D. from the University of Rajasthan. He has been in the teaching profession for the last 26 years and has been associated with many academic institutions of repute in India and abroad. Dr. Goyal has contributed more than fifty research papers to journals of repute and edited or co-authored twelve books. He has completed five funded research projects. He is supervising Ph.D. scholars and has awarded ten Ph.Ds; presently, eight more scholars are pursuing Ph.Ds under his supervision. He has been awarded for Best Paper Presenter, Best Teacher, Best Essay Writer, and Academic Excellence. Prof. Goyal is also awarded the IARE-2020 International Research Excellence Award.

Muhammad Ikhlaas Gurrib holds a PhD in Finance and a Bachelor of Commerce (Economics and Finance) from Curtin University (Australia), a Master of Finance and a Master of Professional Accounting from Victoria State University, Australia. Prior to joining Canadian University Dubai, he was an Assistant Professor at Prince Sultan University, Saudi Arabia, and also taught at Curtin Business School, Australia. Dr. Gurrib is also experienced in the finance industry, having worked as a Finance Manager with Westpac Bank, Australia. He published in various top tier journals including Financial Innovation, International Journal of Neutrosophic Science, and Studies in Economics and Finance. His research interests include portfolio management, investment analysis, and international financial markets. He holds a full Professor rank and serves as the Head of Accounting and Finance programs at Canadian University Dubai.

Bharath H. is a research scholar with a strong academic background and a passion for research. Holding a master's degree in both MBA and MSc Psychology, Bharath has demonstrated a unique blend of business acumen and a deep understanding of human behavior. Currently pursuing a Ph.D. in Management, he is committed to advancing his knowledge and contributing to the academic field. Bharath has enriched his academic journey with a year of industry experience, providing him with practical insights into the dynamics of the business world. This hands-on experience has complemented his theoretical knowledge, equipping him with a well-rounded perspective that he integrates into his research endeavors. Currently, he holds position of Teaching Assistant in the Marketing department at CMS Business School, Jain deemed to be University.

Dr. Ahmed Mohamed Habib works in Accounting and Finance, Independent Research, Zagazig, Egypt. He published numerous articles in high-ranking journals and conferences. His research interests include accounting and finance science; corporate governance; intellectual capital; corporate social responsibility; environmental, social, and governance (ESG) criteria; working capital management; corporate narrative reporting; corporate finance; earnings management; business strategies; corporate investment efficiency; performance optimization; continuous improvement; frontier analysis; data envelopment analysis (DEA); malmquist productivity index (MPI) analysis; DEA and MPI applications; managerial ability; knowledge management; decision support systems and econometric analysis.

Dalia Hemdan holds a PhD in Accounting from Universiti Teknologi MARA (UiTM) Malaysia, a Master of Finance from Canadian University Dubai (CUD) and a Bachelor of Commerce (Accounting) from Helwan University (Egypt). Dr. Dalia has Academic experience in Canadian University Dubai and American University Emirates as an Assistant Professor teaching accounting and finance courses. Dr. Dalia also has more than 20 years of experience in corporate and banking sector as finance manager. She has publications in Scopus journals. Her research interests include earnings management, corporates governance, and earnings quality.

Shatha Hussain possesses a PhD in project management, specializing in finance and accounting, obtained from the British University in Dubai,

UAE. She also holds a master's degree in accounting and a bachelor's degree in accounting from Tishreen University in Syria. With over a decade of academic experience at highly regarded universities, Dr. Hussain has made significant contributions to the fields of accounting, finance, behavioral finance, corporate governance, and auditing through her extensive publications in top-tier international peer-reviewed journals. Her research endeavors have substantially advanced these disciplines. Currently, Dr. Hussain serves as an assistant professor of finance and accounting at City University Ajman, where she continues to share her expertise and knowledge with students and colleagues.

Asha Devi. J is a Research Scholar in Management at the University of Kerala, India. She has completed her M. Phil in Management from the University of Kerala and completed MBA in Finance and HR from the Mahatma Gandhi University, Kerala. She has published a textbook on "History of Management Thoughts Text and Cases". She is engrossed in writing research articles and textbooks and is concerned with refining her skills and unique abilities in the area of Management. She has p resented fifteen research papers at National and International Seminars. She has published ten articles were published in various journals.

Samia Hamed Al Jahwari is working as Lecturer at the Undergraduates department, College of Banking and financial studies since 2018. She has 18 years' experience in the field of academic and research. She has been working at Oman Nursing Institute, MOH as Information Technology Teacher from 2004 until 2011, Then she has worked for TRC (The research Council of Oman) as Research specialist from 2012 until 2018. Currently, she is working as Lecturer UG department since 2018, teaching courses related to Information systems such as Management Information Systems, E Business, Operation Management and Business systems for HND students. She got her BSC. Information systems from SQU in 2004 and her MBA from SQU in 2010.

Dr. Sarfaraz Javed is a full-time Associate Professor at Sohar University. He completed his education at Aligarh Muslim University (AMU), India, where he was honored with the prestigious Laurel Award. Dr. Javed has an impressive academic record, having published over 30+ research papers and articles in reputable journals. His active engagement in the academic community is further demonstrated by his participation in more than 25 seminars and conferences, along with over 40 workshops, both nationally and internationally. His contributions have significantly enriched the fields of his expertise, making him a respected figure in academia.

Shrinivas K. holds a PhD from Pacific Academy of Higher Education and Research (PAHER), Udaipur, a Post-graduation Diploma in Higher Education from KSOU, Mysore, an MBA in Marketing Management and Human Resource Management from Acharya Institute of Management and Sciences, Bangalore, and a BBM in Human Resource Management from KLE's S. Nijalingappa College, Bangalore.

Faisal Khan holds dual PhDs in Accounting and Finance and is a fully qualified Certified Public Accountant (CPA) and Chartered Accountant (CAF). With over 15 years of academic experience at top-ranked universities and 14 years of industrial experience with leading audit firms, he has established himself as a distinguished expert in his field. Dr. Khan has published extensively, with top ranked international peer review journals. His research interests encompass accounting, finance, corporate governance, and auditing, contributing significantly to the advancement of these disciplines. Currently, he is serving as an Associate Professor of Finance and Accounting at City University Ajman.

Dr. Farhina Sardar Khan, D.Phil., M.Com., UGC NET is an Associate Professor in the Department of Commerce and Business Management, Integral University, Lucknow. She is an Alumnus of the University of Allahabad, Prayagraj. Her research areas are Banking and Finance, and HRM. She has 14 years of teaching experience and has published more than 50 research papers in the Scopus, Web of Science, ABDC-B, and UGC CARE journals. She has authored seven books and 11 edited chapters. She had five patents and one seed-money project. She received eight Ph.D. awardees under her supervision. She received six distinct awards for her research and an education excellence award for her teaching. She is a reviewer for the Scopus-indexed and Peer-Reviewed journals of the UGC CARE. Apart from academics, she serves her department as a DQAC Coordinator, NAAC Criteria 3 Coordinator, and Ph.D. Coordinator as well. She is actively involved in organizing activities with NGOs, workshops, FDPs, seminars, and webinars in her department. Dr. Farhina has a lifetime membership in the 'Indian Commerce Association (ICA), 'the Indian Accounting Association (IAA), the Environmental & Consumer

Protection Foundation, Annual Membership in the 'Indian Finance Association (IFA),' and Annual Membership in the International American Council for Research and Development. You can reach her through.

Dr. Azeem Ahmad Khan is Assistant Professor at Al Baha University, Saudi Arabia Having worked in both India and Saudi Arabia, he has vast knowledge in research and instruction. With an eye on financial accounting and International Financial Reporting Standards (IFRS), Dr. Khan's knowledge resides in accounting and finance. He has written many articles in Scopus and Web of Science (WOS) indexed journals, therefore offering insightful analysis to the scholarly community. Dr. Khan also actively participates in intellectual conversation having attended several national and international seminars and conferences.

Dr. Reshmy Krishnan is working as Head of Research and Associate Professor in Computing, Muscat College, Oman. She is having rich academic years for over 29 years in the field of Computer Science. She holds Post-Doctoral Fellowship and PhD in Intelligent systems, Associate fellowship in teaching and learning. She has guided four students for PhD. She has thirteen funded projects and 445 citations in research profile.

Megha Kukreja holds a Master's degree in Business Administration with Finance as her specialization. With over 9 years of teaching experience, she has taught accounting and finance papers to undergraduate students. Currently, she is working as an Assistant Professor at Centre for Management Studies, Jain (Deemed to be) University, Bangalore, India and pursuing her Ph.D in Management.

Raghavendra Prasanna Kumar is Assistant Professor, School of Business and Management, CHRIST (Deemed to be University), Bangalore. He has a full-time Ph. D in Human Resource Management with over ten years of expertise in teaching and research. He has published the research articles in ABDC/Scopus journals and presented 22 research papers at international conferences. He won the "Best Paper Award" at the International Conference organized by the College of Banking and Financial Studies, Muscat, Sultanate of Oman, in 2019. He has participated in several workshops on data analysis and FDPs at premier institutions in India. He is also contributed as a peer reviewer for various institutions' editorial books. He was a reviewer for the Scopus and ABDC-indexed journals.

Karthikeyan M. is a Professor in the Department of Cooperatives at Wollo University, Ethiopia, with 28 years of teaching and research experience. Specializing in areas such as Management, Human Resource Management, Cooperatives, Social Enterprises, and CSR. He has participated in over 100 scientific deliberations globally, authored 27 books, published 80 articles (55 in international journals), and developed 11 course curriculums. He has served as a research advisor for both undergraduate and Ph.D. students and has acted as a foreign examiner for over 50 universities. In addition to his academic contributions, he has organized 20 training programs and presented papers in 9 webinars. His international experience spans several countries, including Italy, the UK, South Africa, and Switzerland.

Sumi A. M. currently pursuing Ph.D. in Management at Institute of Management in Kerala (IMK), University of Kerala. She has completed M. Phil in Management and M.B.A (2015) from the University of Kerala. She has published a textbook published on "History of Management Thoughts; Text and Cases". She has published fourteen articles in various reputed Journals and edited books. She has presented 20 research papers in national and international seminars.

Dr. Priya Makhija is currently working as Associate Professor at the Center for Management Studies, Jain (Deemed to be) University. She has completed her M.Com, M.B.A, M.Phil, Ph.D., PGDHRM, and Executive Financial Data Analytics. She has 16 years of academic work experience in the areas of Teaching, Research, Team building, Academic administration, faculty development & research enhancement. She has published over 28 research papers in journals and presented her research work at various national and international conferences.

Dr. Garima Malik is an Associate Professor of Marketing at Birla Institute of Management Technology, Greater Noida. She is a Fellow of the Xavier School of Management, XLRI Jamshedpur, India, and a recipient of the K.V. Raju Gold Medal granted to an exceptional Ph.D. student. She has more than twenty years of academic experience. Her research interests span various areas, including gamification, marketing analytics, customer engagement, destination marketing, and gaming marketing experience. She authored more than 80+ research papers. In addition to her research contributions, Dr. Malik has authored five books, two of which are textbooks, and four are case study books.

Dr. Syed Shahid Mazhar holds M.Com, MBA, D.Phil degree and is currently working as Associate Professor, DCBM, Faculty of Commerce & Management, Integral University, Lucknow, India. An alumnus of University of Allahabad, he possesses rich teaching experience in the field of Accounting, Finance and International Trade. He has a substantial number of research papers, publications, paper presentations at National & International conferences and has also successfully attended a number of workshops, FDPs, & STCs. He is guiding research scholars in the areas of International Trade, Indian Capital Market, Islamic Banking, etc. 6 PhD Degrees have been awarded under his supervision.

Teena Mertiya is currently working as a research scholar at the Department of Business Finance and Economics at Jai Narain Vyas University in Jodhpur. She has to her credit various publications in renowned journals, besides holding certifications from national and international conferences, webinars, and faculty development programs. Her research interests include international trade and finance and fintech.

Dr. Shelly Mohanty is an educationalist and Human Resource consultant having more than twenty-three years of experience in academic and administrative fields from India and Overseas. She has a number of articles and research paper to her credit in the area of management, human resource management, organizational behavior, stress management etc. in various national and international journals. She contributed as member of the Editorial Board of Cambodian Management Journal. She has authored books on 'Management Principles and applications' and 'Corporate Law'. She has presented papers at several universities and professional training institutions. She is a motivational speaker and as a resource person conducted many workshops and training programs in the national and international arena.

Dr. Mari Anand N. is a seasoned academic luminary with 12 years of expertise in Marketing and Human Resource Management, currently serving as a Faculty Member at the University of Technology & Applied Sciences, Salalah, Oman. Holding an MBA with a prestigious Gold Medal, he previously Headed the Department of Business Studies at SRM University, Chennai. Dr. Mari Anand N. is a prolific researcher with 27 publications in Scopus and UGC Listed Journals, mentoring 2 Ph.D. scholars and supervising numerous research projects. He has held key administrative roles at SRM Institute of Science & Technology,

Chennai, including Chief Superintendent, Academic Council and Board of Studies. Additionally, he contributes as an Editorial Board Member for the International Journal of Advance Research in Commerce Management and Finance (IJARCMF). Dr. Mari Anand N.'s academic influence extends globally through his participation in international conferences and conclave organization. He is revered as a resource person for Faculty Development Programs worldwide and holds affiliations with prestigious organizations such as FICCI and MMA. Notably, he has spearheaded three Funded Research Projects, resulting in two Patents under the auspices of the Government of India. Dr. Mari Anand N.'s international stature is underscored by his chairing of sessions at significant International Conferences organized by IFERP across Australia, Malaysia, and Dubai.

Dr. Girija Narasimhan is currently working as a Lecturer at the University of Technology and Applied Science, Muscat. She has published research articles in various international conferences and journals. She is a regular contributor to scientific journals in Tamil. She has edited two books and contributed three book chapters. She is specialized in databases, data warehousing, data mining, data science, and data visualization. She has over 22 years of academic experience. She completed certifications from Microsoft, Cisco, and Oracle. She serves as a reviewer for international journals, conferences, and research initiatives.

She has conducted workshop on technology for faculty and students and guided the projects of research scholars.

Karthika P. is an Associate Professor of Finance in the Management Department at Kebri Dehar University, Ethiopia. With 13 years of experience in academia and industry, including 12 years of teaching, she specializes in Financial Accounting, Security Analysis, Portfolio Management, and Strategic Management. She has served as a SEBI Financial Education Resource Person, delivering over 120 workshops across various colleges. Also, published 20 research papers in national and international journals, and has presented more than 25 papers at prestigious conferences. Further, her research focused on the impact of future trading and macroeconomic variables on stock price volatility, further cementing her expertise in finance.

Dharen Kumar Pandey is an Assistant Professor in the Indian Institute of Management Sambalpur, Sambalpur, Odisha, India. He previously worked in P. G. Department of Commerce, Magadh University, Bodh Gaya, Bihar, and a Post-Doctoral Researcher at the Faculty of Business, Economics and Social Development, University of Malaysia Terengganu, Malaysia. He has 12+ years of industry and teaching experience. His research interests are financial markets, financial econometrics, market efficiency, etc. He has authored 3 books and more than 50 research and review papers in top-tier journals, indexed in ABDC, Scopus, Web of Science, UGC Care list, including the Economic Letters, International Review of Economics and Finance, Journal of Behavioral and Experimental Finance, Financial Research Letters, Research in International Business and Finance, Journal of Business Research, the International Journal of Financial Markets and Derivatives, the Review of Finance and Banking, the Indian Journal of Commerce, Current Issues in Tourism. His three research papers have been awarded in the International Research Awards hosted by the Institute of Chartered Accountants of India.

Dr. Navaneetha Krishnan Rajagopal a renowned academician and researcher, lives in the Sultanate of Oman and holds a Ph.D. in Management from a reputed university. His research focuses on finance, organizational behavior, and business management, with numerous articles published in Scopus and Web of Science-indexed journals, reflecting his significant impact in the field. Serving as an international Ph.D. examiner for over 140 research scholars and conducting more than 60 workshops for the Securities and Exchange Board of India, he has made substantial contributions to academia and professional development. His achievements have earned him accolades, including the Best Teacher Award, underscoring his dedication to advancing management studies.

Dr. Narayani Ramachandran holds a Ph.D., MBA, MFC degrees with international experience in Stockholm, Sweden & London. With over 20+years of experience in academia, research, and consulting, her expertise includes equity research, financial modelling, valuation, and financial risk management. She holds two patents on Implementing Financial Incentives to improve employee performance in Banking Sector under The Patents Act, of 1970. She has published in national and international journals listed in ABDC & Scopus listing and contributed multiple book chapters. An avid equity market player, she has offered multiple MDPs for various clients including Moody's AMBA, PNB Metlife, TVS Groups of Companies, Bank of Jammu & Kashmir and Britannia India Ltd. etc. She held the position of Finance Committee Member in a Central Government University in India. She is an affiliate member of the Council for Financial Planners—Karnataka.

Dr. Mahalakshmi S. an executive alumna of IIM Vishakhapatnam, is a highly accomplished professional with a strong academic background. She holds a Ph.D. in Management and completed her Engineering in Computer Science from Visvesvaraya Technological University, Belgaum, with distinction. Her MBA from Bangalore University earned her three gold medals and the top state rank. She also holds a Post Graduate Certificate Program (PGCP) in Digital and Social Media Marketing from IIM Vishakhapatnam. With extensive experience as an Associate Project Manager in management consultation and project management, she has worked on projects in India, Germany, and Canada, bringing practical industry insights to her role. Dr. Mahalakshmi is also a certified professional in Marketing and Technology from IIM Madras and serves as a Subject Matter Expert for executive MBA programs at Manipal, JainEx, and upGrad. She has developed and delivered MOOC courses in marketing on platforms such as upGrad, Manipal, and JainEx. Her expertise is recognized through numerous best paper awards, two patents, and publications in Scopus-indexed and Web of Science journals. She has also chaired conference sessions. Currently, Dr. Mahalakshmi serves as a faculty member in the Marketing Area at CMS Business School, Jain (Deemed-to-be) University, and she is also an adjunct faculty member and Subject Matter Expert at the Manipal Centre for Distance Learning.

Jayendira P. Sankar received his PhD from the University of Madras, India. He worked for ten years in India and in Bahrain for seven years. Overall, seventeen years of academic experience, Senior Fellow HEA-UK and Academic Fellow CIPD-UK with many publications in various high-impact journals and conferences. The current research interests include Development Economics: economic growth, poverty, inequality, market failure, fiscal, economic and social condition, healthcare, education, employment sector, industrial and social infrastructure; Human Resource Management: employee welfare, work-family balance, consumer behaviour, retail marketing, corporate social responsibility, sustainability, and teaching-learning and assessments.

Shivam Sharma is currently working in enterprise sales at Fleetx company.

Ahsan Siraj is a PhD scholar at School of Management Engineering, Zhengzhou University, China. He is working as a Visiting Lecturer at MNS University of Agriculture, Multan, and he is also affiliated with the University of Lahore, Pakistan as an Administration Officer. He has diverse research interests including digital banking, FinTech, branding, e-commerce, consumer behaviour, entrepreneurship, sustainable marketing, SMEs, and sustainability. He has got his research works published in various high-impact international journals and conferences. He is serving as the reviewer for reputed international journals and conferences.

Dr. Shilpa Taneja is an Assistant Professor in Marketing at Sheffield University Management School, University of Sheffield, United Kingdom. Recently, she has worked as a Postdoctoral Fellow at Centre for Research Excellence in Marketing, Mudra Institute of Communications Ahmedabad (MICA), India. She has gained over 8 years of academic experience while undertaking teaching and research at different reputed institutes. Her research areas include digital banking, FinTech, marketing, branding, sustainable consumer behaviour, sustainability, and e-commerce. She has published various peer-reviewed articles in the aforementioned areas in high-impact international journals and conferences. She is also serving as the reviewer for reputed high-impact journals and conferences.

Aanchal Nigam Verma holds B. Ed and MBA degree and is currently working as Assistant Professor, Lucknow Public College of Professional Studies Lucknow, India. She is pursuing her PhD from Integral University, Lucknow, India. She has over 7 years of academic experience with specialization in Finance, Communications, and Marketing. Her research areas include financial technology, cyber security, bibliometrical analysis and financial innovation.

List of Figures

List of Tables

Transforming Customer Perception through Green Banking Channels in Electronic Finance

Impact of Green Banking Practices on the Performance of Indian Banks: An Empirical Study

FinTech Adoption Literature: Current State and Future Directions

The Role of Fintech in Financial Inclusion: A Survey of Low-Income Individuals in Kolkata

How Can FinTech Adoption Benefit the MSME Sector in India?

Fintechs as an Enabler of Financial Inclusion: An Empirical Analysis in the Landscape of African Economies

Recent Trends in the Development of Artificial Intelligence Among Banking Sectors in India

Bibliometric Analysis on Digital Financial Inclusion Through Blockchain Technology Crowdfunding

Cryptocurrency Conundrum: Understanding the Dynamics of Indian Consumer Intentions using an Extended UTAUT Model

Impact of AI on Accounting Practices in Saudi Arabia

Perspectives on Electronic Finance and Sustainability

Interplay of Electronic Finance with the Electronic Market

Samia Hamed Al Jahwari

1 Introduction

An electronic market refers to an online market wherein customers access services, products, brands, or enterprises through an online platform. E-market involves marketing performed on the Internet, e-finance and includes marketing conducted via wireless media and e-mail. Electronic marketing can consist of direct and interactive marketing elements or direct response marketing. When e-marketing elements are implemented properly, return on investments (ROI) can be higher than traditional marketing platforms. Although the electronic market concept is a relatively new field, it has witnessed significant growth and development during the past few years.

Moreover, it's an arena that is constantly evolving and always unique. The following chapter introduces the meaning of the electronic market, the establishment of the electronic markets, the growth, the impact on the economy, e-finance, the future of development, and the way of benefits for the MENA Region. Heavy emphasis on future directions for the MENA region will be detailed at the end of this chapter.

S. H. Al Jahwari (✉)
College of Banking and Financial Studies, Muscat, Oman
e-mail: samiacbfs@gmail.com

© The Author(s), under exclusive license to Springer Nature Singapore Pte Ltd. 2025

A. S. et al. (eds.), *Trends and Challenges of Electronic Finance*,
https://doi.org/10.1007/978-981-96-3304-3_1

2 Establishment and Growth of Electronic Market

The concept of a market is both changeable and adaptable to keep pace with technological advancements. Therefore, traditional or physical markets did not depend on divided customer demands according to the market sector segmentation (Adede et al., 2017). Because of the emergence of many variables such as distribution, products, advertising, and prices, electronic marketing aims at increasing the market share and business for institutions. The development of an e-market requires the presence of four variables, namely distribution, individuals, information, and technology, and all these variables are means of developing new offers or attracting new customers (Wang, 2017). The principal objective of the technological-based electronic market is to increase the profit of enterprises and try to achieve customers' personal needs interactively and permanently (Elsayed, 2021).

2.1 E-Market and Artificial Intelligence (AI)

Artificial intelligence refers to the ability of the computer to mimic human behavior in terms of functionality, speed, and availability. The concept of artificial intelligence was mentioned in the last editorial report for electronic markets as a fundamental enabling technological element that converges with other modern technologies, such as the extended reality or technology of distributed ledger (Shahid & Li, 2019). The convergence notion signifies a technological evolutional process to meet the current world standards, and for sure, AI has been on the practitioner's and academia's desks for some time now. At specific points, it consisted of the technological and methodological spectrum. For example, an analysis mentioned in the newspaper and academic sources proves that artificial intelligence has experienced a perfect adoption growth since the 1980s and has experienced a more substantial increase since 2012 (Elsayed, 2021).

According to Thomassey and Zeng (2018), artificial intelligence involves a mix of variables such as deep learning, learning machine, and big data, which are all similar in the application of expensive computing power to perform analysis of big and central data. Consequently, various discussions are opened from the dynamics of numerous differentiated disciplines. For the balancing purposes of the entire debate, intelligence is conceived as having a close relationship with human interactions and skills. This, in turn, supports a survey by Lu (2019), who defined AI as any technique, method, or theory that objectively assists computer-enabled machines that analyze, exploit, explore, and simulate the behavior thinking process of human beings.

Additionally, literature based on different functionalities such as perception, cognition psychology, action, processing, and learning was discovered to be suiting in the structuring of potential AI in the business arena or context. According to Elsayed (2021), other features of AI are perceived anthropomorphism, animacy, intelligence, and particularly, the objective to rime the intelligence of human beings as reflected in various levels of AI systems that range from reactive machines and smart information systems to strong and weak units (Huang & Rust, 2021). As the aspect of intelligence is very fundamental for making decisions across the AI application domains, AI is thus, renamed as a technological general-purpose strategy alleged to create stronger and impacting reforms for digitalized transformation in the world of e-commerce.

2.2. Digital Platforms for Artificial Intelligence

According to Shahid and Li (2019), digital platforms fundamentally provide AI-enabled sources of data and confirm pre-editorial concepts introduced as a special concern on massive data services. Both centralized and decentralized platforms are described as service systems where data originates from interactions and transactions on an individual as well as from aggregated levels. For the systems to be able to process data digitally, they must be digital themselves (Chintalapati & Pandey, 2021); for example, the device type and the operating systems in use must be able to coincide with the digital platforms at stake. The actors and content of data will vary according to the purpose and participants of the platforms, while others are just agonistic applications and cross-domain in nature.

According to Pevzner et al. (2018), data obtained from transactional platforms is more structured compared to those coming from social networking or innovation platforms, where content is likely to be unstructured. Adede et al. (2017) showed that Toyota, Volkswagen, Citibank, or BBVA are doing their best to achieve and establish their own digital platforms. The reason behind having a desire to own a platform is that platform providers possess the ability to monitor the activities going on the platforms and instantly cope with their offerings and strategies. On the same note, providers of digital platform are also able to sell this data to create marginal revenues.

Yeh et al. (2019) show that dedicated platforms for electronic markets emerged purposefully for trading and collection of digital data and platforms. However, in the field of social media analytics (SMA), big data (BD), and business intelligence (BI), two major pitfalls should be considered. One is the existence of massive data amounts that present a potential need for further processing to make it make sense that is amenable in business processes (Pevzner et al., 2018). Much is embedded on the fact that data originates from many application systems and knowledge bases, which basically feature different conventions in terms of data semantics and syntax.

The second one is gatekeeping dependence on platform providers to access data. While in certain scenarios they might decide to sell or share data with third parties, they may keep data for themselves in some cases. This hoarding of data is conducted to monopolize its access by others. As a matter of fact, many big technology-owning companies show patterns of behaviors that raise concerns on the use of their positions and power (Litvinova et al., 2017). Recently, an opinion paper showed that this oligopolistic market structure can endanger user freedom and innovation. According to Adede et al. (2017), the recent investigation against Facebook by European Commission accused Facebook to be illegally advertising data from its flea platforms and online dating accounts to gain competitive advantage for their own service.

3 E-finance as a Trading Platform

E-finance is defined as "Providing financial services and markets using electronic communication and computation" (Franklin Allen, 2002). E-finance, which includes investing, banking, mortgage lending, and insurance, will expand at a breakneck pace in the following years. It is a mirror of the Internet's rapid rise. In just five years, the World Wide Web has progressed from uncharted territory to a pervasive medium for conducting business, exchanging information, and connecting with people all over the world. There are several kinds of e-finance services, such as e-banking, e-payment, e-trade finance, e-credit and e-loans, e-rating, and e-insurance and guarantees.

E-finance will benefit both consumers and companies by allowing them to cut transaction costs, process documentation more quickly than expected, and have rapid access to information. Online finance can drastically increase efficiency and lower the expenses of internal corporate tasks, such as expenditure reporting, contract labor management, and time-and-billing processes for firms. Furthermore, by offering tailored information about customers, the Internet enables businesses to participate in "one-to-one marketing," allowing them to customize the online experience to meet the demands of everyone.

The Internet has evolved as a vital tool for consumers to manage their finances and stay updated on financial news. As a result, there has been an increase in online brokerage businesses and financial news Websites. Online brokerages provide convenience, lower costs than traditional brokerage firms, and the opportunity to track individual accounts. Many large-scale, conventional brokerage companies have entered online investment as technology has altered conventional business methods. These new investors are not passive bystanders; they are actively involved in making their own financial decisions, administering their funds, and analyzing opportunities.

Aside from the stumbling of entrenched interests, there are other hurdles for firms and consumers working in e-finance. Several online insurance providers provide consumers with policies at lower prices than their physical-established counterparts, owing to the lower operating expenses of conducting business via the Internet. They can do that because they do not require a sales team and can handle transactions considerably more inexpensively online than traditional methods. Companies that collect customer information online, especially personal financial information, must be mindful of privacy concerns.

E-finance has an impact on international business in a variety of ways. For example, new virtual network facilitators or electronic markets lessen the requirement for a corporation to have the essential human and financial infrastructures for internationalization. To prevent the danger of volatility and to cut transaction costs, all stock exchanges, bond markets, foreign exchange markets, and financial markets have shifted to electronic trading (Shahrokhi, 2008).

4 Growth of Electronic Commerce

With the rise of e-commerce, many interests have been brought on board about e-commerce domains. Commonly called Internet commerce, electronic business or electronic commerce involves the process or art of buying and selling of services or products over the Internet, including the transfer of money or data to complete the transaction. Electronic commerce has seen accelerated sales growth across the globe. With the unprecedented events around the world, there has been a remarkable rise in the European nations. According to Digital Commerce 360, consumers worldwide spent close to $965.25 trillion on electronic purchase and payment just in 2020, up to 42% over the year. Consequently, e-commerce has empowered online retail for decades now.

Businesses and individuals involved in online commerce want a premium that is a one-word domain, which is brand enabled. According to Wang (2017), recent brokers at Saw.com sold one of the most common domains called cool.com. Globally, e-commerce development differs from country to country. In China and the most developed western markets such as the UK, USA, France, and Germany, the e-commerce penetration of total retail sales surpassed 10% and reached nearly 16% in the case of the UK. In 2018, the MENA e-commerce market reached $8.3 billion. With an average annual growth rate of 25%, e-commerce in the region has been growing slightly ahead of the global average. Egypt alone accounts for 80% of the e-commerce market, and they have been growing at a rate of 30% annually (Yeh et al., 2019).

5 Impact of E-Commerce on the Economy

The spectacular and advent growth of the Internet has spawned claims of a new economy led by new economics. Contrarily, economists rarely endorse such claims stating that basic macroeconomics and microeconomics principles still apply whatsoever (Qasim et al., 2018), as in the case of the classical economic models that advocate for perfect competition and price setting. However, while the underlying economic principles remain unchanged, the concepts of Internet and electronic commerce have greatly altered the economic operations of firms in terms of cost structures and raised the importance of certain economical phenomena, i.e., network economics (Adede et al,. 2017).

Currently, the impact of e-commerce is significant across North American and European nations. The USA covers accreditation of about four-fifths of the worldwide electronic commerce activities. In addition, the figures roughly suggest that Eastern Europe is about 10%, while Asia is 5% of the world's total e-commerce business usage and application. According to Alsaad et al. (2018), the USA has 69% to 85% of top e-commerce sites, followed by Canada at five out of six categories. Surprisingly, nations such as Germany and France (German T-online service and France Mintel) have subjected their citizens to online buying and selling. The benefits have migrated to the Internet only provided services, thus, expanding e-commerce at large in these nations (Qasim et al., 2018).

Despite Bangladesh being an underdeveloped country, its business community has embraced e-commerce immensely (Sahabi et al., 2018). Personal computers and the Internet have emerged to be day-to-day business tools, thus favoring the growth of e-commerce in Bangladesh. Therefore, the development of e-commerce has led to the development of some emerging industries such as logistics and created more jobs in industries such as computers and the Internet, hence stimulating the consumption rate. Since electronic commerce has provided customers with a wider variety of products, more and more consumers have been keen on online shopping than physical purchasing (Wang, 2017).

Consequently, the rapid growth of e-commerce has impacted the regional economic growth of MENA. In Saudi Arabia, there has been 35% to 60% growth in mobile commerce penetration across all aspects of online customers, and close to 4 out of 10 customers shopping online show the potential to make their shopping inquiries on mobile phones (Yeh et al., 2019). Furthermore, high-income earning professionals show the highest efforts to pay more, especially Arab expats, those living in Riyadh, and those in their 30 s and 20 s. Statistics show that Saudis' KSA, travel has the highest in terms of online share of 59%, in the sense that it has reduced the cost of services, particularly in retail and wholesale trade, transportation, finance, and business service levels.

Most importantly, cost savings in services are stimulated via a productive growth scenario that creates room for analysis of macro-economic variables such as GDP, welfare, wages, and terms of trade. Also, a combination of market and technological forces in the MENA region has compelled companies to examine and reinvent their procurement strategies. Most of the transactions and transfers of data are done externally through e-markets. To remain competitive in the market, firms in the region have been forced to search for greater coordination and collaboration among supply chain partners to remove any inefficiencies within a firm's transactions (Rabayah et al., 2021).

Iteration from most research surveys and articles shows that new job creation, contribution to GDP, and production of innovation in technology are some of the major economic growth contributors.

Notably, three factors stimulate the development of e-commerce via e-payment systems: reduced operational and payment processing costs, growing online commerce, and decreased cost of technology. Many online payment strategies drive the economic growth or market, including increased productivity, creation of electronic data, and demand for ICT infrastructure. Small and medium enterprises have immensely adopted e-commerce strategies as a form of doing business in the MENA region, and its penetration effects are felt even at the local level. According to Shahid and Li (2019), online trade facilitates the participation and growth of SMEs in the economy due to lower costs and improved business competitiveness.

In Oman, the local economic reports show that the online customer services system has represented a saving of 20,000 new hires (about 14% of their total labor force) (Al-Abdallah et al., 2021). Just as electronic commerce can significantly reduce selling costs, it can also reduce the costs associated with buying. While the actual buying and selling transactions occur outside the company, the costs associated with supply chain processes consist of high internal costs. In addition, e-commerce has changed the structure of cost, which is a key determinant of a firm's relationship with other businesses in the concept of a value-added chain (Qasim et al., 2018). An intermediary always performs a service that enables this kind of flow of adding value alongside adding cost at every processing stage. E-commerce, especially in intangible products, might reduce the involvement of intermediaries in the value addition chain and cost reduction in the long run.

6 Future of Growth and Way of Benefits for MENA Region

The growth of the e-commerce market in the MENA region has gained momentum over the past few years despite taking off late behind other areas. Notably, the region is still in the cycle of e-commerce adoption, and the future can take many forms, not forgetting the challenges associated with it. Consequently, the growth trajectory of e-commerce has had different varieties depending on the prevailing market. In a well-established market such as the USA, e-commerce growth has been linear, and it took up to two decades for electronic commerce to realize a 12% share of the total retail sales (Rabayah et al., 2021). Also, electronic commerce in MENA is set to experience significant growth should the elements of the ecosystem fall into its place as anticipated early by the environmental fostering agencies such as UNEP, among others (Al-Abdallah et al., 2021).

In other markets such as China, where the physical retail ecosystem has been historically underdeveloped, the growth of e-commerce has been significantly faster, with a share of retail sales going up within eight years (Sahabi et al., 2018). Besides the readiness of consumers and the development of different ecosystem elements, the entry of large electronic commerce players in the market could also help accelerate the e-commerce shift to heights. India is a case at hand that proves a good example of the growth of e-commerce. Before the launch of Amazon, the e-commerce market in India grew by 38% annually from 2010 to 2014. When Amazon entered the Indian market, the e-market in India experienced a significant shift upwards, with the growth of e-commerce more than doubling, averaging 88% annually, between 2013 and 2016 (Alsaad et al., 2018).

Furthermore, the launch of Amazon Prime in 2016 served as a major catalyst for the rapid growth and penetration of e-commerce up to 2.5% in 2017 (Momin, 2020). According to Sultan and Noor (2017), e-commerce in MENA region will have an estimated growth of 3.5% by 2022, reaching a total market size of $29.5 billion, which is the rate of market penetration of 7% of the total retail sales currently observed in continental Europe today. Alzahrani (2018) showed that the forecasted e-commerce growth for the region of MENA trickling down to Oman area was about 27% annually from 2014. The expansion of the middle class, the growing role of women in the workplace, improvements in logistics, and access to online products in Tier 1 and Tier 2 cities and towns in MENA, such as Oman, are key drivers for the growth of growth e-market and commerce.

Likewise, e-commerce has created access to a whole new set of customers in more remote areas than before. Consequently, the modes of payment for the products have also significantly changed with cash on delivery through online platforms coming on board to replace the demanding cash payment. Notably, cash on delivery has been a significant challenge in Oman and MENA as a whole as it can result in higher return rates and higher deliveries (Shehata & Montash, 2019). Furthermore, it adds pressure to working capital requirements while limiting delivery options to logistic firms that accept this payment mode. Currently, about 62% of Oman online shoppers prefer COD as a mode of payment when buying online, unlike the case in UK and France, which is less than 5%. COD is prevalent even in the UAE, where credit card penetration is at 58% (Momin, 2020).

Also, mobile wallets have been gaining traction in the market, with world technology players, telecom operators, and local banks rolling out solutions and driving merchant and user adoption. Favorable legislation and government initiatives are vital in supporting the adoption of mobile wallets. The launch of Emirates Digital Wallet by UAE in partnership with 16 national banks was a great step in e-commerce in the MENA region as well (Alzahrani, 2018). Furthermore, Fawry's mobile wallet has over 5 million users in Oman and the neighboring towns, and it promises to enable digital payment, even for consumers without bank accounts. Therefore, the future of e-commerce in the MENA region is very promising in the growth of digital debit cards, mobile wallets, and bank payments.

According to Elsayed (2021), a growth of at least up to $5.9 billion in sales share is expected in the region by the end of 2022. With markets such as France and UK recording more than 40% penetration into the platform of online markets, the room for growth in the region is significant. An expansion of the selection of products beyond mobile phones into home appliances and other items, such as kitchen wares, clothes, vehicles, and furniture, would be key.

Notably, MENA is still a cash-based economy. In the future, higher and healthy credit card penetration rates are expected to replace cash on delivery payment mode that is embedded in the minds of customers (Sultan et al., 2019). In addressing the issue of customer trust, as far as online markets and payments are concerned, establishing a consistent track record of product delivery that matches consumer expectations and a simple, fast, and reliable return process are crucial components to be considered in the long run.

References

Adede, O. A., Kibera, F. N., & Owino, J. O. (2017). Electronic marketing practices, competitive environment and performance of telecommunications companies in Kenya. *British Journal of Marketing Studies*, 5(5), 60–67.

Al-Abdallah, G. M., Fraser, K. E., & Albarq, A. N. (2021). Internet-based entrepreneurial ventures: An empirical investigation of startup business strategies on firm performance from the MENA region. *Global Journal of Flexible Systems Management, 22*(1), 29–41.

Allen, F., McAndrews, J., & Strahan, P. (2002). E-Finance: An introduction. *Journal of Financial Services Research, 22*, 5–27. https://doi.org/10.1023/A:1016007126394

Alsaad, A., Mohamad, R., Taamneh, A., & Ismail, N. A. (2018). What drives global B2B e-commerce usage: An analysis of the effect of the complexity of trading system and competition pressure? *Technology Analysis & Strategic Management, 30*(8), 980–992.

Alsheibani, S., Cheung, Y., & Messom, C. (2018). Artificial intelligence adoption: AI-readiness at firm-level. In *PACIS* (p. 37).

Alzahrani, J. (2018). The impact of e-commerce adoption on business strategy in Saudi Arabian small and medium enterprises (SMEs). *Review of Economics and Political Science.*

Chintalapati, S., & Pandey, S. K. (2021). Artificial intelligence in marketing: A systematic literature review. *International Journal of Market Research*, 14707853211018428.

Elsayed Fayed, A. (2021). Artificial Intelligence for marketing plan: The case for e-marketing companies. *Marketing and Management of Innovations*, 1, 81–95. https://doi.org/10.21272/mmi.2021.1-07

Huang, M. H., & Rust, R. T. (2021). A framework for collaborative artificial intelligence in marketing. *Journal of the Academy of Marketing Science volume, 49*, 30–50. https://doi.org/10.1007/s11747-020-00749-9

Litvinova, T. N., Tolmachev, A. V., Saenko, I. I., & Iskandaryan, G. O. (2017, December). Role and meaning of the ICT infrastructure for development of entrepreneurial activities in the Russian agricultural machinery market. In *Perspectives on the use of new Information and Communication Technology (ICT) in the modern economy* (pp. 793–799). Springer.

Momin, S. (2020). E-commerce acceptance and implementation among consumers in the UAE: An opportunity to build human capital for future jobs in technology and marketing. In *Human capital in the Middle East* (pp. 253–272). Palgrave Macmillan.

Pevzner, M. N., Petryakov, P. A., Donina, I. A., & Shaydorova, N. A. (2018). Internet marketing as a diversity management tool in education. *European Research Studies Journal, 21*(3), 496–505.

Qasim, D., Mohammed, A. B., & Liñán, F. (2018). The role of culture and gender in e-commerce entrepreneurship: Three Jordanian case studies. In *Entrepreneurship ecosystem in the Middle East and North Africa (MENA)* (pp. 419–432). Springer.

Rabayah, K. S., Maree, M., & Alhashmi, S. M. (2021). Cultural factors that influence the adoption of e-commerce: A Palestinian case study. *Information Development*, 02666669211006887.

Sahabi, B., Shakerpur, P., & Tahmasebi, D. (2018). The impact of E-commerce and ICT on economic growth of using the translog function. Bi-*quarterly Journal of development economics and planning*, *7*(2).

Shahid, M. Z., & Li, G. (2019). Impact of artificial intelligence in marketing: A perspective of marketing professionals of Pakistan. *Global Journal of Management and Business Research, 19*(2), 27–33.

Shahrokhi, M. (2008). E-finance: Status, innovations, resources and future challenges. *Managerial Finance., 34*, 365–398. https://doi.org/10.1108/03074350810872787

Shehata, G. M., & Montash, M. A. (2019). Driving the internet and e-business technologies to generate a competitive advantage in emerging markets: Evidence from Egypt. *Information Technology & People.*

Sultan, A. A., & Noor, S. M. (2017). Absorptive capacity, civil conflict and e-commerce adoption among Iraqi firms. *Advanced Science Letters, 23*(8), 7992–7995.

Thomassey, S., & Zeng, X. (2018). Introduction: Artificial intelligence for fashion industry in the big data era. In *Artificial Intelligence for fashion industry in the big data era* (pp. 1–6). Springer.

Wang, M. (2017). Establishment of an international legal framework for cross-border electronic commerce rules: Dilemmas and solutions. *World Customs Journal, 61.*

Yeh, T. M., Chen, S. H., & Chen, T. F. (2019). The relationships among experiential marketing, service innovation, and customer satisfaction—A case study of tourism factories in Taiwan. *Sustainability, 11*(4), 1041.

Digital Financial Access and Financialization: Panel Evidence from the Selected Countries in Asia–Pacific Region

Savitha Basri

1 Introduction

The financial system acts as an intermediary between savers with excess money and businesses or entrepreneurs who need that money to make investments in the process of production. Financialization is the term used to describe the finance sector's hegemony over other economic sectors and its encroachment upon the actual economy (Davis, 2018; Lin & Tomaskovic-Devey, 2013). It is instrumental in promoting savings, investment, and borrowing for productive activities by providing cost effective and easy access to various financial products and services (Galor & Moav, 2004). There is no denying that financialization can change lives. For instance, a poor person who owns a plot of land can apply for a loan from a bank by pledging it as collateral, and he/she can use that money to fund productive endeavours that enable him/her to transcend poverty. However, marginalized section of the society might be left out if there are barriers to access financial services (Greenwood & Jovanovic, 1990).

S. Basri (✉)
Manipal School of Commerce and Economics, Manipal Academy of Higher Education, Manipal, India
e-mail: savitha.bs@manipal.edu

© The Author(s), under exclusive license to Springer Nature Singapore Pte Ltd. 2025

A. S. et al. (eds.), *Trends and Challenges of Electronic Finance*,
https://doi.org/10.1007/978-981-96-3304-3_2

The redistributive effect of financialization might become negative if it fails to include the poor or disadvantaged section of the society in the financial system (Haan & Sturm, 2017; Huang & Zhang, 2020; Meniago & Asongu, 2018). Rich people benefit from easier access to low-cost financial products and digital technology, as well as from a greater concentration and production of wealth (Daud et al., 2021). Also, income inequality arises when finance sector growth is higher than other sectors leading to wage differentials between individuals working in finance sectors and those employed in non-financial industries (Hyde et al., 2017; Lin & Tomaskovic-Devey, 2013).

The blending of the digital and financial facets, known as digital financialization, is hailed as a vital instrument for promoting financial inclusion where a large percentage of population lack access to financial products and services. Digital communication technology, including smartphones and the internet, is used in the digital domain, whereas financial transactions are included in the financial sphere. Digital platforms connect with people in this new hybrid world that is headed towards financialization. The economic value created due to digital transformation was 45% of the GDP of major economies.

The developing world still lags behind other countries in the adoption and usage of mobile wallets (Asongu & Nwachukwu, 2018; Patil et al., 2017; Sharma et al., 2018). For instance, India's 75% of population own mobile phones yet 60% of population are under-banked. 67% of them prefer cash transactions whereas 10% only use debit or credit cards (Amarante Consulting Group, 2014; Srivastava & Sharma, 2017). The opportunity cost of offline banking is estimated to be around US$2 billion (Manyika et al., 2016). Digital financial access, particularly for the economically disadvantaged, reduces costs and enhances the efficiency of financial service delivery. Previous studies show that the digital divide has a negative impact on income inequality (Noh & Yoo, 2000) because it creates disparities in access to resources that influence mobile connectivity, internet usage, and the outcomes of internet usage (Van Deursen & van Dijk, 2019). One crucial concern that has arisen because of recent advancements in financial technology is: Could digital financial access contribute to financialization?

According to Jain and Gabor (2020), FinTech and tech corporations' profit from the blurring of digital and financial identities at the expense of the public. However, widespread adoption of digital finance in economies with underdeveloped financial infrastructure would improve financialization. The consequent broadening of financial asset base and removal of structural constraints in the financial system would benefit the economy. To counter the disadvantages of digital financialization, the digital platforms should be secured against any cyber frauds and phishing attacks. Nevertheless, excessive financialization especially corporate financialization has been the sole reason for many financial crashes in the past. If the private sector debt reaches 80 to 100 per cent of Gross Domestic Product (GDP), it imposes heavy cost on the economy in terms of slower growth and higher volatility (de Rugy & Salmon, 2020). The misallocation of resources away from actual production and the unequal compensation of those employed in the financial sector have a negative impact on societal output.

Financialization or financial development has been measured by a single index in the previous studies, either as market capitalization of stock market or as total amount of credit dispersed by banks. A multidimensional index of financialization is developed by Svirydzenka (2016) as a combination of separate indices for financial institutions and financial markets. These indices have sub-indices that measure their depth, access, and efficiency. Not only studies that investigate the effect of digital finance on financialization are limited especially in Asia–pacific countries but also financialization was characterized in the previous studies as a single index. The present paper aims to fill this gap by focusing on Asia–pacific countries. Due to the lack of data for all these economies, 11 countries namely Bangladesh, Cambodia, India, Indonesia, Laos, Malaysia, Nepal, Philippines, Singapore, Thailand, Vietnam were considered for this study.

1.1 Financialization in India

India's journey towards financial inclusion in the mid-2000s relied heavily on the commercial banks to meet the unmet banking needs of excluded population. These banks invested more in opening physical branches to supply these services, however, with the advent of digital technologies, there is a paradigm shift in the policy focus. The swift changes in the banking sector have opened the doors to private banks who invented and invested hugely on digitization process and created innovative digital mobile banking apps, adopted artificial intelligence and block chain technology to ensure secure financial transactions and better access to financial services.

In 2015, the Indian government started digitization system with Jan Dhan programme to improve network connectivity and financial inclusion through an efficient structure of unified payment system (Rani, 2016). The depth, accessibility, and effectiveness of financial institutions as well as financial markets have improved through several policy initiatives such as JAM (Jan Dhan accounts, Aadhaar linkages to bank accounts, mobile phones), demonetization, online government services, and electronic transfer of subsidies into bank accounts. The digital financialization was propelled after the demonetization of currency in 2016, the Digital India campaign created awareness, encouraged adoption, and acted as a catalyst for the growth of financialization. The COVID-19 pandemic bolstered the adoption and usage of online and mobile financial services.

In India, everyday financial transactions, such as buying essential goods and services, groceries, paying utility bills, and online banking have been changed by digitalization. The desire for cashless payments has changed primarily because of a fundamental shift in the availability of services that are more digital in nature. However, individuals that does not participate in the financial or digital domains have also increased demand for these services. Due to the greater digital accessibility and robustness of the digital financial ecosystem, the number of individuals adopting online and mobile banking, plastic cards, ATMs, opening up demat accounts, and value of transactions over digital platforms (online insurance, peer-to-peer lending, crowdfunding, mutual funds, derivatives) has increased substantially over a period (Telecom Regulatory Authority of India, 2023).

The digital transactions have increased by 41.7% from INR 141,459,089 crore in 2020–21 to INR 242,823,798 crore in 2023–24 whereas debit card transactions increased by 88.7% from INR 66,491 crore to INR 592,429 crore during the same period. However, unified payment interface (UPI) transactions increased by 99.4% from INR 4,103,658 crore in 2020–21 to INR 19,995,086 crore in 2023–24 (Reserve Bank of India, 2024). To bridge digital divide, the Indian government initiated Aadhaar Enabled Payment System (AePS) to enable transactions without ATM. India's rapid UPI adoption and usage, especially among the poorest segments of society, may be attributed mostly to reasonably priced smartphones, growing digital commerce, and more affordable internet connections.

1.2 Financialization of Saving in India

Because of higher borrowings from banks and non-banks, a decline in net financial savings has been observed in India in 2022–23 to a five-year low of INR 14.16 lakh crore, 5.3% of GDP (MoSPI, 2024). At the same time, banks and non-banks have reported higher household borrowings which increased to 14.21 lakh crore compared to 9.61 lakh crore in 2021–22. Mutual funds investment has increased to INR 1.79 lakh crore in 2022–23 from INR 61,688 crore in 2019–20 whereas investment in shares and debentures has increased to INR 2.06 lakh crore in 2022–23 (INR 94,742 crore in 2019–20). The life insurance funds increased to INR 540,561 crore in 2022–23 (INR 475,850 crore in 2021–22). Thus, financialization of savings and higher risk appetite under which households preferred financial instruments (including insurance, mutual funds, stocks, derivatives) over traditional savings options. India has 1.158 billion mobile subscribers and 936.16 million internet subscribers in 2023, second-largest internet and mobile subscriber base in the world (Telecom Regulatory Authority of India, 2023).

2 Literature Review

Digitalization has been widely defined as an integration of digital technologies, infrastructure, and human resources that significantly influence the way economies and economic and other activities are carried out (Autio et al., 2018). The digital transformation is expected to reduce unequal distribution of income, improve productivity, innovation, and promote economic growth (Akerman et al., 2015; Jaumotte et al., 2013). Canh and Thanh (2020) found negative effect of internet usage on financial development whereas mobile usage positively influences it. Ha (2022) confirms positive effect of digitalization on financial markets and institutions development in 27 European countries. Several studies have documented direct effect of digitalization on reduction in labour and intermediate cost (Herzog et al., 2017; Pop, 2020), open-up new avenues for investment for global firms (Damgaard et al., 2018). Digital fundraiser platforms threaten the role of intermediaries where foreign and domestic investors can invest directly and access new markets using digital infrastructure (Damgaard et al., 2018; World Economic Forum, 2021).

The digitized financial system increases depth, accessibility, and efficiency of financial markets and institutions where savers/investors and deficient units or corporations can access capital at a lower cost and higher efficiency. The transparent information flow among participants increases the depth of financial markets. Internet and communication technologies (ICT) enable interconnected networks between markets and institutions, removing barriers to financial access. The effect of these is seen in an increase in GDP for host and home countries (World Economic Forum, 2021). Thus, digitalization affects financial development or financialization positively.

Financialization or financial development is positively associated with the growth in national income and international trade, foreign direct investment, and growth in stock market or banking sector (Jenkıns & Katırcıoglu, 2010; Katircioglu, 2012). Financial inclusion is influenced by social political and banking factors, domestic saving, inflation, trade, and government expenditure (Ahmed, 2016; Bozkurt et al., 2018; Datta & Singh, 2019; Ng et al., 2016). An emerging aspect of financialization is crowdfunding, which is internet-based digital platform for raising capital for new projects (Roma et al., 2017).

Visser (2019) carried out a study to know the influence of one aspect of digitalization that is internet and mobile phones whereas Ha (2022) considered several dimensions of digitalization while studying its effect on financialization. The researcher concluded direct influence of digitalization on financialization. Digitalization is a broader concept whereas ICT (internet, mobile) is a narrower concept. ICT has reduced time and cost and removed distance barriers while at the same time delivering effective services and communication (Suvankulov et al., 2012). The beneficial effect of digitalization on businesses in managing supply chain, marketing processes, value creation, and increasing resource base is well documented (Ardito et al., 2018; Ceipek et al, 2021; Correani et al., 2020).

Financial institutions (banks, insurance companies, mutual funds) also are an important part of financialization where they oil the wheels of financial markets. Digitalization in finance might reduce the need for intermediaries by shifting their functions to digital platforms and eliminating direct interaction and communication between its agents, brokers, or representatives. However, digitalization is a conduit for communication that reduces the cost and time taken for actual transactions, but financial institution remains relevant by providing digital finance platforms to carry out these transactions (Ha, 2022). The banking penetration in India has significantly increased after digitalization in the economy where financial products and services were offered over smartphones and computers

(Singh & Malit, 2019). However, rural consumers' usage of internet and mobile banking is lower compared to urban counterparts. The advent of FinTech sector aims to bridge this gap; however, there are a few studies on the digital financial access and financialization in India and other Asia–Pacific countries.

3 Methods

Financialization is captured by various dimensions namely accessibility, depth, and efficiency of financial markets and financial institutions. Digital financial access was measured using the data on number of debit and credit cards per 1000 adults and value of transaction volume through internet and mobile platforms as percentage of GDP and Automated Teller Machines (ATMs) per 100,000 adults. Since no data was available on other dimensions of digitalization, the scope of this study is limited to these aspects.

An empirical econometric approach to test the assumption that digital finance access leads to financialization was adopted. Financialization or financial development (FD) was defined in this study as the depth, accessibility, and efficiency of financial institutions (FI) and financial markets (FM), a composite index calculated by IMF. The independent variables were the number of ATMs per 100,000 adults, number of debit cards issued per 1000 adults, the number of credit cards issued per 1000 adults, and value of internet and mobile transactions as percentage of GDP. Dependent variable was FD and financial institution index (FI).

$FD_{it} = \beta_0 + \beta_1 CR + \beta_2 DR + \beta_3 VALUE + \beta_4 ATM + \varphi_t + \omega_i + \varepsilon_{ijt}$.

i represents country, t represents year. ω_i capture country and φ_t year fixed effects.

ε_{ijt} is the error term. FD_{it} is financialization index that considers three sub-indicators namely depth, accessibility, and efficiency of financial institutions (FID, FIA, FIE, respectively) and depth, accessibility, and efficiency of financial markets (FMD, FMA, FME, respectively).

The dummy variable technique is used to estimate the fixed effects model with varied intercepts among countries. These estimate models are commonly known as the Least Squares Dummy Variable approach (LSDV) was also used. A sample of 11 countries in Asia–Pacific region was considered and the data from the year 2012 to 2021 was collected. Since Hausman test was significant, fixed effect model panel regression model was used. Fisher-type unit-root test for FD and FI, number of

ATMs, number of debit and credit cards, value of internet and mobile transactions as per cent of GDP variables based on augmented Dickey–Fuller tests was carried out. Pesaran's test of cross-sectional independence and Modified Wald test was used. Wooldridge test for autocorrelation in panel data was calculated. Breusch–Pagan LM test of independence was to know correlation in residuals was used.

The data was obtained from International Monetary Fund (IMF) Financial Access Survey (FAS), FD index of IMF, and Reserve Bank of India annual reports and databases. The FAS was established in 2009 with the goal of gathering supply-side data on the usage and access indicators associated with financial inclusion. The absence of digitalization index in India is a major drawback of this study. Stata 18 was used for data analysis.

Panel data regression is as follows.

4 Results

The mean number of ATMs per 100,000 adults was 38, number of credit cards per 1000 adults was 250, number of debit cards per 1000 adults was 815 (Table 1). Number of mobile and internet banking transactions per 1000 adults was nearly 97,889 and its value as percentage of GDP was 291.78.

FD index's average value was 0.415, FI index had an average of 0.454, and the mean value of FM index was 0.361. FID index had an average value of 0.36, FIA was 0.285, and FIE was 0.646. FMD index had a mean value of 0.407, FMA was 0.31, and mean value of FME was 0.341. Correlation between the variables was assessed (Table 2). Number of debit cards has high correlation with value of transactions as % of GDP (0.85) and FD with credit cards (0.9175). FI is highly correlated with FD (0.9774) and number of credit cards (0.9663) whereas FM with FD (0.9822) and FI (0.9204).

Fixed effects presuppose that variations in intercepts may account for individual country differences (cross section). Hausman test revealed that the fixed effects model fits the data. The results of the regression are given in Table 3. Fisher-type unit-root test for FD, FI, FM, ATM, debit, and card variables based on augmented Dickey–Fuller tests revealed that at least one panel is stationary ($p < 0.05$). Pesaran's test of cross-sectional independence was not significant (test value = 1.031, $p = 0.3026$) and average absolute value of the off-diagonal elements was 0.409. Modified Wald test was not significant. Wooldridge test for autocorrelation in panel

Table 1 Descriptive statistics

Variable	*Mean*	*Standard deviation*	*Minimum*	*Maximum*
Number of ATMs per 100,000 adults	38	29	6	114
Number of credit cards per 1000 adults	250	445	1	2047
Number of debit cards per 1000 adults	815	660	1	2336
Number of mobile and internet banking transactions per 1000 adults	97,888.86	117,227.4	28.68	381,318.7
Value of mobile and internet banking transactions (% of GDP)	291.787	216.678	0.02	643.46
Financial development index	0.415	0.208	0.133	0.761
Financial institutions index	0.454	0.182	0.159	0.773
Financial markets index	0.361	0.241	0.001	0.735
Financial institutions depth index	0.36	0.291	0.054	1
Financial institutions access index	0.285	0.148	0.0.088	0.647
Financial institutions efficiency index	0.646	0.081	0.311	0.75
Financial markets depth index	0.407	0.309	0.001	0.952
Financial markets access index	0.31	0.223	0	0.82
Financial markets efficiency index	0.341	0.291	0	1

data was not significant, so there was no first-order autocorrelation ($p = 0.1160$, $F = 2.962$). Breusch–Pagan LM test of independence was non-significant (chi-squared value = 22.7), thus residuals were not correlated. Overall R^2 was 0.8307 (within = 0.3994, between = 0.8499).

As given in Tables 3 and 4, number of ATMs has positive and statistically significant effect on the FD and FI whereas number of debit cards affect FD only. Number of credit cards reduces financial institutions' development. Therefore, public adoption of digitalization in terms of use of credit cards contributes lesser development of financial institutions in a country. ATMs improve financialization and institutional development.

Table 2 Correlation matrix

	number	*value*	*atm*	*credit*	*debit*	*fd*	*fi*	*fm*
number	1.0000							
value	0.6176	1.0000						
atm	0.4640	0.2793	1.0000					
credit	0.5713	0.6462	0.7871	1.0000				
debit	0.4270	0.8507	0.3299	0.7183	1.0000			
fd	0.5174	0.5115	0.7624	0.9175	0.6639	1.0000		
fi	0.5151	0.5649	0.8113	0.9663	0.7063	0.9774	1.0000	
fm	0.4999	0.4446	0.6902	0.8394	0.6010	0.9822	0.9204	1.0000

Note fd—Financial development index; fi—Financial institutions index; fm—Financial markets index; number—Number of mobile and internet banking transactions per 1000 adults; value—Value of mobile and internet banking transactions (% of GDP)

On financial institutions index as dependent variable, number of ATMs has positive sign revealing that larger number of ATMs per 1000 adults, higher would be the development of FIs. Number of credit cards per 1000 adults has negative sign indicating that a greater number of these cards would reduce the development of FIs. The overall R^2 was 0.676 (within = 0.541; between = 0.689), Prob > F = 0.01.

The results of Least Squares Dummy Variable approach are given in Table 5. The adjusted R^2 was 0.993 on financialization index. Singapore has higher financialization, followed by Malaysia, Thailand, India, and Philippines.

A sub-sample of selected few countries (Bangladesh, India, Indonesia, Malaysia, Vietnam, and Thailand) for which data on value and number was available was considered for further analysis. Fixed effects regression results are given in Table 6. The adjusted R^2 was 0.691 (within = 0.436, between = 0.725), Prob > F = 0.000. On financial development index, number of ATMs has positive sign suggesting its positive impact on financialization.

As shown in Table 7, financial institutions development index is affected by the number of ATMs and value of mobile and internet banking transactions as % of GDP. Both these variables have positive sign suggesting their positive impact on FI development. Overall R^2 was 0.783 (within = 0.698, between = 0.799).

Table 3 Estimation of fixed effects panel regression: Financialization

Corr (u_i, Xb) = 0.7797				*F(3, 10) = 21.46* *Prob > F = 0.0001*		
		(Std. err. adjusted for 11 clusters in country)				
fd	*Coefficient*	*Robust std. err*	*t*	*P > |t|*	*[95% conf. interval]*	
atm	0.0021801	0.0004702	4.64	0.001	0.0011324	0.0032279
debit	0.0000571	0.000025	2.29	0.045	1.51e-06	0.0001127
credit	−9.48e-06	9.72e-06	−0.98	0.352	−0.0000311	0.0000122
_cons	0.2884624	0.0239687	12.03	0.000	0.2350568	0.3418681
sigma_u	0.14091581					
sigma_e	0.01922687					
Rho	0.98172375	(fraction of variance due to u_i)				

Note fd—Financial development index

Table 4 Estimation of fixed effects panel regression: Financial institutions index

corr(u_i, Xb) = 0.3259				*F(3, 10) = 6.35* *Prob > F = 0.0110*		
		(Std. err adjusted for 11 clusters in country)				
fi	*Coefficient*	*Robust std. err*	*t*	*P > |t|*	*[95% conf. interval]*	
atm	0.003818	0.0010085	3.79	0.004	0.001571	0.006065
debit	0.0000319	0.0000311	1.03	0.329	−0.0000374	0.0001011
credit	−0.0000328	0.000014	−2.35	0.041	−0.000064	−1.70e-06
_cons	0.2904669	0.043006	6.75	0.000	0.1946435	0.3862902
sigma_u	0.11190168					
sigina_e	0.01893488					
rho	0.97216495	(fraction of variance due to u_i)				

Note fi—Financial institutions index

Table 5 Estimation of LSDV approach: Financialization

Linear regression

Number of obs = *100*
F(3, 10) =
Prob > F =
R-squared = *0.09926*
Root MSE = *0.01923*

		(Std. err. Adjusted for 11 clusters in country)				
fd	*Coefficient*	*Robust std, err*	*t*	*P > |t|*	*[95% conf. interval]*	
atm	0.0021801	0.0004968	4.39	0.001	0.0010731	0.0032871
debit	0.0000571	0.0000264	2.17	0.056	−1.63e.-06	0.0001159
credit	−9.48e-06	0.0000103	-0.92	0.378	−0.0000324	0.0000134
country						
1	0.226132	0.0052265	43.27	0.000	0.2144866	0.2377773
2	0.1163597	0.0105526	11.03	0.000	0.0928469	0.1398724
3	0.3845389	0.0188456	20.40	0.000	0.3425483	0.4265295
4	0.2080971	0.0289975	7.18	0.000	0.1434867	0.2727075
5	0.1073318	0.0107416	9.99	0.000	0.083398	0.1312656
6	0.4643842	0.0485109	9.57	0.000	0.3562952	0.5724731
7	0.1320275	0.0099381	13.29	0.000	0.109884	0.1541709
8	0.2672853	0.0189845	14.08	0.000	0.2249852	0.3095854
9	0.4946295	0.0494343	10.01	0.000	0.3844831	0.604776
10	0.4216443	0.0546872	7.71	0.000	0.2997937	0.5434949
11	0.2517312	0.0285043	8.83	0.000	0.1882196	0.3152428

Note fd—Financial development index; 1—Bangladesh, 2—Cambodia, 3—India, 4—Indonesia, 5—Laos, 6—Malaysia, 7—Nepal, 8—Philippines, 9—Singapore, 10—Thailand, 11—Vietnam

Table 6 Estimation of fixed effects panel regression: Financialization in selected countries

corr(u_ij. Xb) = 0.4533				*F(4, 41) = 7.93* *Prob > F = 0.0001*		
fd	*Coefficient*	*Std. err*	*t*	*P > |t|*	*[9556 conf. interval]*	
atm	0.0023766	0.0008848	2.69	0.010	0.0005897	0.0041635
debit	0.0000221	0.0000288	0.77	0.447	−0.0000361	0.0000803
number	1.74e-07	1.18e-07	1.47	0.149	−6.49e-08	4.14e-07
value	0.0000429	0.0000431	1.00	0.325	-0.0000441	0.00013
_cons	0.3450359	0.0354691	9.73	0.000	0.2734046	0.4166671
sigma_u	0.11281097					
Sigma_e	0.02141734					
rho	0.96521033	(fraction of variance due to u_i)				
F test that all u_i = 0: F(5, 41) = 117.85					Prob > F = 0.0000	

Table 7 Estimation of fixed effects panel regression: Financial institutions index of selected countries

Corr (u_i, Xb) = 0.2787				*F(4, 41) = 23.72* *Prob > F = 0.0000*		
fi	*Coefficient*	*Std. err*	*t*	*P > |t|*	*[95% conf. interval]*	
atm	0.002892	0.0003939	7.34	0.000	0.0020966	0.0036874
credit	0.0001334	0.0001097	1.22	0.231	−0.0000882	0.0003551
number	−6.32e-08	6.24e-08	−1.01	0.316	−1.89e-07	6.27e-08
value	0.0000547	0.0000219	2.50	0.016	0.0000106	0.0000989
_cons	0.3329655	0.020316	16.39	0.000	0.2919365	0.3739945
sigma_u	0.08328362					
sigma_e	0.01068108					
rho	0.98381824	(fraction of variance due to u_i)				
F test that all u_i = 9: F(5, 41) = 117.61					Prob > F = 0.0000	

The Least Squares Dummy Variable approach was adopted to see country effects (Table 8). The adjusted R^2 was 0.9867. Malaysia performs better followed by India and Thailand in financial development index.

Table 8 Estimation of LSDV approach: Financialization Index

				R-squared = 0.9867 *Root MSE = 0.02151*		
			(Std. err adjusted for 6 clusters in country)			
fd	*Coefficient*	*Robust std. err*	*t*	*P > |t|*	*[9596 conf*	*interval]*
atm	0.0028749	0.0007316	3.93	0.011	0.0009944	0.0047555
credit	−0.000107	0.00038	−0.28	0.790	−0.0010838	0.0008699
value	0.0000633	0.0000606	1.04	0.345	−0.0000926	0.0002191
number	2.00e-07	1.61e-07	1.24	0.269	−2.14e-07	6.15e-07
country						
1	0.2258555	0.0078795	28.66	0.000	0.2056006	0.2461105
2	0.4099323	0.0180496	22.71	0.000	0.3635344	0.4563302
3	0.2077501	0.0475056	4.37	0.007	0.0856332	0.329867
4	0.5254164	0.1404319	3.74	0.013	0.1644247	0.886408
5	0.409796	0.1476191	2.78	0.039	0.030329	0.7892629
6	0.2799079	0.0333317	8.40	0.000	0.194226	0.3655897

Note fd—Financial development index; 1—Bangladesh, 2—India, 3—Indonesia, 4—Malaysia, 5—Thailand, 6—Vietnam

5 Conclusion

The growth of financial markets and institutions is positively and statistically significantly impacted by digitalization. Average index value of FI was the highest, followed by FD and FM. Therefore, financial markets development is much lower that has to be improved through various digital push measures and policy initiatives. FI efficiency was the highest followed by FI depth. Financial institutions and financial markets accessibility are the lowest. FM depth was much higher than FM efficiency. Digital finance relies on delivery of financial products and services using technologies such as mobile phone solutions, electronic cards, phablets, biometric devices, and structured electronic payment platforms (David-West et al., 2018). Financial services available digitally boost the percentage of individuals using formal banking or financial services in rural areas (Finau et al., 2016).

Out of all the digital access to finance, number of debit cards per 1000 individuals and number of ATMs per 100,000 individuals contribute to the financialization whereas ATMs improve the development of financial institutions. Financial institutions development is impeded by the quantity of credit cards issued. The Least Squares Dummy Variable approach reveals that Singapore has the most financialization, with Malaysia, Thailand, India, and the Philippines following. When additional factors were included and the LSDV approach was applied for five countries for which the data was available, Malaysia performed the best on the financial development index, followed by India and Thailand. The number of ATMs and value of mobile and internet banking transactions as per cent of GDP positively influences the development of financial institutions whereas number of ATMs affects financialization. The data on different measures of digital finance access for a longer time period was not available for most of the countries in Asia–Pacific region, therefore, future studies can look into a larger dataset that provides in-depth information on several dimensions of digitalization.

India lags behind many countries in the Asia–pacific region in financialization and development of financial institutions. Despite a rise in internet usage over the years, a sizable portion of the population in India still does not have access to official banking or financial services. Many persons in lower income categories do have bank accounts, but they are only used once a month, and only for withdrawals. If the value of mobile and internet banking transactions as per cent of GDP increases, the financial institutions would develop at par with other developed countries. Access to financial institutions and financial markets is still low in the sample. Distance from a financial institution (bank branch) remained one of the key reasons why people do not have bank accounts; therefore, the number of ATMs per 100,000 increases financial development and growth of financial institutions especially efficiency and depth.

ATMs provide consumers with a range of financial services quickly and safely, including cash withdrawals, deposits, fund transfers, and balance inquiries. They provide a wide range of services like account information, cash deposits, bill payments, generate mini statement, and PIN changes. If more ATMs are positioned in towns and villages, people will be encouraged to register for bank services, develop trust in digital payments, and ultimately embrace them. Debit cards assist individuals to purchase goods and services, withdraw cash from ATMs, and online fund transfers. It is convenient to use, and the risk of carrying cash or the need to visit bank branches is reduced. They financially empower people to avail of online services, e-commerce, or any electronic transactions on digital platforms. It is essential that the government progressively create awareness about the advantages of owning a bank account such as cash withdrawals via ATMs or use of debit cards for e-commerce or online purchase of financial products. Reducing economic inequalities and promoting financial inclusion in India can be achieved by increasing the ATM network to far-flung locations. ATMs and debit cards may significantly improve the lives of millions of people who do not currently have access to formal financial institutions by giving them swift access to banking services and thereby, encouraging growth in the economy. Public should be educated about the importance of using mobile or internet banking in meeting their financial needs such as e-payments, e-insurance, online trading, or opening fixed deposits online. The number of credit cards per 1000 had negative impact of financial institutions development, this needs to be explored further using larger datasets. India can catch up to its counterparts because of the country's strong internet penetration rate, but it needs to encourage the use of digital payments.

References

Ahmed, A. D. (2016). Integration of financial markets, financial development and growth: Is Africa different? *Journal of International Financial Markets,*

Institutions and Money, 42, 43–59. https://doi.org/10.1016/j.intfin.2016.01.003

Akerman, A., Gaarder, I., & Mogstad, M. (2015). The skill complementarity of broadband internet. *Quarterly Journal of Economics, 130*(4), 1781–1824. https://doi.org/10.1093/qje/qjv028

Amarante Consulting Group. (2014). Market study of digital financial services in India. *A Summary Report by Amarante Consulting Group.* Accessed from http://amaranteconsulting.com/upload/publication/Summary%20DFS%20Report%20India%20June%22014_1.pdf on July 27, 2017 on 12th May 2024.

Ardito, L., Petruzzelli, A. M., Panniello, U., & Garavelli, A. C. (2018). Towards Industry 4.0: Mapping digital technologies for supply chain management-marketing integration. *Business Process Management Journal, 25*(2), 323–346. https://doi.org/10.1108/BPMJ-04-2017–0088

Asongu, S., & Nwachukwu, J. C. (2018). Comparative human development thresholds for absolute and relative pro-poor mobile banking in developing countries. *Information Technology & People, 31*(1), 63–83.

Autio, E., Nambisan, S., Thomas, L. D. W., & Wright, M. (2018). Digital affordances, spatial affordances, and the genesis of entrepreneurial ecosystems. *Strategic Entrepreneurship Journal, 12*(1), 72–95. https://doi.org/10.1002/sej.1266

Bozkurt, I., & Karakus¸ R., & Yildiz, M. (2018). Spatial determinants of financial inclusion over time. *Journal of International Development, 30*(8), 1474–1504. https://doi.org/10.1002/jid.3376

Canh, N. P., Thanh, S. D., & S. D. (2020). Financial development and the shadow economy: A multi-dimensional analysis. *Economic and Political Weekly, 67*, 37–54. https://doi.org/10.1016/j.eap.2020.05.002

Ceipek, R., Hautz, J., Petruzzelli, A. M., De Massis, A., & Matzler, K.. (2021). A motivation and ability perspective on engagement in emerging digital technologies: The case of Internet of Things solutions, Long. *Range Planning, 54*(5),101991. https://doi.org/10.1016/j.lrp.2020.101991

Correani, A., De Massis, A., Frattini, F., & Petruzzelli, A. M. (2020). Natalicchio, Implementing a digital strategy: Learning from the experience of three digital transformation projects. *California Manageent Review, 62*(4), 37–56. https://doi.org/10.1177/0008125620934864

Damgaard, J., Elkjaer, T., & Johannesen, N. (2018). Piercing the Veil, finance & development. https://doi.org/10.5089/9781484357415.022. eISBN: 9781484357415.

Datta, S. K., & Singh, K. (2019). Variation and determinants of financial inclusion and their association with human development: A cross-country analysis. *IIMB Management Review, 31*(4), 336–349. https://doi.org/10.1016/j.iimb.2019.07.013

Daud, S. N. M., Ahmad, A. H., & Ngah, W. A. S. W. (2021). Financialization, digital technology and income inequality. *Applied Economics Letters, 28*(16), 1339–1343. https://doi.org/10.1080/13504851.2020.1808165

David-West, O., Iheanachor, N., & Kelikume, I. (2018). A resource-based view of Digital Financial Services (DFS): An exploratory study of Nigerian providers. *Journal of Business Research, 88*, 513–526.

Davis, L. E. (2018). Financialization and investment: A survey of the empirical literature. *Journal of Economic Surveys, 31*(5), 207–235. https://doi.org/10.1111/joes.12242

Finau, G., Rika, N., Samuwai, J., & McGoon, J. (2016). Perceptions of digital financial services in rural Fiji. *Information Technologies & International Development, 12*(4), 11–21.

Galor, O., & Moav., O. (2004). From Physical to human capital accumulation: Inequality and the process of development. *Review of Economic Studies, 71*, 1001–1026. https://doi.org/10.1111/0034-6527.00312

Greenwood, J., & Jovanovic, B. (1990). Financial development and the distribution of income. *The Journal of Political Economy, 98*, 1076–1107. https://doi.org/10.1086/261720

Ha, L. T. (2022). Effects of digitalization on financialization: Empirical evidence from European countries. *Technology in Society, 68*, 101851. https://doi.org/10.1016/j.techsoc.2021.101851

Haan, J., & Sturm, J. (2017). Finance and income inequality: A review and new evidence. *European Journal of Political Economy, 50*, 171–195. https://doi.org/10.1016/j.ejpoleco.2017.04.007

Herzog, K., Winter, G., Kurka, G., Ankermann, K., Binder, R., Ringhofer, M., Maierhofer, A., & Flick, A. (2017). The digitalization of steel production. *BHM Berg- Hüttenm¨annische Monatsh, 162*(11), 504–513, https://doi.org/10.1007/s00501-017-0673-9

Huang, Y., & Zhang, Y. (2020). Financial inclusion and urban-rural income inequality: Long-run and short-run relationship. *Emerging Markets Finance and Trade, 56*, 457–471. https://doi.org/10.1080/1540496X.2018.1562896

Hyde, A., Vachon, T., & Wallace, M. (2017). Financialization, income inequality and redistribution in 18 affluent democracies, 1981–2011. *Social Currents, 5*, 193–211. https://doi.org/10.1177/2329496517704874

Jain, S., & Gabor, D. (2020). The rise of digital Financialisation: The case of India. *New Political Economy, 25*(5), 813–828. https://doi.org/10.1080/13563467.2019.1708879

Jaumotte, F., Lall, S., & Papageorgiou, C. (2013).Rising income inequality: Technology, or trade and financial globalization? *IMF Economic Review, 61*(2), 271–309. https://doi.org/10.1057/imfer.2013.7

Jenkıns, H. P., & Katırcıoglu, S. T. (2010). The bounds test approach for cointegration and causality between financial development, international trade and economic growth: The case of Cyprus. *Applied Economics, 42*(13), 1699–1707. https://doi.org/10.1080/00036840701721661

Katircioglu, S. T. (2012). Financial development, international trade and economic growth: The case of sub-saharan Africa. *Ekonomista,* 117–127.

Lin, K., & Tomaskovic-Devey, D. (2013). Financialization and U.S. income inequality: 1970–2008. *American Journal of Sociology, 118*, 1284–1329. https://doi.org/10.1086/669499

Manyika, J., Lund, S., Singer, M., White, O., & Berry, C. (2016). *Digital finance for all: Powering inclusive growth in emerging economies (Rep.).* McKinsey Global Institute, McKinsey & Company.

Meniago, C., & Asongu, S. (2018). Revisiting the finance-inequality Nexus in a panel of African countries. *Research in International Business and Finance, 46*, 399–419. https://doi.org/10.1016/j.ribaf.2018.04.012

MoSPI. (2024). *National accounts statistics 2024.* Ministry of statistics and program implementation. https://www.mospi.gov.in/publication/national-accounts-statistics-2024

Ng, A., Ibrahim, M. H., & Mirakhor, A. (2016). Does trust contribute to stock market development? *Econometric Modelling, 52*, 239–250. https://doi.org/10.1016/j.econmod.2014.10.056

Noh, Y., & Yoo, K. (2000). Internet, inequality and growth. *Journal of Policy Modelling, 30*, 1005–1016. https://doi.org/10.1016/j.jpolmod.2007.06.016

Patil, P. P., Dwivedi, Y. K., & Rana, N. P. (Nov, 2017). Digital payments adoption: An analysis of literature. In *Conference on e-Business, e-services and e-society* (13 E) (pp. 61–70). Springer.

Pop, L. D. (2020). Digitalization of the system of data analysis and collection in an automotive company. *Procedia Manufacturing, 46*, 238–243. https://doi.org/10.1016/j.promfg.2020.03.035

Rani, S. (2016). Digital India: Unleashing prosperity. *Indian Journal of Applied Research, 6*(4), 238–243.

Reserve Bank of India. (2024). Payment system indicators. Payment system indicators—Payment & Settlement System Statistics. https://www.rbi.org.in/Scripts/PSIUserView.aspx?Id=34

Roma, P., Petruzzelli, A. M., & Perrone, G. (2017). From the crowd to the market: The role of reward-based crowdfunding performance in attracting professional investors. *Research Policy, 46*(9), 1606–1628. https://doi.org/10.1016/j.respol.2017.07.012

de Rugy, V., & Salmon, J. (2020). *Debt and growth: A decade of studies.* Policy Brief. Mercatus Centre, George Mason University, Fairfax. https://www.mercatus.org/research/policy-briefs/debt-and-growth-decade-studies

Sharma, S. K., Mangla, S. K., Luthra, S., & Al-Salti, Z. (2018). Mobile wallet inhibitors: Developing a comprehensive theory using an integrated model. *Journal of Retailing and Consumer Services, 45*, 52–63.

Singh, R., & Malit, G. (2019). Impact of digitalization on Indian rural banking customer: With reference to payment systems. *Emerging Economy Studies, 5*(1), 31–41. Sage Publishers.

Srivastava, A. K., & Sharma, S. (2017). Social justice through Aadhaar: An e-policy initiative. In L. W. Zacher (Ed.), *Technology, society and sustainability* (pp. 83–97). Springer-Verlag.

Suvankulov, F., Lau, C. K., & Chau, F. H. C. (2012). Job search on the internet and its outcome. *Internet Research, 22*(3), 298–317. https://doi.org/10.1108/10662241211235662

Svirydzenka, K. (2016). Introducing a new broad-based index of financial development (SSRN scholarly paper ID 2754950). In *Social Science Research Network*. https://papers.ssrn.com/abstract=2754950

Telecom Regulatory Authority of India (2023). *Indian telecom services performance indicators*. The Indian Telecom Services Performance Indicator Report October–December. https://www.trai.gov.in/sites/default/files/QPIR_23042024_0.pdf

Van Deursen, A. J. A. M., & van Dijk, J. A. G. M. (2019). The first-level digital divide shifts from inequalities in physical access to inequalities in material access. *New Media and Society, 21*, 354–375. https://doi.org/10.1177/1461444818797082

Visser, R. (2019). The effect of the internet on the margins of trade. *Information Economics and Policy, 46*, 41–54. https://doi.org/10.1016/j.infoecopol.2018.12.001

World Economic Forum. (2021). COVID-19: *How digital investments can help the recovery*. World Economic Forum. Retrieved August 8, https://www.weforum.org/agenda/2020/04/covid-19-digital-foreign-direct-investment-economic-recovery/

Smart Technology Adoption in E-Finance Services

Girija Narasimhan and Reshmy Krishnan

1 Introduction

Artificial intelligence (AI) applications are generally referred to as Smart technology. In recent years, Smart technology has played an essential role in helping businesses analyze, predict, and improve their performance. An enormous corporation seeks the advice and prediction of a financial consultant and fund manager about its market value and customer retention. A forecast is a term coined in meteorology, but this term is common in modern business-like financial forecasts and share-marketing forecasts. Communication and network field technologies such as big data, robotics, and the Internet of Things (IoT) are implemented in E-finance applications. Artificial Intelligence-based technologies make digitized finance more secure. Let us explore each of these topics. FinTech topics define FinTech categories and FinTech companies. It also describes the top four countries where FinTech services are in use. The next part of the chapter is

G. Narasimhan (✉)
IT Department, University of Technology and Applied Science, Muscat, Oman
e-mail: girija.narasimhan@utas.edu.om

R. Krishnan
Muscat College, Muscat, Oman
e-mail: reshmy@muscatcollege.edu.om

© The Author(s), under exclusive license to Springer Nature Singapore Pte Ltd. 2025

A. S. et al. (eds.), *Trends and Challenges of Electronic Finance*,
https://doi.org/10.1007/978-981-96-3304-3_3

a classification of cryptocurrencies and their features. The cryptocurrency-approved and banned country status is discussed in this part. The third topic is financial forecasting. This topic explains how AI predicting applications transform the traditional financial forecasting techniques in the modern E-finance world. The sub-topic Robo-advisor and its services in E-finance. Leading companies that supply Robo-advisor services and their assets under management values are given in Fig. 2.6. One of the prime operations of banking services is lending. Adopting machine-learning technology in lending process flow helps to detect fraud much better than the earlier method. The traditional and technological approaches of market values prediction are discussed under the stock market prediction. Machine-learning algorithms and their accuracy level of market prediction are available in Fig. 10. The latter topic discusses E-finance security challenges, specifically cybersecurity.

2 Financial Technology (FinTech)

FinTech is a technology-based financial service that uses computer technology in banking services using a smartphone. Generally, the consumer uses FinTech for money transfer, balance checking, and deposit status. The pandemic situation insists almost one-third of the consumers use at least two or three FinTech services regularly daily (kagan, 2020). PayPal is one of the leading FinTech companies. Personal Capital, Wealthfront, and Lending Club are also the most well-known FinTech companies. The categories of FinTech services are B2C for small businesses, B2B for banks, business clients, and consumers or end-users in Fig. 1.

The PWC 2020 report statement that 81% of banking CEOs believe technologies are changing finance services rapidly than any other sector (Courbe, 2020). Therefore, from 2014 global investments have increased triple times in FinTech. FinTech influences the banking services to spend more than $215 Billion on IT-enabled services like internal software and hardware services. Because of technological disruption, the FinTech lending loan process in digital lending is helpful for small startup businesses. The FinTech services are digital payment, blockchain, insurance, mobile banking, equity finance, and digital wealth management. The most general FinTech service is money transfer and payments. As per ACI Worldwide and Global Data 2020 report, the top four countries that promote FinTech services are India, China, South Korea, and Thailand (Anil, 2018). Almost 2100 FinTech companies are in India. Most of the

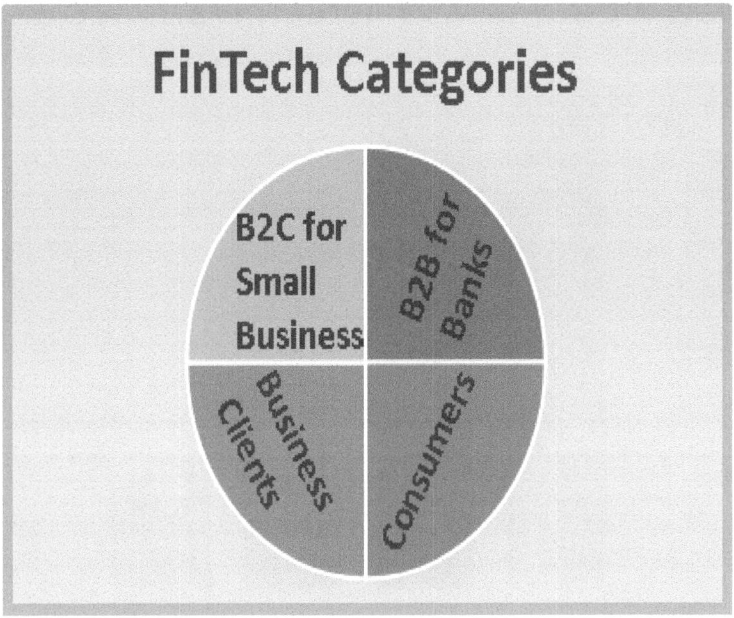

Fig. 1 FinTech categories

companies started within last five years. Due to the pandemic the past two years from 2020, this service became vital in the financial sector (Fig. 2).

3 Crypto Currency

In ancient times, people used gold, silver, and copper coins to remain currency. Once metals are costly, the paper currency started the journey in the financial market. Next are plastic currencies like credit cards and debit cards. Digital technology enrichment is cryptocurrency or crypto. Using blockchain technology, investors can process cryptocurrency transactions in a decentralized system. In 2008, still unclear whether a single person or group of people using the Japanese name Satoshi Nakamoto coined the first cryptocurrency, named Bitcoin (Girija, 2021). From a trading point of view, it is the most volatile asset. Because the price of one Bitcoin in the 2010th year was $0.0008 and currently in 2021, its value is relatively $57,126.80. The various classifications of a cryptocurrency described in

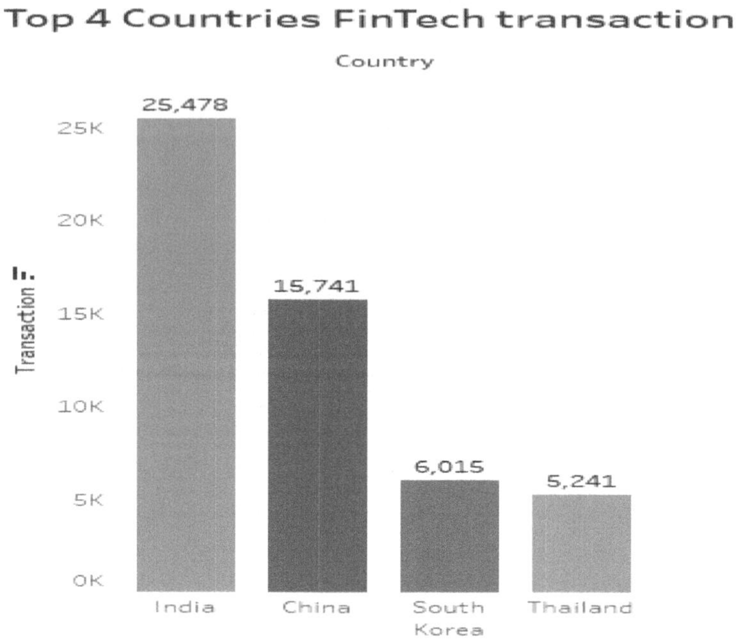

Fig. 2 Top 4 countries using FinTech transaction

Fig. 3. Bitcoin is also referred to as the main coin. The Altcoin word is a combination of the alternative plus coin. The altcoin feature is fixed and based on demand value may increase or decrease. Shit coins no little value or no current purpose used in digital currency (Hyes, 2021).

El Salvador comprises the first country to accept cryptocurrency. Most of the cryptocurrency holding a country stands for the USA. No doubt, this cryptocurrency concept creates a new wave in business transactions. At the same time, most countries are seriously thinking about forming

Fig. 3 Cryptocurrency classification

digital currency in the future. The main difference between digital currency and cryptocurrency—digital currency is a centralized currency and transaction within the regulated network. However, a community of developer(s) regulating cryptocurrency. Those are controlling the network protocol. It is a decentralized system. The given below Fig. 4 shows a few sample countries, which accept and ban the status of the cryptocurrency.

Market capitalization short term is cap. Based on the size of the market cap, companies are in three categories. They are large cap, midcap, and small cap. The cap value is calculated based on the formula—the current stock price multiplied by total outstanding shares. Suppose the current stock price is $2 and the total number of outstanding shares is 10000

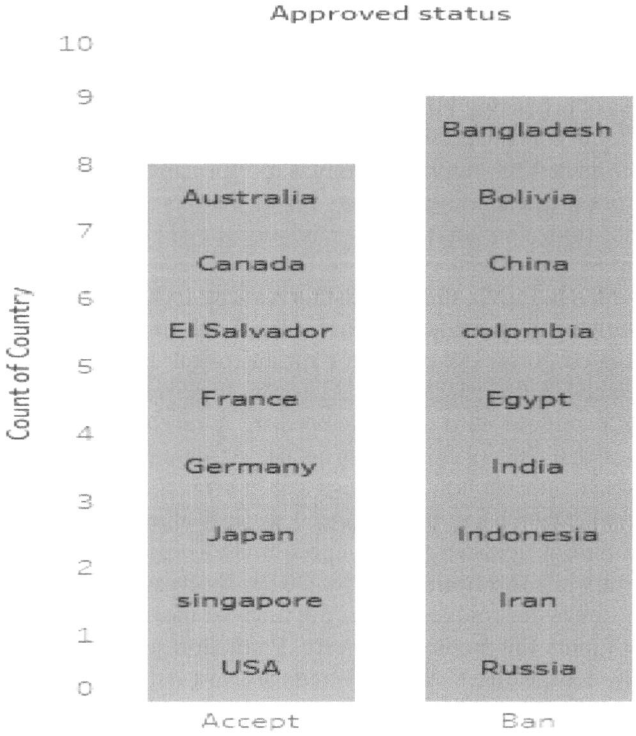

Fig. 4 Cryptocurrency Accept/Ban status

Table 1 Market cap value of cryptocurrency

CryptoCurrency_name	*CryptoCurrency_code*	*Price*	*Market Cap*
Bitcoin	**BTC**	**$58,708.26**	**$1,109,897,825,986**
Ethereum	**ETH**	**$4,448.02**	**$528,333,915,452**
Binance Coin	**BNB**	**$628.40**	**$104,775,240,790**
Tether	**USDT**	**$1.00**	**$73,169,897,606**
Solana	**SOL**	**$212.09**	**$64,498,401,532**

units then 10000 * $2= $20000 is cap value (Company size, 2021). Table 1 shows the market cap value of the top five cryptocurrencies and their approximate price in December 2021.

4 Financial Forecasting

The process of predicting business revenue in any sector is inevitable. This process is termed as financial prognoses. This process is helpful for policy or decision-makers to improve business performance. Business performance is not only generating revenue. It also matters to future investment and organization aim, capital cost, and budget (Financial Forecasting, 2020) (Fig. 5).

As explained in Fig. 5, the financial forecasting techniques are classified into qualitative and quantitative. These classifications execute forecasting based on the corporate establishment and historical data (Borad, 2021).

In the modern financial world, AI technology transforms the earlier forecasting technique into a simple format. A recent Deloitte Insights report states that 70% of financial firms use AI-based predicting applications, especially in cash flow, adjusting credit scores, and detecting fraud (Kaye, 2019). Digitalization in financial services allows a route to enter the AI technology application and algorithms to support a more secured environment while forecasting (Kuder, 2019). Forecasting and predicting are almost similar techniques. Predictive analysis based on the factor and the various inputs will predict the future. Prediction sub-discipline is forecasting. The forecasting technique inputs are vast data or historical data. Based on the given input number, it will make a prediction.

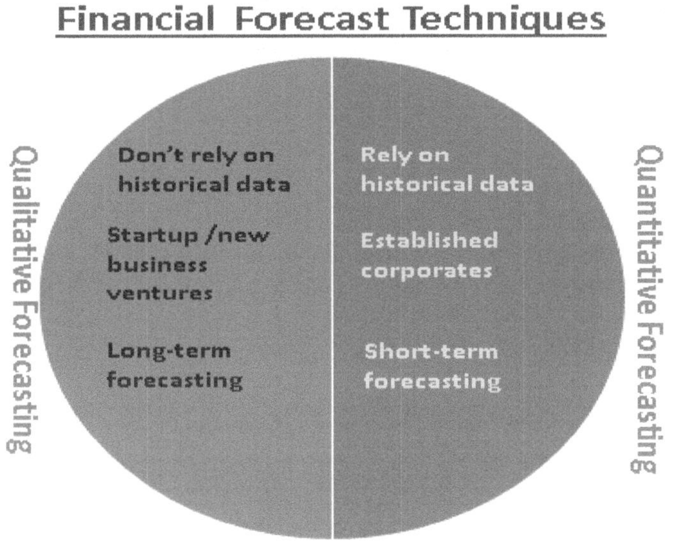

Fig. 5 Financial forecast techniques

4.1 Robo-Advisor

Artificial Intelligence (AI) swaps the finance world smarter and easier to get and invest money. Therefore, AI-enabled applications refer to Smart technology (Schroer, 2021). Robo-advisor is an automated algorithm-based online financial service. The automatic investment of asset management Robo-advisor software algorithms plays a vital role. It distributes the client assets most efficiently and manages the portfolio automatically. The top four Robo-advisor companies and their asset under management (AUM) details are in Fig. 6. All the companies are working from the United States. In the mid of 2020, Charles Schwab bought TD Ameritrade. TD Ameritrade is moreover a well-known popular Robo-advisor AUM. After merging with TD Ameritrade, Charles Schwab gained the prime spot (The Five, 2021).

Each company has the best feature like easy to access in Betterment, nominal fees are Charles Schwab, and college saving plans are best in Wealthfront (Top Robo, 2021). From the technology point of view, Black–Litterman Model is the most often used in Robo-advisor. In 1990, Fischer Black and Robert Litterman developed this mathematical model

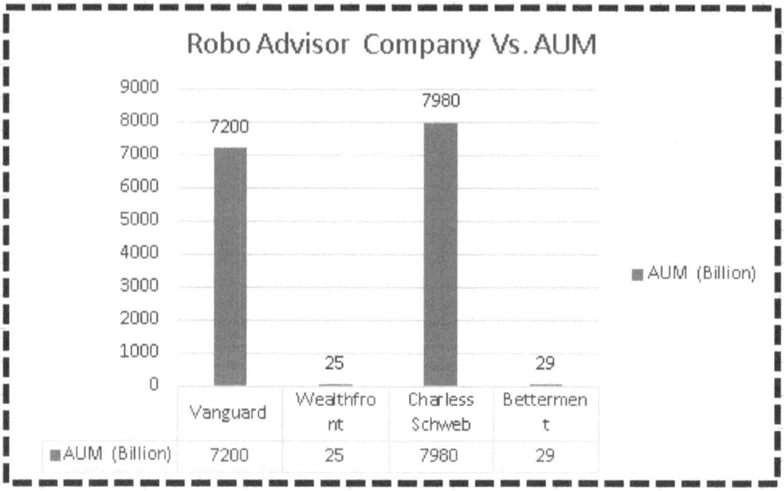

Fig. 6 Robo-advisor company Vs. AUM

for portfolio allocation. This model uses the Bayesian approach in best asset allocation. And then it supplies a former estimation of investor view of awaited returns. It stands for a combination of the Capital Asset Pricing Model (CAPM) and Markowitz's means-variance optimization model. Utilizing this combination, the model calculates the best portfolio expected returns based on given input data. The input data implied returns plus investor views. Figure 7 explains the various service factors of Robo-advisor. The Robo-advisor has aided the investor to identify with minimum investment still there is any financial plan or goal, risk tolerance percentage, and expense ratio.

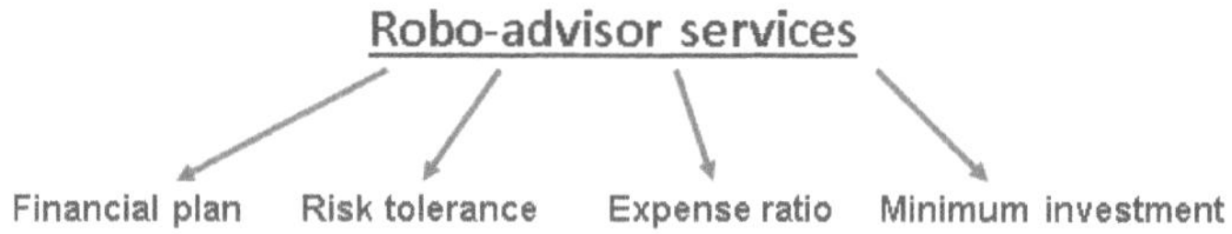

Fig. 7 Robo-advisor services

5 Smart Technology in Banking Lending Services

Lending is still a primary process of banking services. Digital lending reduces paper-based work and time consumption in the loan process. For diamond evaluation, 4 Cs information is needed. In the same manner, lending needs 5 Cs. In general, lending decides the potential of the borrower based on capacity, capital, collateral, conditions, and characters. The lending process supports various steps given in Fig. 8. FinTech helps with the first and second steps. The first step is collecting lender information which is the primary source information. In addition, the second step tracks the financial transaction of the borrower and analyzes user data which is the screening process. The next step is to design a loan contract. These contracts are designed based on both lending and borrower types. Recently most private banks started using distributed Ledger contracts (DLT). The DLT has been implemented using blockchain technology. Fraud detection and detecting anti-money laundering are the most severe challenge in lending services. Monitoring is the foremost process of lending. For constructing a lending policy, tracking suspicious activities and the credit history of the consumer data is very much needed. AI and machine-learning automated processes simplify this challenge more comfortably to the banker. Mostly Artificial Neural Networks (ANN) and Bayesian Belief Networks (BNNs) are popular machine-learning techniques used especially for fraud detection (Sam et al., 2002). The supervised machine-learning algorithm is Logistic Regression. These techniques are helpful for decision-makers to take conclude approval.

Bank branch operations are expensive. Instead of opening more bank branches, adopting Smart technology in banking services is the simplest way to contact rural people. It also improves bank profitability (Digital, 2017). To automate decision-making for credit scoring or credit rating of each customer deep learning analytics aid the bank to take decisions quickly. This pandemic situation increased health-based lending services. Mobile P2P (Peer-to-Peer) payments like Google Pay, Ola Money, and Apple Pay simplify the paid choice (Biswas, 2021). The payment ecosystem security is most significant because past two years in the COVID-19 period, most of the country's bank statistics say 2–3% increased card fraud. NFC is Near-Field Communication, which secures

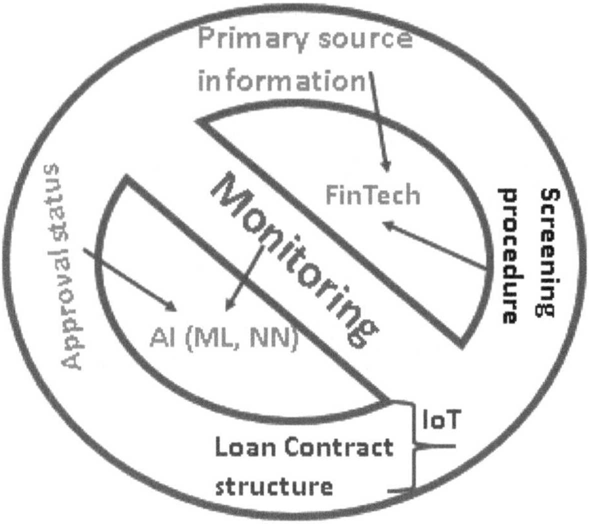

Fig. 8 Lending process

contactless payment. AI/ML techniques prevent fraud by providing security features like voice-activated transactions, biometric authentication, and Smart assistant payment authentication (Smullian, 2021).

6 Stock Market Prediction

The equity market stands for assets and earrings of corporate. Stock index values differ in each stock exchange. Like a network model, entire stock exchanges are interconnected (Chauhan, 2020). Therefore, any rise or down in stock value not only affects the stock exchange index value. It reflects the country's currency value and economic stability. The equity market is always volatile. Therefore, predicting a dynamic market involves a substantial risk for investors. Smart technology assists investors in predicting future stock trends. Machine-learning technology leads to efficient investment to reach minimal risk and high profit.

The stock market prediction approach includes two factors- trading and market time. The fundamental analysis helps to find sustained investment. Technical analysis spots out the short-term investment in the stock market. Two traditional metrics of the fundamental analysis are the P/

E ratio and P/B ratio for predicting stock. Suppose if the P/E ratio is minimum, then future profit is excessive. To detect overestimating or underestimating the stock value P/B ratio is useful. If company value might be down in the future sometimes, then the P/B ratio value is high (Nusrat et al., 2021). The sentiment analysis approach highlights social sentiments in the stock market. The sentimental analysis uses the text-mining concepts. Machine-learning and AI-accordance approaches implement an algorithm to generate the pattern. The generated patterns aid in predicting stock market movement values. Figure 9 gives pictorial representation of overall stock market approaches in detail (Mishra, 2019).

The stock market prediction uses the statistics-based regression analysis approach. The linear regression technique in the predictive analysis. Especially polynomial classifier (PC) used in recognition like voice and image-based applications. The security prices movement in Dubai Financial Market using PC (Al-salkhadi, 2011). Support Vector Machines (SVMs) and Artificial Neural Networks (ANNs) are popular algorithms in pattern learning and predicting share (Fernando, 2021). Currently, the random forest is a supervised learning algorithm that offers a more exact prediction. Time series forecasting is applied by various sectors like weather forecasting, earthquake prediction, pattern recognition, and signal processing. In the stock market, time series analysis is predicted based on the historical data of the stock. The resulting output of the analysis is the future value of a currency. For predicting linear time series, Autoregressive Integrated Moving Average (ARIMA) model is the

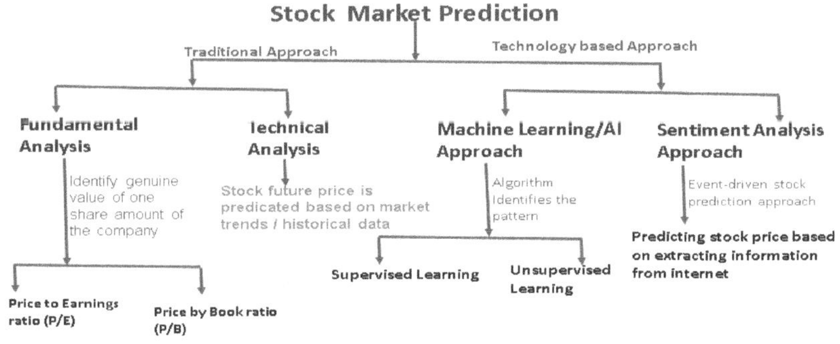

Fig. 9 Stock market prediction Approach

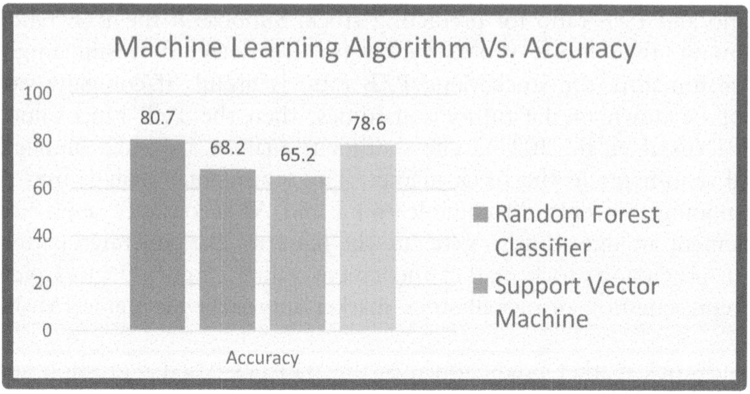

Fig. 10 ML algorithm accuracy

best choice. It is most efficient for predicting short-term share market movement (Dhaduk, 2021). The machine-learning algorithms and stock predictions accuracy level of each algorithm detail are given in Fig. 10 (Ashwini, 2020).

There are 21 major stock exchanges around the globe. These 21 stock exchanges are from various continents like Australia, Europe, Asia, and the United States. Saudi stock exchange (Tadawul) using Random Forest Regressor machine-learning algorithm and Indian stock exchange using ANN (SBI, 2018). The London stock exchange using LSTM-based deep learning models. Australian stock market index predicting using multi-layer feed-forward neural network. Bloomberg launched the Alpaca forecast AI prediction matrix application (Ashley, 2020). It aids the investor in forecasting the price and exact market pattern price movements (Bachinskiy, 2019). Therefore, dominant stock exchanges are using machine-learning techniques and algorithm-based applications.

7 E-finance Security Challenge

Data privacy is a significant challenge in E-finance. AI tools using technology like two-factor authentication and biometric verification ensure security. Voice recognition and fingerprint authentication techniques helped reduce fraud. These techniques prevent fraud in lending services and find the customer's credit score. The cybercrime and cyber-attack cost is 0.08 percent of worldwide GDP, according to 2018 estimation. American Express bank installed NVIDIA TensorRT deep learning models for fraud detection. Robotic Process Automation (RPA) is implemented in the State Bank of India for the internal banking process (Melnychenko, 2020). Bank of Baroda implemented an innovative artificial intelligence Baroda Brainy. It reflects superintelligence, i.e., AI, which is much more secure than human intelligence.

8 Conclusion

Stock market index and banking services reflect the wealth of the nation. AI-enabled Chatbot and virtual assistant helpdesk improve customer service 24/7. Human energy is more needed for gathering and analyzing data. In this context, AI saves human energy and time. The accuracy level of predicting is also very appreciable. In recent days, communication technology introduced FinTech services to easy mobility to the common public. Simultaneously, innovative and unusual fraud happens specifically in E-finance. The thief's identification is easy when the currency is in cash format. The technology-based E-finance challenge is to protect software weaknesses and hardware vulnerabilities at the international level. Therefore, blockchain technology is admired universally in E-finance. From expatriate to trading executive-level expecting quick and secured money transaction in banking service, news channels media increase knowledge awareness of equity market investment to an investor. It influences the investor's curiosity about high profit from equity. Therefore, ML-predicting algorithms and apps are so indeed in demand. Gradually, Robo-advisor vanishes the finance consultant role. In the future, the Robo-advisor task may improve the border much wide in E-finance. Based on the market volatility, it will automatically invest with the help of FinTech services. Next few decades the AI/ML technologies are inevitable in the finance world.

References

Anil Kavuri, A. M. (2018). Fintech and the future of financial services: What are the research gaps? *SSRN Electronic Journal*. https://doi.org/10.2139/ssrn.3215849

Ashley, J. (2020, October 5). *American express adopts NVIDIA AI to help prevent fraud and foil cybercrime*. Retrieved October 10,

2021, from https://blogs.nvidia.com/ website:https://blogs.nvidia.com/blog/2020/10/05/american-express-nvidia-ai/

Ashwini Pathak, S. P. (2020). Study of machine learning algorithms for stock market prediction. *International Journal of Engineering Research & Technology (IJERT)*, *9*(6). https://doi.org/10.17577/IJERTV9IS060064

Assaleh, K., El-Baz, H., & Al-Salkhadi, S. (2011). Predicting stock prices using polynomial classifiers: The case of Dubai financial market. *Journal of Intelligent Learning Systems and Applications*, *3*(2). https://doi.org/10.4236/jilsa.2011.32010

Bachinskiy, A. (2019, February 21). The growing impact of AI in financial services: Six examples. Retrieved October 10, 2021, from https://towardsdatascience.com/ website: https://towardsdatascience.com/the-growing-impact-of-ai-in-financial-services-six-examples-da386c0301b2

Biswas, B. (2021, September 19). Transforming banking with digital lending. In *Finance News*. https://www.cnbctv18.com/finance/transforming-banking-with-digital-lending-10796101.htm

Borad, S. B. (2021, December 17). *Financial forecasting techniques*. Retrieved December 19, 2021, from https://efinancemanagement.com/ website: https://efinancemanagement.com/financial-management/financial-forecasting-techniques

Chauhan, N. S. (2020, January 9). *Stock market forecasting using time series analysis*. Retrieved October 10, 2021, from https://www.kdnuggets.com/ website: https://www.kdnuggets.com/2020/01/stock-market-forecasting-time-series-analysis.html

Company Size: Why Market Capitalization Matters. (n.d.). Retrieved October 2, 2021, from Merrill A Bank of America company website: https://www.merrilledge.com/article/company-size-why-market-capitalization-matters-ose

Courbe, J. (2020). *Financial services technology 2020 and beyond: Embracing disruption*. https://www.pwc.com/gx/en/financial-services/assets/pdf/technology2020-and-beyond.pdf

Dhaduk, H. (2021, July 18). *Stock market forecasting using time series analysis with ARIMA model*. Retrieved October 11, 2021, from https://www.analyticsvidhya.com/blog website: https://www.analyticsvidhya.com/blog/2021/07/stock-market-forecasting-using-time-series-analysis-with-arima-model/

Digital Financial Services: Challenges and Opportunities for Emerging Market Banks. (2017, August). Retrieved November 2, 2021, from www.ifc.org/ThoughtLeadership website: https://www.ifc.org/wps/wcm/connect/067d6a0c-f1b5-4457-97aa-2982a7dfda69/EMCompass+Note+42+DFS+Challenges+updated.pdf?MOD=AJPERES&CVID=lTM-26u

Ferreira, F. G. D. C., Gandomi, A. H., & Cardoso, R. (2021). Artificial intelligence applied to stock market trading: A review. *IEEE Access*, *9*, 30898–30917. https://doi.org/10.1109/ACCESS.2021.3058133

Financial Forecasting. (2020). Retrieved November 11, 2021, from https://www.toolshero.com/. Website: https://www.toolshero.com/financial-management/financial-forecasting/

Girija, N., & Bhuvaneswari, T. (2021). AI emerging communication and computing. In S. Kanimozhi Suguna, M. Dhivya, & Sara Paiva (Ed.), *Artificial Intelligence (AI): Recent trends and applications* (p. 15). https://doi.org/10.1201/9781003005629

Hyes, A. (2021). *10 important cryptocurrencies other than bitcoin*. Retrieved November 2, 2021, from www.investopedia.com website: https://www.investopedia.com/tech/most-important-cryptocurrencies-other-than-bitcoin/

Jaffery, B. (n.d.). *Connecting with meaning Hyper-personalizing the customer experience using data, analytics, and AI*. https://www2.deloitte.com/content/dam/Deloitte/ca/Documents/deloitte-analytics/ca-en-omnia-ai-marketing-pov-fin-jun24-aoda.pdf

Kagan, J. (2020, August 27). *Financial technology—Fintech*. Retrieved September 10, 2021, from https://www.investopedia.com/ website: https://www.investopedia.com/terms/f/fintech.asp

Kaye, N. G. G. (2019). *AI leaders in financial services—Common traits of frontrunners in the artificial intelligence race*. https://www2.deloitte.com/us/en/insights/industry/financial-services/artificial-intelligence-ai-financial-services-frontrunners.html

Kuder, N. G. G. (2019, August 13). *AI leaders in financial services common traits of frontrunners in the artificial intelligence race*. Retrieved October 10, 2021, from https://www2.deloitte.com/ website: https://www2.deloitte.com/us/en/insights/industry/financial-services/artificial-intelligence-ai-financial-services-frontrunners.html

Maes, S., Tuyls, K., Vanschoenwinkel, B., & Manderick, B. (2002). *Credit card fraud detection using Bayesian and neural networks*. https://www.researchgate.net/publication/2524707_Credit_Card_Fraud_Detection_Using_Bayesian_and_Neural_Networks

Rouf, N., Malik, M. B., & Arif, T. (2021). Stock market prediction using machine learning techniques: A decade survey on methodologies, recent developments, and future directions. *MDPI (Special Issue) Recent Advanced Technologies and Applications of Smart Computing and Cyber Security, 10*(21). https://doi.org/10.3390/electronics10212717

SBI, other banks using AI big time to improve efficiency, cut costs. (2018, July 2). *Cio.Economictimes.Indiatimes.Com*. https://cio.economictimes.indiatimes.com/news/strategy-and-management/sbi-other-banks-using-ai-big-time-to-improve-efficiency-cut-costs/64821020

Schroer, A. (2021, July 30). *AI and the bottom line: 20 examples of Artificial Intelligence in finance*. Retrieved October 10, 2021, from https://builtin.com website: https://builtin.com/artificial-intelligence/ai-finance-banking-applications-companies

Selvamuthu, D., Kumar, V., & Mishra, A. (2019). Indian stock market prediction using artificial neural networks on tick data. *Financial Innovation (Springer Open)*, *5*. https://doi.org/10.1186/s40854-019-0131-7

Smullian, N. (2021, February 26). *Tech trends in the payment ecosystem*. Retrieved October 10, 2021, from www.dataart.com website: https://www.dataart.com/blog/tech-trends-in-the-payment-ecosystem

The Five Largest Robo-Advisors Top 5 Robo-advisors by assets under management. (n.d.). Retrieved October 10, 2021, from https://corporatefinanceinstitute.com/ website: https://corporatefinanceinstitute.com/resources/knowledge/trading-investing/the-five-largest-robo-advisors/

Top Robo advisors in 2021: Performance reviews, returns, and comparisons. (2021, July 29). Retrieved September 11, 2021, from insider intelligence website: https://www.insiderintelligence.com/insights/best-robo-advisors/

Employees' Perspective on Interplay of IT-based Banking & Sustainability

Shilpa Taneja, Liaqat Ali, and Ahsan Siraj

1 Introduction

In 2015, the United Nations member states adopted the goals for sustainable development in curbing poverty, protecting the planet, and ensuring peace & prosperity for people under Agenda 2030. Since, the sustainable development encompasses three dimensions—social, economic, and environmental, the 17 sustainable development goals are committed to achieving the objective of sustainable development across three of the dimensions in a balanced as well as integrated manner. As such these

S. Taneja
Sheffield University Management School, The University of Sheffield, Sheffield, UK
e-mail: s.taneja@sheffield.ac.uk

L. Ali
School of Management Studies, Punjabi University, Patiala, India
e-mail: liaqat_sms@pbi.ac.in

A. Siraj (✉)
School of Management, Zhengzhou University, Zhengzhou, China
e-mail: ahsan.siraj@gs.zzu.edu.cn

Department of Technology, The University of Lahore, Lahore, Pakistan

© The Author(s), under exclusive license to Springer Nature Singapore Pte Ltd. 2025

A. S. et al. (eds.), *Trends and Challenges of Electronic Finance*,
https://doi.org/10.1007/978-981-96-3304-3_4

include the goals about people, planet, prosperity, and partnership. For people, the aim is to end poverty and hunger from all across the globe and to ensure the fulfilment of potentials of all the human beings in a dignified, equal, and healthy environment. The goals for the planet intend to ensure responsible and sustainable consumption as well as production to protect the planet from degradation; and to attain prosperity by ensuring flourishing and fulfilling lives to all human beings, and ensuring the active participation of all the stakeholders. The goal of prosperity also embraces that the social, economic, and technological advancements should take place in congruence with nature.

With increased concern for achievement of sustainable development goals, there is an increased pressure on all organisations by the Government and several international agencies and programmes to consider the environmental issues in their operations (Bătae et al., 2021; Klassen & Vereecke, 2012), plans, policies, and strategies (Shen et al., 2020). Undoubtedly, the banks, all around the world, have become conscious of environmental sustainability-related issues concerned with banking (Aracil et al., 2021). They are investing at higher levels to promote sustainability by incorporation of green IT/IS in all of their operations. Besides, there is a huge problem of financial exclusion of the rural and underprivileged people across many countries. There is an upsurge in the requirement of CSR actions, for instance, the actions on issues of sustainability (Shafiq et al., 2017; Walker et al., 2014), environment conservation (Roehrich et al., 2017), sound HR practices (Sen & Bhattacharya, 2001), green product innovation (Song et al., 2020), and ethical consumerism (Jenkin et al., 2011). The implementation of IT/IS (Giramkar, 2018) can affect sustainability in a positive as well as negative manner (Danish Zhang et al., 2019). IT has been contributing largely to increasing carbon footprints of the firms by the way of production of greenhouse gases due to increased use of computers, etc. (Arnold, 2004). Also, it increases the power usage of the firms which is a greater expense for them (Dembo, 2008). On the other hand, implementation 65352of innovative technologies such as Industry 4.0 in the firms can help the businesses to find the ways to cut the overall carbon footprint by the effective and efficient use of these technologies (Javaid et al., 2022), such as with assimilation of green IT (Bose & Luo, 2011; Cai et al., 2013; Jenkin et al., 2011) & IT for green (Butler, 2011; Suki et al., 2022) in the businesses and in the banking and financial service organisations in particular (Merello et al., 2022; Taneja et al., 2021; Yip & Bocken, 2018).

2 IT-based Banking and Sustainability: The Framework

The banks, being a considerable part of the financial services sector in particular and the economy in general, have a considerable effect on the sustainable development (Deutsche Bank, 2019; Jeucken & Bouma, 1999; Luo et al., 2022). However, banks do not have a direct effect on the environment, but they can affect it indirectly such as through usage of paper in large volumes, financing of projects impacting environment, and by the actions of their clients. The size of the banking industry being very large, the environmental impact of this sector cannot be ignored. Further, to attain all-inclusive implementation of the goals for sustainable development, the proper engagement of all the stakeholders is vital (Muzaffar et al., 2019; Nájera-Sánchez, 2020). If the organisations are pursuing environmentally sustainable strategies at a higher level and not communicating these activities to the employees, they are going to miss out on significant opportunities (Berger et al., 2007; Ramus, 2002). Prior researchers have highlighted the significance of understanding the employees' cognition, attitude, and behaviour during the development and the adoption of sustainable initiatives, especially environmentally sustainable initiatives (Carmeli et al., 2007; Freudenreich et al., 2019; Haigh & Griffiths, 2008).

The information acquisition and formation of individuals' attitude are the critical issues at the heart of environment crisis (Bonnedahl et al., 2022; Dumont & Franjeska-Nicole, 2008), which clarifies that in the lack of necessary information; the individual cannot be able to formulate positive or negative attitude towards an issue. Thus, the favourable attitude of the employees concerning such initiatives will be formulated only if they receive complete information on the practices being undertaken by their banks. Also, the technological innovations alone may not be able to achieve ideal outcomes and cannot succeed in the market independently because of the mismatches between their designs and the contexts of their use (Diener & Špaček, 2021; Siraj et al., 2020; Yang et al., 2017), hence, it is crucial to consider employee's perspective concerning if the organisations have truly embraced IT/IS related practices as a component of sustainable and environmental initiatives.

IT/IS have a great deal to do with banking as well as sustainability. As society calls for increased investments & more initiatives concerning multidisciplinary as well as innovative methods to address sustainability issues (Almeida et al., 2013; Nchofoung & Asongu, 2022), this chapter is based on exploring the interplay of IT/IS-based banking and sustainable initiatives undertaken by the banks. Therefore, the current research focussed on employees' perspective of environmentally sustainable IT-related initiatives and strategies adopted by the banks in the context of India. In this respect, the prime aims of the research include the aspects: (a) the various steps undertaken by the banks to incorporate IT-based sustainability, i.e. environmental and social initiatives, (b) the barriers in the successful implementation of such initiatives & strategies, and (c) the level of employees' orientations in terms of their attitudes, cognitions, and behavioural intentions towards the adoption of such initiatives. No prolific attempt has been made by the researchers to study the interrelationship of IT/IS and sustainable banking operations and to understand the level of employees' attitude and engagement in such strategies and practices adopted in the context of banking organisations. Therefore, the chapter is intended for providing the pathways that would have a great impact on the strategies for sustainable development.

3 Methods

The chapter is based on an exploratory approach. Using a survey method through a structured questionnaire, the data were collected from 302 employees of seven banks, out of three leading bank groups in India. The banks selected for the study include top banks based on the investments from each group. The data were collected from the northern regions of India, i.e. Punjab, Haryana, and Chandigarh, and were analysed using descriptive statistics, frequency & percentage analysis, and exploratory factor analysis.

The questionnaire designed for the study consisted of four sections: (a) Demographic profile, (b) Various IT-based sustainable initiatives & strategies undertaken by banks, (c) Barriers in the successful implementation of such strategies, and (d) Employees' perception regarding IT-based environmentally sustainable initiatives & strategies undertaken by the banks. The data about the initiatives undertaken and the perceived barriers were analysed using frequency analysis, percentage analysis, and descriptive statistics. To study the various IT-based environmentally sustainable initiatives and strategies undertaken by the banks, the various items were categorised into prevent/control strategy, sustainable development strategy, preventive strategies, and policy-oriented strategies based on review of literature (Cai et al., 2013; Jenkin et al., 2011; Olson, 2008; Yip & Bocken, 2018). The categorical data concerning this aspect and the barriers in successful implementation of environmentally sustainable IT-based banking practices were analysed using frequency and percentage analysis, and the inferences were made thereupon as discussed in the next section. The data concerning the employees' perception towards such initiatives were analysed using a structural model.

The statements concerning employees' perception regarding these strategies were reduced using exploratory factor analysis and were categorised into the dimensions namely employee cognitions & attitude, and behavioural intentions. Principal Component Analysis (Field, 2009) using varimax rotation was employed and reliability (Cronbach's alpha > 0.7) and validity of the items were confirmed. EFA was applied to reduce a larger set of raw items into more meaningful factors to be used for further investigation. Afterwards, the confirmatory factor analysis was employed to confirm the factor structure extracted in EFA as well as to test the reliability and validity of the scale. Table 1 shows the description of the profile of sample respondents.

Most of the respondents were males, i.e. 64.6 per cent of the valid sample as compared to the females (35.4%). With respect to the age of respondents, the majority of them (32.4%) were aged between 26 and 35 years, where 30.5 per cent of the total sample included those with an age between 36 and 45 years. A larger proportion of the valid sample includes the participants having work experience between 10 and 15 years (34.8%), and a vast majority of the respondents (42.7%) were postgraduate.

The exploratory factor analysis using varimax rotation (Field, 2009) was employed to extract meaningful factors out of the statements derived from review of literature (Cai et al., 2013; Gholami et al., 2013; Jenkin et al., 2011). All the variables were found to yield the factor loadings greater than 0.6 (Field, 2009). The communality value for each factor extracted was found to be greater than 0.5 (Field, 2009). The factors namely employees' cognitions and attitude, and employees' behavioural intention explained 65.57 per cent variance in the observed dataset. Table 2 presents the results of Kaiser–Meyer–Olkin and Bartlett's test of sphericity. The Kaiser–Meyer–Olkin statistic indicates the adequacy of the present sample for using factor analysis. This statistic is considered to be ideal if exceeds the threshold of 0.5 as prescribed by Field (2009) and was found to be 0.831 which depicted that the sample was adequate. The

Table 1 Profile of sample respondents

Variables	*Category*	*Frequency*	*Percentage*
Demographic Characteristics			
Gender	Male	195	64.6
	Female	107	35.4
Age	Up to 25 years	82	27.1
	26–35 years	98	32.4
	36–45 years	92	30.5
	46–55 years	30	10
Experience	Up to 5 years	94	31.1
	5–10 years	103	34
	10–15 years	105	34.8
Education	Undergraduate	6	2
	Graduate	120	39.7
	Post-graduate	129	42.7
	Professional degree	47	15.6
Bank Group & Bank Wise Distribution			
Bank Group Wise Distribution	Bank Group 1	40	13.2
	Bank Group 2	126	41.7
	Bank Group 3	136	45.1
Bank Wise Distribution	Bank 1	40	13.2
	Bank 2	41	13.6
	Bank 3	40	13.2
	Bank 4	45	14.9
	Bank 5	42	13.9
	Bank 6	50	16.6
	Bank 7	44	14.6

Source Primary data compiled using SPSS, 2021

Bartlett's test of sphericity tests whether the correlation matrix is an identity matrix or not. This value was found to be less than 0.05 (Field, 2009) to confirm that the matrix is not an identity matrix.

4 Discussion and Conclusion

The findings revealed that although banks have been undertaking several IT-based environmentally sustainable initiatives, there was a lack of effective incorporation of prevent/control strategy as recommended by Jenkin et al. (2011) by the reduction in printing, reusing & recycling electronic waste (Hart, 1995), substituting e-transactions and e-documents

Table 2 KMO & Bartlett's test of Sphericity

KMO and Bartlett's Test		
Kaiser–Meyer–Olkin Measure of Sampling Adequacy		0.831
Bartlett's Test of Sphericity	Approx. Chi-Square	1441.301
	df	45
	Sig	0.000

Source SPSS survey output 2021

for the paper to reduce the carbon emissions. In respect to sustainable development strategy, the banks need to share environmental knowledge and feedback through IT-based channels and also indulge in the marketing of environmentally sustainable services, i.e. internet banking and mobile banking to promote reduction in paper usage and wastage (Taneja & Ali, 2021). Additionally, the banks should install drive-up ATMs instead of establishing drive-through ATMs to reduce carbon emission due to car idling. However, the banks were found to be performing well concerning PCs management; they must adopt solar energy-based devices at a mass level for lesser energy consumption. Also, there are various preventive strategies banks should adopt by hiring consultants, organising workshops, seminars, and training programmes for employees regarding environmentally sustainable practices since a lower adoption of such strategies has been reported by the employees. The banks need to develop policy-oriented initiatives by separate budget and power consumption of IT than general power consumption.

This research noted positive employee cognitions regarding environmentally sustainable practices being undertaken by their banks, i.e. the employees view environment conservation as a serious issue to be considered by their banks while undertaking business operations. Also, the employees were found to reflect a positive attitude towards getting involved in environment-friendly initiatives being undertaken by their banks, thus depicting optimistic engagement in such practices. On the other hand, the respondents were found to have negative outlook regarding sacrificing their immediate well-being for future benefits and indicated that their convenience was more important to them in comparison to future considerations, thus depicting their negative behavioural intentions. Although, the bank employees reflected favourable and positive cognitions and attitude towards the IT-based environmentally sustainable initiatives but depicted negative behavioural intentions to incorporate those cognitions into their actual behaviour (See Fig. 1); indicating knowing-doing gap (Jenkin et al., 2011; Pfeffer & Sutton, 1999). The present study also pinpointed an opportunity gap in which the employees were found to be aware of the existing environmental activities in their banks but also identified the opportunities available with the banks where they could improve in terms of environmental sustainability.

Additionally, the study highlighted the prevalence of knowledge gaps (Zack, 2005). Knowledge gap can be defined as the difference in the present knowledge of an organisation and required knowledge for implementing a strategy; or between the knowledge of the organisation and its competitor's knowledge (Zack, 2005); and it can be the difference of knowledge between the organisation and the employees (Jenkin et al., 2011). In the present study, it was found that employees were not fully aware of all the activities being undertaken by their banks as presented in their reports, websites, etc. as highlighted by 58 per cent of the respondents. Figure 2 depicts the major barriers respectively indicated by the respondents.

Fig. 1 Employees' orientations (Source: Author's compilation)

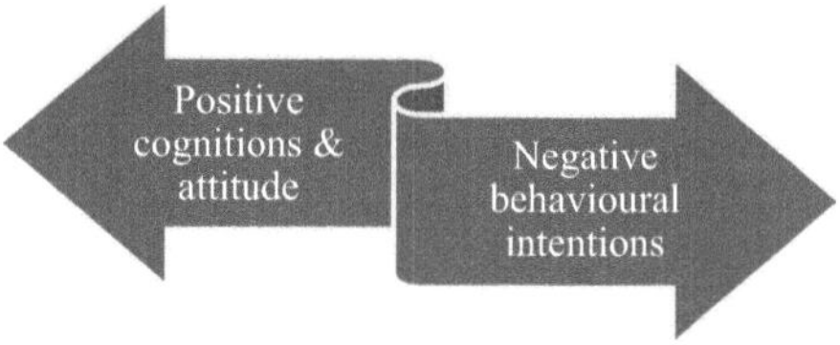

Fig. 2 Major barriers as indicated by respondents (Source: Author's compilation)

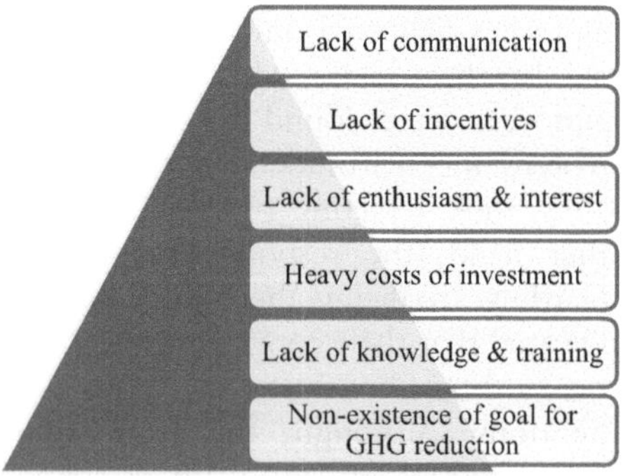

The majority of the respondents (72%) revealed that the greatest barrier in the successful implementation of IT-related sustainable banking strategies has been the lack of communication about the impact of these strategies by the management; followed by lack of a proper incentive system based on their engagement in such strategies (64%). Also, more than half of the respondents believed that barriers in implementing these strategies include lack of employees' enthusiasm & interest (59.3%) and heavy costs of investment (58.6%), followed by lack of sufficient knowledge (58%) & training (51%), and non-existence of goals for GHG reduction (53.3%) respectively. It can be conferred that the banks must communicate their environment or sustainability-related activities to their employees and also must encourage and motivate them for their enthusiastic involvement in such practices through training and counselling programmes, since employee engagement is indispensable for the achievement of sustainable development goals in general and the success of environment-oriented strategies in particular. As suggested by Mohr (2000), the behaviours of persons can be changed by increasing the benefits and reducing the barriers associated with an activity. The bank employees' orientation consisting of their cognitions, attitudes, and behaviour must be stimulated and aligned with the bank's practices, initiatives, and strategies to help close the various gaps and to achieve the goals for sustainable development. Furthermore, the bankers need to find out low-cost alternatives for investing in environmentally sustainable technologies; the banks must set and communicate certain goal for greenhouse gas reduction into their plans and strategies to reduce their carbon footprint.

5 Scope for Future Research

The outcomes of this research open up several avenues for future research. Since it consists of an exploratory investigation, the researchers can undertake to assess the impact of IT usage by banks on their environmental and sustainability performance. Also, assessing the impact of implementing such IT-based sustainable strategies on banks' operational performance can be worthwhile to investigate for the banking industry. Moreover, the examination of employees' attitude towards adopting IT-based banking systems in conjunction with their environmental orientation, for instance, whether there is any significant relationship between the employees' positive or negative attitude towards adopting IT/IS in banking on their orientation concerning IT-based sustainable initiatives, might offer the scope for future research. This study also highlighted some gaps in employees' engagement in environmentally sustainable IT-oriented strategies; further research may ponder upon more ways of aligning the interest of the banks and employees concerning IT-based sustainable banking for filling these gaps.

References

Almeida, C. M. V. B., Bonilla, S. H., Giannetti, B. F., & Huisingh, D. (2013). Cleaner production initiatives and challenges for a sustainable world: An introduction to this special volume. *Journal of Cleaner Production, 47*, 1–10.

Aracil, E., Nájera-Sánchez, J. J., & Forcadell, F. J. (2021). Sustainable banking: A literature review and integrative framework. *Finance Research Letters, 42*(December 2020).

Arnold, C. (2004, June 17). *Computer energy waste a major cause of pollution.* National Public Radio, Morning edition. Retrieved July 8th, 2017, from https://www.npr.org/templates/story/story.php?storyId=1960428

Bătae, O. M., Dragomir, V. D., & Feleagă, L. (2021). The relationship between environmental, social, and financial performance in the banking sector: A European study. *Journal of Cleaner Production, 290.*

Berger, I. E., Cunningham, P. H., & Drumwright, M. E. (2007). Mainstreaming corporate social responsibility: Developing markets for virtue. *California Management Review, 49*(4), 132–157.

Bonnedahl, K. J., Heikkurinen, P., & Paavola, J. (2022). Strongly sustainable development goals: Overcoming distances constraining responsible action. *Environmental Science & Policy, 129*, 150–158.

Bose, R., & Luo, X. (2011). Integrative framework for assessing firms' potential to undertake Green IT initiatives via virtualization—A theoretical perspective. *The Journal of Strategic Information Systems, 20*(1), 38–54.

Butler, T. (2011). Compliance with institutional imperatives on environmental sustainability: Building theory on the role of Green IS. *The Journal of Strategic Information Systems, 20*(1), 6–26.

Cai, S., Chen, X., & Bose, I. (2013). Exploring the role of IT for environmental sustainability in China: An empirical analysis. *International Journal of Production Economics, 146*(2), 491–500.

Carmeli, A., Gilat, G., & Waldman, D. A. (2007). The role of perceived organizational performance in organizational identification, adjustment and job performance. *Journal of Management Studies, 44*(6), 972–992.

Danish Zhang, J., Wang, B., & Latif, Z. (2019). Towards cross-regional sustainable development: The nexus between information and communication technology, energy consumption, and CO 2 emissions. *Sustainable Development, 27*(5), 990–1000.

Dembo, R. (2008). Socially conscious consumerism—A tautology. In *Knowledge Forum on Socially Conscious Consumerism, Toronto, Ontario, Canada.*

Diener, F., & Špaček, M. (2021). Digital transformation in banking: A managerial perspective on barriers to change. *Sustainability, 13*(4), 2032.

Dumont, J., & Franjeska-Nicole, B. C. (2008). Learning about the environment: The role of information technology in shaping attitudes and developing solutions. In *SynEnergy Forum, University of Indianapolis, Indianapolis.* Available online at http://synenergy.teipir.gr/papers/VII_3.pdf)

Field, A. (2009). *Discovering statistics using SPSS* (3rd ed.). Sage Publications Ltd.

Freudenreich, B., Lüdeke-Freund, F., & Schaltegger, S. (2019). A stakeholder theory perspective on business models: Value creation for sustainability. *Journal of Business Ethics, 166*(1), 3–18.

Gholami, R., Sulaiman, A. B., Ramayah, T., & Molla, A. (2013). Senior managers' perception on green information systems (IS) adoption and environmental performance: Results from a field survey. *Information & management, 50*(7), 431–438.

Giramkar, S. (2018, October). Green banking in India: A study for sustainable development. In *Proceedings of economics and finance conferences* (No. 6909452). International Institute of Social and Economic Sciences.

Green IT-Energy Efficiency at work. (May 13, 2019). Deutsche Bank AG, Frankfurt am Main, 2019.

Haigh, N., & Griffiths, A. (2008). The environmental sustainability of information systems: Considering the impact of operational strategies and practices. *International Journal of Technology Management, 43*(1–3), 48–63.

Hart, S. L. (1995). A natural-resource-based view of the firm. *Academy of Management Review, 20*(4), 986–1014.

Javaid, M., Haleem, A., Singh, R. P., Suman, R., & Gonzalez, E. S. (2022). Understanding the adoption of Industry 4.0 technologies in improving environmental sustainability. *Sustainable Operations and Computers, 3*, 203–217.

Jenkin, T. A., McShane, L., & Webster, J. (2011). Green information technologies and systems: Employees' perceptions of organizational practices. *Business & Society, 50*(2), 266–314.

Jeucken, M. H. A., & Bouma, J. J. (1999). The changing environment of banks. *Greener Management International, 27*, 21–35. http://www.sustainability-in-finance.com/gmi-jeucken-bouma.pdf

Klassen, R. D., & Vereecke, A. (2012). Social issues in supply chains: Capabilities link responsibility, risk (opportunity), and performance. *International Journal of Production Economics, 140*(1), 103–115.

Luo, S., Sun, Y., Yang, F., & Zhou, G. (2022). Does Fintech innovation promote enterprise transformation? Evidence from China. *Technology in Society, 68*, 101821.

Merello, P., Barberá, A., la Poza, E., & De. (2022). Is the sustainability profile of FinTech companies a key driver of their value? *Technological Forecasting and Social Change, 174*, 121290.

Mohr, D. (2000). Promoting sustainable behavior: An introduction to community-based social marketing. *Journal of Social Issues, 56*(3), 543–554.

Muzaffar, A., Khurshid, A., Malik, M. N., & Azhar, A. (2019). Sustainable development across the supply chain: The missing link of socio-environmental effect. *Sustainable Development, 27*(5), 976–981.

Nájera-Sánchez, J. J. (2020). A systematic review of sustainable banking through a co-word analysis. *Sustainability, 12*(1).

Nchofoung, T. N., & Asongu, S. A. (2022). ICT for sustainable development: Global comparative evidence of globalisation thresholds. *Telecommunications Policy, 46*(5), 102296.

Olson, E. G. (2008). Creating an enterprise-level "green" strategy. *Journal of Business Strategy, 29*(2), 22–30.

Pfeffer, J., & Sutton, R. I. (1999). Knowing "What" to do is not enough: Turning knowledge into action. *California management review, 42*(1).

Ramus, C. A. (2002). Encouraging innovative environmental actions: What companies and managers must do. *Journal of World Business, 37*(2), 151–164.

Roehrich, J. K., Hoejmose, S. U., & Overland, V. (2017). Driving green supply chain management performance through supplier selection and value internalisation. *International Journal of Operations & Production Management, 37*(4), 489–509.

Sen, S., & Bhattacharya, C. B. (2001). Does doing good always lead to doing better? Consumer reactions to corporate social responsibility. *Journal of Marketing Research, 38*(2), 225–243.

Shafiq, A., Johnson, P. F., Klassen, R. D., & Awaysheh, A. (2017). Exploring the implications of supply risk on sustainability performance. *International Journal of Operations & Production Management, 37*(10), 1386–1407.

Shen, Z., Siraj, A., Jiang, H., Zhu, Y., & Li, J. (2020). Chinese-style innovation and its international repercussions in the new economic times. *Sustainability, 12*(5), 1–17.

Siraj, A., Guo, J., Wajid Kamran, M., Li, Q., Zhu, Y., & Student, P. (2020). Characteristics for E-satisfaction in E-retailing-evidence from Chinese E-commerce. *International Journal of Innovation, Creativity and Change. 12.* www.ijicc.net

Song, W., Wang, G. Z., & Ma, X. (2020). Environmental innovation practices and green product innovation performance: A perspective from organizational climate. *Sustainable Development, 28*(1), 224–234.

Suki, N. M., Suki, N. M., Sharif, A., Afshan, S., & Jermsittiparsert, K. (2022). The role of technology innovation and renewable energy in reducing environmental degradation in Malaysia: A step towards sustainable environment. *Renewable Energy, 182*, 245–253.

Taneja, S., & Ali, L. (2021). Determinants of customers' intentions towards environmentally sustainable banking: Testing the structural model. *Journal of Retailing and Consumer Services, 59*, 102418.

Taneja, S., Ali, L., Hassan, M. K., & Lee, Y. D. (2021). Three decades of research on the demand and supply side perspectives of digital technologies in banking: A review and research agenda. *International Journal of Agile Systems and Management, 14*(4), 543–575.

Walker, H., Klassen, R. D., Sarkis, J., & Seuring, S. (2014). Sustainable operations management: Recent trends and future directions. *International Journal of Operations & Production Management, 34*(5), 1–11.

Yang, M., Evans, S., Vladimirova, D., & Rana, P. (2017). Value uncaptured perspective for sustainable business model innovation. *Journal of Cleaner Production, 140*(3), 1794–1804.

Yip, A. W., & Bocken, N. M. (2018). Sustainable business model archetypes for the banking industry. *Journal of Cleaner Production, 174*, 150–169.

Zack, M. H. (2005). The strategic advantage of knowledge and learning. *International Journal of Learning and Intellectual Capital, 2*(1), 1–20.

Navigating Views on Digital Finance: An In-depth Exploration of Diverse Perspectives

Navaneetha Krishnan Rajagopal, Mari Anand N., and Shelly Mohanty

1 Introduction

In the contemporary landscape of finance, electronic finance, or e-finance, stands as a pivotal force reshaping the traditional paradigms of monetary transactions and economic interactions. Gone are the days when financial transactions were confined to physical cash and paper-based records (Ouk-Heon). Today, in an era characterized by rapid technological advancement and digital transformation, the integration of digital platforms and financial services has become ubiquitous, revolutionizing the way individuals, businesses, and institutions manage their financial affairs (Gomber et al., 2018).

N. K. Rajagopal (✉) · Mari Anand N. · S. Mohanty
College of Economics & Business Administration, University of Technology and Applied Sciences, Salalah, Oman
e-mail: Navaneetha.Rajagopal@utas.edu.om

Mari Anand N.
e-mail: mari.anand@utas.edu.om

S. Mohanty
e-mail: shelly.mohanty@utas.edu.om

© The Author(s), under exclusive license to Springer Nature Singapore Pte Ltd. 2025

A. S. et al. (eds.), *Trends and Challenges of Electronic Finance*,
https://doi.org/10.1007/978-981-96-3304-3_5

The emergence of e-finance represents a seismic shift in the financial landscape, ushering in an era of unprecedented convenience, efficiency, and accessibility. From mobile banking apps to online investment platforms, e-finance has democratized access to financial services, empowering individuals to conduct transactions, manage their savings, and invest in assets with unprecedented ease and flexibility. Moreover, e-finance has catalyzed the emergence of new business models, disruptive technologies, and innovative financial products, reshaping the dynamics of the global economy (Hanna, 2009).

Against this backdrop of rapid technological change and financial innovation, this study embarks on a journey to delve into the multifaceted realm of e-finance, aiming to offer a comprehensive exploration from diverse perspectives. Our objective is not merely to scratch the surface of e-finance but to delve deep into its intricacies, nuances, and implications for various stakeholders. By adopting a multidimensional approach, we seek to unravel the complexities of e-finance, examining its evolution, impact, challenges, and future prospects (Lin et al., 2015).

At its core, e-finance represents more than just a technological innovation; it embodies a fundamental shift in the way we conceptualize, access, and utilize financial services (Carayannis, 2008). No longer bound by the constraints of physical infrastructure or geographical boundaries, e-finance transcends traditional barriers, connecting individuals, businesses, and economies on a global scale (Christiansen, 2001). Whether it's sending money to a family member halfway across the world or investing in a startup through a crowdfunding platform, e-finance has transformed the way we interact with money, capital, and financial markets (Joshi, 2020).

However, the transformative potential of e-finance is not without its challenges and complexities. From cyber security threats to regulatory hurdles, the rapid pace of technological change has raised a host of issues that must be addressed to ensure the sustainability, security, and inclusivity of e-finance (Indjikian et al., 2002). Moreover, the proliferation of digital financial services has underscored the importance of governance, accountability, and ethical considerations in the design and deployment of financial technologies (González Páramo, 2017).

In light of these dynamics, this study seeks to provide a holistic and nuanced understanding of e-finance, drawing upon insights from diverse disciplines, perspectives, and stakeholders (Yadav et al., 2024). By combining rigorous academic research with real-world insights from industry practitioners, regulators, and technology developers, we aim to bridge the gap between theory and practice, offering actionable insights and recommendations for policymakers, financial institutions, and technology innovators alike.

In the subsequent sections of this study, we will delve deeper into the evolution of e-finance, its role in advancing financial inclusion, simplifying payment systems, and widening the accessibility of investment avenues (Mvelase, 2022). Moreover, we will examine the challenges faced by e-finance, implications for stakeholders, and strategies for fostering collaborative governance structures. Ultimately, our aim is to unlock the full potential of e-finance as a catalyst for inclusive economic growth and societal progress in the digital era.

The primary objective of this study is to undertake a thorough examination of electronic finance, unraveling its complexities, evolution, and impact on various stakeholders. By adopting a holistic approach, we seek to shed light on the transformative journey of e-finance, from its nascent stages to its current status as a cornerstone of the global financial ecosystem. Moreover, our goal is to elucidate the myriad roles played by e-finance in advancing financial inclusion, simplifying payment systems, and widening the accessibility of investment avenues.

2 Methodology

To achieve our objective, we employ a combination of systematic literature review and qualitative interactions with industry insiders. This approach allows us to integrate insights from scholarly works with firsthand perspectives from practitioners in the field of e-finance. The systematic literature review provides a comprehensive overview of the existing body of knowledge, identifying key themes, trends, and gaps. By examining academic journals, research papers, books, and reports, we synthesize the collective wisdom on e-finance, laying the groundwork for a nuanced understanding. Complementing this, qualitative interactions through interviews, focus groups, and discussions with stakeholders such as financial regulators, technology innovators, and financial institution executives enrich our analysis with real-world experiences and diverse perspectives. This methodological triangulation enhances the credibility and relevance of our study, offering robust insights and actionable recommendations. Our interdisciplinary approach aims to contribute to the scholarly discourse, inform decision-making, and advance the understanding of e-finance in the digital age. Subsequent sections will explore the evolution of e-finance, its role in financial inclusion, payment system simplification, and widening investment accessibility, as well as the challenges, stakeholder implications, and collaborative governance strategies. Ultimately, we aim to unlock the full potential of e-finance for inclusive economic growth and societal progress.

3 Evolution of E-Finance

Tracing the developmental trajectory of e-finance from its inception to its current status reveals a fascinating journey marked by key milestones, transformative moments, and paradigm shifts in the global financial landscape (refer Fig. 1) (Kaur et al., 2024). In this exploration, we uncover how technological advancements, regulatory changes, and shifts in consumer behavior have shaped the evolution of e-finance, paving the way for its emergence as a cornerstone of the digital economy (Erick & Kasowaki, 2024).

3.1 Inception and Early Developments

E-finance began with the advent of the internet in the late twentieth century, leading to the launch of online banking services in the

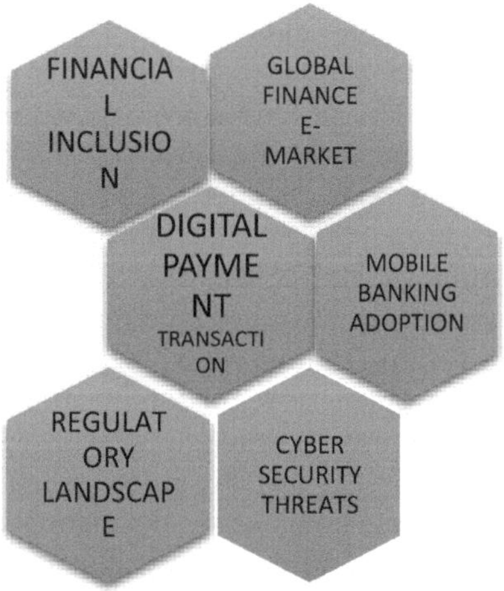

Fig. 1 Evolution of e-financing

1990s. This enabled basic banking transactions such as checking account balances, transferring funds, and paying bills online (Allen et al., 2002).

3.2 The Dot-com Boom and Bust

The late 1990s saw a surge in internet-based businesses, including online brokerage firms and digital payment systems. Although the dot-com bubble burst in the early 2000s led to industry consolidation, it laid the foundation for future e-finance innovations (Mallick, 2022).

3.3 The Rise of Mobile Finance

The proliferation of smartphones in the 2000s propelled mobile finance, with mobile banking apps and digital wallets providing on-the-go financial services. This significantly boosted financial inclusion, especially in underserved regions (Gupta et al., 2019).

3.4 The Emergence of Fintech

The 2010s marked the rise of fintech, where startups leveraged technologies like AI, blockchain, and cloud computing to disrupt traditional banking. This period saw innovations like robo-advisors and peer-to-peer lending platforms, fostering a wave of financial technology advancements (Erman, 2017).

3.5 **Blockchain and Cryptocurrency Revolution**

Blockchain technology, popularized by Bitcoin, introduced a secure, decentralized ledger system, revolutionizing financial transactions (Ahram et al., 2017). Despite skepticism, blockchain's potential in areas like cross-border payments and smart contracts garnered significant interest, expanding e-finance's scope.

3.6 Regulatory Response and Policy Frameworks

Regulators worldwide faced the challenge of balancing fintech innovation with consumer protection and financial stability. While some embraced supportive frameworks, others imposed stringent regulations to mitigate risks, reflecting a dynamic and complex regulatory landscape (Igbinenikaro & Adewusi, 2024).

3.7 Future Prospects and Challenges

E-finance is set to evolve rapidly with advancements in AI, IoT, and digital identity verification. However, challenges like cybersecurity threats, data privacy concerns, and regulatory uncertainties persist. Collaboration among stakeholders is essential to ensure e-finance drives inclusive economic growth and societal progress (Igbinenikaro & Adewusi, 2024).

4 Role in Advancing Financial Inclusion

Financial inclusion, the access to and usage of financial services by individuals and businesses, is widely recognized as a key driver of economic development, poverty reduction, and social empowerment (Refer Fig. 2) (Lal, 2018). However, traditional banking systems often fail to reach underserved populations, particularly in rural areas and developing countries, due to barriers such as physical distance, high transaction costs, and stringent eligibility criteria (Hinson, 2011). In this context, e-finance has emerged as a powerful tool for advancing financial inclusion, bridging the gap between the unbanked and the formal financial system, and empowering individuals to participate in the economy (Bisht & Mishra, 2016). In this section, we will examine how e-finance has contributed to enhancing financial inclusion and discuss its impact on reaching underserved populations and facilitating access to financial services.

4.1 Expanding Access to Banking Services

One of the most significant contributions of e-finance to financial inclusion is its ability to expand access to basic banking services, such as savings accounts, payment services, and credit facilities (Llanto et al., 2018). Through the proliferation of mobile banking apps, digital wallets, and online banking platforms, individuals who were previously excluded from the formal banking system now have access to a wide range of financial products and services. Mobile money platforms, such as M-Pesa in Kenya and Paytm in India, have been particularly successful in reaching underserved populations, enabling users to send and receive money, pay bills, and access credit using their mobile phones (Regragui, 2022). By

Fig. 2 Role in advancing financial inclusion

leveraging existing infrastructure such as mobile networks and digital platforms, e-finance has made banking services more accessible and affordable for millions of people around the world.

4.2 Facilitating Digital Payments and Remittances

E-finance has revolutionized the way financial transactions are conducted, making digital payments and remittances faster, cheaper, and more convenient than ever before (Seetharaman & Raj, 2009). With the rise of digital payment platforms and mobile money services, individuals can now transfer money instantly to family members, friends, and businesses across borders at a fraction of the cost of traditional remittance channels (Metzger et al., 2019). This has had a transformative impact on migrant workers, who rely on remittances to support their families back home. By reducing transaction costs and increasing the speed and transparency of remittance transfers, e-finance has helped to alleviate poverty, improve livelihoods, and promote financial resilience among underserved communities.

4.3 Empowering Microentrepreneurs and Small Businesses

E-finance has democratized access to credit and capital for microentrepreneurs and small businesses, who often struggle to obtain financing from traditional banks due to lack of collateral or credit history (Swarupa et al). Peer-to-peer lending platforms, crowdfunding platforms, and digital lending apps have emerged as alternative sources of funding for entrepreneurs, enabling them to access capital quickly and efficiently (Omarini, 2018). Moreover, e-finance has enabled microentrepreneurs to accept digital payments from customers, expand their customer base, and manage their finances more effectively. This has helped to stimulate entrepreneurship, create jobs, and drive economic growth in underserved communities.

4.4 Promoting Financial Literacy and Education

In addition to expanding access to financial services, e-finance has played a crucial role in promoting financial literacy and education among underserved populations (Llanto et al., 2018). Digital financial literacy initiatives, such as online tutorials, mobile apps, and interactive tools, have empowered individuals to make informed financial decisions, manage their money effectively, and build a better future for themselves and their families. Moreover, e-finance has facilitated access to financial education resources and training programs for microentrepreneurs, enabling them to develop the skills and knowledge needed to succeed in the digital economy (Ozili, 2020).

4.5 Addressing Regulatory and Technological Barriers

Despite its potential to advance financial inclusion, e-finance faces a number of regulatory and technological barriers that must be addressed to ensure its widespread adoption and impact (Shahrokhi, 2008). Regulatory challenges such as limited interoperability, inadequate consumer protection, and cybersecurity risks can hinder the growth of e-finance and undermine its potential to reach underserved populations (Kihamba, 2020). Moreover, technological barriers such as lack of internet connectivity, digital literacy, and access to affordable smartphones can limit the adoption of e-finance in rural and remote areas. By addressing these challenges through targeted policy interventions, investment in infrastructure, and collaboration among stakeholders, governments, financial institutions, and technology providers can unlock the full potential of e-finance to advance financial inclusion and promote inclusive economic growth.

The point taken here is that the e-finance has emerged as a powerful tool for advancing financial inclusion, empowering underserved populations, and driving inclusive economic growth. By expanding access to banking services, facilitating digital payments and remittances, empowering microentrepreneurs and small businesses, promoting financial literacy and education, and addressing regulatory and technological barriers, e-finance has the potential to transform the lives of millions of people around the world. However, realizing this potential will require concerted efforts from governments, financial institutions, technology providers, and civil society organizations to ensure that e-finance is accessible, affordable, and inclusive for all (Gautam et al., 2022).

5 Simplifying Payment Systems

The advent of electronic finance (e-finance) has ushered in a new era in payment systems, revolutionizing how transactions are conducted, processed, and settled. In this section, we explore the role of e-finance in streamlining payment systems, focusing on the emergence of digital payment platforms and their impact on traditional banking systems. E-finance offers unparalleled efficiency and speed in payment processing, eliminating the need for intermediaries and reducing transaction times from days to seconds (Lin et al., 2015). Whether it's paying bills, transferring money, or making purchases online, e-finance provides convenience and accessibility with just a few clicks or taps on mobile devices (Punjabi, 2016). Moreover, e-finance offers significant cost savings compared to traditional methods, with lower fees, competitive exchange rates, and transparent pricing structures. This accessibility and inclusivity democratize access to financial services, enabling individuals of all backgrounds to participate in the digital economy and empowering marginalized populations to gain access to financial services for the first time (refer Fig. 3).

The emergence of e-finance has spurred innovation and disruption in the payment industry, challenging traditional banking systems and paving the way for new business models and technologies (Godard, 2022).

Fig. 3 Simplifying payment methods

Digital payment platforms have transformed peer-to-peer transactions and introduced new forms of digital currency like cryptocurrencies. However, this transformation also poses challenges for traditional banking systems, forcing them to adapt to remain competitive (Mensah, 2019). While some banks have embraced e-finance to expand their reach and grow their customer base, others have struggled to keep pace with technological change, leading to consolidation and closures in the banking industry. Overall, e-finance has emerged as a powerful force in streamlining payment systems, offering efficiency, speed, cost savings, accessibility, and innovation. However, realizing its full potential will require collaboration and regulatory clarity to ensure secure, reliable, and inclusive payment systems for all.

6 Widening Accessibility of Investment Avenues

The evolution of electronic finance (e-finance) has not only transformed payment systems but has also revolutionized the landscape of investment opportunities. Through e-finance platforms, retail investors now have access to a diverse array of investment options, ranging from traditional assets like stocks and bonds to alternative investments such as peer-to-peer lending, real estate crowdfunding, and digital assets. This diversification not only allows investors to spread risk across different asset classes but also enables them to capitalize on emerging trends and opportunities in the global economy (Bartram & Dufey, 2001). E-finance has democratized access to investment opportunities, empowering individuals of all backgrounds and income levels to build wealth and achieve their financial goals.

One of the key benefits of e-finance in widening accessibility to investment avenues is its ability to lower entry barriers for individual investors. E-finance platforms offer low-cost, user-friendly solutions that enable investors to buy, sell, and manage investments with ease. From commission-free trading platforms to robo-advisors and social trading networks, e-finance has democratized access to investment opportunities, particularly benefiting underserved populations, such as young investors, women, and minority groups. Moreover, e-finance has played a crucial role in promoting financial literacy and education among retail investors by providing access to educational resources, research tools, and interactive tutorials. This emphasis on financial literacy empowers investors to navigate the complexities of financial markets and make informed decisions about their money.

Beyond providing access to investment opportunities and promoting financial literacy, e-finance has democratized access to capital for entrepreneurs, startups, and small businesses seeking funding (Abu Amuna, 2019). Crowdfunding platforms, peer-to-peer lending networks, and digital investment marketplaces enable entrepreneurs to raise capital directly from individual investors, bypassing traditional intermediaries (Wales, 2017). This democratization of access to capital has leveled the playing field for entrepreneurs of all backgrounds and industries, enabling them to bring their ideas to market and drive economic growth (Wilson et al., 2009). However, while e-finance has widened accessibility to investment opportunities, it also poses regulatory and compliance challenges that must be addressed to ensure investor protection and market integrity (Claessens et al., 2002). Regulatory frameworks governing e-finance platforms vary widely across jurisdictions, raising concerns about investor rights, transparency, and accountability. Addressing these challenges will require collaboration among regulators, policymakers, industry stakeholders, and investors to develop robust regulatory frameworks that promote innovation while safeguarding investor interests and maintaining market stability.

7 Challenges Faced By E-Finance

The rapid expansion of electronic finance (e-finance) has brought about unprecedented opportunities for financial inclusion, innovation, and economic growth (refer Fig. 4). However, along with these opportunities come significant challenges that threaten the sustainability and security of e-finance systems (Kandpal et al., 2023). One of the most pressing challenges is cybersecurity vulnerabilities. As financial transactions increasingly move online and data becomes more digitized, e-finance platforms have become prime targets for cyberattacks, data breaches, and fraud (Albshaier et al., 2024). Sophisticated cybercriminals employ a variety of tactics, such as phishing scams, malware attacks, and ransomware extortion, to exploit vulnerabilities in e-finance systems and compromise the integrity, confidentiality, and availability of financial data (Lagouvardou, 2018). These cyber threats not only pose financial risks to individuals and institutions but also erode trust and confidence in e-finance platforms, undermining their long-term viability and adoption.

In addition to cybersecurity vulnerabilities, e-finance also faces regulatory complexities that can hinder its growth and scalability. The regulatory landscape surrounding e-finance is complex and fragmented, with

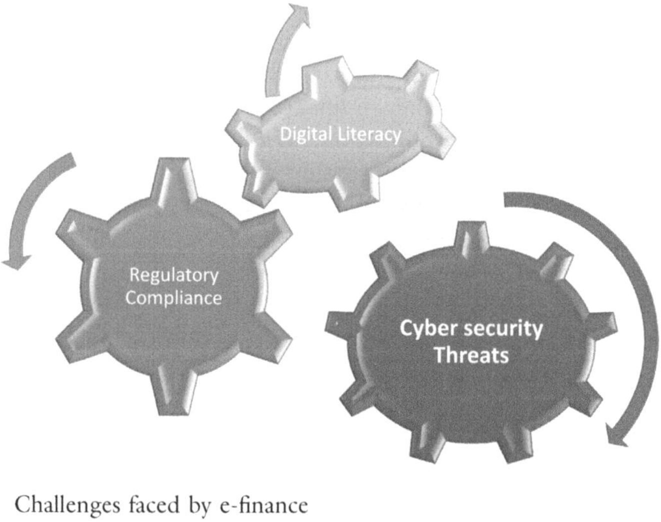

Fig. 4 Challenges faced by e-finance

different jurisdictions implementing varying rules, standards, and compliance requirements (Christiansen, 2001). This regulatory fragmentation creates challenges for financial institutions and technology providers operating across borders, as they must navigate a patchwork of regulations and ensure compliance with multiple regulatory regimes (Ahern, 2021). Moreover, regulatory uncertainty and ambiguity can stifle innovation, deter investment, and impede the development of e-finance solutions, limiting their potential to drive economic growth and financial inclusion (Ganbold, 2008). As governments and regulators grapple with the evolving nature of e-finance, there is a need for greater harmonization, coordination, and collaboration to develop clear and consistent regulatory frameworks that promote innovation while safeguarding consumer protection and financial stability.

The implications of these challenges on the sustainability of e-finance are profound and far-reaching. Cybersecurity vulnerabilities not only pose financial risks to individuals and institutions but also threaten the integrity and stability of financial systems (Westby, 2004). A successful cyberattack on a major e-finance platform could result in significant financial losses, reputational damage, and disruption to economic activities, undermining trust and confidence in digital financial services (George & Nagadeepa, 2023). Moreover, regulatory complexities and uncertainties can create barriers to entry, inhibit competition, and limit the adoption of e-finance solutions, particularly in emerging markets and underserved communities where regulatory oversight may be lacking or inadequate. This regulatory uncertainty can deter investment, slow innovation, and impede the development of e-finance ecosystems, hampering their ability to drive inclusive economic growth and financial empowerment (Agenyi, 2013).

Addressing these challenges will require a coordinated and multipronged approach involving collaboration among governments, regulators, financial institutions, technology providers, and other stakeholders (Oriji et al., 2023). First and foremost, cybersecurity must be treated as a top priority, with investments in robust cybersecurity infrastructure, threat detection and prevention mechanisms, and incident response capabilities (Diogenes & Ozkaya, 2018). Financial institutions and technology providers must implement rigorous cybersecurity protocols, adhere to industry best practices, and continuously monitor and update their systems to stay ahead of emerging threats (Mullet et al., 2021). Moreover, collaboration and information sharing among stakeholders are essential to combatting cyber threats effectively and enhancing the resilience of e-finance systems against cyberattacks.

Furthermore, regulatory frameworks governing e-finance must be modernized and harmonized to foster innovation while ensuring consumer protection and financial stability (Ababu, 2019). Governments and regulators should work together to develop clear, consistent, and technology-neutral regulations that promote innovation, encourage competition, and safeguard consumer interests (Koops, 2006). This may involve establishing regulatory sandboxes, promoting cross-border cooperation, and adopting principles-based regulatory approaches that accommodate the dynamic nature of e-finance while addressing emerging risks and challenges (Michael, 2021). By fostering an enabling regulatory environment and promoting collaboration among stakeholders, governments and regulators can help unlock the full potential of e-finance to drive inclusive economic growth, financial inclusion, and societal progress in the digital era.

In conclusion, while e-finance offers tremendous opportunities for financial inclusion, innovation, and economic development, it also faces significant challenges that must be addressed to ensure its sustainability and security. Cybersecurity vulnerabilities and regulatory complexities pose formidable obstacles to the growth and scalability of e-finance systems, threatening their viability and adoption. However, by prioritizing cybersecurity, modernizing regulatory frameworks, and promoting collaboration among stakeholders, governments, regulators, financial institutions, and technology providers can overcome these challenges and unlock the full potential of e-finance to drive inclusive economic growth and financial empowerment.

8 Implications for Stakeholders

The study on electronic finance (e-finance) reveals significant implications for policymakers, financial entities, and technology innovators, emphasizing the necessity for collaboration, innovation, and regulatory clarity to maximize the potential of e-finance in the digital era (Gomber et al., 2017). Policymakers must create regulatory environments conducive to innovation while ensuring consumer protection and financial stability. By adopting principles-based regulatory approaches and promoting cross-border cooperation, policymakers can drive innovation in e-finance while mitigating risks. Financial entities must embrace technology and invest in digital infrastructure to remain competitive, exploring new business models and partnership opportunities enabled by e-finance. For technology innovators, developing secure and user-friendly e-finance solutions is crucial, prioritizing cybersecurity and compliance with regulations. Collaboration among stakeholders is vital to establish robust governance structures that ensure the reliability of electronic financial platforms (Avci, 2020). By fostering an enabling regulatory environment, promoting competition and innovation, and investing in cybersecurity, stakeholders can harness the transformative potential of e-finance to drive inclusive economic growth and financial inclusion in the digital era.

9 Collaborative Governance Structures

In the dynamic realm of electronic finance (e-finance), robust governance structures are essential to ensure the reliability and longevity of digital financial platforms. This necessitates collaborative efforts among policymakers, financial entities, technology innovators, and regulatory bodies to address the diverse challenges and opportunities inherent in e-finance. Through collaborative governance, stakeholders can foster innovation, promote competition, and safeguard consumer protection while maintaining financial stability and integrity (Igbinenikaro & Adewusi, 2024). Policymakers play a crucial role in shaping regulatory frameworks that govern e-finance, requiring collaboration with industry stakeholders to develop clear, technology-neutral regulations. Financial entities must collaborate with technology innovators to develop secure and user-friendly e-finance solutions, prioritizing investment in digital infrastructure and cyber security. Technology innovators, in turn, should engage in open dialogue and collaboration with stakeholders to develop responsible technology solutions that address consumer needs and regulatory concerns (Sutcliffe, 2011). By fostering a culture of innovation, collaboration, and responsible technology development, stakeholders can harness the potential of e-finance to drive inclusive economic growth, financial inclusion, and societal progress in the digital era.

10 Realizing Inclusive Economic Growth

Overcoming hurdles and leveraging the potential of electronic finance (e-finance) is pivotal for achieving inclusive economic growth in the digital era (Refer Fig. 5). By addressing challenges like cybersecurity vulnerabilities, regulatory complexities, and technological barriers, stakeholders can unlock e-finance's transformative power to drive economic development, foster financial inclusion, and promote broader societal progress.

E-finance holds promise in expanding access to financial services, particularly among underserved populations such as women, youth, and rural communities, empowering them to build assets, manage risk, and improve financial well-being (Satpathy et al., 2024). Moreover, e-finance facilitates entrepreneurship and innovation by providing platforms for funding, market access, and scalability, driving job creation, economic dynamism, and global competitiveness. Additionally, e-finance initiatives can promote financial literacy, education, and empowerment, aiding individuals in making informed financial decisions and contributing to social cohesion and human development. By embracing e-finance, stakeholders can build an inclusive, resilient, and sustainable financial ecosystem

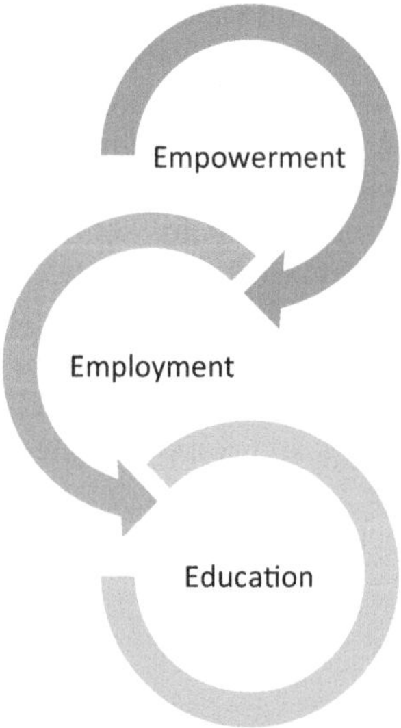

Fig. 5 Inclusive economic growth

that benefits individuals, businesses, and societies, advancing economic prosperity and societal progress in the digital age.

11 Conclusion

In conclusion, the exploration of electronic finance (e-finance) illuminates its transformative potential to reshape financial landscapes and foster societal progress in the digital era. While e-finance offers diverse investment opportunities, simplified payment systems, and enhanced financial inclusion, it also presents significant challenges, including cybersecurity vulnerabilities and regulatory complexities. Collaborative governance structures among policymakers, financial entities, technology innovators, and regulatory bodies are imperative to ensure the dependability and durability of e-finance platforms. Overcoming these challenges and leveraging the potential of e-finance can lead to inclusive economic growth by promoting entrepreneurship, job creation, and poverty reduction. By expanding access to financial services, fostering innovation, and promoting financial literacy, e-finance can drive broader societal progress, advancing social cohesion and human development. Thus, e-finance represents not only a technological evolution but also a catalyst for positive change, offering the promise of a more inclusive, resilient, and sustainable financial ecosystem for the future.

References

Ababu, B. (2019). LL. M in business law.

Abu Amuna, Y. M. (2019). Crowdfunding financing model effect on entrepreneurship aspirations. *International Journal of Academic Accounting, Finance & Management Research (IJAAFMR).*

Agenyi, B. (2013). Mobile banking and entrepreneurship in developing countries: A case study of Nigeria.

Ahern, D. (2021). Regulatory lag, regulatory friction and regulatory transition as FinTech disenablers: Calibrating an EU response to the regulatory sandbox phenomenon. *European Business Organization Law Review, 22*(3), 395–432.

Ahram, T., Sargolzaei, A., Sargolzaei, S., Daniels, J., & Amaba, B. (2017, June). Blockchain technology innovations. In *2017 IEEE technology & engineering management conference (TEMSCON)* (pp. 137–141). IEEE.

Albshaier, L., Almarri, S., & Hafizur Rahman, M. M. (2024). A review of blockchain's role in e-commerce transactions: Open challenges, and future research directions. *Computers, 13*(1), 27.

Allen, F., McAndrews, J., & Strahan, P. (2002). E-finance: An introduction. *Journal of Financial Services Research, 22*, 5–27.

Avci, S. B. (2020). A new era in the risk management of financial firms. *Ecological, Societal, and Technological Risks and the Financial Sector*, 389–417.

Bartram, S. M., & Dufey, G. (2001). International portfolio investment: Theory, evidence, and institutional framework. *Financial Markets, Institutions & Instruments, 10*(3), 85–155.

Bisht, S. S., & Mishra, V. (2016). ICT-driven financial inclusion initiatives for urban poor in a developing economy: Implications for public policy. *Behaviour & Information Technology, 35*(10), 817–832.

Carayannis, E. G. (Ed.). (2008). *Innovation, technology, and knowledge management*. Springer.

Christiansen, H. (2001). Electronic finance: Economics and institutional factors. *Occasional Paper, 2*.

Claessens, S., Glaessner, T. C., & Klingebiel, D. (2002). *Electronic finance: A new approach to financial sector development?* (Vol. 431). World Bank Publications.

Diogenes, Y., & Ozkaya, E. (2018). *Cybersecurity-attack and defense strategies: Infrastructure security with red team and blue team tactics*. Packt Publishing Ltd.

Erick, J., & Kasowaki, L. (2024). *Navigating the future: A comprehensive guide to internet banking in e-commerce* (No. 11806). EasyChair.

Erman, C. (2017). Financial technologies effect on financial services from an open innovation perspective.

Ganbold, B. (2008). *Improving access to finance for SME: International good experiences and lessons for Mongolia* (Vol. 438). Institute of Developing Economies.

George, S., & Nagadeepa, C. (2023). A study on the rising impacts of cybercrimes in electronic financing. *Role of Management and Business Practices for Sustainable Development, 63*.

Gautam, R. S., Rastogi, S., Rawal, A., Bhimavarapu, V. M., Kanoujiya, J., & Rastogi, S. (2022). Financial technology and its impact on digital literacy in India: Using poverty as a moderating variable. *Journal of Risk and Financial Management, 15*(7), 311.

Godard, J. J. (2022). *Impact of Fintech solutions on traditional banks by 2035: Qualitative e-Delphi study* (Doctoral dissertation). University of Phoenix.

Gomber, P., Kauffman, R. J., Parker, C., & Weber, B. W. (2018). On the fintech revolution: Interpreting the forces of innovation, disruption, and transformation in financial services. *Journal of Management Information Systems, 35*(1), 220–265.

Gomber, P., Koch, J. A., & Siering, M. (2017). Digital finance and FinTech: Current research and future research directions. *Journal of Business Economics, 87*, 537–580.

González Páramo, J. M. (2017). Financial innovation in the digital age: Challenges for regulation and supervision. *Revista de Estabilidad Financiera/Banco de España, 32 (mayo 2017), p. 9–37.*

Gupta, Y., Khanwalker, S., & Uiversity, I. U. (2019). Accelerating financial inclusion in India with digital products and services. *Gurukul Business Review-Gbr, 15*, 61–75.

Kihamba, J. S. (2020). E-Financing and the quest for financial inclusion in Tanzania. *Tanzania Journal for Population studies and Development*, *26*(1).

Hanna, N. K. (2009). *Enabling enterprise transformation: Business and grassroots innovation for the knowledge economy*. Springer Science & Business Media.

Hinson, R. E. (2011). Banking the poor: The role of mobiles. *Journal of Financial Services Marketing, 15*, 320–333.

Indjikian, R., Branch, E. C., & SITE, U. (2002). E-finance for SMEs: Global trends and national experiences. *Journals of Electronic Commerce, 1*, 1–38.

Joshi, V. C. (2020). Digital finance, bits and bytes. *Springer Books.*

Kaur, G., Lekhi, P., & Popli, S. (Eds.). (2024). *Exploring central bank digital currencies: Concepts, frameworks, models, and challenges: Concepts, frameworks, models, and challenges*. IGI Global.

Lin, Z., Whinston, A. B., & Fan, S. (2015). Harnessing internet finance with innovative cyber credit management. *Financial Innovation, 1*, 1–24.

Mallick, M. K. (2022). *Essentials of e-commerce B. Com 2nd semester—Syllabus prescribed by national education policy*. SBPD Publishing House.

Mvelase, S. K. (2022). *Performance evaluation of FinTech applications in emerging market economies: A case of TelPay.*

Igbinenikaro, E., & Adewusi, A. O. (2024). Financial law: Policy frameworks for regulating Fintech innovations: Ensuring consumer protection while fostering innovation. *Finance & Accounting Research Journal, 6*(4), 515–530.

Kandpal, V., Chandra, D., Dalei, N. N., & Handoo, J. (2023). Expanding financial inclusion through Fintech and e-governance. *Financial inclusion in circular economy: A bumpy road towards sustainable development* (pp. 103–129). Springer International Publishing.

Koops, B. J. (2006). Should ICT regulation be technology-neutral? *Starting points for ICT regulation. Deconstructing prevalent policy one-liners, it & law series, Bert-Jaap Koops, Miriam Lips, Corien Prins & Maurice Schellekens*, eds, *9*, 77–108. T.M.C. Asser Press.

Lagouvardou, S. (2018). *Maritime cyber security: Concepts, problems and models.* Kongens Lyngby.

Lal, T. (2018). Impact of financial inclusion on poverty alleviation through cooperative banks. *International Journal of Social Economics, 45*(5), 808–828.

Llanto, G. M., Rosellon, M. A. D., & Ortiz, M. K. P. (2018). E-finance in the Philippines: Status and prospects for digital financial inclusion.

Omarini, A. E. (2018). Peer-to-peer lending: Business model analysis and the platform dilemma. *International Journal of Finance, Economics and Trade, 2*(3), 31–41.
Oriji, O., Shonibare, M. A., Daraojimba, R. E., Abitoye, O., & Daraojimba, C. (2023). Financial technology evolution in Africa: A comprehensive review of legal frameworks and implications for AI-driven financial services. *International Journal of Management & Entrepreneurship Research, 5*(12), 929–951.
Ouk-Heon, S. I Impact of it Revolution on the financial structure of the seacen countries:. Challenges facing.
Ozili, P. K. (2020). Contesting digital finance for the poor. *Digital Policy, Regulation and Governance, 22*(2), 135–151.
Mensah, J. M. (2019). The impact of technological change (Digital currency) on traditional banking. *Pentvars Business Journal, 12*(12), 50–58.
Metzger, M., Riedler, T., & Pédussel Wu, J. (2019). *Migrant remittances: Alternative money transfer channels* (No. 127/2019). Working Paper.
Michael, B. (2021). How should public procurement law deal with FinTech?. *University of Hong Kong Faculty of Law Research Paper*, (2021/56).
Mullet, V., Sondi, P., & Ramat, E. (2021). A review of cybersecurity guidelines for manufacturing factories in industry 4.0. *IEEE Access, 9*, 23235–23263.
Punjabi, H. (2016). Innovative payment systems-core to India's e-finance Revolution. *BVIMSR Journal of Management Research, 8*(1).
Regragui, M. K. (2022). The African mobile wallets: An empirical analysis of the services and the anticipated trends.
Satpathy, I., Nayak, A., Baral, S. K., Islam, M., & Patnaik, B. C. M. (2024). e-Financial strategies as a catalyst for poverty alleviation and financial inclusion. In *E-Financial Strategies for Advancing Sustainable Development: Fostering Financial Inclusion and Alleviating Poverty* (pp. 235–251). Springer Nature Switzerland.
Seetharaman, A., & Raj, J. R. (2009). Evolution, development and growth of electronic money. *International Journal of E-Adoption (IJEA), 1*(1), 76–94.
Shahrokhi, M. (2008). E-finance: Status, innovations, resources and future challenges. *Managerial Finance, 34*(6), 365–398.
Swarupa, S. G., Vijaya, E., & Reddy, K. V. SME financing approaches and strategies: Global Perspective.
Sutcliffe, H. (2011). A report on responsible research and innovation. *MATTER and the European Commission.*
Wales, K. (2017). *Peer-to-Peer lending and equity crowdfunding: A guide to the new capital markets for job creators, investors, and entrepreneurs*. Bloomsbury Publishing.

Westby, J. R. (2004). *International guide to cyber security*. American Bar Association.

Wilson, K. E., Vyakarnam, S., Volkmann, C., Mariotti, S., & Rabuzzi, D. (2009, April). Educating the next wave of entrepreneurs: Unlocking entrepreneurial capabilities to meet the global challenges of the 21st century. In *World economic forum: A report of the global education initiative*.

Yadav, N., Mathur, A., & Thanvi, J. (2024). Fusion of AI and ethical finance: Changing the outlook of financial companies and society. In *Fintech applications in Islamic finance: AI, machine learning, and blockchain techniques* (pp. 24–34). IGI Global.

Transforming Customer Perception through Green Banking Channels in Electronic Finance

Garima Malik

1 Introduction

Green banking is a banking practice in which factors related to both environment and society are considered. Green banking is also denoted as ETHICAL BANKING. The aim of ethical banks is to protect the environment. Similar to traditional these banks are also governed and controlled by authorities, the only difference being that they ethical banks also aim to protect the environment (see Table 1). The term green banking in general denotes how much committed a bank is to green and ethical policies i.e., How much the bank cares for environment? In this study, we will see what is the impact of green banking channels on customer perception:

I. **Aims of Green Banking**

- Reservation and efficient usage of natural resources
- Diminish and reutilize waste at source
- Proposal of environmental-friendly products
- Intensification of resource savings and energy effectiveness

G. Malik (✉)
Birla Institute of Management Technology, BIMTECH, Greater Noida, India
e-mail: garima.malik@bimtech.ac.in

© The Author(s), under exclusive license to Springer Nature Singapore Pte Ltd. 2025

A. S. et al. (eds.), *Trends and Challenges of Electronic Finance*,
https://doi.org/10.1007/978-981-96-3304-3_6

Table 1 Difference between green banking and a normal bank

Green banking	*Regular banking*
Environmental factors are considered	Financial factors are considered
Loan is given only when all the environmental standards are satisfied	Loan is given based upon the ability of the customer to repay the loan

- Encourage scientifically and technologically developed processes to prevent environmental contamination and endlessly improve its eco-friendliness
- Rise in the alertness of bank employees, suppliers, and customers toward environment

II. **Benefits of Green Banking**

- Basically, Ethical banking maintains a strategic distance from paperwork as much as possible; one becomes environmentally friendly by using credit cards, green mortgages, and furthermore every one of the exchanges done through the web.
- Creating attention to agents about natural and social obligation empowering them to complete an ecological well-disposed business practice.
- Using green banking means providing loans to only those firms or companies which pursue environmental and ecological standards. It makes green banking a smart move to make entrepreneurs change their business strategy to an environment friendly model and will help our future generations.
- When loans are taken for companies that choose methods which conserve environment then the interest on such loans is usually less than those provided by normal banks, in light of the fact that green banks give more significance to natural neighborly factors they don't work with high premium.

2 Green Banking in India

India's GDP has been growing for the past fifteen years and the credit for such a change goes to the industrial sector as it plays the most vital role in India's road to progress. Still, the Indian industry undergoes a major challenge of monitoring the impact of environment on the business i.e., pollution reduction and reducing emission of the client organizations. The government is making an effort to work on this subject of concern by forming environmental laws and by also taking a step to encourage the industry to implement technologies and practices related to environment. So, green banking is one such practice that government is following to conserve environment by making sure industries which use environment friendly equipment will be encouraged and thus will be provided with loans from various private and public sector banks all over the county.

2.1 *Review of Literature*

(Naidu, 2015) Industrialization around the globe has set off the location of consistently expanding necessities and requests of the people and it has turned out to be representative of flourishing and improvement of an economy. Then again, it has brought about the misuse of the regular habitat, which thus has disturbed ecological balance.

(Raj, 2017) Banks are not directly associated with environmental degradation but they indirectly contribute to environmental degradation. Banking activities and internal operations carried out by the banks are not harmful for the environment. Their operations don't cause any kind of pollution or discard hazardous waste into environment. In any case, banks give loans to the enterprises and different firms who thus carry out the business that effects nature. The study intends to recognize the view and responsiveness of bank personnel and clients in reference to their perception toward green banking in both private and public sector banks. It is essential to categorize numerous efforts which banks take on the subject of green banking so as to motivate the customer and make them eco-friendly. We will study the effect of gender on initiatives taken by public and private sector banks to encourage green banking (Menon & Shivdas, 2017). The study shows how energy preservation and stability in the environment are important for survival of all businesses. Sustainability of economy is important in long term for businesses. The lenders should provide loans to those borrowers who prefer methods of energy conservation because these methods will help the firm to be stable and sustainable for long time and eventually, they will be able to pay off their debt. This will help both economy and the environment. The study also examines various green banking initiatives in various banks of India.

(Vadrale & Katti, 2016) They quoted that green banking is a banking business that is managed in such a technique which leads to reduction of overall external carbon emission as well as that of internal carbon footprint. The study helps to understand how green banking products are valuable in banking sector and it also helps in examining the green banking initiatives taken by the top three private and also top three public sector banks of India. It also came to the conclusion that both private and public banks are effective in initiation of green banking, but it is also to be noted that the public sector banks are performing better than the private banks to the degree that the green banking practices are concerned.

(Deka, 2018) Banks as reliable companies are in like manner getting significant advances wherever all through the world to address this issue. They are receiving many green monetary practices with the objective that they can make little duty toward the earth. Green practices of banks are the undertakings of the budgetary division to keep the earth green and to restrict nursery impact. The paper discusses client's perspectives on the determination and use of various green budgetary practices displayed by the banks in the area of Assam in India. It is seen that green budgetary practices have beneficial outcome on nature since allocation of these practices by the customers may result saving of essentialness, fuel, paper, water, time, and furthermore cash. The examination wraps up with the clarification that 'green financial practices are not just plausible, they are currently getting to be basic.'

(Joshi & Shah, 2017) An important term which define practices and guidelines to make all commercial banks eco-friendly, cost-effective and responsible toward society is green banking. Banks finance green technology and non-polluting projects to make sure there's a decline in external carbon emissions. Banks and other financial institutes implement strategies to deal with environmental problems and contribute toward sustainable eco-development. The banking industry acts as a mediator between environment security and economic progress by bringing out socially responsible and environmentally stable deal. The paper identifies various levels of green banking initiatives which commercial banks took, and it also gives out various green banking strategies followed by them and also it proposes a model for green banking in India.

(Veena & Nayana, 2017) The idea green banking encourages bank to find a way to decrease the immediate influence of its processes on the earth. The study gives the dimension of customer awareness and satisfaction with respect to 'Green financial administrations' activity taken by

State Bank of India. SBI presents 'green-channel banking' at more divisions to advance paperless work and to encourage quicker exchanges for clients. The study aims to identify the estimation and consciousness of clients with respect to green financial idea at SB. It is important to distinguish different activities taken by bank on green banking all together to impact on understanding of clients. By and large, the banks are utilizing Internet banking rather than branch banking.

(Ganesh & Geetha, 2017) Change is the need of the hour; change is important in all areas of societies. Change is important in both rural and urban areas. Urban areas have been using green banking technologies for long but the case is not the same when rural areas are concerned. It's the need of the hour for the banks to become the backbone of the economy in the rural areas by promoting and using green banking techniques. Day-to-day banking in rural areas should be green to form a low-carbon economy. The study shows the strategies of green banking used by Grameen banks and how they are giving their helping hand in order to protect the planet.

3 Objective and Scope of the Study

- To understand the green banking concept and to learn the green banking practices.
- To identify the different levels of strategies which are adopted by various commercial banks to promote green banking.
- To discuss how green banking practices have an impact on sustainability by evaluation of benefits.
- To investigate and find the customers' awareness levels of green banking practices and what is their adoption level for the same.

3.1 *Research Methodology & Design*

A descriptive research design is used in order to discover the primary factors relating to the green banking and its impact on consumer perception. A quantitative research is done in order to understand attitudes and behaviors of consumers toward various green banking principles. Also, a qualitative research is done which tells us how people from different age groups and different genders vary in results.

For primary data collection, a questionnaire with 21 questions has been designed with the multiple-choice questions and 319 people all over

Table 2 Variable mean rank table

Variables/ Statement	*Mean*	*Rank*
Green banking cell is established for promoting & monitoring green banking activities	4.01	9
Banks should associate with NGOs, environmentalist, and corporate bodies to create awareness among the customers about green banking	3.98	10
Banks should adopt green banking as a business model for sustainable banking	4.03	7
Rbi should frame strict regulations to promote green banking	4.03	7
Banks should shift its motive from 'profit profit profit' to 'planet people profit'	4.16	3
Banks should reward customers who carry out their transactions in eco-friendly manner	4.11	4
Green banking should become essential element to preserve natural resources	4.18	2
Banks should conduct green banking audit for the project which is financed	4.08	6
Banks should make customers aware by promoting green banking	4.11	4
Green banking is corporate social responsibility of every bank	4.24	1
What green banking channels you are likely to use the most? Kindly rate on order of preference [cash deposit]	2.78	15
What green banking channels you are likely to use the most? Kindly rate on order of preference [cash withdrawal]	3.01	14
What green banking channels you are likely to use the most? Kindly rate on order of preference [online transfer]	3.12	12
What green banking channels you are likely to use the most? Kindly rate on order of preference [green finance]	3.09	13
What green banking channels you are likely to use the most? Kindly rate on order of preference [green infrastructure]	3.26	11

Delhi have been surveyed (refer Table 2). Most of the questions have been planned on five points on the Likert Scale namely Strongly Agree, Agree, Neutral, Disagree, and Strongly Disagree. Where 'Strongly Agree' denotes the highest level of trust, and 'Strongly Disagree' denotes the lowest level of trust. The data processing has been done using SPSS.

3.2 Method of Sampling

Various statistical techniques such as mean, standard deviation, and standard error of deviation are employed in the analysis. These methods help in summarizing and understanding the central tendencies, dispersion, and reliability of the data collected. Additionally, frequency tables are utilized to examine how respondents have answered the survey questions, providing a clear overview of the distribution of responses. Crosstabulations are particularly useful for determining the duration people have held bank accounts and identifying their preferred banking sectors. By employing these methods, we can gain a comprehensive understanding of the survey data and uncover meaningful patterns and insights.

4 Data Analysis

- As per Table 3, we can see that almost all respondents think that green banking is corporate social responsibility of every bank.
- It also shows that customers are least likely to deposit cash through machines or without using paper or cash deposit receipts.
- Ranks of various other statements are given in the table.

- This shows that approximately 44% of people are unlikely to perform cash deposit using green methods (See Fig. 1).
- It shows that people are neutral toward withdrawing money using green methods.
- It shows that approximately 40% of people are likely to use online transfer.
- It shows that approximately 43% of people are likely to use green financing services.
- It shows that approximately 30% of people are most likely to use green infrastructures.

4.1 Crosstabs

- It shows that people holding accounts from less than 10 years prefer private sector banks as compared to public sector banks (refer Table 4).
- It also shows that people holding accounts for more than 20 years i.e., senior citizens prefer their old tried and tested public sector banks.
- Overall preference for private sector banks is more because of their faster service.

Table 3 Results of green banking channels

What green banking channels you are likely to use the most? Kindly rate on order of preference

	Cash Deposit		Cash Withdrawal		Online Transfer		Green finance		Green Infrastructure	
	Frequency	Percent	Frequency	Percent	Frequency	Percent	Frequency	Percent	Frequency	Percent
1	72	22.6	40	12.5	55	17.2	49	15.4	46	14.4
2	66	20.7	79	24.8	54	16.9	64	20.1	56	17.6
3	82	25.7	82	25.7	78	24.5	69	21.6	79	24.8
4	59	18.5	74	23.2	61	19.1	82	25.7	45	14.1
5	40	12.5	44	13.8	71	22.3	55	17.2	93	29.2
Total	319	100.0	319	100.0	319	100.0	319	100.0	319	100.0

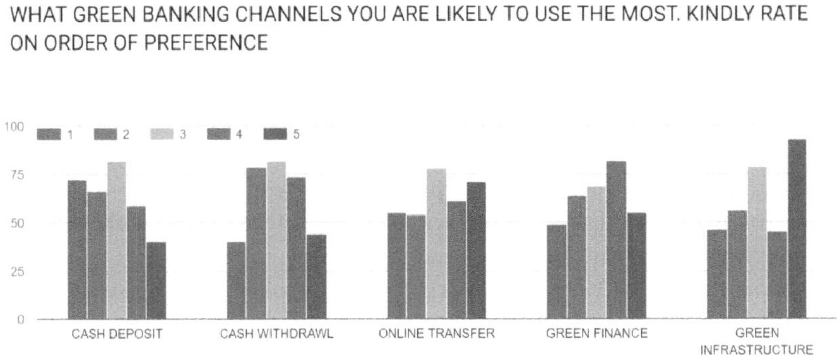

Fig. 1 Preference for usage of green banking channels

Table 4 Preference for different types of banks

*Which banks do you prefer? * how long you have been holding a bank account cross tabulation*

		How long you have been holding a bank account						*Total*
		Less than a year	*1 yr–5 yr*	*5 yr–10 yr*	*10 yr–15 yr*	*15 yr–20 yr*	*20 yr and above*	
Which banks do you prefer?	Private sector banks	15	78	77	21	13	3	207
	Public sector banks	5	49	31	10	6	11	112
Total		20	127	108	31	19	14	319

5 Findings

- Two thirds of respondents prefer private sector banks over public sector banks.
- Three fourth of population have been holding bank accounts for the past 1 to 10 years.
- Approx. 63% of respondents say their banks follow an implement green banking principle and 32% are not sure about their answer.

- Three fourth respondents agree to switch to net banking, online transfer, and e-receipts to save paper and environment.
- Approx. 60% of the respondents are quite aware of various green banking channels.
- About 75% of people agree to the fact that a green banking cell is established by their banks for promoting green tech.
- About 72% of respondents want banks to associate with NGOs, environmentalists, etc.
- Almost 95% of people want that banks should opt for sustainable banking business model.
- Most of the respondents (74% agree or strongly agree and 20% are neutral) want RBI to frame strict rules for green banking promotion.
- 78% respondents want banks to shift their motive to planet, people, and profit rather than just focusing on profits.
- 78% of respondents want banks to reward them for using green banking channels.
- 75% of respondent wants audit to check whether industries which took loans are following green banking principles or not.
- 75% of people want banks to promote green banking and make customer well aware of the same.
- Approx. 4.5% of people do not consider green banking a corporate social responsibility of every bank.

6 Conclusion & Recommendations

This study comes to the conclusion, that green banking has direct and positive impact toward being sustainable. Following green banking practices customers can save energy, fuel, paper, water, time, and even money. It also results in reduction of the carbon footprint from banking practices. Green banking practices are very appropriate, easy, and economical for the customers of the banks. It saves journeys to the bank. Customers need not to go to the bank for transactions, thereby, saving not only time but also money. It is a type of anytime, anyplace banking. Green banking practices are also profitable to the banks because they cause less cost due to postage and handling services. And it also reduces the workload from the bank staff.

As a result, one must say that a small 'GREEN' step implemented today will be a stepping stone to a long path in structuring a greener future and directing us to a healthier global environment. 'Go Green' is the need of the hour and is a huge initiative to lead banks, banking processes, and customers of various banks to an efficient automatic and cost-effective way. Thus, carbon footprint will be reduced and also an awareness and insight will be built about nation, environment and society.

The green banking as a concept is clear to all sections of society; it is recommended that more people should follow green banking concepts and both private and public sector banks should have a green channel counter where they avoid wastage of paper, etc. Banks should finance projects, which are green, i.e., those which avoid degradation of environment. A larger audience can be used for the study as a survey can be also conducted in rural or semi-urban places to get a better overall outcome. It is recommended that there should be an adequate number of publications both from the government and banks to spread awareness about the ecological effects of different green banking practices. Course and workshops are to be organized by the banks to make individuals aware of green banks.

7 Limitations

A major limitation is lack of involvement of people from rural or semi-urban areas. Also, a limitation is that major responses are from people who are in well-to-do families. For a wider picture, people from all sections of society must be considered. Green banking as a concept is gaining popularity but it is not as popular as traditional banking. Banks prefer to earn profits and finance those projects which are not green thus making it a major limitation. Hence, we need to take steps for proper implementation of these principles and make earth a better place.

References

Naidu, V. K. (2015, Jan-June). *A study on green banking trends in india*. https://www.researchgate.net/publication/310973098_A_STUDY_ON_GREEN_BANKING_TRENDS_IN_INDIA

Raj, D. G. (2017, July). *A study on the customer awareness on green banking*. https://www.researchgate.net/profile/Pappu_Rajan/publication/318760489_A_STUDY_ON_THE_CUSTOMER_AWARENESS_ON_GREEN_BANKING_INITIATIVES_1/links/597c49a0aca272d568e2ac27/A-STUDY-ON-THE-CUSTOMER-AWARENESS-ON-GREEN-BANKING-INITIATIVES-1.pdf?origin=publication_

Ganesh. K. T., & Geetha, V. D. (2017). Adoption of green banking in RRB'S: With reference to Kaveri Grameen Bank. *Peer Reviewed & Indexed Journal*, 234–237.

Menon, D. G., Sreelakshmi, S. G., & Shivdas, A. (2017). Green banking initiatives: A review of Indian banking sector. *2017 IEEE international conference on technological advancements in power and energy (TAP Energy)*.

Vadrale, K. S., & Katti, V. P. (2016). *Green banking initiatives by Indian public and private sector banks*. Conference Paper.

Deka, G. (2018). Customers' perception on green banking practices of state bank of India: A SWOC analysis. *International Journal of Management Studies*, 29–42.

Joshi, D. N., & Shah, P. S. (2017). Green banking: a tool for sustainable development in 21st century. *IJEMR*.

Veena, K. P., & Nayana, N. (2017). A study on customer perception towards green banking—A special reference to State Bank of India—Bangalore and Mysore City. *Journal of Exclusive Management Science*. *6*(2), 1–7.

Fintech and Sustainability: Perspectives from Emerging Markets

Ahmed Mohamed Habib

1 Introduction

When developing economic models, the reality of resource scarcity and the importance of preserving and managing resources in a way that does not negatively affect the environment must be considered. Additionally, the impact of resource availability on economic growth is highly dependent on the adopted growth model (Walker et al., 2023). According to de Ferranti et al. (2002), successful natural resource developers and current theory should consider improving human capital and fostering the ability to learn and innovate. Developing intellectual capital can also promote overall performance (Habib & Dalwai, 2023; Habib & Mourad, 2023a) and mitigate potential risks (Shahwan & Habib, 2020). In this context, most economic historians believe that US industrial success was mainly due to resource availability in a wide range of minerals and aggressive investment in intellectual capital and knowledge management (Huynh et al., 2024; Nkambule et al., 2022).

In addition, if countries cannot effectively utilize their resource bases, indicators of resource reliance may broadly indicate a lack of development

A. M. Habib (✉)
Department of Accounting and Finance, Independent Research, Zagazig, Egypt
e-mail: dr_ahmedhabib@yahoo.com

© The Author(s), under exclusive license to Springer Nature Singapore Pte Ltd. 2025

A. S. et al. (eds.), *Trends and Challenges of Electronic Finance*,
https://doi.org/10.1007/978-981-96-3304-3_7

success (Stijns, 2006). Unfortunately, mass production techniques and the realization of economies of scale have resulted in excessive utilization of natural resources and pollution generation (Schoenmaker & Schramade, 2019). In addition, environmental and socioeconomic issues, including global warming and climate change, ocean acidification, ozone depletion, poverty and hunger, child labor, and gender discrimination, worsen if not promptly addressed (Habib, 2023a; Walker et al., 2019). Governments and politicians have recently concocted public policies, such as the Sustainable Development Goals (SDGs) and 2030 agenda, to effectively handle this shift (Gutterman, 2021; Habib, 2023b). Hence, a seamless transition to a sustainable economy is the only way to address these issues.

Sustainable finance includes ESG criteria for investment choices. Investments in sustainable projects and activities have increased over time. Figure 1 depicts the current universe of companies that are aware of ESG. An effective financial system can guarantee that financial resources are allocated to sustainable firms (Walker et al., 2023). Financial support, such as investment or financing, directed toward sustainable objectives can significantly boost sustainable initiatives and expedite the shift toward a sustainable society (Habib, 2022; Habib & Mourad, 2023b). Sustainable investment or financing represents a fundamental change in the role of financial services in promoting an environment-friendly, fair, and sustainable future. Unlike traditional investment or financing, which tends to disregard environmental and social implications, sustainable investment or financing incorporates them into financial decision-making (Edmans & Kacperczyk, 2022; Scott Cato, 2022). Sustainable investment or financing encompasses various concepts, including green finance, green bonds, sustainable finance, environmental finance, ESG finance, climate finance, sustainable investment, green fintech, and green innovation.

Targets 17.1 to 17.5 within SDG 17 focus on finance for sustainability. Moreover, new technologies and developments have transformed financial systems. Digitalization and advanced technologies have enhanced fintech industry growth. Fintech investments have transformed financial service operations. Fintech has a significant ambition of facilitating payment automation and granting instant digital access to financial resources. Fintech can enable institutions to adopt a sustainable approach by mitigating the adverse environmental effects and providing sustainable investment options. Thus, green fintech can promote sustainability. Fintech can help financial organizations improve the accuracy of green process data, reduce costs, and increase ESG efficiency (Chen et al.,

Fig. 1 Current universe of companies with ESG data awareness

2023; Galeone et al., 2024; Tang et al., 2023). This entails developing digital tools and platforms for green investments, ESG reporting transparency, and eco-friendly financial products and services (Walker et al., 2023). Fintech also promotes sustainability by investing in green bonds and crowdfunding initiatives (Mirza et al., 2023; Wan et al., 2023).

From a macroeconomic perspective, fintech can be used to achieve sustainability. Figure 2 illustrates the ESG dimensions and scope. Fintech can help orient ESG policies and provide effective platforms for monitoring and managing regulatory activities. Fintech tools can be adapted to construct water waste reduction and carbon dioxide (CO_2) emission control systems and provide effective platforms for monitoring and managing regulatory activities. Furthermore, although fintech offers many benefits, environmentalists are worried about its potential impacts. Opponents are concerned that fintech advancements may have more disadvantages than advantages. Thus, the intersection between fintech and sustainability presents opportunities and risks, necessitating comprehensive re-evaluation and notable considerations.

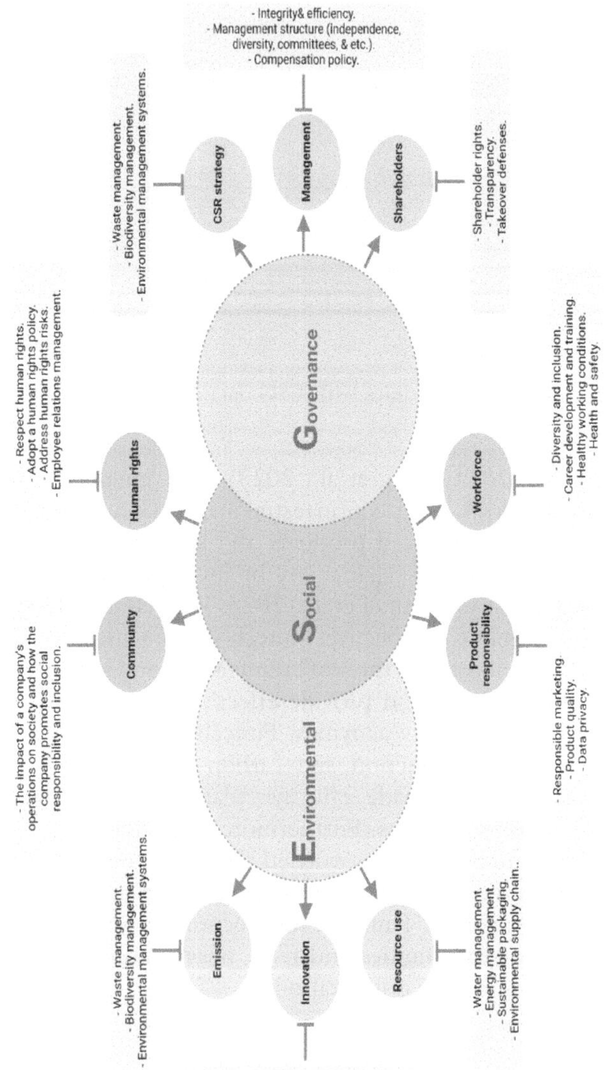

Fig. 2 ESG dimensions and scope

2 Fintech and Environmental Sustainability.

The Paris Agreement, launched in 2015, has devised a shared global target for countries on climate change. It seeks to constrain the rise in the worldwide average temperature to a level significantly lower than $2^{\circ C}$ over the temperatures observed pre-industrial levels and to pursue efforts to cap the temperature increase to $1.5^{\circ C}$. To restrain global warming, greenhouse gas (GHG) emissions, particularly CO_2 emissions, must be reduced by 43 percent by 2030. It was ratified by 196 parties in Paris on December 12, 2015, at the United Nations (UN) Climate Change Conference (COP[21]) and became effective on November 4, 2016.

In addition, the Paris Agreement confirms for the first time that affluent countries should provide financial aid to less-developed and vulnerable countries and encourage voluntary contributions from other parties. Massive investment is required to reduce emissions; therefore, climate financing is necessary for mitigation. Environmental adaptation requires substantial financial resources to mitigate the adverse effects of the changing environmental conditions. However, developing nations face a significant financing shortfall in addressing climate change, although developed countries have committed to COP[15] in Copenhagen to finance developing countries by approximately US$100 billion annually to adapt to and reduce climate change (Timperley, 2021). The Paris Agreement confirms the significance of fully implementing technological development and knowledge management to improve climate change resilience and reduce GHG emissions. However, according to a recent UN report, national climate action plans are still inadequate in their efforts to restrict global warming and achieve the objectives of the Paris Agreement (UN, 2023). Despite the increasing efforts of certain countries, the report indicates a pressing need for more substantial action to significantly reduce global emissions and prevent the most severe consequences of climate change.

According to a recent UN report, GHG emissions must be reduced by 43 percent by 2030 compared with the 2019 levels recorded. The increase in temperature must be restricted to $1.5^{\circ C}$ to prevent the most severe consequences of climate change, such as frequent and intense droughts, heatwaves, and rainfall (UN, 2023). The report also specifically examined strategies developed by countries to transition to net-zero emissions by or around the mid-century period. The analysis suggests that if all long-term initiatives are adequately executed on time, these countries might achieve a reduction of approximately 63 percent in GHG emissions by 2050 compared to 2019. However, the investigation highlighted that numerous net-zero targets are still unknown, delaying the urgent action that must be taken (UN, 2023).

Furthermore, the 26th UN Conference (COP^{26}) in Glasgow, UK, between October 31 and November 12, 2021, gathered world leaders and climate experts to agree on policies to remain below $1.5^{\circ C}$. COP^{26} objectives show that finance, technology, and sustainability intersect. This intersection can help to achieve environmental sustainability. During this conference summit, several objectives were discussed, including mitigation of emissions, adaptation to the consequences of climate change, and financing from developed to developing. They also discussed securing funding to ensure that developing nations receive US$100 billion in climate finance annually and collaborating to expedite efforts to address climate change through the involvement of governments, businesses, and civil society.

Typically, initiatives encompassed by green fintech or climate fintech taken by organizations play a vital role in addressing climate change. Globally, green or climate fintech developments are the most prevalent in consumer behavior, investing, and risk analysis. AI can be utilized in green fintech or climate fintech applications to synthesize data swiftly and improve decision-making. Fintech integrated with AI and IoT can shift consumer inclination toward environmentally friendly products. Fintech is expected to continue allocating resources to sustainable projects to expand its market in a fiercely competitive financial industry.

Additionally, fintech solutions substantially contribute to the progress of environmental goals by offering innovative tools for monitoring and reducing the carbon footprint. BC technology can provide transparent and immutable records of carbon emissions, enabling the measurement and verification of the environmental impacts of businesses and investments. Fintech platforms enable individuals and companies to compute their carbon footprints and offset emissions by investing in renewable energy initiatives. These platforms make it easier for individuals to actively reduce their environmental impact by using user-friendly interfaces and automated procedures.

3 Fintech and Social Sustainability

Fintech is crucial to advancing sustainability and societal transformation in a dynamic digital environment. There is growing emphasis on sustainable finance, as investors and consumers increasingly seek greater transparency and accountability from financial institutions. Owing to its groundbreaking technological solutions, fintech can become a potent instrument for advancing social objectives. These technologies can enhance accessibility to information, streamline financial transactions, and empower individuals to make informed decisions that align with their specific needs.

The UN General Assembly (UNGA) endorsed the 2030 Agenda for Sustainability in September 2015. The agenda aims to achieve 17 general sustainable development goals (SDGs), including 169 subgoals. These 17 development goals balance the economic, social, and environmental challenges. This agenda prioritizes equitable and inclusive growth. Macroeconomic growth has also been linked to social growth. Thus, socioeconomic growth can help achieve new development goals and reduce poverty, especially in emerging markets. In addition, with increasing global awareness of the importance of sustainable practices, fintech is leading the path toward a more environmentally friendly and socially accountable future. Utilizing these capabilities can expedite the shift toward a more environmentally friendly and equitable global economy. However, poverty and lack of economic resources are significant concerns. External and appropriate financing can support disadvantaged groups in imperfect credit markets with knowledge asymmetry.

Improving financial access can reduce poverty and inequality. Financial inclusion is a critical issue that must be considered to achieve socioeconomic development in disadvantaged groups. Fintech has also significantly promoted financial inclusion. Fintech platforms offer digital payment solutions and mobile banking services to individuals, not part of the traditional banking system or with limited access to financial services. The enhanced availability of financial resources can empower individuals and communities, reduce poverty, and promote economic development. Financial inclusion also shows promise for the financial system's stability and enhanced worldwide awareness of the urgent financial demands of disadvantaged groups (Hussain et al., 2024; Ofosu-Mensah Ababio et al., 2023).

In addition to financial inclusion, optimizing procedures, and offering user-friendly interfaces, fintech is propelling the advancement and acceptance of sustainable financial projects. Fintech is transforming the financial industry by incorporating environmental and social considerations into the investment decision-making processes. These include the use of green bonds, impact investing, carbon footprint tracking, and ESG grading systems (Galeone et al., 2024). In addition to environmental objectives, fintech is propelling the advancement of social goals. For example, fintech platforms enable the provision of microfinance, which offers small loans to entrepreneurs in less-developed and vulnerable countries that may not have access to conventional banking services. By using technology, these platforms can access and serve neglected populations, allowing them to initiate or enhance their companies and quality of life. Therefore, this technology may have a positive social influence if well-adapted.

4 4. Fintech and Governance Sustainability

Fintech can contribute to sustainable development by facilitating ESG investments and promoting financial inclusion efforts that cater to the financial requirements of those with limited or no access to traditional banking services. The COVID-19 pandemic has had varying impacts on the macro or micro level for countries (Habib & Kayani, 2024; Nuta et al., 2024; Zimon et al., 2024), leading to increased dependence on digital banking systems (Yıldırım & Erdil, 2024). However, the absence of unified governance and regulatory systems for fintech poses a challenge to attaining the UN Sustainable Development Goals. Hence, enhanced governance is required, and establishing regulatory frameworks is necessary to mitigate the risks linked to fintech while maximizing its advantages over time.

Fintech can contribute to sustainable development by facilitating ESG investments and promoting financial inclusion efforts that cater to the financial requirements of those with limited or no access to traditional banking services. The COVID-19 pandemic has resulted in heightened dependence on digital banking systems. However, the absence of unified governance and regulatory systems for fintech poses a challenge to attaining the UN Sustainable Development Goals. Hence, enhanced governance is required, and establishing regulatory frameworks is necessary to mitigate the risks linked to fintech while maximizing its advantages over time.

Intergovernmental organizations mandate that financial institutions and fintech startups implement robust governance frameworks that are capable of adapting to a dynamic environment. Given the increasing engagement among fintech startups, incumbent banks, and other financial entities, ensuring strong corporate governance is crucial for preserving shareholders' rights and preventing the banking system from new threats. In addition, the updated principles of the Group of Twenty (G20) and the Organization for Economic Cooperation and Development (OECD) recognize the capacity of digitalization and fintech to develop conventional financial systems and introduce novel challenges to corporate governance frameworks (G20, 2018; OECD, 2021, XX2022). Policymakers and regulators strive to optimize the benefits of fintech companies in the financial industry while reducing possible risks to the financial system by encouraging the adoption of effective governance procedures (FSB, 2017). Figure 3 depicts guidance on regulatory approaches to fintech.

It is essential to note that the regulatory environment for financial technologies is continuously developing. Several jurisdictions have worked on setting unique frameworks, norms, and guidelines to handle the raised fintech opportunities and challenges. Policies, regulatory regimes, and government programs are the fundamental strengths of fintech's success in the United Kingdom. Under the Financial Services and Markets Act (FSMA) of 2000, the Prudential Regulation Authority (PRA) and the Financial Conduct Authority (FCA) regulate financial firms, including fintech companies, to ensure safe and sound operations.

In addition, several federal and state regulators oversee financial organizations in the US. For instance, the Consumer Financial Protection Bureau (CFPB) ensures that fintech companies' consumer financial services and products are equitable, transparent, and follow federal consumer finance rules. Additionally, under the supervision and regulation of the Office of the Comptroller of the Currency (OCC), national banks, federal savings organizations, and fintech companies are all subject to oversight. Moreover, securities markets, including crowdfunding platforms and other fintech companies that offer investment-related financial products, are regulated by the Securities and Exchange Commission (SEC) following federal law.

In addition, fintech regulation in European Union (EU) countries is a cooperative effort among several regulatory agencies. For instance, the European Banking Authority (EBA) ensures that prudential regulation

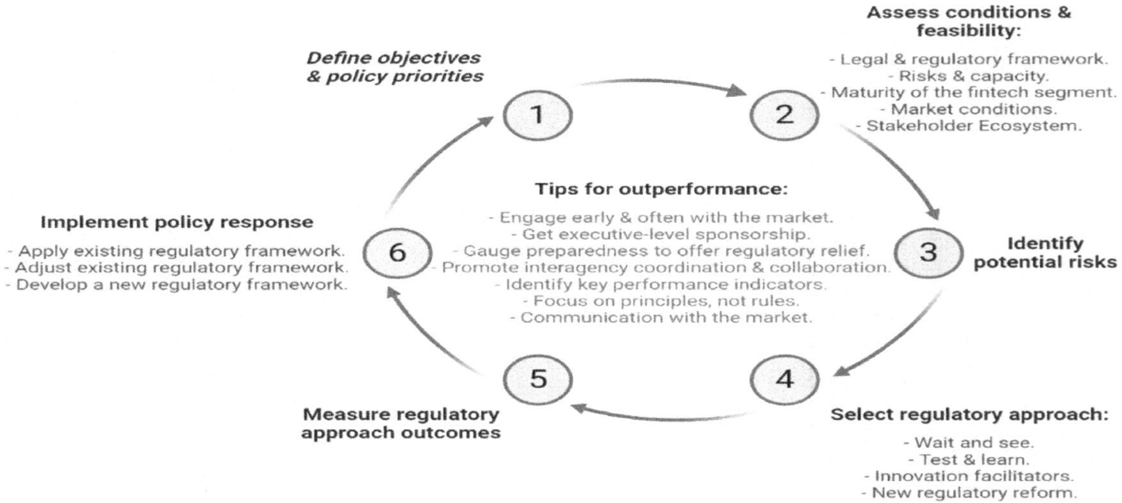

Fig. 3 Guidance on regulatory approaches toward fintech

and control of fintech activities are conducted efficiently and consistently. The European Securities and Markets Authority (ESMA) also monitors investment businesses and securities markets concerned with fintech activities. Moreover, each member state has national regulatory agencies that collaborate with EU authorities to regulate fintech within their jurisdictions. One such body is the Federal Financial Supervisory Authority in Germany, known as the Federal Financial Supervisory Authority (BaFin), which oversees the safety, stability, integrity, and protection of the financial sector and consumers' collective interests in Germany.

In the Middle East, as an emerging market, Habib (2024) confirms that as global capital markets and globalization trends integrate, emerging market authorities must embrace sensible macroeconomic policies and structural changes for financial services development. Moreover, the United Arab Emirates (UAE) has increased significantly, from 39 percent in 2018 to 73 percent in 2023. However, the usage of digital banking among Middle Eastern customers is barely 17 percent, in contrast to the significantly higher rate of approximately 60 percent in the US. In the UAE, regulatory authorities, such as the Central Bank of the UAE (CBUAE), Virtual Assets Regulatory Authority (VARA), Securities and Commodities Authority (SCA), and Dubai Financial Services Authority (DFSA), play a crucial role in administering financial services frameworks and regulating the fintech market. The Saudi Arabian Monetary Authority (SAMA) regulates licenses and develops the fintech industry in the Kingdom of Saudi Arabia (KSA). The Central Bank of Oman (CBO) actively prioritizes fintech development and enhances innovation in the financial sector. The Financial Regulatory Authority (FRA) licenses and regulates fintech companies in Egypt.

Moreover, regulatory bodies exist in different regions and countries. For instance, the FSB, an international organization known as the Financial Stability Board, monitors and recommends reforms to the global financial system. The Financial Services Agency (FSA) also regulates the financial services provided by fintech companies. The Australian Securities and Investments Commission (ASIC) oversees fintech companies' activities. The Monetary Authority of Singapore (MAS) is a leading regulatory authority in the financial sector that provides a sandbox for fintech companies to test their services and products in a controlled environment. HKMA, the Hong Kong Monetary Authority, regulates Hong Kong's financial industry.

5 Conclusion

Governments and politicians have developed public policies, such as the SDGs and 2030 agenda, to address environmental and socioeconomic issues. SDG 17 focuses specifically on finance for sustainability and adopting and executing investment promotion regimes for the least developed countries. A seamless transition to a sustainable economy is critical in this context. Sustainable investment or financing encompasses various concepts, including green finance, green bonds, sustainable finance, environmental finance, ESG finance, climate finance, sustainable investment, green fintech, and green innovation. Moreover, sustainable finance incorporates ESG factors into investment choices, and adequate financial support, such as investment or financing, directed toward sustainable objectives can significantly boost sustainable initiatives and support the shift toward a sustainable society.

On the other hand, new technologies and developments, such as BD, AI, ML, BI, BC technology, IoT, CR, and CBS, have enhanced the fintech industry's growth. Fintech can enable institutions to adopt a sustainable approach by mitigating the adverse environmental effects and providing sustainable investment options. Thus, green fintech can promote sustainability. Fintech can help financial organizations improve the accuracy of green process data, reduce costs, and increase ESG efficiency. This entails developing digital tools and platforms for green investment, ESG reporting transparency, and eco-friendly financial products/services. Fintech promotes sustainability by investing in green bonds and crowdfunding. Fintech can help design ESG policies, norms, and regulations and provide effective platforms for monitoring and managing regulatory activities. Fintech tools can be adapted to construct water waste reduction and CO_2 emission control systems and provide effective platforms for monitoring and managing regulatory activities.

Fintech is crucial to advancing sustainability and societal transformation in a dynamic digital environment. There is growing emphasis on sustainable finance, as investors and consumers increasingly seek greater transparency and accountability from financial institutions. Due to its groundbreaking technological solutions, Fintech has become a potent instrument for advancing social objectives. Fintech companies are transforming sustainable financing by using advanced technologies. These technologies enhance accessibility to information, streamline financial transactions, and empower individuals to make informed decisions that align with their specific needs. Furthermore, fintech offers many benefits but may lead to more risks. Thus, the intersection between fintech and sustainability presents opportunities and risks, necessitating comprehensive re-evaluation and notable considerations. The regulatory landscape of fintech is evolving constantly. Therefore, it is imperative, in general, and in emerging markets in particular, to develop and regulate novel opportune frameworks and policies to effectively tackle these issues and capitalize on the potential of the fintech business. Enhanced governance and the establishment of regulatory frameworks are essential to mitigate the risks linked to fintech while maximizing its advantages over time.

References

Chen, W., Wu, W., & Zhang, T. (2023). Fintech development, firm digitalization, and bank loan pricing. *Journal of Behavioral and Experimental Finance, 39*, 100838. https://doi.org/10.1016/j.jbef.2023.100838

de Ferranti, D., Perry, G. E., Lederman, D., & Maloney, W. E. (2002). From natural resources to the knowledge economy. *The World Bank*. https://doi.org/10.1596/0-8213-5009-9

Edmans, A., & Kacperczyk, M. (2022). Sustainable Finance. *Review of Finance, 26*(6), 1309–1313. https://doi.org/10.1093/rof/rfac069

FSB. (2017). *Financial stability implications from FinTech*. https://www.fsb.org/wp-content/uploads/R270617.pdf

G20. (2018). *G20 policy guide: Digitisation and informality—Harnessing digital financial inclusion for individuals and MSMEs in the informal economy*. https://www.oecd.org/g20/G20-Policy-Guide-Digitisation-and-Informality.pdf

Galeone, G., Ranaldo, S., & Fusco, A. (2024). ESG and FinTech: Are they connected? *Research in International Business and Finance, 69*, 102225. https://doi.org/10.1016/j.ribaf.2024.102225

Gutterman, A. S. (2021). *Sustainable finance and impact investing*. Business Expert Press. https://www.oreilly.com/library/view/sustainable-finance-and/9781637420034/

Habib, A. M. (2022). Does the efficiency of working capital management and environmental, social, and governance performance affect a firm's value? Evidence from the United States. *Financial Markets, Institutions and Risks, 6*(3), 18–25. https://doi.org/10.21272/fmir.6(3).18-25.2022

Habib, A. M. (2023a). Do business strategies and environmental, social, and governance (ESG) performance mitigate the likelihood of financial distress? A multiple mediation model. *Heliyon, 9*(7), e17847. https://doi.org/10.1016/j.heliyon.2023.e17847

Habib, A. M. (2023b). Does real earnings management affect a firm's environmental, social, and governance (ESG), financial performance, and total value? A moderated mediation analysis. *Environment, Development and Sustainability*. https://doi.org/10.1007/s10668-023-03809-6

Habib, A. M. (2024). *Financial development and corporate governance efficiency: An overview of MENA* (pp. 147–169). https://doi.org/10.1142/9781800614734_0006

Habib, A. M., & Dalwai, T. (2023). Does the efficiency of a firm's intellectual capital and working capital management affect its performance? *J Knowl Econ, ahead-of-print* (ahead-of-print), 1–28. https://doi.org/10.1007/s13132-023-01138-7

Habib, A. M., & Kayani, U. N. (2024). Price reaction of global economic indicators: Evidence from the COVID-19 pandemic and the Russia-Ukraine conflict. *SN Business & Economics, 4*(19), 1–21. https://doi.org/10.1007/s43546-023-00619-w

Habib, A. M., & Mourad, N. (2023a). Analyzing the efficiency of intellectual capital: A new approach based on DEA-MPI technology. *Benchmarking: An International Journal, ahead-of-print* (ahead-of-print). https://doi.org/10.1108/BIJ-06-2022-0384

Habib, A. M., & Mourad, N. (2023b). The influence of environmental, social, and governance (ESG) practices on US firms' performance: Evidence from the coronavirus crisis. *J Knowl Econ, ahead-of-print* (ahead-of-print), 1–20. https://doi.org/10.1007/s13132-023-01278-w

Hussain, S., Rehman, A. U., Ullah, S., Waheed, A., & Hassan, S. (2024). Financial inclusion and economic growth: Comparative panel evidence from developed and developing asian countries. *SAGE Open, 14*(1). https://doi.org/10.1177/21582440241232585

Huynh, N., Le, Q. N., & Tran, Q. T. (2024). Firm-level political risk and intellectual capital investment: Does managerial ability matter? *International Review of Financial Analysis, 91*, 103020. https://doi.org/10.1016/j.irfa.2023.103020

Mirza, N., Umar, M., Afzal, A., & Firdousi, S. F. (2023). The role of fintech in promoting green finance, and profitability: Evidence from the banking sector in the euro zone. *Economic Analysis and Policy, 78*, 33–40. https://doi.org/10.1016/j.eap.2023.02.001

Nkambule, N. A., Wang, W.-K., Ting, I. W. K., & Lu, W.-M. (2022). Intellectual capital and firm efficiency of US multinational software firms. *Journal of Intellectual Capital, 23*(6), 1404–1434. https://doi.org/10.1108/JIC-02-2021-0041

Nuta, A. C., Habib, A. M., Neslihanoglu, S., Dalwai, T., & Rangu, C. M. (2024). Analyzing the market performance of Romanian firms: Do the COVID-19 crisis and classification type matter? *International Journal of*

Emerging Markets, ahead-of-print (ahead-of-print), 1–32. https://doi.org/10.1108/IJOEM-05-2023-0842

OECD. (2021). The future of corporate governance in Capital markets following the COVID-19 crisis. *OECD*. https://doi.org/10.1787/efb2013c-en

OECD. (October, 2022). *Digitalisation and corporate governance: Background note for the OECD-Asia roundtable on corporate governance*. https://www.oecd.org/corporate/background-note-Asia-roundtable-digitalisation-and-corporate-governance.pdf

Ofosu-Mensah Ababio, J., Yiadom, E. B., Sarpong-Kumankoma, E., & Boadi, I. (2023). Financial inclusion: A catalyst for financial system development in emerging and frontier markets. *Journal of Financial Economic Policy, 15*(6), 530–550. https://doi.org/10.1108/JFEP-06-2023-0155

Schoenmaker, D., & Schramade, W. (2019). *Principles of sustainable finance*. Oxford University Press. https://global.oup.com/academic/product/principles-of-sustainable-finance-9780198826606?cc=ca%26lang=en%26

Scott Cato, M. (2022). Sustainable finance. *Springer International Publishing*. https://doi.org/10.1007/978-3-030-91578-0

Shahwan, T. M., & Habib, A. M. (2020). Does the efficiency of corporate governance and intellectual capital affect a firm's financial distress? Evidence from Egypt. *Journal of Intellectual Capital, 21*(3), 403–430. https://doi.org/10.1108/JIC-06-2019-0143

Stijns, J.-P. (2006). Natural resource abundance and human capital accumulation. *World Development, 34*(6), 1060–1083. https://doi.org/10.1016/j.worlddev.2005.11.005

Tang, X., Yao, X., Miao, Y., & Yu, L. (2023). "Cost Reduction" or "Profit Increase"?: The impact of Fintech on the operating efficiency of securities companies from the perspective of absorptive capacity. *Proceedings of the 2023 14th international conference on e-business, management and economics*, 229–236. https://doi.org/10.1145/3616712.3616781

Timperley, J. (2021). The broken $100-billion promise of climate finance—and how to fix it. *Nature, 598*(7881), 400–402. https://doi.org/10.1038/d41586-021-02846-3

UN. (2023). *New analysis of national climate plans: Insufficient progress made, COP28 must set stage for immediate action*. https://unfccc.int/news/new-analysis-of-national-climate-plans-insufficient-progress-made-cop28-must-set-stage-for-immediate

Walker, J., Walker, G., & Pekmezovic, A. (2019). *Sustainable development goals: Harnessing business to achieve the SDGs through finance, technology and law reform*. John Wiley & Sons, Inc. https://www.wiley.com/en-ie/Sustainable+Development+Goals%3A+Harnessing+Business+to+Achieve+the+SDGs+through+Finance%2C+Technology+and+Law+Reform-p-9781119541813

Walker, T., Turtle, H. J., Kooli, M., & Nikbakht, E. (2023). Fintech and sustainability: An overview. In *fintech and sustainability* (pp. 3–9). Springer Nature. https://doi.org/10.1007/978-3-031-40647-8_1

Wan, S., Lee, Y. H., & Sarma, V. J. (2023). Is Fintech good for green finance? Empirical evidence from listed banks in China. *Economic Analysis and Policy, 80*, 1273–1291. https://doi.org/10.1016/j.eap.2023.10.019

Yıldırım, A. C., & Erdil, E. (2024). The effect of Covid-19 on digital banking explored under business model approach. *Qualitative Research in Financial Markets, 16*(1), 87–107. https://doi.org/10.1108/QRFM-08-2021-0142

Zimon, G., Habib, A. M., & Haluza, D. (2024). Does the quality management system affect working capital management efficiency? Evidence from polish firms. *Cogent Business & Management, 11*(1), 1–18. https://doi.org/10.1080/23311975.2023.2292787

Impact of Green Banking Practices on the Performance of Indian Banks: An Empirical Study

Dharmendra Singh and Garima Malik

1 Introduction

Over the previous decade, mindfulness has developed about boundless natural corruption and the intricate issue confronting the present reality, environmental change. Progressing endeavors have been made around the planet to quantify and relieve the danger of environmental change brought about by human exercises. Numerous nations, including India, have focused on it. Since Socially Responsible Corporate Citizens (SRCC) banks are viewed as harmless to the ecosystem and don't altogether affect the climate through their own inside tasks, the outside sway on the climate through the exercises of your clients has an effect. The financial area is one of the fundamental wellsprings of financing for modern undertakings like steel, paper, concrete, synthetic compounds, manures, energy, materials, and so on that cause the most extreme fossil fuel byproducts.

D. Singh
Modern College of Business and Science, Muscat, Oman
e-mail: dharmendra@mcbs.edu.om

G. Malik (✉)
Birla Institute of Management Technology (BIMTECH), Greater Noida, India
e-mail: garima.malik@bimtech.ac.in

© The Author(s), under exclusive license to Springer Nature Singapore Pte Ltd. 2025

A. S. et al. (eds.), *Trends and Challenges of Electronic Finance*,
https://doi.org/10.1007/978-981-96-3304-3_8

Hence, the financial area can play a mediator job between monetary turn of events and natural security to advance ecologically stable and socially capable ventures. Banks likewise make an immediate and roundabout natural commitment through ventures/advances in their customers' organizations. Thus, they should assume a vital part in improving/lessening the carbon impression. It is said that what isn't estimated isn't overseen.

Green banking is a similarly innovative advancement in the monetary world. It is a type of banking that considers social and natural effects and whose principle rationale is to secure and safeguard the climate. When all is said in done, the present worldwide economy is confronting a significant test to beat natural issues and their outcomes. Notwithstanding organizations, purchasers and the overall population know about the significance of natural assurance for guaranteeing environmental manageability. Subsequently, shopper request has driven business relationship to change their business exercises and techniques to guarantee the assurance of normal assets and the climate. The monetary area, especially banks, can possibly assume a significant part in advancing ecological manageability, which is one of the principle drivers of strategy making in the business world. Nonetheless, the current ecological corruption circumstance must be improved through the planned endeavors of government, the private area, and the populace. Banks and monetary organizations are backing and supplementing these greener endeavors in various manners. In December 2007, the Reserve Bank of India (RBI) gave a roundabout featuring the significance of dependable banks' conduct and their commitment to manageable turn of events and the requirement for Indian banks to set up institutional instruments to secure maintainability.

1.1 Green Banking

Government offices, financial bankers, and the overall population are requesting that organizations give more data about their carbon impression and their natural activities and accomplishments. Banks by implication affect the climate by financing delegates who are the principle wellspring of long haul financing for different ventures that are exceptionally dirtying. Consequently, it is critical to comprehend the requirement for reasonable financial practices.

Green financial alludes to the activity of banks to support green speculation, focusing on ventures that have effectively become environmentally viable or are attempting to do as such, in this way assisting with reestablishing the common habitat. This green financial activity is commonly valuable for banks, industry, and organizations. Also, green financial will guarantee that the characteristics of banks' resources improve later on. As opposed to mainstream thinking, harmless to the ecosystem advances bode well for the business and furthermore decrease its monetary weight. The dirtying business faces expanded obstruction and is regularly compelled to close down or face enormous public resistance. This enormously builds your expenses.

1.2 Green Practices

1.2.1 Online or Mobile Banking

Web-based banking permits you to deal with your financial balance over the Internet utilizing a PC or cell phone. There is no compelling reason to visit a bank office and you can finish all your financial undertakings when it is generally advantageous for you, even external ordinary financial hours.

The adoption of paperless banking has led to a reduction in the carbon footprint of internal banking operations. This additionally converts into cost investment funds for the bank, as computerization can dodge the expense of paper stockpiling, just as the expense of fuel utilization and emanations from messenger vehicles.

1.2.2 Green Finance

Bank should fund climate amicable undertakings and climate-agreeable items like sun-based supplies, reused furniture, vehicle money for low fossil fuel byproducts vehicles, home account for green structures, and so forth with giving a few concessions in handling expense and concessional pace of revenue.

1.2.3 Green Infrastructure

Utilization of force saving supplies: Use of sun-oriented controlled UPS, GSL/LED bulbs, downpour water reaping by banks, setting up sunlight-based fueled ATMs, and so on. Utilization of green and reused solid like office entryways and cabinetry which are produced using wheat sheets or covers which are produced using waste solid;

- Use of energy proficient items like double flush latrines, low stream spigots, reflecting roofing material, sun-based shades that square immediate daylight without killing light, and sun-based warming framework.

- Reusing of development waste like steel, cardboard, and wood. Green Building Construction improves advertising and representative fulfillment and in this manner diminishes the pace of mileage among workers.

1.2.4 Green Banking Products

Green advances: implies giving credits to an undertaking or organization that is viewed as harmless to the ecosystem.

- Green Mortgage - Refers to a home loan in which you are given a rebate to set aside cash or a bigger credit than is ordinarily permitted to make energy proficiency enhancements or to purchase a home that satisfies certain energy effectiveness guidelines.
- Green Credit Cards - Whether it's as green prizes or the utilization of biodegradable Visa material or advancing paperless banking, Visas are becoming environmentally viable.
- Green Savings Accounts - With Green Savings accounts, banks are dependent on client reserve funds. The more you save, the more the climate will profit by bank commitments or gifts.

2 Literature Review

Naidu and Paramasivan (2018) have indicated that the important agenda in the international community is environmental protection and sustainable development. Shaumya and Anton (2021) suggested that in terms of emissions and waste, the banking sector is commonly regarded as environmentally friendly. Green banking has a substantial effect on banks' environmental efficiency. So, banks can enhance their environmental performance by green banking practices. It helps banks, as good corporate citizens, to protect the environment and to create a picture. Green banking may also be an avenue for reducing emissions and preserving the world. While several research studies have been carried out on green banking, the effect of green banking on the environmental performance of banks has not been explored so far. Laxman (2014) depicted the significance of green banking, varieties of green banking products, and furthermore framed boundless survey of related writing. She had discovered that, there has not been a lot of activity in such manner by the banks and other monetary organizations in India. In this way, ideas identified with likely strategy activities and activity to advance green banking in India were given. Jinwala (2013) depicted the significance of green banking and featured global encounters. This paper added new mark of drivers and patterns in green item improvement, contrasted with above paper of Laxman (2014). He inferred the end that there has not been a lot of activity by the banks and other monetary establishments in India thus he recommended conceivable approach measures to advance green banking in India. Ruchi (2014) zeroed in on the best way to practice environmental awareness in different utilitarian units and exercises like CRM, SCM, Procurement and PLC the board and different green financial techniques. Again which is headway to the above investigation of Jinwala (2013) she featured IndusInd Bank's progressive activity in "Green Banking" project, by turning first bank in Maharashtra to dispatch a sun-oriented force ATM. She inferred that the Indian banks are as yet stepping into this technique for banking. Islam and Das (2013) broke down the green financial practices in Bangladesh. They gathered auxiliary information from bank sites and examined the measurements on Green 46 asset portion, online banking, and Mobile banking. They inferred that, idea of green banking is new in Bangladeshi banks but should be created.

Shaumya and Arulrajah (2017) has included auxiliary just as essential study identified with green financial practices in Sri Lanka. They gave an outline 47 about the four significant banks of Sri Lanka with respect to green activities. Afterward, they considered making of Instrument for estimating green financial practices among investors. They distinguished 98 green financial acts of absolute four banks in the initial step, and at that point examination was done based on similitudes and contrasts, which led to 16 green financial practices with class of four measurements—daily activity related practices, client orientated, representative arranged, and bank strategy-related practices. Later pilot study was refined and solid scale was created with inputs got. It was concluded that the scale developed so far is solid and substantial. Bankers have become more aware of their initiatives compared to others and will be able to improve the relevant areas. This will motivate banks and make investors more informed about green initiatives. Sweta et al. (2012) investigated idea of green monetary items. They studied in Mumbai to distinguish the mindfulness and mentality of client and client for green monetary items. This gave them thought regarding the likely interest identified with these items. Brokers' assessment was additionally taken about the green items through poll. Key findings from the bankers' side revealed that green initiatives were introduced partly for reputational purposes, with green home loans being particularly popular; charge motivating force is the great instrument to advance the green items. According to perspective on customers, lion's share knew about green home credits; they like to go for green items if there are financial advantages. It was inferred that, monetary establishments and banks have a significant task to carry out by sponsorship to the creation productive low-carbon economy. Masukujjaman and Aktar (2013) considered the situation with green banking in Bangladesh and it was contrasted and worldwide activities in similar lines. It was discovered that Bangladeshi banks are exceptionally delayed in the usage of the idea of green banking against different banks in world. Yet, at the same time, they considered in-house and other than in-house green exercises, wherein banks zeroed in on the online compensation, E-delicate, and so on. It was presumed that green structure and developments can guarantee the ecological maintainability. Barhate and Mohasin (2016) considered the hypothesis with respect to green banking and zeroed in on reasonable clarification. They covered strategies like paperless banking, green MasterCards, energy assets, and so forth for becoming environmentally friendly. They discovered there exists numerous chances like establishing climate-agreeable items, appropriation of carbon impression configuration, Inventory wastage arranging, and so forth. Hardly any difficulties incorporate recently opened banks would discover challenges, skilled and experienced staff required, and credit chances. It was suggested that administration should assume dynamic part and form green arrangement.

Zhelyazkova and Kitanov (2015) have endeavored to make a green financial plan of action based on the applied comprehension of green banking and its extension. They featured that, in different pieces of the world from recent years, numerous definitions for the idea were authored, yet no accuracy in that was accomplished. The portrayed the green banking is need for the banking, as bank is dynamic financial exchange for bringing in cash, while they think such green items diminishes down their edge thus they are less roused to start. Considering the scope of green banking, the respondents believed that offering simple green products is not sufficient; rather, incorporating environmental indicators into risk assessment and management control systems is essential. The Business Model proposed by them consolidates steps: First they recommend banks to create green items and give more revenue to make it appealing that will prompt asset receipts, which again can be given to organizations for doing green exercises; so issue is if there is higher financing cost on store, banks can remunerate by keeping high rate in green credits, reserves gathered from this, ought to be utilized for giving more green advances. They inferred that green banking is getting more thought and initial ones to receive will acquire market.

Board, clients to spur them for green activities which will be helpful to build up the better green practices around the world. Alsheikh and Bojei (2014), "Determinants Affecting Customer's Intention to Adopt Mobile Banking in Saudi Arabia". Portable advances and administrations are imagined as the conceivable main impetus that will make an assortment of significant indicators for receiving portable financial administrations in the underlying reception stage. The key end is that versatile financial administrations should offer imaginative administrations contrasted with existing rivalry administrations in a comparative zone, for example, electronic banking administrations. As illustrated, separation can be achieved by incorporating more advantage factors than penance factors that make apparent benefit of receiving versatile financial administrations later on. Jyotsna (2014), "Portable Banking: A Pioneering Tool in the Hands of Customer". The fast development of electronic trade gives a test to advertisers in light of the fact that "as shoppers embrace new advancements, their practices change". Seeing how organizations ought to connect with their clients and convey administrations in electronic climate is of conclusive significance. Customer's utilization of versatile specialized gadgets is expanding quickly, and gadgets dependent on new innovation are presently typical in regular day-to-day existence. Quite possibly the most arising and spearheading instrument in the possession of the client is versatile banking. In 43 this paper an endeavor has been made to examine the different parts of versatile banking. Ratten Vanessa (2012), "Business E-Finance and Mobile Banking". This examination centers around the part of business venture and e-money in estimating an individual's point of view to embrace M-banking and furthermore decide mindfulness and information on client's about M- banking and advertising. This paper centers on the part of business and e-account in deciding an individual's expectation to embrace portable banking. The methodology used in this paper is to build up a reasonable system that incorporates various recommendations that are created and supported by the writing. The fundamental discoveries of this paper are that individuals' innovative tendency and learning inclination will decide how they react to showcasing and information about portable banking. The down-to-earth suggestions are that monetary organizations engaged with e-money can center their advertising endeavors at expanding individuals' openness to versatile banking. Malarvizhi and Rajeshwari (2012), "Client's Criteria for Selecting Mobile Banking Services in Coimbatore: Empirical Evidence". The study centers on mindfulness and utilization of M financial administrations and furthermore identifies the standards for choosing these administrations in Coimbatore city. It is discovered that clients are educated and have a place with business gathering and center pay gathering. M financial is more helpful, secure, and furthermore meet assumption to customers.19 Beiginia et al. (2011), "Assessing the Mobile Banking Adoption Based on the Decomposed Theory of Planned Behaviors". Saleem and Rashid (2011) explored the connection between customer satisfaction and mobile banking adoption in Pakistan. This study aimed to identify the key factors of mobile technology adoption that influence customer satisfaction in the country. The discoveries show that client's interests about security, validness, and dependability of the innovation are of importance. The outcomes suggest that organizations should center upon IT application, creative administrations, security, client trust, and danger as these are the critical markers of innovation reception. The examination proposes that versatile banking has a brilliant future in Pakistan. This investigation clarifies M-banking basic issues in financial industry. The discoveries additionally show that portable financial appropriation requires innovatively productive just as modest, dependable, and secure innovation improvement. Sharma (2011), "Versatile Banking as Technology Adoption and Challenges". This paper centers on different advantages of M-banking like its attainability, accommodation, ease, and taking care of record at home solaces, and furthermore clarifies MPSP {mobile installment administration provider} or characterizes procedures for its advancement. This paper analyzes shopper reception of another electronic installment administrations as portable banking and the variables affecting the selection of versatile banking in India. This examination shows that purchasers get dispirited by the convoluted capacities while evaluating the versatile financial administrations which lead them to disappointment level as no appropriate direction is to be given to them. The truth of the matter is that the factor danger and security are the main elements for banking administration appropriation and especially according to "new" electronic environment. All partners like controllers, govt., and telecom specialist organizations. Akhras et al. (2011), "Inventive Secure Mobile Banking Services". The term portable banking portrays the financial administrations that the clients can perform through a cell phone at whenever and anyplace. With the end goal for clients to get to their records, they need a cell phone and organization network. This paper proposed M financial security, accessibility, and ease of use and furthermore presented framework front of m banking (a) the client administrations, (b) the security administrations or hindrances and advantages of utilizing cell phone for banking exchange. This office saves time even individual in emergency clinic line or in holding up zone. This paper investigates the chances of utilizing portable innovation in the electronic banking (e-banking) area to improve existing financial administrations by moving toward versatile financial utilizing cell phones and remote media that can give freedoms to existing wherever admittance to the financial administrations as versatile advances can be utilized at whenever and anyplace. This investigation presents a portable framework that exhibits the adaptability acquired out of this innovation and covers the significant parts of such sort of utilization. The proposed framework covers two sections: the client support and security angle. The finding of this examination is that the indicators' impact preposterous factors were distinctive for each gathering of portable financial clients and non-clients. The study recommends that the proposed incorporated structure offers a more profound comprehension of the factors that impact the reception of portable banking. Aggarwal Manav (2014), "A Study on Importance of Mobile Banking.

3 Research Methodology

Exploration is the main prerequisite to make due in the present serious time. It is properly said that "the client is the ruler of the market" and it is important to consider the requirements, tastes, and inclinations of clients corresponding to the item. It isn't the time of large-scale manufacturing where a result of this kind has no time span of usability without distinguishing the need, and the item that will be advertised. Today, organizations should go through advertising tests prior to dispatching the item or adding new highlights to the current item, as the acknowledgment of such developments falls on the clients. On the off chance that they are not acknowledged on the lookout, there is essentially an extraordinary misfortune borne by the organization. Given the danger and achievement, research is fundamental.

The fundamental reason for this section is to picture the work finished concerning the territory and extent of the examination. Any examination is truly founded on the incredible work of exploration procedure. Without research approach, research is pointless. It fundamentally portrays the dependability and legitimacy of the examination. The start of this section featured the presentation of the examination, the clarification of the issue, the motivation behind that exploration, the speculation of the investigation, the significant of the examination, the survey of the writing, the plan of the examination, the devices for gathering information. information, and the primary impediment of the investigation.

Examination for the most part implies a quest for information. It tends to be characterized as a logical and orderly quest for data on a particular point. Examination implies a nitty gritty investigation of a point, particularly to find new data or to acquire another arrangement. Exploration is a coordinated and deliberate method of discovering answers to questions. Methodical on the grounds that there is a characterized set of strategies and steps that we follow. Coordinated as in there is a strategy structure for directing an examination. It is an arranged cycle, not an unconstrained one. 34 Finding an answer is the finish, all things considered. Examination is fruitful when we discover answers. Questions are key to the examination. On the off chance that there are no inquiries, the appropriate response is pointless. Hence, the examination is a cautious examination or a deliberate investigation and a unique commitment to the current information for its further turn of events. It alludes to the speculation of improvement, hypotheses, or standards and identifies with destiny and potentially extreme control of occasions. Summary of hypotheses is given in Table 1

3.1 Objectives of the Study

Research objectives are primarily to provide the final term for carrying out the research. It should be closely related to the explanation of the problem. The objectives of present research are:

- To identify the green banking practices adopted by Indian banks
- To examine the impact of green banking practices on environmental performance of Indian banks

Table 1 Summary of hypothesis

H1	There is a significant impact of online banking on environmental performance
H2	There is a significant impact of online banking on organizational performance
H3	There is a significant impact of green finance on environmental performance
H4	There is a significant impact of green finance on organizational performance
H5	Thereisa significant impactofgreeninfrastructureonenvironmental performance
H6	Thereisa significant impactofgreeninfrastructureonorganizational performance
H7	There is a significant impact of green product on environmental performance
H8	There is a significant impact of green product on organizational performance

- To examine the impact of green banking practices on business performance of Indian banks

3.2 Data Collection

3.2.1 Sources

Primary data: traditional data collected directly by the researcher through questionnaires are supported by bank employees. This study analyzed bank employees' perceptions on bank performance.

Secondary data: Secondary data is owned by journals, textbooks, magazines, news, newspapers, and the Internet. Different websites. And also from banking websites.

3.2.2 Data Collection and Sample

An online survey—GOOGLE FORMS has been used for the current research. Employees working the banks between the ages of 28 and 49 and above were considered for the study. The survey was circulated using online platforms such as LinkedIn and Facebook. The data collection took a period of 1.5 months and accounted for 240 responses from 19 banks including both public and private banks.

3.3 Research Process

The research strategy utilized in the current examination is the questionnaire technique. It is utilized to gather information from representatives who work in chosen public and private banks. The existing previous literature have been studied in detail for formulating the questionnaire. Bank

Table 2 Sample design

Universe of Study:	Banking Industry
Research Design:	Descriptive Research Design
Sample Unit:	Employees of Indian banks
Sampling Area:	All over India
Respondents:	Employees of Indian banks
Sample Size:	240
Sampling Technique	Convenience Sampling

employees were viewed as a feature of the populace for the investigation. For this process following points have been included (see Table 2):

- Universe of the study
- Selection of the sample
- Selection of research tools
- Data collection
- Statistical tools employed for analysis and interpretation

Universe of this Study:

The universe of this study includes all the public and private sector banks operating all over India.

Selection of study area:

As the research has been conducted through online platforms, it was possible to collect data from banks operating throughout India.

Selection of Sample:

Sample is a part of population which represents the entire population. The researcher collected data as his convenience. Sample size (of employees): The sample size was 240.

Sampling Technique:

The researcher has circulated questionnaire to the employees of the bank who were easily available. Due to busyness of bank employees, convenient sampling method was adopted for research. The universe of customers was considered as infinite hence it was not possible to take employees of each bank.

4 Data Analysis

The flow chart of demographic variables is given in Fig. 1. A three-stage procedure was utilized to assess the outcomes. Then, all changed scales were brought down by Exploratory Factor Analysis (EFA), and afterward Structural Equation Modeling (SEM) was executed in the size of components created by EFA utilizing SPSS AMOS 22.0, with the examination proceeded as a Confirmatory Factorial first (AFC) to check that there are two stages. The legitimacy, dependability, and nature of the model are reliable with this. At long last, the direction examination is performed to approve the proposed connections between the different designs in the theoretical model.

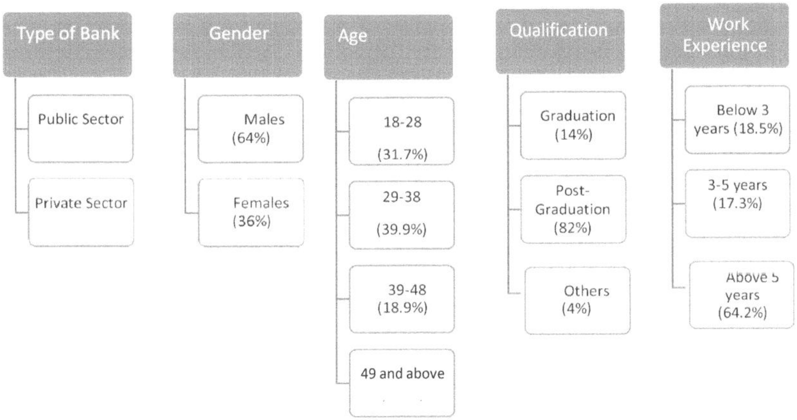

Fig. 1 Flowchart of demographic variables

I. Exploratory Factor Analysis

Exploratory Factor Analysis (EFA) is a statistical approach for determining the correlation between variables in a dataset. For this data, EFA was carried out using the Principal component and the Varimax rotation. All of the 24 statements were used for factor analysis that provided more than 0.5 factor loadings. Cronbach alpha was used to verify the reliability of the designs and all values were between 0.812 and 0.898, which was more than the cutoff value of 0.7. The Kaiser-Meyer-Olkin measure, which was also above 0.7, was used to determine the adequacy of the constructions (see Table 3). And the Bartlett Sphericity Test, which is designed to test the significance and correlation between items, was also used, the sig<0.005 of which was used.

I.I Confirmatory Factor Analysis

Confirmatory Factor Analysis is the next step to evaluate the structure of the factor. This model was used to determine convergent validity, discriminatory validity, and fitness of the model.

I.II Convergent Validity

Convergent Validity refers to the degree to which two constructions are associated. For this function, two parameters were used, namely AVE and Composite reliability (see Table 4). Average Variance Extracted of Environmental performance, online banking, green infrastructure, and green product is more than 0.5 while the remaining two constructs i.e., organizational performance and green finance are less than the defined criteria of 0.5. The composite reliability of all the constructs is more than

Table 3 KMO and Bartlett's test

Kaiser–Meyer–Olkin Measure of Sampling Adequacy		0.841
Bartlett'sTestof Sphericity	Approx. Chi-Square	3362.4 24
	Df	276
	Sig	0.000

the defined criteria of 0.7 signifying that the constructs are reliable and consistent.

Discriminating validity is shown by evidence that systemic measures which, ideally, should not be very closely related to each other are, in fact, not found to be strongly correlated. Discriminant validity is calculated by comparing the square root items of the AVE indicated on the diagonal

Table 4 Statistics of the constructed items

Constructs	*Statements*	*Loadings*	*Composite Reliability*	*Cronbach Alpha*	*AVE*
Organizational Performance	OP1	0.796			
	OP2	0.756	0.849	0.843	0.201
	OP3	0.824			
	OP4	0.715			
Environmental Performance	EP1	0.739			
	EP2	0.873	0.902	0.898	0.902
	EP3	0.838			
	EP4	0.829			
Green Finance					
	GF1	0.819			
	GF2	0.790	0.811	0.812	0.112
	GF3	0.753			
	GF4	0.746			
Online Banking	OB1	0.814			
	OB2	0.798			
	OB3	0.846	0.843	0.828	0.524
	OB4	0.630			
	OB5	0.595			
Green Infrastructure	GI1	0.644			
	GI2	0.899	0.887	0.880	0.668
	GI3	0.926			
	GI4	0.842			
Green Product					
	GP1	0.718			
	GP2	0.900	0.875	0.866	0.703
	GP3	0.906			

Table 5 Discriminant validity

CR	*OB*	*EP*	*GI*	*OP*	*GF*	*GP*	
OB	0.874	**0.724**					
EP	0.912	0.454***	**0.835**				
GI	0.926	0.291***	0.133†	**0.817**			
OP	0.874	0.439***	0.449***	0.307***	**0.767**		
GF	0.849	0.317***	0.334***	0.154*	0.333***	**0.725**	
GP	0.907	0.256***	0.475***	0.114	0.270***	0.191*	**0.838**

side of Table 5 with the other inter-construct correlation items listed on the non-diagonal side of Table 5.

Model Fitness

To quantify the reasonableness of the model, different recommended files were utilized, for example, B. Chi-Square/Degree of Freedom (CMIN/DF), which compares to the most extreme number of consistently self-governing qualities, which values the opportunity to recognize the decency of fit record (GFI) in the informational collection, which is a proportion of the fit between the speculative model and the noticed covariance framework. The Adjusted Goodness Fitness Index (AGFI) rectifies the GFI, which is influenced by the quantity of estimations of each inert variable. The standardized file of fit (NFI) dissects the contrast between the chi-square estimation of the theoretical model and the chi-square estimation of the invalid model. The

Comparative Fit Index (CFI) dissects the reasonableness of the model by examining the error between the outcomes and the speculative model. Change for test size issues inborn in the chi-square model's proportion of fit and the ordinary list of fit. Exhaust Lewis Index (TLI), which demonstrates the decency of attack of the model, and the root mean square estimation blunder (RMSEA), which shows the helpless attack of the model. The lists recorded in Table 6 show the appropriateness of the model and the reasonableness of the outcomes for additional investigations.

Table 6 Fitness of model indices

Fit Indices	*Research model*	*Recommend criteria*
$\chi 2/df$	2.075	< 3.0
GFI	0.853	> 9.0
SRMR	0.075	< 0.5
RMSEA	0.067	< 0.08
TLI	0.908	> 9.0
CFI	0.921	> 9.0
NFI	0.902	> 9.0
AGFI	0.814	> 0.8

4.1 *Hypothesis Testing*

The justification of the model in the most famous sort of SEM is to consider the variety and covariance of the deliberate variables (MV). Way examination (e.g., relapse) tests the model and the associations between VMs. Corroborative factor examination tests models of the associations between inactive factors (LV or typical factors) and MV, which are markers of regular components. The CFA, which was characterized to assess the association between the developments, was performed utilizing three principles: the degree of importance (gauge < 0.05), the basic list (CR > 1.96), and the relapse investigation. The summed up outcomes of the hypothetical tests are appeared in Table 7. Moreover, the investigation of the direction with the assessed relapse coefficients appeared in Fig. 2.

Table 7 Hypothesis testing results

Hypothesis		*Standardized estimates*	*C.R*	*SE*	*P value*	*Hypothesis decision*
H1	OP < –- OB	0.321	5.333	0.063	0.001	Supporting
H2	OP < –- GI	0.182	3.263	0.039	0.001	Supporting
H3	OP < –- GF	0.202	3.536	0.066	0.001	Supporting
H4	OP < –- GP	0.142	2.571	0.039	0.01	Supporting
H5	EP < –- OB	0.34	6.087	0.075	0.001	Supporting
H6	EP < –- GI	-0.042	-0.806	0.047	0.421	Not Supporting
H7	EP < –- GF	0.175	3.301	0.079	0.001	Supporting
H8	EP < –- GP	0.386	7.498	0.047	0.001	Supporting

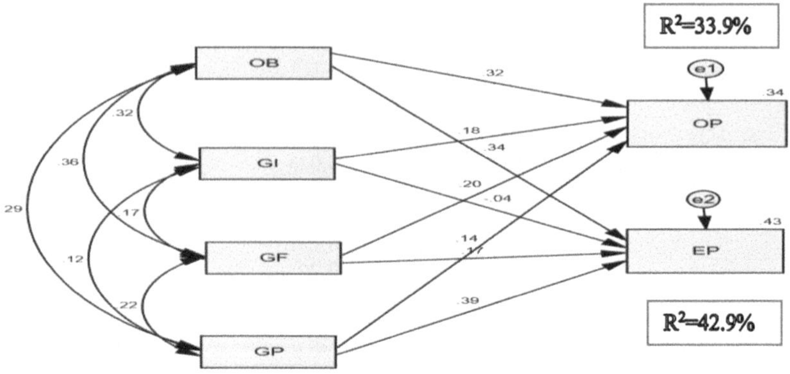

Fig. 2 Structural model test results

5 Findings

Financial regulatory and banks, specifically, assume a significant part in such a manner, adding to the improvement of a solid and fruitful low-carbon economy. As green banking turns into a significant requirement for banks to annihilate or alleviate natural corruption, scholastics and experts the same have called for additional investigations. Utilizing the above boundaries, the proposed hypothesis of H1–H5 and H7–H8 are measurably upheld as they have a significant value under 0.05 and a Critical Ratio more than 1.96. H6 has a p-value more than 0.05, which shows that it doesn't essentially affect environmental performance. The outcomes propose that online banking, green products, and green finance fundamentally affect the bank's overall performance, yet green infrastructure doesn't have a critical effect. Moreover, contrasted with the outcomes, it is accepted that internet banking has the best impact on the overall performance of banks. The proposed model has a total explained variance of 42.9% in anticipating the effect of green finance practices on environmental performance and 33.9% of variance in evaluating the effect of green being practices on Organizational performance. Table 7 shows the outline table of the consequences of the speculation tests. In light of speculation testing, this examination has affirmed a positive and measurably huge impact of harmless to the ecosystem banking rehearses on the bank's natural exhibition. The more prominent the green financial practices, the better the bank's natural exhibition. Moreover,

Exploratory Factor Analysis and Confirmatory Factor Analysis have shown that internet banking, green account, and green items are connected and positive practices that have positive and huge impacts on the bank's environmental and Organizational performance. In any case, the green infrastructure framework practice was not a vital pointer of the bank's environmental exhibition.

6 Conclusion

Green banking is the arising idea in India; universally, it is being acknowledged on tremendous level, while Indian banks still have a large approach. Green banking might be truly considered as an answer for the crucial circumstance of an unnatural weather change because of fast consumption of worldwide climatic adjustments. Banking area is the foundation of any monetary frameworks which guarantee the improvement through the compelling channelization of monetary assets. Developing urbanization, over utilization of petroleum products, abundance fossil fuel byproduct, and the intermittent finishing to obliterate the woods for everyday use are pushing us to the perilous lopsidedness of the natural framework. These issues acquire more prominent consideration for all enterprises including monetary areas giving higher needs for green activities.

Contrasted with the previous a very long time there are sure significant developments that lead to gigantic upgrades in financial administrations and activities. Quick development in the productive and simpler. Through the green financial practices, all the financial administrations and items are accessible at the fingertips now. Simultaneously green financial practices make the financial establishments a mindful corporate resident.

Dominant parts of the banks are demanding money-free and paperless exchanges to appreciate the advantages of advancements in innovation. Innovation-based tasks assist saves money with improving their effectiveness, to reduce down their exchange expenses, and diminish carbon impression in order.

The consolidation of social and natural situated activities and loaning measure into the advancement objective of the banks causes them for accomplishing the viable ecological administration framework. As indicated by Krebs Bach, the banks which are received. Yet, the creator had recommended that banks ought to embrace the green loaning standards so that a client base won't be influenced. The credibility comes from maintaining high standards. However, if the regulations are raised too high too quickly, it may discourage some banks from lending and negatively impact businesses that require capital. By and by more number of banks is guaranteed for moral and natural practices, to lessen the nursery outflow, yet the broadening and developing strategic approaches of banking area, requesting more representatives working in the exceptional workplaces nonstop on more PCs, expanded interest for power which was regularly made the consuming of carbon dioxide in the climate. Currently, we have the globally recognized Equator Principles—a framework for managing environmental and social risks. A total of 82 financial institutions across 36 countries, including those in emerging markets, have adopted these principles. Be that as it may, a large portion of the Indian monetary organizations are not showing a lot of interest for following the equator standards by absolving their benefit.

Despite the fact that the money-free financial frameworks are valuable to purchasers, workers, and enterprises and economy all in all. It will accommodate to customers for decreasing by and large exchange cost, simple stores and withdrawals, simple approaches specific ventures will actuate the financial specialists for beginning their unit in a natural well-disposed way which will be gainful to the group of people yet to come as well.

In a country like India, the lack of infrastructure, technical training, and cooperation from the banking workforce may hinder the widespread adoption of green banking practices. It is the time now India should find some significant ways to cling to the idea of making strides toward environmental friendliness rehearses by receiving ecological delicate boundaries to assess the danger required prior to putting resources into various social situated tasks via Environmental Impact Assessment (EIA), Annual Reporting System (ARS), Environmental Management Audit (EMA), and so on.

Despite the fact that a ton of Indian banks have not yet carried out green financial practices, theories banks are passing up a great opportunity for the genuine need of such practices and their advantages. Hence, for economical banking, Indian banks ought to receive green banking as a plan of action immediately. There is unquestionably an immense chance in perfect, sustainable power innovations, discharges decrease, and diminished carbon transportation which can be gradually and consistently be accomplished in the event that we get participation from all areas of the economy and bank being a basic piece of our economy should lead from the front.

From our insightful outcomes, it tends to be reasoned that banks should show new drive. Green banking would guarantee the compelling utilization of the country's money to guarantee an energy-cognizant climate. Banks would comprehend green banking to be a need as opposed to allure.

7 Limitations and Future Scope

The suggested computational model has been active in showing the importance of green banking activities on the overall efficiency of banks. There are some shortcomings in this report.

1. The current analysis is focused on information obtained only from selected banks in India.
2. The sample size of the analysis is small due to limited circulation of the survey. The survey was limited to only banking sector.
3. This analysis is primarily of the data gathered through the questionnaire on online platforms only. There was no personal interaction with any respondents
4. As green banking is relatively a new concept in the banking industry and the information received is exceptionally limited.
5. Also there can be lack of information on the respondent about the theme. Financial and time goals were also a limitation
6. There can be chances of one-sided or biased response by the respondent.
7. Finally, the antecedent factors are not taken into account. Despite these shortcomings, this research is believed to make an important contribution to the current Green Banking literature.

For future examination, it is additionally important to test current outcomes in longitudinal constructions, which might be more appropriate than cross-over structures. The momentum work just identifies with the quantitative idea of the examination. Future exploration will likewise consider gathering more inside and out information from respondents. Moreover, future examines offer extra freedoms to think about significant going before factors for this investigation. The aftereffects of this report are methodologically restricted to public and private banks and not to unfamiliar bank offices working in India. At last, future exploration should empower diverse differentiation to recognize contrasts in customer discernment in an assortment of settings.

References

Biswas, N. (2011). Sustainable green banking approach: The need of the hour. *Business spectrum 1*, (1), 32–38.

Janakiraman, R. (2016). A study on green banking in India—An Overview. 5(11).

Shaumya, K., & Arulrajah, A. (June, 2017). The impact of green banking practices on bank's environmental performance: Evidence from Sri Lanka. Journal of Finance and Bank Management, 5(1), 77–90.

Empowering Rural Banking for Sustainability: Exploring Fintech Solutions with Equitas Small Finance Bank

Karthika P., Karthikeyan M., and Jayendira P. Sankar

1 Introduction

In the rapidly changing world of financial innovation, the intersection of technology and banking, known as Fintech, has emerged as a pioneering force for modernization (Feyen et al., 2021). In the same way, envision a scenario in which conventional banking ideas converge with Silicon Valley's disruptive prowess, subsequently transforming the tapestry of financial services (Onunka et al., 2023). Furthermore, this narrative occurs within the dynamic realm of financial technology (Fintech), where

Karthika P.
Department of Management, University of Kebridehar, Kebri Dehar, Ethiopia
e-mail: karthika@kdu.edu.et

Karthikeyan M.
Cooperative Studies, College of Business & Economics, Wollo University, Dessie, Ethiopia
e-mail: karthikeyan@wu.edu.et

J. P. Sankar (✉)
College of Administrative and Financial Sciences, University of Technology Bahrain, Salmabad, Bahrain
e-mail: jpsankar@utb.edu.bh

© The Author(s), under exclusive license to Springer Nature Singapore Pte Ltd. 2025

A. S. et al. (eds.), *Trends and Challenges of Electronic Finance*,
https://doi.org/10.1007/978-981-96-3304-3_9

cooperation between Fintech firms and traditional banks ushers in a new era of possibilities (Harsono & Suprapti, 2024). At the epicenter of this evolving landscape lies the question: Does the collaboration between Fintech companies and small finance banks (SFBs) result in Sustainable Finance in India? This inquiry is not solely academic; it delves into the heart of financial inclusion and innovation, addressing the needs of millions of unbanked or underbanked individuals in one of the world's fastest-growing economies. Grasping the intricacies of this collaboration is crucial for industry stakeholders and policymakers in fostering inclusive economic growth.

Fintech, a term derived from the combination of finance and technology, represents a significant transformation in the banking industry by harnessing technological advancements to improve financial services (Barroso & Laborda, 2022). In India, where a substantial proportion of the population has limited access to essential banking services, Fintech has emerged as a vital force, connecting financial institutions with underserved communities (Asif et al., 2023). Thus, the emergence of SFBs in India is a strategic initiative by the Reserve Bank of India (RBI) to expand financial inclusion and meet the diverse needs of low-income individuals (Chaturvedi, 2022). Hence, given India's growing population and thriving Fintech market, the country presents an ideal setting to explore the complexities of Fintech collaboration in small finance banking (Kaur et al., 2019). While over 500 million individuals lack access to formal financial services, the landscape offers ample opportunities for innovation and intervention (Gomber et al., 2018). Although microfinance institutions (MFIs) have historically played a crucial role in extending financial services to rural populations, the advent of SFBs represents a paradigm shift toward more comprehensive financial inclusion strategies (Abrar et al., 2021; Sankar, 2024).

This study evaluates the benefits of cooperation between Fintech companies and SFBs, specifically Equitas Small Finance Bank (ESFB), regarding risks and opportunities in Fintech applications and customer services. The study assessed the advantages of such collaboration and then examined the potential risks and opportunities of exploiting banking operations and customer services in Fintech collaboration. Lastly, the study promoted sustainable finance assessment to improve Fintech adoption and increase customer usage of these services. The research design utilized in this study was exploratory, focusing on the ESFB in Tamil Nadu. Both descriptive and analytical methods were employed, with data collected through surveys. A mixed research approach was used to gather quantitative and qualitative data that meets the research objectives. A multistage procedure was followed to select areas, branches, and customers for sampling. The analysis aims to investigate the benefits, risks, and opportunities for collaboration between Fintech companies and ESFB. Additionally, the study employs a logical model and theory of change (TOC) to measure and design short- and long-term outcomes related to collaboration.

The subsequent sections of this study delve into various aspects of Fintech collaboration in small finance banking. Also, the study investigates this partnership's benefits, risks, and opportunities and sheds light on its implications for sustainable finance in India. Furthermore, the study examines the regulatory framework, consumer attitudes, and technological advancements driving this transformative agenda. Additionally, this study comprehensively explores the evolving landscape of Fintech collaboration in small finance banking, focusing on its implications for sustainable finance in India. Through a detailed analysis of this partnership's intricacies, this study aims to contribute to the academic discourse on financial inclusion, innovation, and sustainability, ultimately facilitating informed decision-making and policy interventions in the financial services sector.

2 Literature Review

2.1 Fintech and Small Finance Bank Collaboration

Collaboration between Fintech companies and traditional banks transforms the financial industry by combining banks' trust and resources with Fintech's innovation (Harsono & Suprapti, 2024). Furthermore, this partnership has increased transaction volume and improved customer experience through personalized digital solutions while addressing regulatory challenges (Kraus et al., 2021). In addition, obstacles such as cultural differences and cybersecurity threats must still be addressed (Willie, 2023). Despite these challenges, collaboration in payment systems and credit distribution is evident, and Fintech is helping to promote financial inclusion, particularly in underserved areas (Amnas et al., 2024). Correspondingly, Samarasinghe (2023) pointed out that these efforts can also benefit the stock returns of traditional banks. Also, Fahy (2022) states that to fully realize this collaboration's potential, regulators need to provide support and foster innovation and competition in the industry. Likewise, Nabiyev and Ovenc (2023) study in Turkey revealed that traditional banks have responded to Fintech disruptions by forming alliances with Fintech companies rather than making investments, with large banks often partnering with non-payment Fintech companies in Istanbul. However, Frederica et al. (2021) studies have shown that bank-Fintech collaboration has not significantly impacted banking performance. Further, this suggests the need for specific Fintech regulations and customer data protection policies. Klus et al. (2019) mentioned that established financial firms collaborate with startups to innovate and digitalize rapidly. Fintech companies seek resources and regulatory support, and banks pursue innovation benefits.

2.2 *Benefits of Fintech Collaboration, Applications, and Usage*

Collaboration between banks and Fintech entities yields mutual benefits, particularly in promoting financial inclusion and fostering economic growth (Heng & Tok, 2022). Furthermore, Fintech's digital prowess complements traditional banks, facilitating their transition into digital service providers (Feyen et al., 2021). Similarly, this transformation expands the banking market reach, particularly into underserved segments like SFBs, and improves accessibility to financial services (Jayadev et al., 2017). Additionally, the collaboration enhances banks' customer databases and fosters public trust in Fintech, improving customer access, convenience, and cost-effective borrowing options (Aldboush & Ferdous, 2023). Also, Varma et al. (2022) mentioned that Fintech integrates technology and finance, revolutionizing banking through innovations like blockchain, despite challenges such as security risks and job losses, with collaboration between Fintech and banks offering potential solutions for enhanced stability. Likewise, Ruhland and Wiese (2023) explored strategic cooperation between financial institutions and Fintechs, identifying motives like financial return and customer satisfaction through literature review and expert interviews, offering practical guidance despite limitations in sample size and geographical focus. Correspondingly, Basdekis et al. (2022) revealed the impact of Fintech expansion on the Greek banking sector, revealing consumer trust in traditional banks over Fintech, with security concerns among consumers and education level influencing employees' readiness for new technologies.

2.3 Risks Involved in Fintech Adoption in Financial Institutions and Banks

Despite the benefits, bank-Fintech collaborations pose inherent risks, including data breaches, cyber-attacks, and challenges associated with outsourcing (Najaf et al., 2021). Furthermore, regulatory gaps in data protection increase vulnerability to data leaks, highlighting the need for robust legislation (Doblas et al., 2023). Similarly, the escalating cyber-attack threat necessitates proactive crisis management and cyber-security measures. Moreover, traditional risk management frameworks face new challenges in the Fintech era, such as peer-to-peer lending, necessitating innovative approaches (Jain et al., 2023; Natarajan et al., 2022; Yoganandham & Sankar, 2022). Hence, technological advancements, changing customer expectations, and emerging risks demand reevaluating risk management practices in banks (Natarajan et al., 2021; Shetty & Nikhitha, 2022). In addition, Al-Shari and Lokhande (2023) pointed out the risks of adopting Fintech in banks and their impact on performance, finding cyber and operational risks negatively affect performance while outsourcing risks have a positive effect. Further, He et al. (2023) highlight that Fintech affects their risk management, finding that Fintech adoption reduces risk-taking, particularly among state-owned, small and medium-sized banks and those with high non-interest income, by enhancing internal control quality. Again, Wu et al. (2024) exposed that novel Fintech index derived from media sources examine how Fintech adoption impacts bank liquidity creation for the top 300 US banks from Q1 2015 to Q2 2021, finding a consistent negative association even during the COVID-19 pandemic, supported by rigorous tests, highlighting Fintech's transformative effect on traditional banking liquidity creation.

While existing literature sheds light on various aspects of Fintech adoption and collaboration, research on small finance banking remains limited. The present study aims to fill this gap by comprehensively exploring Fintech applications, risks, opportunities, and sustainable practices in small finance banking operations and customer services.

3 Research Methodology

This study adopted an exploratory research design, and ESFB, located in Tamil Nadu, was selected. Both descriptive and analytical research methods were adopted in this study. The survey method was adopted for data collection. A mixed research approach was followed for data collection and data analysis. Quantitative and quantitative data were gathered and analyzed to fulfill the research objectives (Creswell, 2003). Further, the sampling procedure adopted a multistage sampling (Sedgwick, 2015) to select the area regarding district, branches, and sample customers. Since this study intended to explore financial inclusion and Fintech applications in rural banking, three rural branches of ESFB in the Erode District were chosen as sample study units. The required data was collected from 12 employees using an interview schedule and 100 customers using a semi-structured questionnaire survey method. In addition, a statistical package for social sciences (SPSS) (Stacks, 1989) was used for data analysis. Descriptive statistics (Fisher & Marshall, 2009) were used to analyze and interpret the data regarding investigating the benefits of collaboration between Fintech companies and ESFB, examining the risks involved and opportunities for Fintech application in ESFB. The logical model and TOC were used to measure and design the short-term and long-term outcomes regarding ESFB and Fintech companies' collaboration.

4 Major Findings of the Study

4.1 Profile of the Customers

This study surveyed 100 respondents, 51.7% of whom were male and 48.3% of whom were female. The bulk of respondents, 52%, are between the ages of 18 and 25, followed by 33% between the ages of 26 and 35, 11% between the ages of 36 and 45, 3.7% between the ages of 46 and 55, and 0.3% over the age of 55. Most respondents have an income of 31.3% less than Rs.1000, 25.7% Rs.1001–2500, 25% Rs.2501–4000, and 18% more than Rs.4001. Most participants, 35%, are single, while others are married 62.6%, widowed 1.7%, or divorced 0.7%. According to the respondents' educational attainment, 50% have a bachelor's degree, 15.3% have a master's degree, 12.3% have a primary degree, 9% have a secondary degree, 6.7% have a high school diploma, 6.3% have a professional certificate, and 0.3% have a post-professional certificate.

4.2 *Fintech Companies and Equitas Small Finance Bank Collaboration*

ESFB is a new-generation bank that offers a new banking experience to children, youth, families, and small business owners across India. During its tenure as a microfinance institution, the ESFB quietly enabled livelihoods and elevated lives. Today, as a small financing bank, it is also reimagining, delivering, and experiencing banking with trust as the primary motivator. Also, ESFB is one of India's largest SFBs. As a new-generation bank in one of the world's fastest-developing economies, it offers a portfolio of products and services targeted to the needs of its customers, individuals with limited access to formal finance channels, and wealthy and mass-affluent individuals, small and medium enterprises, and corporates. It has a well-established strategy that is focused on providing credit to unbanked and underbanked micro and small entrepreneurs, developing products that address the growing aspirations of the bottom of the pyramid, fueled by granular deposits and providing a 'value for money' banking relationship for its customers and stakeholders. The asset products offered by ESFB are suitable for diverse customers with various characteristics. These include the provision of small business loans to micro-entrepreneurs, including secured loans, housing loans, and agriculture loans; microfinance to joint liability groups dominated by women; used and new commercial vehicle loans to drivers and micro-entrepreneurs; micro-small entrepreneurs loans to proprietorships; and loans to non-bank financial companies. On the liability side, the target consumers are middle- and upper-class persons to whom the bank offers current accounts, salary accounts, savings accounts, and a range of deposit accounts.

Additionally, it offers non-credit goods such as automatic teller machine (ATM) debit cards, third-party insurance, mutual fund products, and FASTag issuance. Apart from being technologically agile, ESFB has established a Pan-India footprint, touching clients' lives through diversified loan portfolios, complete banking services, and non-credit offers. While the business model has evolved, primary objective of delivering sustainable credit to unserved and underserved populations remains the same. Equitech is another initiative ESFB developed to help scale the Fintech startup. Equitech is a portal for startups to innovate and incubate by cooperating with ESFB and co-creating meaningful and creative financial solutions. To add value and service to the lives of Indian consumers through innovative banking products and technology, as well as customer experience. A platform for Startups to display their idea to investors and industry experts and pitch for funding. Equitech provides an excellent opportunity for Fintechs to have ESFB as the strategic partner. Scale up the ideas into outcome-driven collaboration in Payment Tech, Lending Tech, Liability Tech, Corporate Tech, Agritech, Health Tech, Edutech, Regulatory Tech, and Wealth Tech.

4.3 Fintech-Equitas Small Finance Bank Collaboration Benefits

ESFB and Google Pay have embarked on a groundbreaking collaboration, enabling Google Pay users to invest in ESFB's particular fixed deposit without the need for a traditional bank account. This innovative one-year deposit scheme offers investors an attractive interest rate of 6.35%, mirroring the benefits available to ESFB's account holders. Moreover, this pioneering partnership signifies the dawn of a new era in banking, where traditional financial institutions join forces with tech giants to unlock unprecedented opportunities. While banks typically rely on their subscriber base or attempt to attract new customers, ESFB has chosen to leverage the expansive reach of Google Pay's user network. Murali Vaidyanathan, senior president of ESFB, emphasized the bank's commitment to democratizing financial products through strategic alliances, stating that Equitas uses the Google distribution channel to democratize the deposit product. Further, in Fintech, collaborations between banks and technology firms extend beyond payment gateways to encompass fund collection and credit distribution. While these transactions may yield lower profits than direct customer lending, they are pivotal in extending financial services to previously underserved populations. ESFB's partnerships with Fintech entities like Niyo, Groww, and Neokred further underscore its dedication to embracing technological innovations to drive financial inclusion.

Integrating Fintech solutions into ESFB's operations brings many benefits, as revealed by the bank's employees. First, Fintech partnerships empower ESFB to penetrate previously untapped markets by leveraging cutting-edge technologies. This expansion opens up avenues for diverse financial transactions while enhancing transaction security. Second, by embracing Fintech solutions, ESFB gains access to advanced technologies without the burden of maintaining costly infrastructure. This bolsters transaction security and frees up resources for other strategic initiatives.

Third, Fintech collaborations offer a cost-effective alternative to in-house technology development and maintenance. ESFB benefits from reduced total cost of ownership, allowing for optimal resource allocation. Fourth, collaborating with Fintech firms equips ESFB with adaptable and secure technology solutions, enabling the bank to stay competitive amid evolving market dynamics. This agility ensures resilience and fosters customer trust. Fifth, collaborating with Fintech firms fosters a culture of innovation within ESFB, laying a solid foundation for continuous improvement and adaptation to market trends. Sixth, Fintech partnerships enable ESFB to engage its customer base through advanced digital offerings, enhancing customer satisfaction and loyalty. Finally, ESFB can efficiently introduce new services without incurring additional risks or operational costs, leading to potential revenue growth opportunities. Likewise, the collaboration between ESFB and Fintech entities epitomizes the transformative potential of merging traditional banking expertise with technological innovation. By embracing this paradigm shift, ESFB enhances its market relevance and fulfills its mission of fostering financial inclusion on a broader scale.

5 Risks and Opportunities of Fintech Applications and Usage in Banking Operations and Customer Service

The study found that though ESFB expanded its reach to rural customers by applying Fintech in banking services, Fintech brought new risks into the banking business, like liquidity, cybersecurity, and legal and reputational risks. As for risks involved in Fintech and ESFB collaboration, Fintech applications in ESFB's banking operations and customer services, the respondents sampled 100 customers who reported their difficulties in using Fintech financial services offered by the ESFB. The multiple responses given by the customers are as follows.

5.1 Risks Involved in Using Fintech Financial Services by Equitas Small Finance Bank Collaboration

First, 65.5% of respondents believed Fintech products received less protection than traditional financial products due to gaps in the country's financial consumer protection regulation and financial sector oversight.

Second, the majority 68% of respondents indicated that factors such as the novelty, opaqueness, or complexity of specific Fintech business models and Fintech entities' responsibilities, as well as a lack of consumer familiarity, result in new or increased risks of loss from financial service providers or third parties fraud or misconduct. Third, in some cases, the Fintech platform or other systems underpinning a Fintech offering are unreliable or vulnerable to external threats; 57% of respondents reported that this exposes consumers to increased risks of loss and other harm. Fourth, consumers whose funds are held or administered by a Fintech entity run the risk of losing those funds if the entity goes bankrupt or their business ceases to operate, and factors such as inexperienced entrants and riskier or novel business models can exacerbate these risks. Hence, this was felt by 76.4% of the study's respondents.

Fifth, according to the majority, 64% of respondents, the standard risks associated with consumers not receiving adequate product information can be exacerbated when new types of pricing, product features, and risks are introduced or when digital channels of communication present difficulties for consumer comprehension. Sixth, Fintech can increase access to riskier or more complex financial products for consumers who may lack the knowledge or experience necessary to properly assess or use them, resulting in increased risks of harm from product unsuitability. Thus, this was the opinion of most % of the bank's respondents, 52%. Seventh, 68% of ESFB respondents indicated that Fintech business models may create conflicts of interest in new circumstances not anticipated by regulators or consumers. Algorithmic decision-making: 55% of respondents believe that the use of algorithms to make consumer-related decisions is becoming increasingly prevalent, particularly in highly automated Fintech business models, and that some scoring choices may result in unfair, discriminatory, or biased outcomes. Finally, most customers 79% believe that data privacy is a critical consideration for Fintech, which has heavily data-driven offerings.

5.2 *Opportunities*

The ESFB has opportunities for advanced Fintech technologies such as the use of biometrics, which would assist in reducing fraud and identifying potential security threats, Agent Banking Solutions, establishing solar-powered ATMs in rural areas, Health tech for the rural population via mobile banking, which can be exploited to offer better banking services to rural customers. More opportunities, such as outcomes and impact, can be found in the logical model and TOC.

6 Results from the Logical Model and Theory of Change

A TOC and a Logic model are very similar in many ways. Both serve as a roadmap for the resources needed, the primary activities undertaken, the products delivered, and the results aiming for outcomes and impact. They diverge because a TOC focuses on why a change will occur rather than on what will happen. As a result, they are frequently more complex and must account for the intervention's context and the influence of external factors. Whichever is appropriate will depend on the intervention's significance, the scenario's complexity, and the time, resources, and skills available. The logical model and TOC result show that this collaboration entails better customer services, expanded digital banking functions, lower operation costs, and improved real-time customer reach through online or mobile platforms. The study found that ESFB expanded its reach to rural customers by applying Fintech in banking services. Hence, this study uses the logical model and TOC, considering their importance in understanding how and why the Fintech intervention is used in ESFB's banking operations and customer services.

6.1 Logical Model Designed for Equitas Small Finance Bank

A logic model is a table or diagram that illustrates how the project or program will operate to address a specific need. Similar to a TOC, it aims to identify the resources required, the primary activities to be undertaken, and, finally, the desired outcome. Based on the preceding analysis, the author designed the logical model sequence for ESFB, as shown in Fig. 1 below.

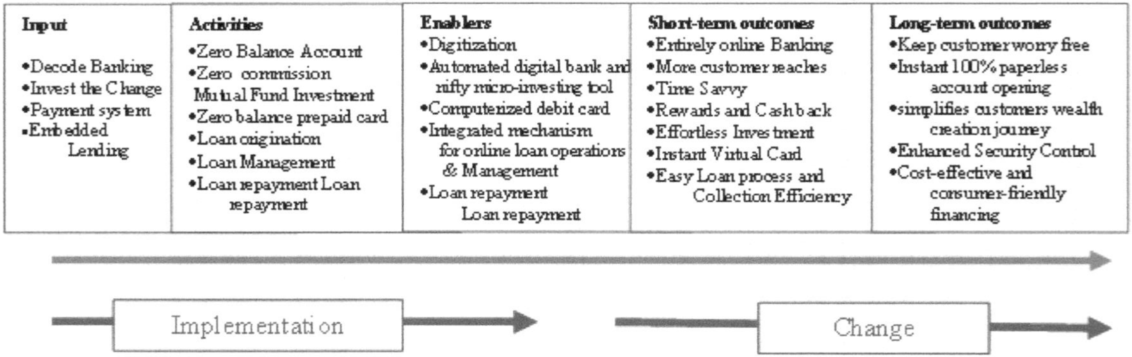

Fig. 1 Logic model for Equitas Small Finance Bank (Source: Self-made by the authors)

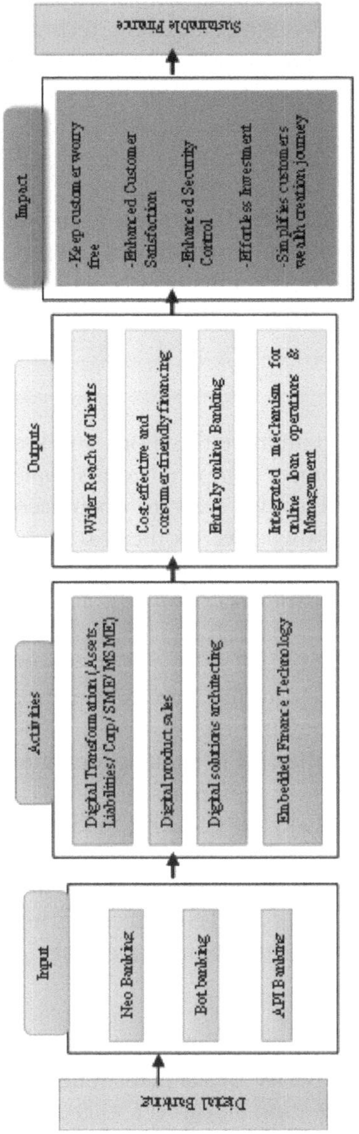

Fig. 2 Digital strategy framework of TOC for Equitas Small Finance Bank (Source: Self-made by the authors)

6.1.1 *Inputs*

The ESFB has collaborated with Niyo, Groww, Neokred, banking operations, and customer services by using an existing technology infrastructure and supporting Fintech companies. Metrics can be applied to inputs: decoding banking, investing the change, payment system, and embedded lending.

6.1.2 *Activities*

The Fintech companies collaborated, supported, and delivered necessary applications to process ESFB's inputs. Metrics can be applied to activities like zero-balance accounts, commission-free mutual fund investments, zero-balance prepaid cards, loan origination and management, and loan repayment.

6.1.3 *Enablers*

The ESFB's objective was to improve the short- and long-term outcomes of a control group of customers compared to a sample set that was not a part of the ESFB. The objectives were to open accounts and provide services to 80% of customers who were otherwise unbanked at the time of the ESFB's inception and complete the digitization process compared to a comparison group of customers.

6.1.4 *Short-Term Outcomes*

The ESFB was a success, reinvesting new venture capital into Fintech firms to continue and expand the digitization process. Equitech was a project developed to scale the ESFB banking operations and customer service model. However, these outcomes are not quantifiable in the ESFB logic model. Additionally, there is no follow-up measurement of customers who participated in the digitization program, even though the collaborated Fintech companies' products effectively demonstrated the value of enrolling customers as ESFB account holders, creating an incentive for customer segments to maintain their relationship with ESFB.

6.1.5 *Long-Term Outcomes*

The ESFB has the potential to contribute to addressing broader customer needs and improving the quality of services available to all customers through technological innovation. However, this was not quantified in the ESFB.

6.2 *Theory of Change Framework for Equitas Small Finance Bank*

A TOC is best described as a flow chart, diagram, or explanation of how the activities engaged will result in the change desired in the world. It aims to ascertain the resources that will be required, the primary activities that will be undertaken, and the end products or services (outputs) that will be delivered. It then identifies the necessary step changes (outcomes) to accomplish a long-term goal or mission. According to the study's findings, the effects of Fintech applications on bank operations and customer service are depicted using the TOC as a framework.

Figure 2 demonstrates an example TOC that addresses the ESFB's digital strategy framework for banking operations and customer service. As with a logic model, it is a sequential process model that progresses from activities to outcomes. The TOC, on the other hand, significantly complicates the logic model by including additional variables and multiple pathways to impact outcomes. Additionally, the TOC contains more gritty details about specific banking operational activities and their anticipated impact on customer service. As a strategic management model, the TOC requires more care than a logic model but may be more useful in project-level decision-making. The focus is given on ESFB's Digital Banking, Neo Banking, Bot Banking, and Application Programming Interface Banking as inputs, activities (digital transformation, digital product sales, digital solution architecting, and embedded finance technology), outputs (wider reach of clients, cost-effective and consumer-friendly financing, entirely online banking, and integrated mechanism for online operations and management) with corresponding impact (keep customer worry-free, enhanced customer satisfaction, and security control, effortless investment, simplified customer wealth creation journey, and cost-effective & consumer-friendly financing) in line with the mission statement of the ESFB, and the outcome impact would be sustainable finance.

7 Conclusion

In a nutshell, the findings of this study suggest several points that may benefit various stakeholders in terms of increasing consumer intention to adopt Fintech. Financial services providers and regulators can use the findings as a guide to encourage customer participation in using Fintech in financial services applications. The findings revealed that there were numerous benefits to be gained from working together, such as increased efficiency and innovation. However, there were also risks involved, including data security concerns and regulatory challenges. Despite these potential obstacles, the study concluded that the benefits of collaboration outweighed the risks and recommended further exploration of this partnership model in future. As such, financial services providers should design and provide consumers with a technological tool that is user-friendly, efficient, and effective at its job. Additionally, financial services providers should integrate their technology with increased peer interaction to encourage participation in Fintech.

8 Recommendations

Based on the findings, the following recommendations are forwarded: First, effective oversight of any regulatory measures implemented, as well as monitoring of Fintech developments and consumer risks more broadly, will be critical to achieving the policy objectives underlying such measures (Bains & Wu, 2023; Restoy, 2021). Second, supervisors will require new strategies and technological tools to monitor financial sectors that are expanding and changing due to Fintech entrants and offerings, including unregulated providers and restructured businesses of some regulated entities (Anifa et al., 2022; Feyen et al., 2021). Third, complementary measures will be required to supplement regulatory actions. While regulatory measures are frequently necessary, they are far from the only ones (Khan et al., 2023; Varma et al., 2022). Finally, complementary measures, for example, will be required to increase consumers' digital and financial literacy and raise market participants' awareness and understanding of responsible business practices (Koskelainen et al., 2023; Yang et al., 2023). Raising consumer awareness and enhancing financial capability for both consumers and industry will also be critical for maximizing the impact of regulatory measures and addressing consumer risks more broadly. At the outset, it is recommended that an assessment be made of the economic, social, and environmental impact of Fintech applications on banking operations and customer services, enabling the ESFB to offer sustainable finance to improve rural customer services.

References

Abrar, U. H. M., Asad, M., Natarajan, V., Sankar, J. P., & Asif, M. U. (2021). Microfinance and empowerment: A case study on beneficiaries of a community development program. *Turkish Journal of Computer and Mathematics Education, 12*(10), 5408–5415.

Al-Shari, H. A., & Lokhande, M. A. (2023). The relationship between the risks of adopting FinTech in banks and their impact on the performance. *Cogent Business and Management, 10*(1), 1–35. https://doi.org/10.1080/23311975.2023.2174242

Aldboush, H. H. H., & Ferdous, M. (2023). Building trust in Fintech: An analysis of ethical and privacy considerations in the intersection of big data, AI, and customer trust. *International Journal of Financial Studies, 11*(3), 1–18. https://doi.org/10.3390/ijfs11030090

Amnas, M. B., Selvam, M., & Parayitam, S. (2024). FinTech and financial inclusion: Exploring the mediating role of digital financial literacy and the moderating influence of perceived regulatory support. *Journal of Risk and Financial Management, 17*(3), 1–20. https://doi.org/10.3390/jrfm17030108

Anifa, M., Ramakrishnan, S., Joghee, S., Kabiraj, S., & Bishnoi, M. M. (2022). Fintech innovations in the financial service industry. *Journal of Risk and Financial Management, 15*(7), 1–19. https://doi.org/10.3390/jrfm15070287

Asif, M., Khan, M. N., Tiwari, S., Wani, S. K., & Alam, F. (2023). The impact of Fintech and digital financial services on financial inclusion in India. *Journal of Risk and Financial Management, 16*(2), 1–12. https://doi.org/10.3390/jrfm16020122

Bains, P., & Wu, C. (2023). Institutional arrangements for fintech regulation: Supervisory monitoring. In *Fintech Notes* (Vol. 2023, Issue 004, pp. 1–52).

Barroso, M., & Laborda, J. (2022). Digital transformation and the emergence of the Fintech sector: Systematic literature review. *Digital Business, 2*(2), 100028. https://doi.org/10.1016/j.digbus.2022.100028

Basdekis, C., Christopoulos, A., Katsampoxakis, I., & Vlachou, A. (2022). FinTech's rapid growth and its effect on the banking sector. *Journal of Banking and Financial Technology, 6*(2), 159–176. https://doi.org/10.1007/s42786-022-00045-w

Chaturvedi, P. (2022). The role of small finance banks in promoting financial inclusion in India. *Research Review International Journal of Multidisciplinary, 7*(5), 8–15. https://doi.org/10.31305/rrijm.2022.v07.i05.002

Creswell, J. W. (2003). Research design qualitative quantitative and mixed methods approaches. In *Research design qualitative quantitative and mixed methods approaches* (6th ed.). Sage Publication. https://doi.org/10.3109/08941939.2012.723954

Doblas, M. P., Natarajan, V. K., & Sankar, J. P. (2023). Revisiting the autoregressive integrated moving average approach to modelling volatility using Bahrain all share index daily returns. *Middle East J. of Management, 10*(6), 619–636. https://doi.org/10.1504/mejm.2023.133757

Fahy, L. A. (2022). Fostering regulator—Innovator collaboration at the frontline: A case study of the UK's regulatory sandbox for Fintech. *Law and Policy, 44*(2), 162–184. https://doi.org/10.1111/lapo.12184

Feyen, E., Frost, J., Gambacorta, L., Natarajan, H., & Saal, M. (2021). Fintech and the digital transformation of financial services: Implications for market structure and public policy. In *BIS Papers* (Vol. 117, Issue 117).

Fisher, M. J., & Marshall, A. P. (2009). Understanding descriptive statistics. *Australian Critical Care, 22*(2), 93–97. https://doi.org/10.1016/j.aucc.2008.11.003

Frederica, D., Augustine, Y., Murwaningsari, E., & Mayangsari, S. (2021). The effect of Fintech and bank collaboration on banking performance in Indonesia moderated by the implementation of regulations. *International Journal of Business, Economics and Law, 24*(1), 113–118.

Gomber, P., Kauffman, R. J., Parker, C., & Weber, B. W. (2018). On the Fintech revolution: Interpreting the forces of innovation, disruption, and transformation in financial services. *Journal of Management Information Systems, 35*(1), 220–265. https://doi.org/10.1080/07421222.2018.1440766

Harsono, I., & Suprapti, I. A. P. (2024). The role of Fintech in transforming traditional financial services. *Accounting Studies and Tax Journal (COUNT), 1*(1), 81–91. https://doi.org/10.62207/gfzvtd24

He, M., Song, G., & Chen, Q. (2023). Fintech adoption, internal control quality and bank risk taking: Evidence from Chinese listed banks. *Finance Research Letters, 57*, 104235. https://doi.org/10.1016/j.frl.2023.104235

Heng, D., & Tok, Y. W. (2022). Fintech: Financial inclusion or exclusion? In *IMF Working Papers* (WP/22/80) https://doi.org/10.5089/9798400208645.001

Jain, R., Kumar, S., Sood, K., Grima, S., & Rupeika-Apoga, R. (2023). A systematic literature review of the risk landscape in Fintech. In *Risks* (Vol. 11, Issue 2, pp. 1–15). https://doi.org/10.3390/risks11020036

Jayadev, M., Singh, H., & Kumar, P. (2017). Small finance banks: Challenges. *IIMB Management Review, 29*(4), 311–325. https://doi.org/10.1016/j.iimb.2017.10.001

Kaur, C., Sharma, A., & Singh, T. P. (2019). FinTech in India: opportunities and challenges. *Fintech in India-Opportunities and Challenges, 8*(8), 42–54. https://doi.org/10.5958/2319-1422.2019.00002.x

Khan, H. H., Khan, S., & Ghafoor, A. (2023). Fintech adoption, the regulatory environment and bank stability: An empirical investigation from GCC economies. *Borsa Istanbul Review, 23*(6), 1263–1281. https://doi.org/10.1016/j.bir.2023.10.010

Klus, M. F., Lohwasser, T. S., Holotiuk, F., & Moormann, J. (2019). Strategic alliances between banks and Fintechs for digital innovation: Motives to collaborate and types of interaction. *The Journal of Entrepreneurial Finance, 21*(1), 1–23. https://doi.org/10.57229/2373-1761.1346

Koskelainen, T., Kalmi, P., Scornavacca, E., & Vartiainen, T. (2023). Financial literacy in the digital age—A research agenda. *Journal of Consumer Affairs, 57*(1), 507–528. https://doi.org/10.1111/joca.12510

Kraus, S., Jones, P., Kailer, N., Weinmann, A., Chaparro-Banegas, N., & Roig-Tierno, N. (2021). Digital transformation: An overview of the current state of the art of research. *SAGE Open, 11*(3), 1–25. https://doi.org/10.1177/21582440211047576

Nabiyev, A. B., & Ovenc, G. (2023). The symbiotic relationship and collaboration between commercial banks and fintechs in Turkey. *Humanities and Social Sciences Communications, 10*(1), 1–7. https://doi.org/10.1057/s41599-023-02429-9

Najaf, K., Mostafiz, M. I., & Najaf, R. (2021). Fintech firms and banks sustainability: Why cybersecurity risk matters? *International Journal of Financial Engineering, 08*(02), 1–15. https://doi.org/10.1142/s2424786321500195

Natarajan, V. K., & Abrar ul Haq, M., Akram, F., & Sankar, J. P. (2021). Dynamic relationship between stock index and asset prices: A long-run analysis. *Journal of Asian Finance, Economics and Business, 8*(4), 1–16.

Natarajan, V. K., & Abrar ul Haq, M., & Sankar, J. P. (2022). Causality between public expenditure and economic growth in the kingdom of Bahrain. *Middle East Journal of Management, 9*(2), 209–225. https://doi.org/10.1504/MEJM.2022.121393

Onunka, T., Raji, A., Nkemchor Osafiele, A., Daraojimba, C., Afeyokalo Egbokhaebho, B., & Chinazo Okoye, C. (2023). Banking: A comprehensive review of the evolution and impact of innovative banking services on entrepreneurial growth. *Economic Growth and Environment Sustainability, 2*(2), 66–78. https://doi.org/10.26480/egnes.02.2023.66.78

Restoy, F. (2021). Fintech regulation: How to achieve a level playing field. In *Occasional Paper* (Vol. 17, Issue 17, pp. 1–27). Financial Stability Institute. 1020–9999.

Ruhland, P., & Wiese, F. (2023). FinTechs and the financial industry: Partnerships for success. *Journal of Business Strategy, 44*(4), 228–237. https://doi.org/10.1108/JBS-12-2021-0196

Samarasinghe, A. (2023). Stock market liquidity and bank stability. *Pacific Basin Finance Journal, 79*, 102028. https://doi.org/10.1016/j.pacfin.2023.102028

Sankar, J. P. (2024). Sustainable microfinance principles in sustainable development goals for the economic resilience. In R. Nafea, S. Faizal, D. Jelonek, N. Kumar, J. P. Sankar, & I. Paweloszek (Eds.), *Sustainable Innovations in Management in the Digital Transformation Era* (pp. 163–172). Routledge. https://doi.org/10.4324/9781003450238

Sedgwick, P. (2015). Multistage sampling. In *BMJ (Online)* (Vol. 351, pp. 1–2). https://doi.org/10.1136/bmj.h4155

Shetty, M. D., & Nikhitha, M. K. (2022). Impact of information technology on the banking sector. *International Journal of Management, Technology, and Social Sciences*, *7*(2), 634–646. https://doi.org/10.47992/ijmts.2581.6012.0241

Stacks, D. W. (1989). Statistical package for the social sciences/pc + v3.0. In *Communication Education* (Vol. 38, Issue 4, pp. 387–393). https://doi.org/10.1080/03634528909378780

Varma, P., Nijjer, S., Sood, K., Grima, S., & Rupeika-Apoga, R. (2022). Thematic analysis of financial technology (Fintech) influence on the banking industry. In *Risks* (Vol. 10, Issue 10, pp. 1–17). https://doi.org/10.3390/risks10100186

Willie, M. M. (2023). The role of organizational culture in cybersecurity: Building a security-first culture. *Journal of Research, Innovation and Technologies (JoRIT)*, *2*(16), 179–198. https://doi.org/10.57017/jorit.v2.2(4).05

Wu, Z., Pathan, S., & Zheng, C. (2024). FinTech adoption in banks and their liquidity creation. *British Accounting Review*, *In-press*, 1–22. https://doi.org/10.1016/j.bar.2024.101322

Yang, J., Wu, Y., & Huang, B. (2023). Digital finance and financial literacy: Evidence from Chinese households. *Journal of Banking and Finance, 156*, 107005. https://doi.org/10.1016/j.jbankfin.2023.107005

Yoganandham, G., & Sankar, J. P. (2022). Organizational credit facilities for microfinance entrepreneurs: An Indian context. *Remittances Review*, *7*(1), 117–130. https://doi.org/10.47059/rr.v7i1.2401

Regulatory Frameworks: Balancing Security and Innovation in Electronic Finance Across Gulf Cooperation Council Markets

Shatha Hussain, Faisal Khan, and Dalia Hemdan

1 Introduction

The accelerated tech advancement has now become a global trend, particularly in the parts of the world such as the Gulf Cooperation Council (GCC) regions (Melovic et al., 2020). These advancements have been affecting every aspect of the business finance such as in the form of electronic finance (commonly known as e-finance) in GCC regions. E-finance, covering a wide range of digital financial services and transactions, has evolved as the main driver of innovation and economic growth in GCC countries (Al-Jabri & Sohail, 2012). However, this rise in e-finance does not come without strings, such as privacy issues, regulatory challenges regarding security, and financial stability (Popovska-Kamnar, 2014). In

S. Hussain · F. Khan (✉)
College of Business, City University Ajman, Ajman, UAE
e-mail: f.khan@cu.ac.ae

S. Hussain
e-mail: s.hussain@cu.ac.ae

D. Hemdan
School of Management, Canadian University Dubai, Dubai, UAE
e-mail: dalia-hemdan@hotmail.com

© The Author(s), under exclusive license to Springer Nature Singapore Pte Ltd. 2025

A. S. et al. (eds.), *Trends and Challenges of Electronic Finance*,
https://doi.org/10.1007/978-981-96-3304-3_10

this chapter, we explore the regulatory frameworks governing e-finance in GCC regions and investigate the ways regulators balance the imperative of fostering innovation with the need to maintain security and stability in financial systems (Alshubiri et al., 2019).

2 Regulatory Landscape of E-Finance in GCC Markets.

Immense digital transformation has been taking place in the GCC markets, particularly in the financial industry. The initiation of e-finance became the foundation of this transformation that led to both innovation and economic growth in the GCC regions (GCC Financial Landscape, 2022; Arab News, 2023; Gulf News, 2023; Khaleej Times, 2023). E-finance encompasses a large range of digital financial services, such as Fintech solutions, online banking, cryptocurrency transactions, and digital banking payments to name a few of them (Burlacu et al., 2021; Gomber et al., 2018). Nonetheless, this rapid spread and expansion in e-finance do not come alone as there are many challenges including security threats, the privacy of the stakeholders, and financial stability (Zalan & Toufaily, 2017) to deal with. On the other hand, the regulatory landscape of e-finance in GCC markets is formed by a mixture of domestic regulations, international standards, and regional initiatives. While each GCC country has its regulatory framework, some common trends and principles underpin regulatory approaches to e-finance across the region are listed below:

2.1 Licensing and Authorization in GCC

For the e-finance service providers, getting permissions and licenses from the regulatory authorities is essential to operate legally in GCC markets. This licensing would ensure the stability and integrity of the financial system, discourage financial crimes including terrorist financing and money laundering, and protect regional customers, etc. The following are the essential components of licensing and authorization in the context of GCC countries:

2.1.1 Prudential Standards

Prudential e-finance standards that are required to be followed by e-finance businesses in GCC include maintenance of sufficient capital reserves, implementation of robust risk management frameworks, and assurance of operational resilience (Goldstein et al., 2019; Thakor, 2020). The purpose of these prudential standards is to safeguard the financial system against market risks and to trust these institutions can withstand financial shocks. For instance, in the UAE, the Central Bank requires financial institutions to adhere to specific capital adequacy ratios and risk management protocols as part of its licensing process (Central Bank of UAE, 2022). Researchers have also reported that these standards help reduce financial risks and raise the financial stability of these institutions in the GCC regions (Khan et al., 2023).

2.1.2 Anti-Money Laundering (AML) Regulations

Another important element of the licensing process in GCC countries is compliance with anti-money laundering (AML) regulations. In this regard, e-finance companies must implement comprehensive AML programs which include reporting suspicious activities, customer due diligence, and transaction monitoring (Reurink, 2019). These elements are crucial to avert money laundering activities from the financial systems along with other illegal activities. The regulators in GCC countries also get help from the guidelines provided by the Financial Action Task Force (FATF, 2021) with local implementation as and where deemed appropriate (Levi, 2017; Reurink, 2019). Hence, robust AML frameworks have a significant role in maintaining the integrity of financial systems and prevention of financial crimes.

2.1.3 Know-Your-Customer (KYC) Requirements

Know-your-customer (KYC) is one of the significant requirements that is designed to verify the customers, understand the nature of their financial activities, and prevent fraud, and identity theft. For example, in Bahrain, the Central Bank of Bahrain (CBB) obligates that all licensed entities comply with KYC protocols as an integral part of their operational procedures (Parate et al., 2023). The framework for KYC implemented by CBB comprises regular monitoring and updates regarding customer information to ensure ongoing compliance (CBB, 2023). In a nutshell, the effective KYC procedure not only prevents financial misconduct but also promotes trust in financial markets (Albahar & Thanoon, 2022).

2.1.4 *Bahrain Fintech Regulatory Sandbox*

Bahrain Fintech regulatory sandbox is a prominent example of a regulatory framework, which is directed by the CBB. Under this sandbox, the Fintech firms and payment service providers may test their innovative products and exchange their services in a very relaxed and supportive regulatory environment. However, it is still mandatory for the participants in a sandbox to get a license from the CBB that guarantees compliance with essential prudential (such as AML and KY). Hence, on the one hand, this sandbox boosts innovation, on the other hand, it also ensures consumer protection and financial stability (Central Bank of Bahrain, 2023). Similarly, as reported by Khan et al. (2023), the regulatory sandbox might also be influential in promoting Fintech innovation by providing a safe space for experimentation and development.

In short, gaining licenses and authorizations to function as an e-finance provider in GCC countries involves rigorous compliance with prudential standards, AML regulations, and KYC requirements. These initiatives are critical to maintaining the integrity of the overall financial system and protecting consumers from committing financial crimes. These regulatory frameworks, for instance, the Bahrain Fintech Regulatory Sandbox, exemplify the balance between promoting financial innovation and ensuring robust regulatory oversight.

2.2 *Consumer Protection in GCC*

The regulators in GCC markets are particularly interested in enhancing consumer protection. Hence, through regulatory frameworks, e-finance providers are directed to implement measures that safeguard the interests of consumers, such as pricing transparency, treating customers fairly, and mechanisms for dispute resolution.

2.2.1 *Transparency in Pricing*

In the e-finance sector, pricing transparency is central to consumer protection, and e-finance providers are bound to reveal all fees linked to their services clearly and comprehensively. This guarantees that consumers are completely aware of the costs they will bear and hence, prevents them from hidden and unexpected fees. For example, the Saudi Arabian Monetary Authority (SAMA) has published comprehensive guidelines on pricing transparency, guaranteeing that consumers might have to compare various financial products and services effectively (SAMA, 2022). Likewise, Ramady (2015) has highlighted the significance of transparency in constructing consumer trust and fostering a competitive market environment.

2.2.2 *Fair Treatment of Customers*

By fair treatment of customers, regulators mean to ensure they have equitable access to financial services, their complaints are addressed promptly, and that the prevailing market prices are not misleading (Farooq & Moon, 2020; Pan & Mishra, 2018). For this purpose, regulators design policies to protect these customers from exploitation and guarantee that they receive fair value for the services provided. In this connection, we see the UAE Central Bank which has already implemented policies that necessitate the financial institutions to treat customers fairly, for instance, the provisions for non-discriminatory practices (Central Bank of the UAE, 2023). As also stated by Alshamsi et al. (2023) treating customers fairly is critical for maintaining the reputation and integrity of the financial sector.

2.2.3 *Mechanisms for Dispute Resolution*

As effective dispute resolution mechanisms are an essential part of consumer protection, e-finance providers have to establish clear procedures for handling complaints and dispute resolutions. Moreover, these mechanisms must also guarantee that in case customers face any issue they have some forum to consult so that their problems are resolved effectively. For instance, in the case of Saudi Arabia, provisions for dispute resolutions are available in SAMA's regulations, particularly on electronic payments and bill presentations. This warrants that customers' grievances are fairly and quickly addressed (SAMA, 2022). Moreover, these mechanisms not only remove the issues on hand but also enhance the trust and confidence of the customers in the system (Alshathri, 2022).

2.2.4 *The Saudi Arabian Monetary Authority (SAMA) Regulations*

SAMA regulations are one excellent example in the context of Saudi Arabia, a regulatory framework that prioritizes consumer protection in the regulations issued on electronic payments and bill presentations (Belwal et al., 2021). These regulations comprise a large number of consumer protection measures, such as requirements for transparency, effective dispute resolution, and fair treatment. SAMA has the goal to increase trust and guarantee that the financial system functions transparently and fairly by setting high standards for e-finance providers (SAMA, 2022). The comprehensive approach adopted by SAMA to safeguard the consumers has also set examples for other regulators to act the same (AlBenJasim et al., 2023). Hence, it has been proven now that consumer protection is the base of regulatory frameworks for e-finance providers in the GCC countries, and measures including transparency in pricing, fair treatment of customers, and effective dispute resolution mechanisms are crucial for safeguarding consumer interests (Belwal et al., 2021). In this regard, regulatory initiatives such as establishing SAMA regulations have played an important role in the overall commitment of the GCC regulators to secure the financial environment of the regions.

2.3 *Cybersecurity and Data Privacy in GCC*

With the increasing digitization of financial services, the regulators in GCC countries also facing cybersecurity and data privacy issues. Hence, the regulatory frameworks have made it compulsory for e-finance providers to properly implement robust cybersecurity measures to protect the users of the services from cyber threats and guarantee the confidentiality and integrity of the customer data and information. The following are the important measures taken in this regard:

2.3.1 *Importance of Cybersecurity Measures*

Securing the financial systems from cyber threats is not only vital in gaining and retaining the consumer trust but also for the stability of financial institutions (Mızrak, 2023). Therefore, e-finance providers must establish a comprehensive cybersecurity framework that covers risk assessment, incident response plan, and continuous monitoring of threats (Akintoye et al., 2022). In this regard, the UAE's Telecommunications Regulatory Authority (TRA) has supplied guidelines on cybersecurity for financial institutions that emphasize the significance of risk management and incident response (TRA, UAE, 2021). Hence, effective cybersecurity practices are significant for reducing the risks created by increasingly complex cyber-attacks.

2.3.2 *Data Privacy Regulations*

The privacy of data is not short than important as other factors and ensures that consumer information is dealt with highest standards of integrity and confidentiality (Everson, 2016). Here, the regulatory framework might cover the encryption of data, control access, and audit to restrict unauthorized access and breaches of data. The "Personal Data Protection Law (PDPL)" in Bahrain dictates strict compliance with data privacy standards, necessitating e-finance providers to apply robust data protection measures (DLA Piper, 2019). Research has shown that following data privacy regulations enhances the credibility of financial institutions as well as protects consumers (Al-Marzouqi et al., 2020).

2.3.3 Risk Management and Incident Response

Developing comprehensive risk management and incident response are essential on the part of e-finance providers as these are the core of cybersecurity and data privacy frameworks and help in identifying potential threats, measuring the vulnerabilities, and minimizing the risks (Akintoye et al., 2022). Moreover, devising a well-structured incident response strategy is crucial for promptly addressing cyber incidents and getting recover from them (Mızrak, 2023). As discussed above, the TRA guidelines denote particular requirements for risk handling such as regular risk assessment, continuous monitoring, and effective communication while facing these incidents (TRA, UAE, 2021). In light of the conclusion derived by Jasur (2023), the proactive approach of managing the risk and incident response is the main idea to reduce the impact of cyber threats in financial institutions.

2.3.4 The UAE Telecommunications Regulatory Authority (TRA) Guidelines

The UAE's TRA has always been active in resolving cybersecurity and data privacy issues through its comprehensive guidelines for financial institutions. The guidelines are driven by a holistic approach to cybersecurity and comprise data privacy, incident response, and risk management (Akintoye et al., 2022; Mızrak, 2023). The TRA guidelines ensure the protection of consumers from cyber threats and guarantee the integrity and confidentiality of these consumers' data (TRA, UAE, 2021). As cybersecurity and data privacy are the pressing issues for GCC regulators; hence, these guidelines serve as a yardstick for the rest of the regulatory bodies in the GCC regions and promote a secure and resilient financial ecosystem. Moreover, they address risk management, data privacy, and incident response in securing the financial system and the protection of consumers' interests (Mızrak, 2023).

3 Balancing Security and Innovation

Presently, the regulators operating in GCC regions are encountering the challenge of balancing the imperatives of security and innovation in e-finance. Hence, they have to promote innovation as it is imperative for the economic growth of the regions. However, they also have to ensure the stability and security of the financial systems in order to maintain the confidence and trust among both the investors and consumers (Jasur, 2023). To achieve the right level of balance between the two, the regulators need to implement a risk-based approach to these regulations which might involve the following elements:

3.1 Proportionate Regulation in E-Finance

Proportionate regulations in e-finance refer to setting various levels of regulatory requirements depending upon the features of the e-finance providers (Jenik & Lauer, 2017). This approach identified that the financial landscape is dissimilar and that a "one-size-fits-all" regulatory framework is generally insufficient to address the unique challenges and opportunities offered by various e-finance activities (Khan et al., 2023). The mandate of this approach is to match the regulatory requirements concerning a firm's size, complexity, and significance. All this will help the regulators to minimize the risks but at the same time, innovation would not suffer. Hence, proportionate regulations are crucial for effectively handling the risk associated with e-finance activities while fostering innovation and competition in the financial sector.

3.2 Tailoring Regulatory Requirements

"Proportionate" regulatory requirements mandate the regulators to tailor to the size, complexity, and systematic importance of the e-finance provider. In other words, without unduly burdening or stifling innovation, smaller firms operating in a less complex and lower systematic risk must be burdened with fewer regulatory requirements in contrast to larger and more complex entities (Khan et al., 2023). For example, the Basel Committee on Banking Supervision has acclaimed a differentiated approach while following Basel-III standards. This approach permits the regulatory frameworks for proportionality in the regulation of smaller banks versus larger, systematically important financial institutions (Parate et al., 2023) and ensures effective as well as fair playing field while acknowledging the diversity within the e-finance sector (Khan et al., 2023). This approach is significant for promoting innovation and competition as overly burdensome regulations may hamper the growth of small firms and smother technological advancement (Arner et al., 2016).

3.3 *Balancing Complexity and Systemic Importance*

The complexity and systemic importance of e-finance providers are other critical factors in appropriate regulations. As the complexity of institutions increases they become indulgent in a large range of financial services and have substantial market impacts that require robust regulatory initiatives to handle the potential risk effectively (Ramady, 2015). In contrast, firms low on complexity and have limited market influence could get an advantage from even lighter regulatory initiatives which allow them to make innovations and grow even without excessive compliance costs (Jenik & Lauer, 2017). Hence, balanced regulatory approaches that consider the above elements may increase the resilience of the financial system along with the support of sustainable growth (Zetzsche et al., 2017). Likewise, the International Monetary Fund (IMF) has also declared the requirement for increased supervision and higher capital requirements for SIFIs to minimize systemic risks (Mizrak, 2023).

3.4 *Avoiding Regulatory Burdens*

As discussed above, the main purpose of proportionate regulation is to avoid undue burden on the e-finance providers (and this should be according to the size and complexity of the firms) otherwise innovation might be compromised and discouraged in these firms (Akintoye et al., 2022; Zavolokina et al., 2017). More so, this undue regulatory burden would also increase the compliance costs and entry to the market, especially in the growing firms and new start-ups (Pan & Mishra, 2018). Small and young firms often lack in resources and expertise and hence, the complex regulatory framework may hamper their struggle for innovation and growth. Through the implementation of proportionate regulatory frameworks, the regulators might ensure that the compliance requirements are manageable and do not inhibit the dynamism and creativity essential for the evolution of the e-finance sector (Pan & Mishra, 2018).

The existing relevant literature (such as Broeders & Prenio, 2018) has also shown that "proportionate" regulation not only reduces the unnecessary burden and barriers on the e-finance providers but also encourages them to make innovations. Similarly, a study conducted by Arner et al. (2015) also concluded that a calibrated regulatory framework may encourage competition and innovation by permitting Fintech start-ups to experiment with the latest technologies and business models without any pressures of compliance with complicated regulatory frameworks (also stated by Zetzsche et al., 2017). In addition, Ehrentraud et al. (2020) focused on the significance of regulatory sandboxes and innovation hubs as tools for the implementation of proportionate regulation. These initiatives allow the regulators to collaborate with Fintech companies in a controlled environment, enabling the testing of new products and services while ensuring that regulatory objectives are met.

3.5 Regulatory Sandboxes

One of the classical examples of proportionate regulation in real world is the application of regulatory sandboxes (Zetzsche et al., 2017). Sandboxes allow e-finance providers to evaluate any new product or service in a controlled environment with relaxed regulatory requirements (Jenik & Lauer, 2017). On the other hand, these sandboxes also enable the regulators to make assessment about the risk and benefit of innovative financial solutions without compromising the consumer safety and financial stability (Broeders & Prenio, 2018). The success and effectiveness of sandboxes across various developed countries (such as UK and Singapore) of the world are an evidence that proportionate regulations are significant to foster innovation while ensuring robust oversight (Jenik & Lauer, 2017). Looking to these successes, the notion of regulatory sandboxes is also getting popularity and being adopted at large scale in the GCC countries in turn shows the commitment to proportionate and innovation-friendly regulations (Khan et al., 2023). In short, proportionate regulation is important for effective oversight of the diverse e-finance sector that tailors the regulatory requirements to the specific features and risks of various e-finance activities, increases competition, and regulators can endorse innovation, and the integrity of the financial system.

3.6 Dynamic Supervision

Regulators need to adopt a dynamic supervisory approach that keeps pace with technological advancements and evolving risks in e-finance. This involves leveraging technology, data analytics, and supervisory tools to monitor e-finance activities, detect emerging risks, and take timely corrective actions to mitigate risks to financial stability and consumer protection. Dynamic supervision allows regulators to be proactive rather than reactive, addressing potential issues before they escalate into significant problems (Bholat et al., 2016). For instance, the use of artificial intelligence (AI) and machine learning (ML) can enhance the ability to analyze large datasets in real time, providing insights into unusual patterns or behaviors that may indicate fraudulent activities or systemic risks (McWaters, 2016; Finck, 2018).

Additionally, the integration of RegTech (regulatory technology) solutions can streamline compliance processes and reduce the burden on financial institutions, allowing them to focus more on innovation and customer service (Arner et al., 2016). By continuously updating their supervisory frameworks and investing in advanced technologies, regulators can maintain a robust oversight mechanism that adapts to the fast-paced nature of e-finance. This approach not only ensures financial stability but also promotes consumer trust and confidence in digital financial services (Philippon, 2016).

3.7 Collaborative Governance

Effective and workable regulation framework of e-finance necessitates collaboration and coordination among multiple stakeholders, such as industry participants, regulators, and other relevant authorities (Ehrentraud et al., 2020). So, the regulators are required to engage the industry stakeholders in a dialogue and understand the new trends, share the prevailing practices, and formulate regulator standards that incurs a suitable balance between innovation and security. This collaborative governance nurtures a holistic understanding of the e-finance ecosystem and ensures regulatory measures are properly worked out and practical in nature (Black, 2008). Establishing the public–private partnership (PPP) is one such approach to collaborative governance that assists in constant interaction and cooperation among the regulatory bodies and e-finance sectors. These collaborations might help identify potential regulatory gaps where innovation could bring new risks (Zavolokina et al., 2017). Moreover, as argued by Arner et al. (2016), international cooperation among regulators is critical to addressing the global nature of e-finance (where financial transactions and services generally transcend national borders). The formation of regulatory sandboxes where Fintech firms may assess new services and products under the regulations of regulators is yet another workable tool. These sandboxes encourage innovation along with financial stability and consumer protection (Jenik & Lauer, 2017). Through nurturing an atmosphere of open communication and trust, collaborative governance assists in building regulatory frameworks and supports sustainability and resilience in the e-finance industry (Abbas et al., 2016).

4 Conclusion

The main objective of this chapter was to explore how e-finance providers are regulated in the GCC markets. In particular, this chapter focused on the ways regulators strive to harmonize innovation along with security and regulatory frameworks that govern the e-finance sector. The rapidly changing and developing e-finance sector of GCC countries has the ability to drive immense economic growth and improve financial inclusion of every segment of these markets. Hence, if sensibly managed, these advancements could reduce the risks and uncertainties regarding cybersecurity, data privacy, and financial instability in these regions. Our analysis of the GCC regions has disclosed that regulators are fully committed to implementing such frameworks which are capable of securing the interests of consumers along with maintaining the integrity of the financial environment through robust authorization processes and licensing. Moreover, if the e-finance providers comply with AML regulations, KYC requirements, and prudential standards, they can surely secure their digital processes. In addition, the protection of consumers' rights including transparent pricing, fair treatment, and effective dispute resolution system must be the top priority of the regulators in GCC countries. We observed that in most of the GCC countries, the regulators have somehow achieved these by implementing their models and institutions. For example, the "SAMA" in Saudi Arabia mainly focuses on consumer rights and protection. Similarly, regulatory frameworks in the UAE and other GCC countries require e-finance providers to impose robust cyber security measures to ensure the protection of consumers. Moreover, the regulators in GCC markets are also implementing "proportionate" regulations by the e-finance firms. In general, this chapter has identified, that "dynamic supervision," "technological leverage," and "data analytics" may allow regulators to monitor e-finance activities effectively. Likewise, collaborative governance is crucial for effective regulation. Finally, the regulators in GCC markets are trying to develop a financial framework for e-finance that signifies a strategic approach to couple with the economic benefits of digital financial services while reducing potential risks. We conclude that by integrating robust regulatory frameworks, dynamic supervision, and collaborative governance, regulators in GCC markets can create a balanced environment where e-finance can thrive safely and sustainably and hence, it will support ongoing innovation and economic growth in the GCC regions.

References

Abbasi, A., Sarker, S., & Chiang, R. H. (2016). Big data research in information systems: Toward an inclusive research agenda. *Journal of the Association for Information Systems, 17*(2), 3.

Akintoye, R., Ogunode, O., Ajayi, M., & Ambibola, A. J. (2022). Cyber security and financial innovation of selected deposit money banks in Nigeria. *Universal Journal of Accounting and Finance, 10*(3), 643–652.

Albahar, M., & Thanoon, M. (2022). Privacy regulations in the Middle East: Challenges & solutions. *International Transaction Journal of Engineering, Management, & Applied Sciences & Technologies, 13*(5), 01–11.

AlBenJasim, S., Dargahi, T., Takruri, H., & Al-Zaidi, R. (2023). Fintech cybersecurity challenges and regulations: Bahrain case study. *Journal of Computer Information Systems*, 1–17.

Al-Jabri, I., & Sohail, M. S. (2012). Mobile banking adoption: Application of diffusion of innovation theory. *Journal of Electronic Commerce Research, 13*(4), 379–391.

Al Marzouqi, A. H., Khan, M., & Hussain, M. (2020). Employee social sustainability: Prioritizing dimensions in the UAE's airlines industry. *Social Responsibility Journal, 16*(3), 349–367.

Alshamsi, A., Nor, M. Z. M., & Long, M. N. H. (2023). *Sharia laws and regulations that govern the residential financing at Ajman Bank in the UAE. Remittances Review, 8*(4).

Alshathri, S. A. (2022). *Online dispute resolution as a mechanism to enhance consumer trust in e-commerce: How can Saudi Arabian law be improved?* (Doctoral dissertation). Newcastle University.

Alshubiri, F., Jamil, S. A., & Elheddad, M. (2019). The impact of ICT on financial development: Empirical evidence from the Gulf cooperation council countries. *International Journal of Engineering Business Management, 11*, 1847979019870670.

Arner, D. W., Barberis, J. N., & Buckley, R. P. (2015). The evolution of fintech: A new post-crisis paradigm? *Georgetown Journal of International Law, 47*, 1271–1319.

Arner, D. W., Barberis, J., & Buckley, R. P. (2016). FinTech, Regtech, and the reconceptualization of financial regulation. *Northwestern Journal of International Law and Business, 37*(3), 371–413.

Belwal, R., Al Shibli, R., & Belwal, S. (2021). Consumer protection and electronic commerce in the Sultanate of Oman. *Journal of Information, Communication and Ethics in Society, 19*(1), 38–60.

Bholat, D., Hansen, S., Santos, P., & Schonhardt-Bailey, C. (2016). Text mining for Central Banks: Handbook. *Centre for central banking studies, Bank of England*, (33), 1–19.

Black, J. (2008). Constructing and contesting legitimacy and accountability in polycentric regulatory regimes. *Regulation & Governance, 2*(2), 137–164.

Broeders, D., & Prenio, J. (2018). *Innovative technology in financial supervision (suptech)—The experience of early users*. Financial stability institute insights on policy implementation, 9. Bank for International Settlements.

Burlacu, S., Ciobanu, G., Troaca, V. A., & Gombos, C. C. (2021). The digital finance–Opportunity of development in the new economy. In *Proceedings of the International Conference on Business Excellence 15*(1), 392–405.

Central Bank of Bahrain. (2023). *Bahrain Fintech regulatory sandbox*. Central Bank of Bahrain

Central Bank of the UAE. (2023). *Guidelines on fair treatment of customers.* Central Bank of the UAE

Central Bank of the United Arab Emirates. (2022). *Prudential Standards.* CBUAE.

DLA Piper. (2019). Data protection laws of the world: Bahrain. Retrieved from https://www.dlapiperdataprotection.com/index.html?t=law&c=BH

Ehrentraud, J., Ocampo, D. G., Garzoni, L., & Piccolo, M. (2020). *Policy responses to Fintech: A cross-country overview*. FSI Insights on Policy Implementation, No 23. Bank for International Settlements.

Everson, E. (2016). Privacy by design: Taking ctrl of big data. *Cleveland State Law Review, 65*, 27.

Farooq, A., & Moon, M. A. (2020). Service fairness, relationship quality and customer loyalty in the banking sector of Pakistan. *Pakistan Journal of Commerce and Social Sciences (PJCSS), 14*(2), 484–507.

Financial Action Task Force. (2021). *International standards on combating money laundering and the financing of terrorism & proliferation.* FATF.

Finck, M. (2018). *Blockchain regulation and governance in Europe*. Cambridge University Press.

GCC Financial Landscape. (2022). *The impact of digital transformation on GCC economies*. [example.com]

Goldstein, I., Jiang, W., & Karolyi, G. A. (2019). To Fintech and beyond. *The Review of Financial Studies, 32*(5), 1647–1661.

Gomber, P., Kauffman, R. J., Parker, C., & Weber, B. W. (2018). On the fintech revolution: Interpreting the forces of innovation, disruption, and transformation in financial services. *Journal of Management Information Systems, 35*(1), 220–265.

Jasur, A. (2023). *Cybersecurity and risk management in the financial sector. International Bulletin of Young Scientist, 1*(1).

Jenik, I., & Lauer, K. (2017). *Regulatory sandboxes and financial inclusion*. CGAP Working Paper.

Khan, H. H., Khan, S., & Ghafoor, A. (2023). Fintech adoption, the regulatory environment and bank stability: An empirical investigation from GCC economies. *Borsa Istanbul Review, 23*(6), 1263–1281.

Levi, M. (2017). Assessing the trends, scale and nature of economic cybercrimes: Overview and Issues. In cybercrimes, cybercriminals and their policing, in crime, law and social change. *Crime, Law and Social Change, 67*, 3–20.

McWaters, R. J., Galaski, R., & Chatterjee, S. (2016). *The future of financial infrastructure: An ambitious look at how blockchain can reshape financial services*. In *World Economic Forum* (Vol. 49, pp. 368–376).

Melovic, B., Jocović, M., Dabić, M., Vulić, T. B., & Dudic, B. (2020). The impact of digital transformation and digital marketing on the brand promotion, positioning and electronic business in Montenegro. *Technology in Society, 63*, 101425.

Mızrak, F. (2023). Integrating cybersecurity risk management into strategic management: A comprehensive literature review. *Research Journal of Business and Management, 10*(3), 98–108.

Arab News. (2023). *The impact of e-finance on economic growth in the GCC*.

Gulf News. (2023). *Digital transformation in the GCC: E-Finance Leads the Way*.

Pan, L., & Mishra, V. (2018). Stock market development and economic growth: Empirical evidence from China. *Economic Modelling, 68*, 661–673.

Parate, S., Josyula, H. P., & Reddi, L. T. (2023). Digital identity verification: Transforming KYC processes in banking through advanced technology and enhanced security measures. *International Research Journal of Modernization in Engineering Technology and Science, 5*(9), 128–137.

Philippon, T. (2016). *The FinTech opportunity* (NBER Working Paper No. 22476). National Bureau of Economic Research.

Popovska-Kamnar, N. (2014). The use of electronic money and its impact on monetary policy. *Journal of Contemporary Economic and Business Issues, 1*(2), 79–92.

Ramady, M. A. (2015). Effective regulatory regimes: A comparative analysis of GCC financial regulators. *Journal of Financial Regulation and Compliance, 23*(1), 2–17.

Reurink, A. (2019). *Financial fraud: A literature review. Contemporary topics in finance: A collection of literature surveys*, 79–115.

Saudi Arabian Monetary Authority. (2022). *Regulations on electronic payments and bill presentment*. SAMA.

Telecommunications Regulatory Authority, UAE. (2021). *Cybersecurity guidelines for financial institutions*. TRA UAE.

Thakor, A. V. (2020). Fintech and banking: What do we know? *Journal of Financial Intermediation, 41*, 100833.

Khaleej Times. (2023). *Technological advancements and digital transformation in the GCC financial sector.*

Zalan, T., & Toufaily, E. (2017). The promise of fintech in emerging markets: Not as disruptive. *Contemporary Economics, 11*(4), 415–430.

Zavolokina, L., Dolata, M., & Schwabe, G. (2017). The FinTech phenomenon: Antecedents of financial innovation perceived by the popular press. *Financial Innovation, 3*(1), 1–16.

Zetzsche, D. A., Buckley, R. P., Barberis, J. N., & Arner, D. W. (2017). Regulating a revolution: From regulatory sandboxes to smart regulation. *Fordham Journal of Corporate & Financial Law, 23*(1), 31–103.

Fintech Adoption

FinTech Adoption Literature: Current State and Future Directions

Dharen Kumar Pandey

1 Introduction

Financial Technology (FinTech) has initiated a transformative wave in financial services, reshaping traditional banking, investment, and payment systems (Abad-Segura et al., 2020; Javaid et al., 2022; Sangwan et al., 2019). This amalgamation of finance and technology has streamlined processes and introduced innovative solutions, challenging conventional practices and offering unparalleled convenience to consumers and businesses alike (Chen, 2018; Li & Xu, 2021; Qin & Hao, 2023). As FinTech continues to burgeon, understanding the dynamics of its adoption becomes imperative, prompting researchers to delve into its multifaceted dimensions.

This paper embarks on a comprehensive exploration of the literature surrounding FinTech adoption, aiming to delineate its current state while shedding light on future trajectories. The landscape of FinTech adoption is characterized by a complex interplay of factors encompassing technological advancements, regulatory frameworks, consumer behavior, and institutional dynamics. By scrutinizing existing research, this paper

D. K. Pandey (✉)
Indian Institute of Management Sambalpur, Sambalpur, Odisha, India
e-mail: dharenp@gmail.com

© The Author(s), under exclusive license to Springer Nature Singapore Pte Ltd. 2025

A. S. et al. (eds.), *Trends and Challenges of Electronic Finance*,
https://doi.org/10.1007/978-981-96-3304-3_11

endeavors to discern patterns, identify gaps, and propose avenues for future inquiry, thereby contributing to the evolving discourse on FinTech adoption.

The inception of FinTech marks a paradigm shift in the financial services sector, challenging conventional norms and fostering innovation (Ali et al., 2020). Historically, financial transactions were predominantly conducted through traditional banking channels, characterized by brick-and-mortar branches and cumbersome processes. However, digital technologies have revolutionized this landscape, offering alternative avenues for accessing financial services. From peer-to-peer lending platforms to robo-advisors, FinTech solutions have democratized finance, empowering individuals and businesses to manage their finances with unprecedented ease and efficiency (Anshari et al., 2022; Belanche et al., 2019; Rabbani et al., 2022).

The adoption of FinTech is influenced by technological, regulatory, socio-economic, and psychological dimensions (Belanche et al., 2019; Chan et al., 2022; Hasan et al., 2021; Singh et al., 2020). At the forefront, technological advancements play a pivotal role in shaping the adoption landscape (Gomber et al., 2018; Gupta et al., 2022). Innovations like blockchain, artificial intelligence, and big data analytics underpin various FinTech applications, offering enhanced security, efficiency, and personalization (Awotunde et al., 2021; Hosen et al., 2023). Concurrently, regulatory frameworks 1wield significant influence, as they dictate the permissible scope of FinTech operations and safeguard consumer interests (Murinde et al., 2022; Ng & Kwok, 2017). The interplay between technological innovation and regulatory compliance forms the cornerstone of FinTech adoption dynamics, delineating the boundaries within which FinTech firms operate and consumers engage (Gao & McDonald, 2022; Han et al., 2022; Kazan et al., 2018).

Moreover, socio-economic factors and consumer behavior patterns also profoundly impact FinTech adoption (Daragmeh et al., 2021; Kraiwanit et al., 2024). Demographic variables such as age, income, and education level influence individuals' propensity to adopt FinTech solutions, with younger, tech-savvy cohorts exhibiting higher adoption rates (Jain & Raman, 2022; Jain et al., 2023; Nayak Kini & Basri, 2022; Yi et al., 2023). Additionally, consumer attitudes toward risk, trust, and privacy shape their willingness to embrace FinTech innovations (Ali et al., 2021; Gupta et al., 2023; Stewart & Jürjens, 2018). Understanding these socio-economic dynamics is imperative for elucidating the nuances of FinTech adoption and devising targeted strategies to enhance uptake.

Despite the myriad benefits offered by FinTech, its widespread adoption is not devoid of challenges. Chief among these is the issue of digital divide, wherein certain demographic groups face barriers to accessing and utilizing FinTech services due to factors such as lack of internet connectivity, digital literacy, or financial exclusion (Friedline et al., 2020; Morgan, 2021; Odei-Appiah et al., 2022). Bridging this divide is essential for ensuring equitable access to financial services and harnessing the full potential of FinTech to foster inclusive growth.

Furthermore, concerns regarding data privacy, cybersecurity, and regulatory compliance loom large in the FinTech landscape (Anagnostopoulos, 2018; Lim et al., 2019; Ng & Kwok, 2017; Stewart & Jürjens, 2018). As FinTech firms amass vast amounts of sensitive consumer data, ensuring robust data protection mechanisms and compliance with evolving regulatory standards becomes paramount. Failure to address these concerns may engender distrust among consumers and stifle FinTech adoption, underscoring the need for proactive measures to mitigate risks and bolster consumer confidence.

Amidst these challenges, however, lie abundant opportunities for innovation and growth. FinTech promises to revolutionize financial inclusion by extending services to underserved populations, facilitating seamless cross-border transactions, and fostering greater transparency and accountability in financial systems (Cumming et al., 2023; Roszkowska, 2021; Xie & Zhu, 2022). Moreover, the convergence of FinTech with emerging technologies such as the Internet of Things (IoT) and distributed ledger technology (DLT) presents novel avenues for creating value and enhancing efficiency across diverse domains, from supply chain finance to healthcare payments.

Amid the burgeoning literature on FinTech adoption, synthesizing existing knowledge and discerning emerging trends can be daunting. Bibliometric analysis provides a systematic and rigorous approach to tackle this challenge by quantitatively analyzing scholarly publications, citations, and keywords (Boubaker et al., 2023; Donthu et al., 2021; Goodell et al., 2023; Khan et al., 2022). By mapping the intellectual landscape of FinTech adoption research, bibliometric analysis enables researchers to identify influential authors, seminal works, research hotspots, and emerging topics (Donthu et al., 2021). Moreover, it facilitates the identification of gaps in the literature, thereby guiding future research agendas and scholarly inquiry.

Against this backdrop, the primary objective of this paper is to conduct a comprehensive bibliometric analysis of the FinTech adoption literature, encompassing publications from academic journals, conference proceedings, and scholarly repositories. Specifically, the study aims to achieve the following objectives:

RO1. Identify the core themes, subdomains, and disciplinary perspectives within the FinTech adoption literature.
RO2. Determine the most-cited publications and prolific authors shaping the discourse on FinTech adoption.
RO3. Explore the interconnections between seminal works, research clusters, and intellectual lineages through citation analysis.
RO4. Detect emerging topics, research gaps, and novel avenues for future research in FinTech adoption.
RO5. Synthesize the findings to propose actionable insights and research directions for scholars, practitioners, and policymakers in FinTech adoption.

Through a comprehensive review of existing literature, this paper seeks to unravel the intricacies of FinTech adoption, delineating its current state and charting future directions for research. By fostering a deeper understanding of the factors influencing FinTech adoption, researchers and practitioners can harness the transformative potential of FinTech to drive positive change and foster inclusive prosperity.

2 Bibliographic Data and Tools

For the corpus, this study relies upon the Scopus database due to its comprehensiveness (Bartol et al., 2014; Pandey et al., 2024; Vieira & Gomes, 2009). The search string "(TITLE-ABS-KEY ("fintech" OR "financial technology") AND TITLE-ABS-KEY ("adoption"))" was applied to retrieve 921 documents. Further, automatic filters to apply subject restrictions have been used—"LIMIT-TO (SUBJAREA, "BUSI") OR LIMIT-TO (SUBJAREA, "ECON") OR LIMIT-TO (SUBJAREA, "SOCI"))," limiting the number of documents to 658. Following other bibliometric studies (Chen et al., 2023; Khan et al., 2022; Pandey, Hunjra et al., 2023a, 2023b; Pandey, Lucey, et al., 2023a, 2023b), I also restrict the document type, source type, and language using the search string

"(LIMIT-TO (DOCTYPE, "ar") OR LIMIT-TO (DOCTYPE, "re")) AND (LIMIT-TO (SRCTYPE, "j")) AND (LIMIT-TO (LANGUAGE, "English"))." Thus, 525 documents were retrieved for the analysis. Furthermore, the corpus was manually filtered by reading the title, abstract, and full text, which yielded 489 documents relevant to the theme.[1] The inclusion–exclusion process is visualized in Fig. 1.

A bibliometric analysis was used to achieve the objectives of the study. Initially, the data has been examined to yield descriptive statistics (using the Biblioshiny in R studio, vosViewer, and MS Excel) (Aria & Cuccurullo, 2017; van Eck & Waltman, 2017), including the publication and citation trends, top-productive and impactful documents, journals, authors, and affiliated nations. Thereafter, the science mapping of the corpus is done, including the keyword analysis, co-authorship analysis, and bibliographic coupling of authors, journals, affiliated countries, and documents. The bibliographic coupling of documents provides the intellectual connection between the documents to segregate the available literature into different focused thematic clusters. While Biblioshiny is used to generate the keyword cloud, vosViewer is used for the rest of the analysis. Additionally, Gephi improves the visualization of the networks generated by vosViewer (Bastian et al., 2009).

3 Descriptive Results

3.1 Year-wise Publication and Citation Trends

The completeness of the bibliographic metadata presented in Fig. 2 indicates that the corpus is fit for bibliometric analysis. A summary of the corpus is presented in Fig. 3, indicating that 489 documents are spread over 258 journals and 1375 authors. The annual publication growth is 21.49%, with an average citation of 15.12.

Table 1 and Fig. 4 present the publication and citation trends. From a single published document in 2000–187 in 2023 and 107 documents

[1] Title, abstract and full text reading filtered 36 documents. Additionally, 28 review papers have not been eliminated because on full text reading it is found that they talk about fintech adoption.

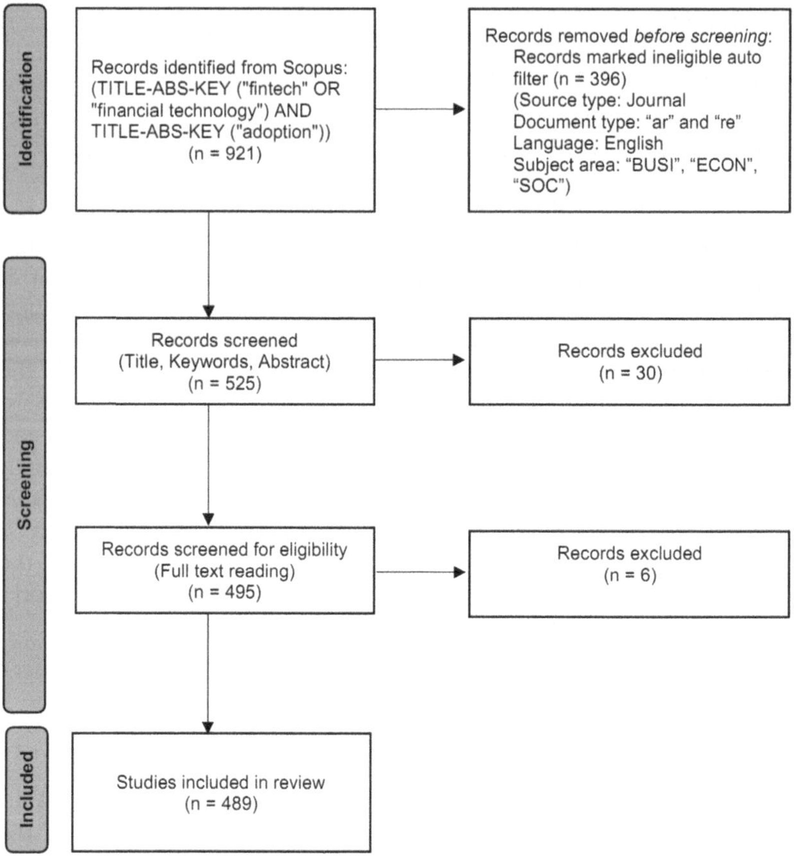

Fig. 1 Inclusion–exclusion process for the analysis

by May 10, 2024, the literature on FinTech adoption has significantly grown. Interestingly, 453 documents (92.64%) have been published from 2020 to May 10, 2024, accumulating 5435 citations (76.65%).

3.2 *Top-cited Documents*

Table 2 presents the list of impactful documents. These publications deal with different aspects of FinTech adoption. The top-most impactful

Metadata	Description	Missing Counts	Missing %	Status
AB	Abstract	0	0.00	Excellent
AU	Author	0	0.00	Excellent
DT	Document Type	0	0.00	Excellent
SO	Journal	0	0.00	Excellent
LA	Language	0	0.00	Excellent
PY	Publication Year	0	0.00	Excellent
TI	Title	0	0.00	Excellent
TC	Total Citation	0	0.00	Excellent
C1	Affiliation	1	0.20	Good
CR	Cited References	5	1.02	Good
DE	Keywords	11	2.25	Good
DI	DOI	24	4.91	Good
RP	Corresponding Author	69	14.11	Acceptable
ID	Keywords Plus	395	80.78	Critical
WC	Science Categories	489	100.00	Completely missing

Fig. 2 Completeness of bibliographic metadata. (Source: Biblioshiny)

Fig. 3 Summary of the sample documents. (Source: Biblioshiny)

article, Au and Kauffman (2008), having been cited 324 times, highlights the economic forces shaping the emergence of new technologies like mobile payments and emphasizes the need for strategic foresight among senior management in navigating issues related to standards, adoption, security, and business value. Belanche et al. (2019), with 313 citations, delve into the adoption dynamics of robo-advisors, a prominent application of artificial intelligence in financial services, underscoring

Table 1 Publication and citation trend

Year	*TP*	*TC*	*TCP*	*AC*
2000	1	71	1	71.00
2008	1	324	1	324.00
2014	1	0	0	0.00
2017	2	86	2	43.00
2018	9	335	9	37.22
2019	20	840	17	42.00
2020	33	1635	33	49.55
2021	48	1191	46	24.81
2022	80	1549	75	19.36
2023	187	936	137	5.01
2024 (May 10)	107	124	30	1.16
Total	489	7091	351	14.50
%	100		71.78	

Notes TP— Total publications, TC— Total citations, TCP— Total cited publications, AC— Average citations

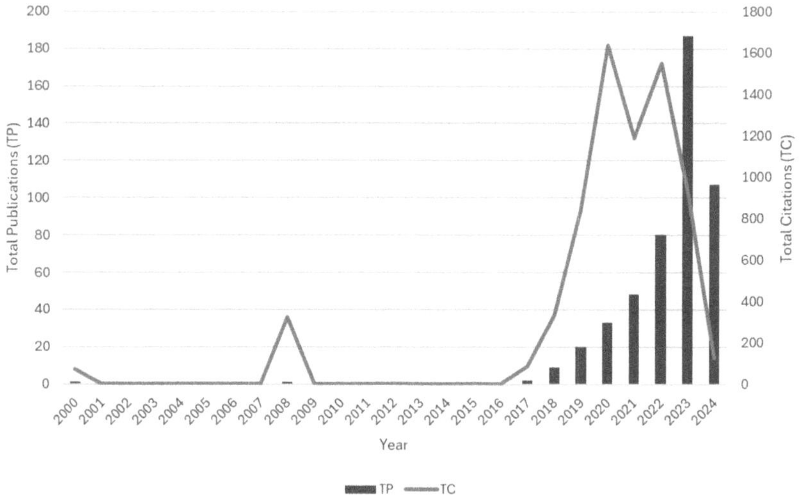

Fig. 4 Publication and citation trend

the significance of consumer attitudes, subjective norms, and sociodemographic factors in driving adoption. The third most impactful article, Chang et al. (2020), having cited 300 times, unravels critical challenges and ethical considerations surrounding blockchain adoption. Milian et al. (2019), the fourth top-cited article, with 239 citations, undertakes a systematic literature review to demystify the concept of FinTech and delineate key research themes. They highlight that the FinTech literature dealt with several key technologies driving adoption in the financial sector, including neural networks, artificial intelligence, the Internet of Things, and Bitcoin hardware evolution. Albayati et al. (2020), having cited 200 times, integrate the Technology Acceptance Model (TAM) with external variables and identify regulatory support and user experience as pivotal factors influencing trust and intention to adopt blockchain technologies.

3.3 Top-productive and Cited Journals

Table 3 presents the list of top-productive and top-cited journals, respectively. The "*Journal of Risk and Financial Management*"—7, "*Sustainability (Switzerland)*"— 17, "*Technological Forecasting and Social Change*"—14, "*International Journal of Bank Marketing*" — 13, and "*Resources Policy*"—11 are the top-five most productive journals. Concomitantly, "*Electronic Commerce Research and Applications*" — 730, "*Technological Forecasting and Social Change*"—609, "*International Journal of Bank Marketing*"—331, "*Journal of Open Innovation: Technology, Market, and Complexity*"—306, and "*Sustainability (Switzerland)*"—263 are the top-five most-cited journals. The results indicate that these journals' aims and scope align most with the FinTech research.

3.4 Top-productive and Cited Authors

Table 4 presents the list of top-prolific and top-cited authors, respectively. *Okoli, T.T.* (with 7 documents and 23 citations), *Alsmadi, A.A.* (with 5 documents and 23 citations), and *Setiawan, B.* (with 4 documents and 132 citations) are the top-three most prolific authors. The rest of the authors in Table 4 are equally prolific, with three documents each. Conversely, Belanche, D., Casaló, L.V., and Flavián, C. are the top-three most-cited authors sharing two common documents with 434 citations.

Table 2 Impactful publications

Authors	*Title*	*Source title*	*TC*
Au and Kauffman (2008)	The economics of mobile payments: Understanding stakeholder issues for an emerging financial technology application	Electronic commerce research and applications	324
Belanche et al. (2019)	Artificial Intelligence in FinTech: understanding robo-advisors adoption among customers	Industrial management and data systems	313
Chang et al. (2020)	How Blockchain can impact financial services—The overview, challenges and recommendations from expert interviewees	Technological forecasting and social change	300
Milian et al. (2019)	Fintechs: A literature review and research agenda	Electronic commerce research and applications	239
Albayati et al. (2020)	Accepting financial transactions using blockchain technology and cryptocurrency: A customer perspective approach	Technology in society	200
Akpan et al. (2022)	Small business awareness and adoption of state-of-the-art technologies in emerging and developing markets, and lessons from the COVID-19 pandemic	Journal of small business and entrepreneurship	161
Garg et al. (2021)	Measuring the perceived benefits of implementing blockchain technology in the banking sector	Technological forecasting and social change	153
Jünger and Mietzner (2020)	Banking goes digital: The adoption of FinTech services by German households	Finance research letters	149
Stewart and Jürjens (2018)	Data security and consumer trust in FinTech innovation in Germany	Information and computer security	134

(continued)

Table 2 (continued)

Authors	*Title*	*Source title*	*TC*
Pizzi et al. (2021)	Fintech and SMEs sustainable business models: Reflections and considerations for a circular economy	Journal of cleaner production	133
Singh et al. (2020)	What drives FinTech adoption? A multi-method evaluation using an adapted technology acceptance model	Management decision	133

Notes TC–Total citations

3.5 *Top-productive and Cited Affiliated Countries*

Table 5 presents the list of top-productive and top-cited affiliated countries, respectively. "*India*" (with 73 documents having cited 818 times), "*China*" (with 59 documents having cited 899 times), "*Malaysia*" (with 57 documents having cited 605 times), the "*United States*" (with 54 documents having 1342 times), and "*Indonesia*" (with 40 documents having cited 457 times) are the top-productive affiliated nations. The results indicate growing interest in FinTech adoption research in developing nations (Fahlevi et al., 2024; Murinde et al., 2022; Pandey et al., 2024; Persaud & Thaffe, 2023). At the same time, the "*United States,*" the "*United Kingdom*" (with 39 documents and 1201 citations), "*China,*" "*India,*" and "*France*" (with 14 documents and 618 citations) are the top-cited affiliated nations.

4 Network Analysis

4.1 *Keyword Co-occurrence Network*

Figure 5 presents the keyword co-occurrence network of keywords occurring at least 10 times. From a total of 1430 keywords, 28 met the threshold of 10 occurrences. The keywords "*FinTech*"—235, "*Financial Technology*"—57, "*Blockchain*"—39, "*Financial Inclusion*"—38, "*Trust*"—31, "*Technology Adoption*"—29, "*Technology Acceptance Model*"— 28, "*FinTech Adoption*"—27, "*UTAUT*"—22, and "*Artificial Intelligence*"—19 are the most prominent in terms of occurrence. The

Table 3 Top-productive journals

(a) Top-productive journals

Source title	*TLS*	*TP*	*TC*	*AC*	*PGRK*
Journal of risk and financial management	754	17	128	7.53	0.030515
Sustainability (Switzerland)	1106	17	263	15.47	0.086342
Technological forecasting and social change	843	14	609	43.50	0.123023
International journal of bank marketing	1183	13	331	25.46	0.019919
Resources policy	162	11	123	11.18	0.062473
Journal of open innovation: technology, market, and complexity	734	10	306	30.60	0.026353
Electronic commerce research and applications	370	6	730	121.67	0.014615
Finance research letters	168	6	175	29.17	0.021036
Cogent business and management	462	5	54	10.80	0.014046
Qualitative research in financial markets	238	5	123	24.60	0.039016
Research in international business and finance	466	5	85	17.00	0.053339

(b) Top-cited journals

Source title	TLS	TP	TC	AC	PGRK
Electronic commerce research and applications	370	6	730	121.67	0.014615
Technological forecasting and social change	843	14	609	43.50	0.123023
International journal of bank marketing	1183	13	331	25.46	0.019919
Journal of open innovation: technology, market, and complexity	734	10	306	30.60	0.026353
Sustainability (Switzerland)	1106	17	263	15.47	0.086342
Technology in society	134	2	213	106.50	0.221203
Finance research letters	168	6	175	29.17	0.021036
Journal of cleaner production	136	2	147	73.50	0.022425
Information and computer security	349	2	143	71.50	0.01719
Management decision	246	2	133	66.50	0.035952

Notes: TLS—Total link strength, TP—Total publications, TC—Total citations, AC—Average citations, PGRK—PageRank

Table 4 Top prolific authors

(a) Top prolific authors

Authors	*TLS*	*TP*	*TC*	*AC*	*PGRK*
Okoli, T.T	377	7	23	3.29	0.013728
Alsmadi, A.A	620	5	23	4.60	0.008407
Setiawan, B	584	4	132	33.00	0.025405
Al-Okaily, M	541	3	34	11.33	0.006537
Bakri, M.H	284	3	31	10.33	0.006732
Bin-Nashwan, S.A	316	3	31	10.33	0.007221
Nathan, R.J	506	3	131	43.67	0.013213
Okello Candiya Bongomin, G	189	3	60	20.00	0.0142
Sibindi, A.B	99	3	13	4.33	0.029539
Tewari, D.D	278	3	9	3.00	0.044042
Zhang, X	35	3	64	21.33	0.048962

(b) Top-cited authors

Authors	TLS	TP	TC	AC	PGRK
Belanche, D	735	2	434	217.00	0.007059
Casaló, L.V	735	2	434	217.00	0.007426
Flavián, C	735	2	434	217.00	0.008605
Setiawan, B	584	4	132	33.00	0.025405
Nathan, R.J	506	3	131	43.67	0.013213
Faccia, A	7	2	110	55.00	0.006398
Nugraha, D.P	433	2	103	51.50	0.014773
Afzal, A	230	2	102	51.00	0.005968
Huang, W	209	2	95	47.50	0.010126
Zhang, X	35	3	64	21.33	0.048962

Notes: TLS—Total link strength, TP—Total publications, TC—Total citations, AC—Average citations, PGRK—PageRank

results highlight that the extant FinTech adoption research has widely employed the "*Technology Acceptance Model*" and the "*Unified Theory of Acceptance and Use of Technology.*" The keyword cloud in Fig. 6 visualizes the prominent themes in FinTech adoption research.

4.2 *Authors' Collaboration Network*

Of 1375 authors, 28 met the threshold of at least 2 documents and 25 citations. Figure 7 presents the co-authorship network of authors in the FinTech adoption research of the 28 authors, only three are

Table 5 Top-productive affiliated nations

(a) Top-productive affiliated nations

Country	*TLS*	*TP*	*TC*	*AC*	*PGRK*
India	20384	73	818	11.21	0.01224
China	12832	59	899	15.24	0.00866
Malaysia	19115	57	605	10.61	0.014587
United States	9576	54	1342	24.85	0.104117
Indonesia	9932	40	457	11.43	0.011597
United Kingdom	8723	39	1201	30.79	0.073817
South Africa	3067	23	154	6.70	0.022168
Jordan	7291	22	222	10.09	0.012452
Saudi Arabia	5780	21	117	5.57	0.019432
United Arab Emirates	5887	19	210	11.05	0.057528

(b) Top-cited affiliated nations

Country	*TLS*	*TP*	*TC*	*AC*	*PGRK*
United States	9576	54	1342	24.85	0.104117
United Kingdom	8723	39	1201	30.79	0.073817
China	12,832	59	899	15.24	0.00866
India	20,384	73	818	11.21	0.01224
France	3873	14	618	44.14	0.009604
Spain	6127	17	608	35.76	0.025909
Malaysia	19,115	57	605	10.61	0.014587
Germany	2745	13	534	41.08	0.009868
South Korea	5541	13	487	37.46	0.02388
Indonesia	9932	40	457	11.43	0.011597

Notes: TLS—Total link strength, TP—Total publications, TC—Total citations, AC—Average citations, PGRK—PageRank

connected: *Umar, M., Afzal, A.,* and *Hasnaoui, A.* The rest 25 do not form any co-authorship cluster, indicating the authors are not connected directly. Although no direct co-authorship connection exists, they may be connected intellectually. The intellectual connection is analyzed through the bibliographic coupling of authors, wherein a connection is established if two authors cite a third author in their documents (Donthu et al., 2021; Lal et al., 2022). In simple words, the intellectual connection is established through the common references used. Figure 8 presents the bibliographic coupling network of authors. *Xiao, S., Zhang, X., Tewari,*

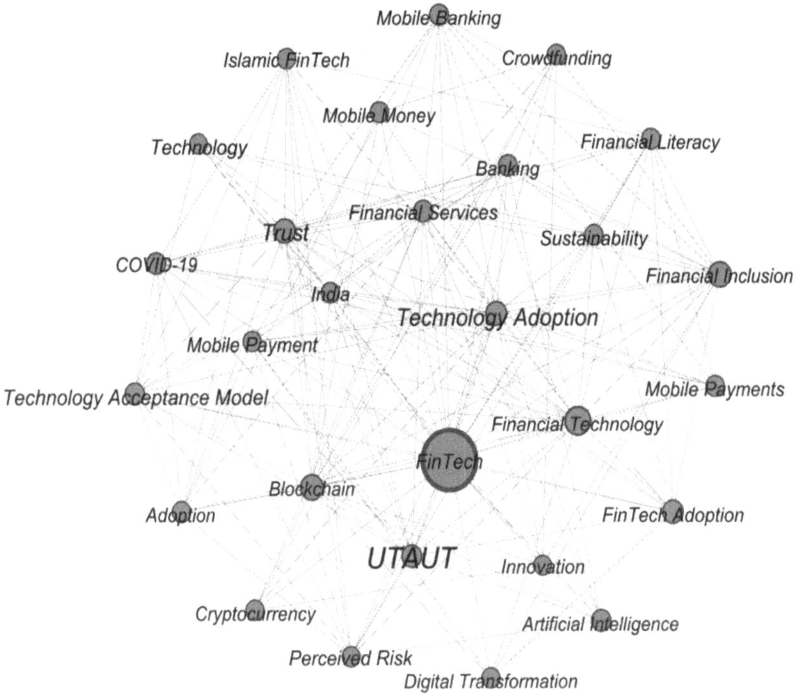

Fig. 5 Keyword co-occurrence network—Total keywords 1430, 28 met threshold of 10 occurrences. (Source: VOSviewer; Visualization: Gephi)

D.D., *Solarz, M.*, and *Umar, M.* are authors with high PageRanks,[2] indicating that these authors are highly co-cited.

4.3 Bibliographic Coupling of Journals

Of 258 journals, 25 met the threshold of at least two documents and 50 citations. Figure 9 presents the bibliographic coupling of the publication outlets. "*International Journal of Bank Marketing*" —1183, "*Sustainability (Switzerland)*" — 1106, "*Technological Forecasting and*

[2] PageRank reflects that an author is cited in highly cited publications and measures the authors' overall status in the domain (Fiala et al., 2015; Yan & Ding, 2011).

Fig. 6 Word cloud of top-50 author keywords. (Source: Biblioshiny)

Social Change" — 843, "*Journal of Risk and Financial Management*" – 754, and "*Journal of Open Innovation: Technology, Market, and Complexity*" —734 are the journals with highest total link strength, indicating that documents in these journals cited common references.

4.4 Bibliographic Coupling of Affiliated Countries

The bibliographic coupling of affiliated countries reveals how these nations are intellectually connected. Of 82 countries, 38 met the threshold of at least two documents and 50 citations. Figure 10 presents the intellectual network of the authors' affiliated countries. "*India*" —20,384, "*Malaysia*" — 19,115, "*China*" — 12,832, "*Indonesia*" — 9932, the "*United States*" — 9576, and the "*United Kingdom*" — 8723 have strong connections in the extant literature. The results indicate that, in FinTech adoption research, developing nations are strongly connected owing to the pace of technology adoption in these countries.

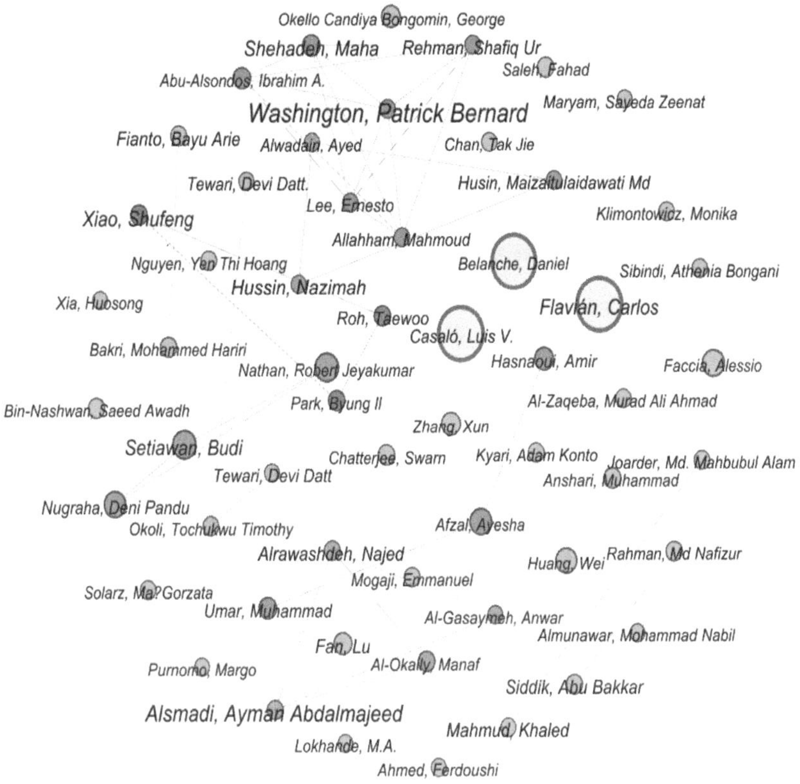

Fig. 7 Co-authorship network—28 authors met threshold of 2 documents and 25 citations. (Source: VOSviewer; Visualization: Gephi)

5 Thematic Clusters

When two documents cite a third document, the intellectual similarity between these two documents is exposed (Donthu et al., 2021). In the given corpus, 40 documents met the threshold of 50 citations, but only 37 are connected intellectually. Figure 11 presents the network of these 37 highly cited documents, segregated across four clusters represented by different colors. Table 6 presents the top-cited documents from each cluster. The content analysis of these documents shows the thematic alignments and future research directions.

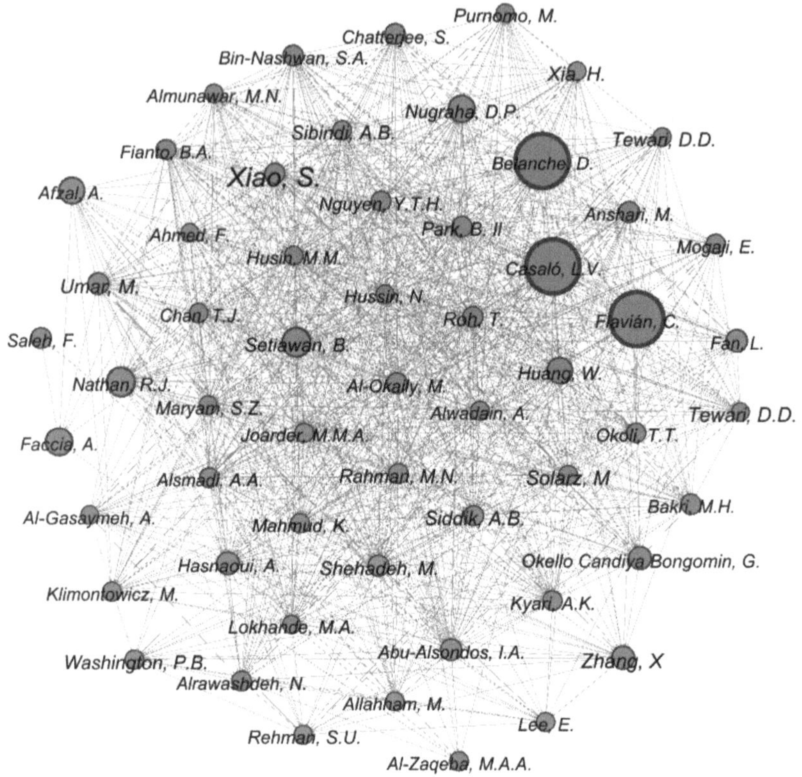

Fig. 8 Bibliographic coupling of authors—28 met threshold of 2 doc and 25 citations. (Source: VOSviewer; Visualization: Gephi)

5.1 *Cluster 1. (Purple Color) Blockchain, FinTech, and Sustainability*

Cluster 1 contains 12 papers focusing on "*FinTech*" and "*Blockchain.*" The most-cited paper in this cluster, Chang et al. (2020), discusses challenges, ethical issues, and motivations for banks to adopt Blockchain, based on interviews with sixteen experts and proposes recommendations to overcome adoption issues, contributing to understanding Blockchain in entrepreneurial finance. Garg et al. (2021) assess the perceived business benefits of Blockchain implementation in banking, focusing on security, values, and standards. Pizzi et al. (2021) focus on the intersection of

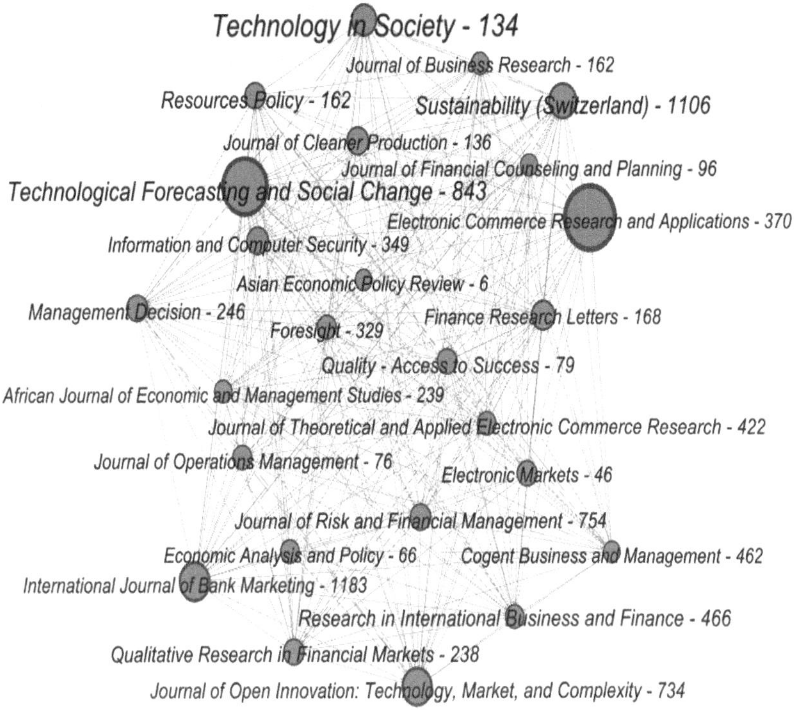

Fig. 9 Bibliographic coupling of journals—25 journals met threshold of 2 documents and 50 citations. (Source: VOSviewer; Visualization: Gephi)

FinTech, Industry 4.0, and sustainable business models, analyzing case studies to demonstrate how FinTech can facilitate SMEs' transition to sustainable business models, particularly in integrating circular economy practices. Mosteanu and Faccia (2020) explore how technologies benefit finance, accounting, and auditing by reducing errors, fraud, and costs while improving reliability in financial reporting, emphasizing the importance of digital transformation and the role of AI in creating a safer business environment. Soni et al. (2022) focus on improving SME efficiency through supply chain finance (SCF) and FinTech, highlighting the role of Industry 4.0 technologies in enhancing SCF, leading to sustainable SCF. The papers in this cluster collectively contribute to understanding the intersection of technology, finance, and sustainability, offering insights

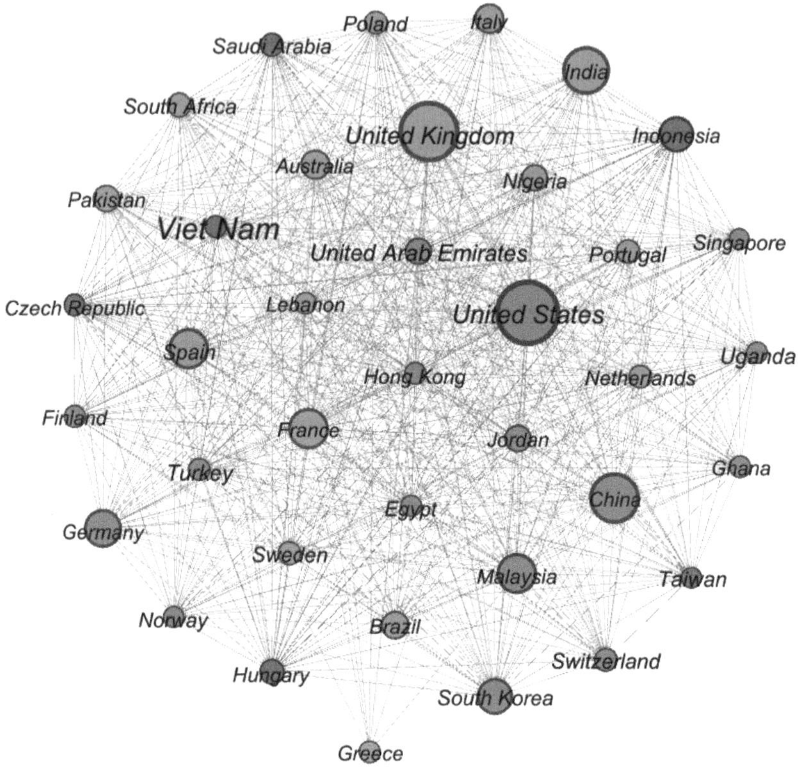

Fig. 10 Bibliographic coupling of affiliated nations- 38 countries met threshold of 2 documents and 50 citations. (Source: VOSviewer; Visualization: Gephi)

into the opportunities and challenges presented by emerging technologies like Blockchain and FinTech.

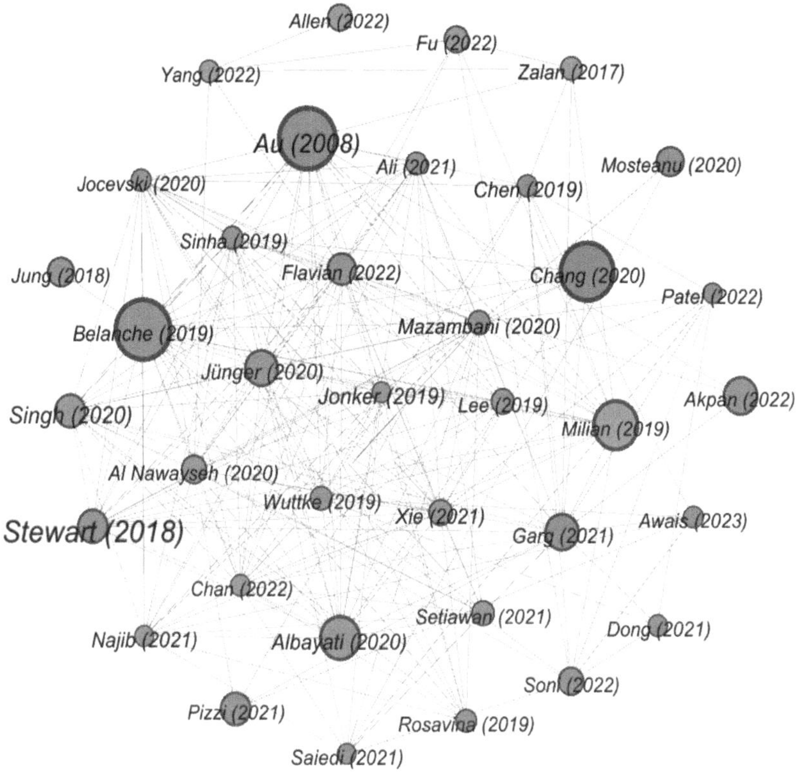

Fig. 11 Bibliographic coupling of documents—40 documents met threshold of 50 citations—37 connected. (Source: VOSviewer; Visualization: Gephi) (Cluster 1: Purple, Cluster 2: Green, Cluster 3: Orange, Cluster 4: Blue)

5.2 *Cluster 2. (Green Color) FinTech Adoption: Insights into Robo-Advisors, Blockchain, and AI Services*

This cluster contains 11 documents focusing on various aspects of FinTech, particularly the adoption and usability of innovative technologies such as robo-advisors and blockchain. The top-cited document in this cluster, Belanche et al. (2019) explore the adoption of robo-advisors

Table 6 Bibliographic coupling based thematic clusters

Authors	Title	Source title	TC	AC
Cluster 1. FinTech adoption in financial services, and SMEs				
Chang et al. (2020)	How Blockchain can impact financial services—The overview, challenges and recommendations from expert interviewees	Technological forecasting and social change	300	75.00
Garg et al. (2021)	Measuring the perceived benefits of implementing blockchain technology in the banking sector	Technological forecasting and social change	153	51.00
Pizzi et al. (2021)	Fintech and SMEs sustainable business models: Reflections and considerations for a circular economy	Journal of cleaner production	133	44.33
Mosteanu and Faccia (2020)	Digital systems and new challenges of financial management—fintech, XBRL, blockchain and cryptocurrencies	Quality—access to success	109	27.25
Soni et al. (2022)	A decision-making framework for Industry 4.0 technology implementation: The case of FinTech and sustainable supply chain finance for SMEs	Technological forecasting and social change	96	48.00
Cluster 2. FinTech adoption and artificial intelligence in services				
Belanche et al. (2019)	Artificial intelligence in FinTech: understanding robo-advisors adoption among customers	Industrial management and data systems	313	62.60
Albayati et al. (2020)	Accepting financial transactions using blockchain technology and cryptocurrency: A customer perspective approach	Technology in society	200	50.00
Singh et al. (2020)	What drives FinTech adoption? A multi-method evaluation using an adapted technology acceptance model	Management decision	133	33.25

(continued)

Table 6 (continued)

Cluster 1. FinTech adoption in financial services, and SMEs				
Authors	*Title*	*Source title*	*TC*	*AC*
Flavián et al. (2022)	Intention to use analytical artificial intelligence (AI) in services—the effect of technology readiness and awareness	Journal of service management	121	60.50
Jung et al. (2018)	Designing a robo-advisor for risk-averse, low-budget consumers	Electronic markets	105	17.50
Cluster 3. FinTech adoption and user perceptions				
Authors	Title	Source title	TC	AC
Au and Kauffman (2008)	The economics of mobile payments: Understanding stakeholder issues for an emerging financial technology application	Electronic commerce research and applications	324	20.25
Akpan et al. (2022)	Small business awareness and adoption of state-of-the-art technologies in emerging and developing markets, and lessons from the COVID-19 pandemic	Journal of small business and entrepreneurship	161	80.50
Jünger and Mietzner (2020)	Banking goes digital: The adoption of FinTech services by German households	Finance research letters	149	37.25
Stewart and Jürjens (2018)	Data security and consumer trust in FinTech innovation in Germany	Information and computer security	134	22.33
Lee et al. (2019)	A study on the reciprocal relationship between user perception and retailer perception on platform-based mobile payment service	Journal of retailing and consumer services	81	16.20

(continued)

Table 6 (continued)

Cluster 1. FinTech adoption in financial services, and SMEs				
Authors	*Title*	*Source title*	*TC*	*AC*
Cluster 4. Fintech Horizons: Exploring Innovation, Adoption, and Impact				
Milian et al. (2019)	Fintechs: A literature review and research agenda	Electronic commerce research and applications	239	47.80
Allen et al. (2022)	Fintech, Cryptocurrencies, and CBDC: Financial Structural Transformation in China	Journal of international money and finance	91	45.50
Fu and Mishra (2022)	Fintech in the time of COVID – 19: Technological adoption during crises	Journal of financial intermediation	88	44.00
Zalan and Toufaily (2017)	The promise of fintech in emerging markets: Not as disruptive	Contemporary economics	68	9.71
Yang and Zhang (2022)	FinTech adoption and financial inclusion: Evidence from household consumption in China	Journal of banking and finance	60	30.00

Notes TC—Total citations, AC—Average citations

among potential customers. The authors suggest that attitudes, subjective norms, and perceived usefulness influence adoption, with marketing tactics needing to consider customers' familiarity with robots. Albayati et al. (2020) investigate the behavioral elements influencing customers' intentions toward blockchain-based transactions, using the TAM with additional variables such as trust, regulatory support, and experience. Regulatory support and experience are crucial factors enhancing customer trust and promoting acceptance of blockchain technology. Singh et al. (2020) examine FinTech adoption from a technology acceptance perspective, highlighting perceived usefulness and social influence as key determinants of behavior intention, with age significantly affecting perceptions of security among older users. Flavián et al. (2022) examine how customers' technology readiness and service awareness impact their intention to use AI investment services and reveal that technological optimism increases intention to use robo-advisors, while feelings of technological discomfort surprisingly positively influence adoption. Jung et al. (2018) address the slow adoption of robo-advisory despite its potential advantages and emphasize the importance of usability in customer willingness to interact with decision support tools. The papers in this cluster contribute to understanding the adoption and usability of FinTech innovations, providing insights for both researchers and practitioners in the finance industry.

5.3 *Cluster 3. (Orange Color) Economic, Technological, and Social Perspectives in FinTech Adoption*

With nine papers, this cluster is the third biggest cluster, covering various aspects of financial technology (FinTech) adoption and its implications. The top-cited document by Au and Kauffman (2008) highlights the importance of understanding the economic forces and stakeholders involved. They also propose an evaluative framework to guide senior management in dealing with the economic aspects of mobile payments. Akpan et al. (2022) focus on the challenges hindering the adoption of digital technologies, particularly among SMEs in emerging markets and developing economies, emphasizing the need for SMEs to adopt advanced technologies to improve operations and competitiveness, especially in light of challenges such as the COVID-19 pandemic. Jünger and Mietzner (2020) analyze the adoption of FinTech services by households in Germany, identifying trust, financial literacy, and transparency as key factors influencing adoption. They find that households with low trust, good financial education, and a preference for transparency are more likely to adopt FinTech. Stewart and Jürjens (2018) highlight the importance of customer trust, data security, and user interface design in driving FinTech adoption in Germany. Lee et al. (2019) examine the factors influencing the adoption of financial technology from both consumer and retailer perspectives, proposing an integrated model considering the dynamics of a two-sided market. The papers in this cluster contribute to understanding the economic, technological, and social factors shaping the adoption of FinTech, with implications for businesses, consumers, and policymakers.

5.4 *Cluster 4. (Blue Color) Fintech Landscape: Definitions, Impacts, and Regulatory Considerations*

This is the smallest cluster with only five papers and covers various aspects of fintech, including its definition, impact on financial inclusion, regulatory considerations, and effects on household consumption and consumption inequality. The top-cited document, Milian et al. (2019), conducts a systematic literature review and highlights topics such as financial service innovations, regulation, and risks, with emerging themes including technology adoption, blockchain, and security. Allen et al. (2022) reviewed recent literature on fintech, cryptocurrencies, stablecoins, and central bank digital currencies (CBDCs), emphasizing the importance of effective regulation for cryptocurrency markets and the potential global impact of CBDCs in China. Fu and Mishra (2022) analyzed the effects of the COVID-19 pandemic on fintech adoption, finding a significant increase in finance app downloads during lockdowns. Zalan and Toufaily (2017) investigated how stakeholders in the Middle East and North Africa perceive fintech's disruptive potential and the strategies adopted by incumbents. They found that while the fintech sector is still nascent, it can potentially disrupt selected product and customer segments. Yang and Zhang (2022) provide micro-level evidence on how fintech adoption affects household consumption and consumption inequality and suggest that higher fintech adoption increases household consumption and reduces consumption inequality, highlighting fintech's role in enhancing financial inclusion. The papers in this cluster contribute to understanding fintech's definition, impact, regulatory considerations, and implications for various stakeholders.

6 Future Research Avenues

The existing literature on FinTech adoption provides valuable insights into consumer behavior, organizational dynamics, and socio-economic factors influencing the adoption and diffusion of financial technologies. However, several areas remain underexplored, offering avenues for future research to enrich our understanding of FinTech adoption and its implications. Drawing from the discussed papers, the following future research directions are suggested:

6.1 Cross-cultural and Regional Variations

While some studies focus on specific regions or countries (Allen et al., 2022; Jünger & Mietzner, 2020; Rosavina et al., 2019), there is a need for comparative research across different cultural and regional contexts to understand how socio-cultural factors influence FinTech adoption differently. Comparative studies could investigate adoption patterns, drivers, and barriers in both developed and emerging markets, providing insights into the role of cultural norms, regulatory environments, and socio-economic conditions.

6.2 Cryptocurrency Adoption

The adoption of cryptocurrencies, such as Bitcoin, remains a topic of interest (Gupta et al., 2023; Saiedi et al., 2021), especially in emerging markets. Future research could explore the determinants of cryptocurrency adoption among consumers and businesses, considering factors such as perceived benefits, risks, regulatory frameworks, and technological infrastructure. Additionally, longitudinal studies could track the evolution of cryptocurrency adoption over time and its impact on financial inclusion and economic development.

6.3 Supply Chain Finance (SCF) Adoption

SCF has emerged as a significant area of interest (Soni et al., 2022; Wuttke et al., 2019), particularly in understanding supplier adoption dynamics. Future research could delve deeper into the motivations and challenges faced by suppliers in adopting SCF solutions, considering both financial and non-financial factors. Moreover, comparative studies across industries and regions could shed light on the contextual factors shaping SCF adoption and its implications for supply chain resilience and performance.

6.4 Integration of FinTech and Sustainability

With growing concerns about environmental sustainability and social responsibility (Al-Okaily et al., 2021; Arner et al., 2020; Awais et al., 2023), there is a need to explore the role of FinTech in promoting sustainable economic development. Future research could investigate how FinTech innovations, such as peer-to-peer lending platforms and digital payment systems, contribute to sustainable finance, resource allocation, and inclusive growth. Moreover, studies examining the environmental impact of FinTech infrastructure and adopting green FinTech solutions could inform policy initiatives to promote sustainable financial practices.

6.5 *Open Banking Adoption*

Open banking presents new opportunities and challenges for financial institutions and consumers (Chan et al., 2022; Zachariadis & Ozcan, 2016). Future research could explore the determinants of consumer adoption of open banking services, considering factors such as perceived risk, trust, and financial literacy. Additionally, studies investigating the impact of open banking on competition, innovation, and consumer welfare could provide valuable insights for policymakers and industry stakeholders.

6.6 *Small and Medium Enterprises (SMEs) Adoption*

SMEs play a crucial role in driving economic growth and innovation, yet their adoption of FinTech remains understudied (Pizzi et al., 2021; Soni et al., 2022). Future research could examine the factors influencing SMEs' adoption of FinTech solutions, including access to financing, technological capabilities, and organizational readiness. Moreover, longitudinal studies tracking the adoption journey of SMEs and the impact of FinTech adoption on business performance could provide actionable insights for policymakers and business owners.

Future research in FinTech adoption should adopt a multidisciplinary approach, integrating insights from economics, finance, technology, and social sciences to address complex challenges and opportunities in the rapidly evolving FinTech landscape. By exploring underexplored areas and advancing theoretical frameworks, researchers can contribute to developing evidence-based strategies to promote inclusive, sustainable, and resilient financial systems.

7 Conclusions

This study embarked on a meticulous journey to unravel the multifaceted landscape of FinTech adoption through a rigorous bibliometric analysis bolstered by the comprehensive Scopus database and an array of analytical tools. By scrutinizing the corpus of 489 relevant documents, this research sought to provide nuanced insights into the trends, patterns, and dynamics shaping the discourse on FinTech adoption.

The descriptive results unveiled a compelling narrative of growth and evolution within the FinTech research domain. The exponential increase in publications, with an annual growth rate of 21.49%, underscores the burgeoning interest and significance of FinTech adoption in contemporary discourse. The comprehensive examination of publication and citation trends, top-cited documents, productive journals, authors, and affiliated nations unveiled the intricate fabric of the FinTech research landscape, delineating key players and knowledge dissemination channels.

This study elucidated the intricate web of intellectual connections among authors, journals, and countries, unraveling collaborative patterns and knowledge diffusion mechanisms within the FinTech research community through network analysis. The study provided a panoramic view of the interconnectedness and interdependence inherent in the FinTech research ecosystem, from keyword co-occurrence networks to authors' collaboration networks and bibliographic coupling of journals and countries.

Thematic clustering emerged as a powerful tool for discerning distinct research trajectories within the FinTech adoption domain. From blockchain sustainability to robo-advisors, economic perspectives, and regulatory implications, each thematic cluster offered unique insights into the complexities and nuances of FinTech adoption dynamics. This study laid the groundwork for deeper explorations into emerging trends, critical challenges, and future research directions by dissecting highly cited documents and delineating thematic clusters.

Looking ahead, the study identified several promising avenues for future research, each offering fertile ground for scholarly inquiry and practical application. Cross-cultural and regional variations, cryptocurrency adoption, supply chain finance, integration of FinTech and sustainability, open banking, and SME adoption represent a few of the rich veins waiting to be tapped by curious minds and innovative thinkers. By embracing interdisciplinary approaches and leveraging cutting-edge methodologies, researchers can continue to push the boundaries of knowledge in the FinTech landscape, ultimately shaping the future trajectory of financial innovation and inclusion.

This study is a testament to the transformative potential of FinTech adoption and the power of rigorous empirical analysis in unraveling its complexities. By shedding light on key trends, patterns, and future research directions, this research lays the groundwork for a deeper understanding of FinTech adoption dynamics and paves the way for evidence-based strategies to foster inclusive, sustainable, and resilient financial systems in the digital age.

References

Abad-Segura, E., González-Zamar, M. D., López-Meneses, E., & Vázquez-Cano, E. (2020). *Financial technology: review of trends, approaches and management*. Mathematics, *8*(6), 951. https://doi.org/10.3390/math8060951

Akpan, I. J., Udoh, E. A. P., & Adebisi, B. (2022). Small business awareness and adoption of state-of-the-art technologies in emerging and developing markets, and lessons from the COVID-19 pandemic. *Journal of Small Business & Entrepreneurship, 34*(2), 123–140. https://doi.org/10.1080/08276331.2020.1820185

Albayati, H., Kim, S. K., & Rho, J. J. (2020). Accepting financial transactions using blockchain technology and cryptocurrency: A customer perspective approach. *Technology in Society, 62*, 101320. https://doi.org/10.1016/j.techsoc.2020.101320

Ali, O., Ally, M., & Clutterbuck, & Dwivedi, Y. (2020). The state of play of blockchain technology in the financial services sector: A systematic literature review. *International Journal of Information Management, 54*, 102199. https://doi.org/10.1016/j.ijinfomgt.2020.102199

Ali, M., Raza, S. A., Khamis, B., Puah, C. H., & Amin, H. (2021). How perceived risk, benefit and trust determine user Fintech adoption: A new dimension for Islamic finance. *Foresight, 23*(4), 403–420. https://doi.org/10.1108/FS-09-2020-0095

Allen, F., Gu, X., & Jagtiani, J. (2022). Fintech, Cryptocurrencies, and CBDC: Financial structural transformation in China. *Journal of International Money and Finance, 124*, 102625. https://doi.org/10.1016/j.jimonfin.2022.102625

Al-Okaily, M., Al Natour, A. R., Shishan, F., Al-Dmour, A., Alghazzawi, R., & Alsharairi, M. (2021). Sustainable fintech innovation orientation: a moderated model. *Sustainability, 13*(24), 13591. https://doi.org/10.3390/su132413591

Anagnostopoulos, I. (2018). Fintech and regtech: Impact on regulators and banks. *Journal of Economics and Business, 100*, 7–25. https://doi.org/10.1016/j.jeconbus.2018.07.003

Anshari, M., Almunawar, M. N., & Masri, M. (2022). Digital twin: financial technology's next frontier of Robo-Advisor. *Journal of Risk and Financial Management, 15*(4), 163. https://doi.org/10.3390/jrfm15040163

Aria, M., & Cuccurullo, C. (2017). Bibliometrix : An R-tool for comprehensive science mapping analysis. *Journal of Informetrics, 11*(4), 959–975. https://doi.org/10.1016/j.joi.2017.08.007

Arner, D. W., Buckley, R. P., Zetzsche, D. A., & Veidt, R. (2020). Sustainability, FinTech and Financial Inclusion. *European Business Organization Law Review, 21*(1), 7–35. https://doi.org/10.1007/s40804-020-00183-y

Au, Y. A., & Kauffman, R. J. (2008). The economics of mobile payments: Understanding stakeholder issues for an emerging financial technology application. *Electronic Commerce Research and Applications, 7*(2), 141–164. https://doi.org/10.1016/j.elerap.2006.12.004

Awais, M., Afzal, A., Firdousi, S., & Hasnaoui, A. (2023). Is fintech the new path to sustainable resource utilization and economic development? *Resources Policy, 81*, 103309. https://doi.org/10.1016/j.resourpol.2023.103309

Awotunde, J. B., Adeniyi, E. A., Ogundokun, R. O., & Ayo, F. E. (2021). *Application of big data with fintech in financial services* (pp. 107–132). https://doi.org/10.1007/978-981-33-6137-9_3

Bartol, T., Budimir, G., Dekleva-Smrekar, D., Pusnik, M., & Juznic, P. (2014). Assessment of research fields in Scopus and Web of Science in the view of national research evaluation in Slovenia. *Scientometrics, 98*(2), 1491–1504. https://doi.org/10.1007/s11192-013-1148-8

Bastian, M., Heymann, S., & Jacomy, M. (2009). Gephi: An open source software for exploring and manipulating networks. *Proceedings of the International AAAI Conference on Web and Social Media, 3*(1), 361–362.

Belanche, D., Casaló, L. V., & Flavián, C. (2019). Artificial Intelligence in FinTech: Understanding robo-advisors adoption among customers. *Industrial Management & Data Systems, 119*(7), 1411–1430. https://doi.org/10.1108/IMDS-08-2018-0368

Boubaker, S., Goodell, J. W., Kumar, S., & Sureka, R. (2023). COVID-19 and finance scholarship: A systematic and bibliometric analysis. *International Review of Financial Analysis, 85*, 102458. https://doi.org/10.1016/j.irfa.2022.102458

Chan, R., Troshani, I., Rao Hill, S., & Hoffmann, A. (2022). Towards an understanding of consumers' FinTech adoption: The case of Open Banking. *International Journal of Bank Marketing, 40*(4), 886–917. https://doi.org/10.1108/IJBM-08-2021-0397

Chang, V., Baudier, P., Zhang, H., Xu, Q., Zhang, J., & Arami, M. (2020). How Blockchain can impact financial services—The overview, challenges and recommendations from expert interviewees. *Technological Forecasting and Social Change, 158*, 120166. https://doi.org/10.1016/j.techfore.2020.120166

Chen, K. (2018). Financial innovation and technology firms: A smart new world with machines. *International Symposia in Economic Theory and Econometrics, 25*, 279–292. https://doi.org/10.1108/S1571-038620180000025012

Chen, X.-Q., Ma, C.-Q., Ren, Y.-S., Lei, Y.-T., Huynh, N. Q. A., & Narayan, S. (2023). Explainable artificial intelligence in finance: A bibliometric review. *Finance Research Letters, 56*, 104145. https://doi.org/10.1016/j.frl.2023.104145

Cumming, D., Johan, S., & Reardon, R. (2023). Global fintech trends and their impact on international business: A review. *Multinational Business Review, 31*(3), 413–436. https://doi.org/10.1108/MBR-05-2023-0077

Daragmeh, A., Lentner, C., & Sági, J. (2021). FinTech payments in the era of COVID-19: Factors influencing behavioral intentions of "Generation X" in Hungary to use mobile payment. *Journal of Behavioral and Experimental Finance, 32*, 100574. https://doi.org/10.1016/j.jbef.2021.100574

Donthu, N., Kumar, S., Mukherjee, D., Pandey, N., & Lim, W. M. (2021). How to conduct a bibliometric analysis: An overview and guidelines. *Journal of Business Research, 133*, 285–296. https://doi.org/10.1016/j.jbusres.2021.04.070

Fahlevi, M., Asdullah, M. A., et al., (2024). *The influence of information and communication technology on trade in developing countries and partners*. Cogent Business & Management, *11*(1). https://doi.org/10.1080/23311975.2024.2320814

Fiala, D., Šubelj, L., Žitnik, S., & Bajec, M. (2015). Do PageRank-based author rankings outperform simple citation counts? *Journal of Informetrics, 9*(2), 334–348. https://doi.org/10.1016/j.joi.2015.02.008

Flavián, C., Pérez-Rueda, A., Belanche, D., & Casaló, L. V. (2022). Intention to use analytical artificial intelligence (AI) in services—The effect of technology readiness and awareness. *Journal of Service Management, 33*(2), 293–320. https://doi.org/10.1108/JOSM-10-2020-0378

Friedline, T., Naraharisetti, S., & Weaver, A. (2020). Digital redlining: poor rural communities' access to fintech and implications for financial inclusion. *Journal of Poverty, 24*(5–6), 517–541. https://doi.org/10.1080/10875549.2019.1695162

Fu, J., & Mishra, M. (2022). Fintech in the time of COVID−19: Technological adoption during crises. *Journal of Financial Intermediation, 50*, 100945. https://doi.org/10.1016/j.jfi.2021.100945

Gao, C., & McDonald, R. (2022). Shaping nascent industries: innovation strategy and regulatory uncertainty in personal genomics. *Administrative Science Quarterly, 67*(4), 915–967. https://doi.org/10.1177/00018392221112641

Garg, P., Gupta, B., Chauhan, A. K., Sivarajah, U., Gupta, S., & Modgil, S. (2021). Measuring the perceived benefits of implementing blockchain technology in the banking sector. *Technological Forecasting and Social Change, 163*, 120407. https://doi.org/10.1016/j.techfore.2020.120407

Gomber, P., Kauffman, R. J., Parker, C., & Weber, B. W. (2018). On the fintech revolution: interpreting the forces of innovation, disruption, and transformation in financial services. *Journal of Management Information Systems, 35*(1), 220–265. https://doi.org/10.1080/07421222.2018.1440766

Goodell, J. W., Oriani, M. E., Paltrinieri, A., & Patel, R. (2023). The importance of ABS 2 journals in finance scholarship: Evidence from a bibliometric case study. *Finance Research Letters, 55*, 103828. https://doi.org/10.1016/j.frl.2023.103828

Gupta, S., Ghardallou, W., Pandey, D. K., & Sahu, G. P. (2022). Artificial intelligence adoption in the insurance industry: Evidence using the technology–organization–environment framework. *Research in International Business and Finance, 63*, 101757. https://doi.org/10.1016/j.ribaf.2022.101757

Gupta, S., Pandey, D. K., El Ammari, A., & Sahu, G. P. (2023). Do perceived risks and benefits impact trust and willingness to adopt CBDCs? *Research in International Business and Finance, 66*, 101993. https://doi.org/10.1016/j.ribaf.2023.101993

Han, J., Zhou, H., Lowik, S., & de Weerd-Nederhof, P. (2022). Enhancing the understanding of ecosystems under innovation management context: Aggregating conceptual boundaries of ecosystems. *Industrial Marketing Management, 106*, 112–138. https://doi.org/10.1016/j.indmarman.2022.08.008

Hasan, R., Ashfaq, M., & Shao, L. (2021). *Evaluating drivers of fintech adoption in the Netherlands*. Global Business Review, 097215092110274. https://doi.org/10.1177/09721509211027402

Hosen, M., Thaker, H. M. T., Subramaniam, V., Eaw, H.-C., & Cham, T.-H. (2023). *Artificial Intelligence (AI), Blockchain, and Cryptocurrency in Finance: Current Scenario and Future Direction* (pp. 322–332). https://doi.org/10.1007/978-3-031-25274-7_26

Jain, N., Raman, T. V., & Bhardwaj, G. N. (2023). *Do Behavioural Biases Drive Adoption of Digital Banking Services? The Moderating Role of User Type. Global Business Review*. https://doi.org/10.1177/09721509231160865

Jain, N., & Raman, T. V. (2022). The interplay of perceived risk, perceive benefit and generation cohort in digital finance adoption. *EuroMed Journal of Business*. https://doi.org/10.1108/EMJB-09-2021-0132

Javaid, M., Haleem, A., Singh, R. P., Suman, R., & Khan, S. (2022). A review of Blockchain Technology applications for financial services. *BenchCouncil Transactions on Benchmarks, Standards and Evaluations, 2*(3), 100073. https://doi.org/10.1016/j.tbench.2022.100073

Jung, D., Dorner, V., Weinhardt, C., & Pusmaz, H. (2018). Designing a robo-advisor for risk-averse, low-budget consumers. *Electronic Markets, 28*(3), 367–380. https://doi.org/10.1007/s12525-017-0279-9

Jünger, M., & Mietzner, M. (2020). Banking goes digital: The adoption of FinTech services by German households. *Finance Research Letters, 34*, 101260. https://doi.org/10.1016/j.frl.2019.08.008

Kazan, E., Tan, C.-W., Lim, E. T. K., Sørensen, C., & Damsgaard, J. (2018). Disentangling digital platform competition: the case of UK mobile payment platforms. *Journal of Management Information Systems, 35*(1), 180–219. https://doi.org/10.1080/07421222.2018.1440772

Khan, A., Goodell, J. W., Hassan, M. K., & Paltrinieri, A. (2022). A bibliometric review of finance bibliometric papers. *Finance Research Letters, 47*, 102520. https://doi.org/10.1016/j.frl.2021.102520

Kraiwanit, T., Limna, P., & Wattanasin, P. (2024). *Digital Wallet Dynamics: Perspectives on Potential Worldcoin Adoption Factors in a Developing Country's FinTech Sector.* Journal of Open Innovation: Technology, Market, and Complexity, 100287. https://doi.org/10.1016/j.joitmc.2024.100287

Lal, M., Kumar, R. B., Kumar, A., Saud, H. S., & Rai, V. K. (2022). Corporate social responsibility, accounting, and auditing: A retrospective review. *International Journal of Accounting, Business and Finance, 1*(2), 47–74.

Lee, J., Ryu, M. H., & Lee, D. (2019). A study on the reciprocal relationship between user perception and retailer perception on platform-based mobile payment service. *Journal of Retailing and Consumer Services, 48*, 7–15. https://doi.org/10.1016/j.jretconser.2019.01.007

Li, B., & Xu, Z. (2021). Insights into financial technology (FinTech): A bibliometric and visual study. *Financial Innovation, 7*(1), 69. https://doi.org/10.1186/s40854-021-00285-7

Lim, S. H., Kim, D. J., Hur, Y., & Park, K. (2019). An empirical study of the impacts of perceived security and knowledge on continuous intention to use mobile fintech payment services. *International Journal of Human-Computer Interaction, 35*(10), 886–898. https://doi.org/10.1080/10447318.2018.1507132

Milian, E. Z., Spinola, M. de M., & Carvalho, M. M. de. (2019). *Fintechs: A literature review and research agenda.* Electronic Commerce Research and Applications, *34*, 100833. https://doi.org/10.1016/j.elerap.2019.100833

Morgan, P. J. (2021). *Fintech, financial literacy, and financial education.* In The Routledge handbook of financial literacy (pp. 239–258). Routledge. https://doi.org/10.4324/9781003025221-21

Mosteanu, N. R., & Faccia, A. (2020). Digital systems and new challenges of financial management–FinTech, XBRL, blockchain and cryptocurrencies. *Quality-Access to Success, 21*(174), 159–166.

Murinde, V., Rizopoulos, E., & Zachariadis, M. (2022). The impact of the FinTech revolution on the future of banking: Opportunities and risks. *International Review of Financial Analysis, 81*, 102103. https://doi.org/10.1016/j.irfa.2022.102103

Nayak Kini, A., & Basri, S. (2022). *An empirical examination of customer advocacy influenced by engagement behaviour and predispositions of FinTech customers in India. F1000Research, 11*, 27. https://doi.org/10.12688/f1000research.74928.2

Ng, A. W., & Kwok, B. K. B. (2017). Emergence of Fintech and cybersecurity in a global financial centre. *Journal of Financial Regulation and Compliance, 25*(4), 422–434. https://doi.org/10.1108/JFRC-01-2017-0013

Odei-Appiah, S., Wiredu, G., & Adjei, J. K. (2022). Fintech use, digital divide and financial inclusion. *Digital Policy, Regulation and Governance, 24*(5), 435–448. https://doi.org/10.1108/DPRG-09-2021-0111

Pandey, D. K., Hunjra, A. I., Hassan, M. K., & Rai, V. K. (2023). Venture capital financing during crises: A bibliometric review. *Research in International Business and Finance, 64*, 101856. https://doi.org/10.1016/J.RIBAF.2022.101856

Pandey, D. K., Hassan, M. K., Kumari, V., Zaied, Y. B., & Rai, V. K. (2024). Mapping the landscape of FinTech in banking and finance: A bibliometric review. *Research in International Business and Finance, 67*, 102116. https://doi.org/10.1016/j.ribaf.2023.102116

Pandey, D. K., Lucey, B. M., & Kumar, S. (2023). Border *disputes, conflicts, war, and financial markets research: A systematic review.* Research in International Business and Finance, 101972. https://doi.org/10.1016/j.ribaf.2023.101972

Persaud, A., & Thaffe, W. (2023). The state of financial inclusion research on developing countries. *Transnational Corporations Review, 15*(4), 22–34. https://doi.org/10.1016/j.tncr.2023.08.002

Pizzi, S., Corbo, L., & Caputo, A. (2021). Fintech and SMEs sustainable business models: Reflections and considerations for a circular economy. *Journal of Cleaner Production, 281*, 125217. https://doi.org/10.1016/j.jclepro.2020.125217

Qin, Z., & Hao, H. (2023). Adopting environment friendly technology model for green consumer adoption: Is financial access important? *Environmental Science and Pollution Research*. https://doi.org/10.1007/s11356-023-28293-3

Rabbani, M. R., Bashar, A., Hawaldar, I. T., Shaik, M., & Selim, M. (2022). What Do We Know about Crowdfunding and P2P Lending Research? A Bibliometric Review and Meta-Analysis. *Journal of Risk and Financial Management, 15*(10), 451. https://doi.org/10.3390/jrfm15100451

Rosavina, M., Rahadi, R. A., Kitri, M. L., Nuraeni, S., & Mayangsari, L. (2019). P2P lending adoption by SMEs in Indonesia. *Qualitative Research in Financial Markets, 11*(2), 260–279. https://doi.org/10.1108/QRFM-09-2018-0103

Roszkowska, P. (2021). Fintech in financial reporting and audit for fraud prevention and safeguarding equity investments. *Journal of Accounting & Organizational Change, 17*(2), 164–196.

Saiedi, E., Broström, A., & Ruiz, F. (2021). Global drivers of cryptocurrency infrastructure adoption. *Small Business Economics, 57*(1), 353–406. https://doi.org/10.1007/s11187-019-00309-8

Sangwan, V., Harshita, H., Prakash, P., & Singh, S. (2019). Financial technology: A review of extant literature. *Studies in Economics and Finance, 37*(1), 71–88. https://doi.org/10.1108/SEF-07-2019-0270

Singh, S., Sahni, M. M., & Kovid, R. K. (2020). What drives FinTech adoption? A multi-method evaluation using an adapted technology acceptance model. *Management Decision, 58*(8), 1675–1697. https://doi.org/10.1108/MD-09-2019-1318

Soni, G., Kumar, S., Mahto, R. V., Mangla, S. K., Mittal, M. L., & Lim, W. M. (2022). *A decision-making framework for Industry 4.0 technology implementation: The case of FinTech and sustainable supply chain finance for SMEs.* Technological forecasting and social change, *180*, 121686. https://doi.org/10.1016/j.techfore.2022.121686

Stewart, H., & Jürjens, J. (2018). Data security and consumer trust in FinTech innovation in Germany. *Information & Computer Security, 26*(1), 109–128. https://doi.org/10.1108/ICS-06-2017-0039

van Eck, N. J., & Waltman, L. (2017). Citation-based clustering of publications using CitNetExplorer and VOSviewer. *Scientometrics, 111*(2), 1053–1070. https://doi.org/10.1007/s11192-017-2300-7

Vieira, E. S., & Gomes, J. A. N. F. (2009). A comparison of scopus and web of science for a typical university. *Scientometrics, 81*(2), 587–600. https://doi.org/10.1007/s11192-009-2178-0

Wuttke, D. A., Rosenzweig, E. D., & Heese, H. S. (2019). An empirical analysis of supply chain finance adoption. *Journal of Operations Management, 65*(3), 242–261. https://doi.org/10.1002/joom.1023

Xie, X., & Zhu, X. (2022). FinTech and capital allocation efficiency: Another equity-efficiency dilemma? *Global Finance Journal, 53*, 100741. https://doi.org/10.1016/j.gfj.2022.100741

Yan, E., & Ding, Y. (2011). Discovering author impact: A PageRank perspective. *Information Processing & Management, 47*(1), 125–134. https://doi.org/10.1016/j.ipm.2010.05.002

Yang, T., & Zhang, X. (2022). FinTech adoption and financial inclusion: Evidence from household consumption in China. *Journal of Banking & Finance, 145*, 106668. https://doi.org/10.1016/j.jbankfin.2022.106668

Yi, T. Z., Rom, N. A. M., et al. (2023). *The Adoption of Robo-Advisory among Millennials in the 21st Century: Trust, usability and knowledge perception.* Sustainability, *15*(7), 6016. https://doi.org/10.3390/su15076016

Zachariadis, M., & Ozcan, P. (2016). The API economy and digital transformation in financial services: The case of open banking. *SSRN Electronic Journal*. https://doi.org/10.2139/ssrn.2975199

Zalan, T., & Toufaily, E. (2017). The promise of fintech in emerging markets: Not as disruptive. *Contemporary Economics, 11*(4), 415–430.

The Rise of FinTech in India's Financial Ecosystem

Kavitha Desai, Narayani Ramachandran, and Mahalakshmi S.

1 Introduction

Artificial Intelligence (AI) has been a transformative force in the finance industry, catalyzing profound changes in operations, risk management, and investment strategies (Arner et al., 2021; Hill, K., 2020). The Indian financial services industry has embarked on a digital transformation journey, rapidly closing the gap with its international counterparts in technology adoption. India ranks among the fastest-growing FinTech markets globally, with the FinTech domain surging as a robust global entity and maintaining its momentum as one of the leading FinTech markets worldwide.

K. Desai (✉) · N. Ramachandran
SVKM's Narsee Monjee Institute of Management Studies, Mumbai, India
e-mail: kavitha.desai@nmims.edu

N. Ramachandran
e-mail: narayani.ramachandran@nmims.edu

Mahalakshmi S.
Faculty of Management Studies, CMS Business School, JAIN (Deemed-to-be University), Bengaluru, India

© The Author(s), under exclusive license to Springer Nature Singapore Pte Ltd. 2025

A. S. et al. (eds.), *Trends and Challenges of Electronic Finance*,
https://doi.org/10.1007/978-981-96-3304-3_12

The Indian FinTech sector has experienced remarkable growth and transformation over the past decade, fundamentally reshaping the global financial services landscape by leveraging emerging technologies and innovative solutions (Arner et al., 2022). India is now recognized as having the third-largest FinTech ecosystem globally, boasting one of the highest adoption rates among global populations (Government of India, 2023). The FinTech market's value stood at INR 3.70 trillion in FY 2023, with projections indicating a surge to INR 11.36 trillion by FY 2028, marking a robust compound annual growth rate (CAGR) of approximately 24.95% during the period spanning FY 2024 to FY 2028 (PricewaterhouseCoopers, 2021). With a flourishing ecosystem of over 9000 FinTech companies, India secures the third position globally in terms of the highest number of FinTech entities, commanding a noteworthy 14% share of startup funding in the country. India leads the charge in FinTech adoption, with an impressive adoption rate of 87%, significantly exceeding the global average of 64% (CFTE, 2023).

The growth of the Indian FinTech sector is driven by a range of supportive initiatives spearheaded by the government and regulators, a thriving funding environment, and the integration of emerging technologies. However, there are several challenges to address, such as potential data security and privacy risks, disparities in the adoption of digital financial services among different demographic segments, and inadequate financial literacy and awareness, among others, which demand constant vigilance from FinTech companies (Economic Times BFSI, 2022; RBI, 2023a).

Despite these challenges, substantial opportunities within the FinTech sector outweigh them. In recent years, the FinTech sector in India has witnessed a remarkable surge in funding, drawing substantial investment from major venture capital and private equity firms (RBI, 2023b). Technologies such as Artificial Intelligence (AI), Machine Learning (ML), and Blockchain are expected to play a significant role in shaping the future of FinTech, enabling customization of financial services, fraud detection and prevention, and enhancing overall customer experience (Arner et al., 2022; Fernandez et al., 2019; OECD, 2021).

2 FinTech Sector Transforming the Financial Industry

New financial technologies (FinTech) have rapidly emerged and transformed financial services around the world, swiftly reshaping various aspects of the financial services sector, including lending, wealth management, insurance, digital payments, regulation, capital markets, supervision, and underlying enabling technologies (Kavuri, A. S., & Milne, A., 2018). In India, digital payments have been leading the FinTech sector and have received the majority of venture capital funding compared to other segments, presenting a unique set of challenges and opportunities (Adithya, S., 2019). The focus on digital payments intensified after the Government's demonetization initiative. The FinTech landscape (See Fig. 1) in India can be categorized into the following segments: Lending and Credit, Payments and Digital Wallets, Investment and Wealth Management, Insurance Technology (InsurTech), and Regulatory Technology (RegTech).

2.1 *Lending and Credit*

The emergence of FinTech has led to the digital transformation of the traditional "bricks-and-mortar" banking model, fundamentally altering

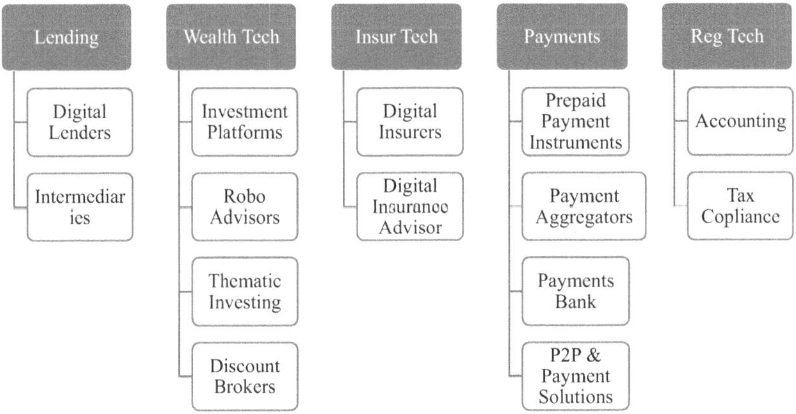

Fig. 1 Fintech landscape in India. (Source: By the author)

the delivery of financial services (Agarwal & Zhang, 2020). Lending and credit can be broadly categorized into two main subsegments: digital lending and intermediaries. Both segments leverage data and technologies like artificial intelligence and machine learning for loan screening, approval, and aggregation of services (EY, 2020).

FinTech has transformed lending in India by using innovative methods to bridge the credit gap. Platforms like Lendingkart, Capital Float, and Cred provide loans to individuals and small businesses (Deloitte, 2021). Peer-to-peer lending platforms such as Faircent and LenDenClub directly connect borrowers with individual lenders, fostering a more inclusive credit ecosystem. Digital lending has gained significant momentum, with FinTechs introducing innovative business models to extend credit to underserved segments. This sector has evolved in response to unmet credit demand through traditional lending mechanisms, serving as a significant provider of credit to small businesses and playing a crucial role in the recovery from the 2008 financial crisis (Manasa & Philipp, 2022).

In India, digital lending has been influenced by three major shifts: increased smartphone accessibility, demonetization prompting a shift to digital payments, and government initiatives. These factors have transformed the credit value chain, allowing digital lenders to streamline processes, acquire customers digitally at lower costs, and develop alternative data-driven underwriting models (RBIC Advisory, 2022).

Key developments in the Lending space include Embedded Finance, Crypto Lending, ESG Loans, and Virtual Collateral Assessment, which leverage technology to enhance accessibility, cater to different risk profiles, promote sustainability, and streamline valuation processes (Arner et al., 2022; Deloitte, 2023a, 2023b, 2023c; Ernst & Young, 2021; PwC, 2022a, 2022b, 2022c).

2.2 Payments and Digital Wallets

India's financial landscape is undergoing a profound transformation driven by its digital payment revolution, a phenomenon rewriting the country's financial narrative at a remarkable pace. The phenomenal success of the Unified Payments Interface (UPI) has catalyzed an unprecedented surge in digital transactions, with over 100 billion recorded in the financial year 2023 (Livemint, 2023). FinTech has emerged as a pivotal force in this evolution, particularly in the realm of payments, facilitating significant growth in cashless transactions over the past five years (NITI

Aayog, 2022a, 2022b). Payment apps and services like Paytm, PhonePe, and Google Pay have played instrumental roles in revolutionizing the way financial transactions are conducted in India (The Economic Times, 2023). The digital payments market in India was estimated to be worth INR 63 trillion in FY21 and is expected to grow at a CAGR of 29% to reach INR 385 trillion by the end of FY26 (Deloitte, 2023a, 2023b, 2023c).

3 Key Developments in the Digital Payments Space:

- **Rise of Super Apps**: Multi-purpose apps, often referred to as "super apps," have gained significant traction by offering a comprehensive suite of services, including digital payments, alongside other features like e-commerce, ride-hailing, and more. These apps have facilitated the growth of digital payments by providing users with a convenient, one-stop solution for various needs (EY, 2022).
- **Buy Now, Pay Later (BNPL)**: The BNPL model, which allows consumers to make purchases and pay for them in installments, has witnessed widespread adoption in India. FinTech companies identified a demand for accessible credit options, particularly among consumers in smaller towns or those new to credit, leading to the proliferation of BNPL services for smaller purchases (KPMG, 2021).
- **Regulatory Framework for Prepaid Payment Instruments (PPIs)**: In late 2021, the Reserve Bank of India (RBI) introduced new regulations for PPIs, which are instruments that facilitate the purchase of goods and services against the value stored on them. These regulations aim to enhance financial inclusion by making PPIs more accessible and user-friendly (Reserve Bank of India [RBI], 2021).

3.1 *Investment and Wealth Management*

Advancements in the WealthTech space in India can be attributed to several factors, including the growth of the working population, increased participation by young salaried professionals, rising disposable incomes, and higher retail participation in equity and mutual fund investments (Bain & Company, 2022a, 2022b). Robo-advisors like Kuvera and

Scripbox have made investing more accessible by leveraging algorithms to recommend portfolios and offering affordable investment options (CFTE, 2023). These platforms cater to both experienced investors and beginners, democratizing wealth management services.

WealthTech solutions not only streamline digital onboarding processes but also provide enhanced visual insights, informative analysis, and transparent operations. This transparency and ease of use have contributed significantly to the rapid adoption of WealthTech technologies (Deloitte, 2023a, 2023b, 2023c).

4 Key Developments in the Wealth Management Space:

- **Digital Wealth Management Platforms**: These startups offer clients a comprehensive overview of their investment portfolios, along with tools and advisory services to help optimize investments and achieve financial goals (Ernst & Young, 2022).
- **Robo Advisory and Mutual Fund Distribution**: These platforms leverage technology to deliver financial advice with minimal human intervention, while also serving as distribution channels for mutual fund companies to offer their products (KPMG, 2021).
- **Thematic Investing and Alternative Investment Platforms**: These startups empower retail investors with advanced tools to create customized stock baskets based on specific themes or sectors, enabling them to pursue alternative investment strategies with fixed-income returns (Bain & Company, 2022a, 2022b).
- **Simplification of Complex Trading/Algorithmic Trading**: These platforms aim to simplify the trading of complex financial instruments like futures and options, allowing users to execute automated trades using proprietary algorithms (Deloitte, 2023a, 2023b, 2023c).
- **Digital Discount Brokers**: These technology-driven brokerage firms offer affordable services and provide retail investors and traders with the necessary tools and resources for investing and trading activities (Ernst & Young, 2022).

4.1 *Insurance Technology (Insurtech)*

Insurtech is revolutionizing the insurance sector by utilizing technology to streamline and personalize insurance offerings, gaining significant traction in India. The digital transformation in the Indian insurance industry has highlighted the substantial impact of blockchain technology and data security on the sector. These digital innovations have considerably and favorably influenced the profitability of insurance businesses (Satuluri, 2021). Platforms like PolicyBazaar and Coverfox enable users to compare and purchase policies online, offering a seamless digital experience (KPMG, 2020). Companies are also exploring the potential of the Internet of Things (IoT) and data analytics to offer usage-based insurance and tailored risk assessment (Bain & Company, 2021). Insurtech aims to enhance the customer journey, products, and services by leveraging technology across the value chain.

In India, the insurance technology industry is rapidly evolving, driven by the growing demand for insurance services and products in the post-COVID-19 era. The National Health Stack initiative by the Indian government is anticipated to play a pivotal role in accelerating the adoption of digital technology in the insurance sector (PwC, 2022a, 2022b, 2022c; NITI Aayog, 2021).

5 Key Developments in the Insurance Technology Space

- Digital policy issuance and aggregation of insurance providers' details, enabling customers to compare and purchase policies online (EY, 2022).
- Innovative distribution channels to cater to the preferences of digital-savvy customers and adapt to changing business environments (KPMG, 2020).
- Product ecosystem integration, allowing customers to meet multiple needs through an interconnected user experience (Bain & Company, 2021).
- Collaborations between insurers, intermediaries, and service providers to ensure profitable growth and product customization for mass appeal (Deloitte, 2023a, 2023b, 2023c).

5.1 *Regulatory Technology (RegTech)*

The growth of financial technology (FinTech) has led to an increased need for regulatory compliance, and Regulatory Technology (RegTech) provides a solution by automating compliance processes and reducing the cost and complexity associated with compliance (Jadhav, 2023). In the dynamic FinTech landscape, RegTech has emerged as a powerful force, leveraging digital tools and processes to assist organizations in managing their regulatory compliance obligations (Deloitte, 2022). Financial institutions are increasingly turning to new technology solutions to alleviate the burden of regulatory requirements. RegTech has firmly established itself within the FinTech ecosystem, offering solutions tailored to address the challenges posed by new and complex regulations, litigation, and regulatory remediation, leading to an overall reduction in compliance costs.

One notable example of RegTech is the emergence of electronic Know Your Customer (eKYC) for customer onboarding. Other examples include tax assistance platforms (e.g., ClearTax), credit scoring platforms, and accounting platforms like KhataBook and EasyGST (KPMG, 2020). The primary goal of implementing RegTech solutions is to minimize the costs associated with non-compliance, enhance process efficiency, and boost confidence in reporting accuracy (Deloitte, 2022).

6 Key Developments in the Regulatory Technology Space

- Anti-money laundering (AML) solutions assist financial institutions in adhering to AML regulations, such as the Prevention of Money Laundering Act (PMLA) in India (EY, 2022).
- Know-your-customer (KYC) solutions streamline the customer onboarding process, aiding financial institutions in complying with KYC regulations and minimizing fraud risk (KPMG, 2021).
- Data privacy and security solutions ensure compliance with data privacy and security regulations, including the Personal Data Protection Bill in India (PwC, 2022a, 2022b, 2022c).
- Compliance management solutions offer a centralized platform for overseeing compliance, enabling financial institutions to more effectively monitor and manage their compliance processes (Deloitte, 2023a, 2023b, 2023c).

7 Factors Impacting FinTech Sector in India

The growth and success of Indian FinTech companies can be attributed to several key factors that have collectively fostered an environment conducive to innovation, expansion, and value delivery in the rapidly evolving financial landscape.

7.1 *Government & Regulator Initiatives*

Numerous government initiatives and regulatory measures have played pivotal roles in nurturing the growth of the FinTech sector in India. Some notable programs and measures include:

- Digital India Campaign: Launched by the Government of India, this initiative aims to transform the country into a digitally empowered society and knowledge economy. It has provided the necessary infrastructure and framework for the growth of digital services, including FinTech (Chaudhuri, 2020; Government of India, 2023). To further enhance service delivery and public participation, the government should prioritize digital efforts in governance (Sakolkar, 2023).
- **Unified Payment Interface (UPI)**: Introduced by the National Payments Corporation of India (NPCI), UPI is a real-time payment system that enables instant money transfers between bank accounts. It has revolutionized digital payments in India and created a fertile ground for FinTech innovation (NPCI, 2023).
- **Jan Dhan Yojana**: This financial inclusion program aimed to provide every Indian citizen with a bank account, significantly expanding the customer base for FinTech companies by bringing millions of previously unbanked individuals into the formal financial system (Government of India, 2023).
- **Goods and Services Tax (GST)**: The implementation of GST has streamlined the taxation system in India, making it easier for FinTech companies to comply with tax regulations and conduct business across state borders (PwC, 2021).
- **Regulatory Sandboxes**: Regulatory sandboxes, such as the one introduced by the Reserve Bank of India (RBI), allow FinTech startups to test their products and services in a controlled environment, fostering innovation while ensuring regulatory compliance (RBI, 2023a).

- **Startup India Initiative**: Launched to promote entrepreneurship and innovation, this initiative provides various incentives and support mechanisms for startups, including those in the FinTech sector (Startup India, 2023). A survey revealed that security, creditworthiness, and compliance are crucial for the success of regulatory sandboxes and FinTech startups in India, creating significant business opportunities (Shukla & Dubey, 2022).
- Financial Inclusion **Initiatives**: The government has implemented various schemes and programs to promote financial inclusion, such as the Pradhan Mantri Jan Dhan Yojana (PMJDY) and Direct Benefit Transfer (DBT) schemes, creating opportunities for FinTech companies to offer innovative services to underserved segments (Government of India, 2023).
- **Regulatory Framework for P2P Lending**: The RBI has introduced regulations for peer-to-peer (P2P) lending platforms, providing a legal framework for these platforms to operate and ensuring the protection of investors and borrowers (RBI, 2023b).

7.2 India Stack

India Stack is a groundbreaking initiative that aims to revolutionize service delivery in India by leveraging digital infrastructure. It provides a set of APIs (Application Programming Interfaces) that enable various stakeholders, including governments, businesses, startups, and developers, to build innovative solutions for societal challenges (India Stack, 2023).

8 The Key Components of India Stack Include:

- **Aadhaar**: A digital identity platform enabling secure authentication for various services (Government of India, 2023).
- e-KYC (Know Your Customer): Allows individuals to digitally verify their identity and share personal information with service providers, streamlining processes (Mehta, 2021).
- **Digital Locker**: Provides a secure digital space for individuals to store and share documents electronically, enabling paperless transactions (Government of India, 2023).

- **Unified Payment Interface (UPI)**: A real-time payment system that simplifies digital payments and enables cashless transactions across platforms (NPCI, 2023).
- **e-Signature**: An electronic signature framework that provides a legally valid alternative to physical signatures, facilitating paperless transactions (Government of India, 2023).

By leveraging these components, India Stack aims to achieve presence-less, paperless, and cashless service delivery, representing a significant step toward leveraging technology to address societal challenges and drive digital transformation (PwC, 2021).

8.1 Funding Environment

Over the past five years, the FinTech sector in India has witnessed a significant surge in funding, driven by the emergence of new startups and technological advancements. A supportive financial environment, with access to venture capital and private equity investments, has provided FinTech startups with the necessary capital to develop and scale their operations (Startup India, 2023; KPMG, 2022).

8.2 Technology & IT Infrastructure

Advanced technologies and robust IT infrastructure enabled FinTech companies to create innovative solutions, streamline processes, and offer seamless user experiences (CFTE, 2023).

8.3 Adoption of Technology by Banks

The continuously increasing collaboration between banks and FinTech startups, in the form of supplementary offerings, partnerships, acquisitions, incubators, and investments, is also a key driver of India's FinTech growth (Economic Times BFSI, 2022).

8.4 Greater Adoption on the Consumer End

Customer adoption and retention are paramount for the success of FinTech companies in the digital era. Key considerations and strategies include:

- **Building Trust**: FinTech companies must prioritize transparency, security, and reliability to build and maintain trust with customers (Verma, 2020).
- **Seamless User Experience**: Providing an intuitive and user-friendly experience is essential for driving adoption (PwC, 2022a, 2022b, 2022c).
- **Personalization**: Tailoring services to individual customer needs and preferences can enhance engagement and loyalty (RBI, 2023a).
- **Value Proposition**: Clearly articulating the value proposition of FinTech offerings is crucial for attracting and retaining customers (Mukherjee, 2021).
- **Continuous Innovation**: Companies must continuously innovate and adapt to emerging technologies and market trends to stay ahead in the rapidly evolving FinTech landscape (Verma, 2020; PwC, 2022a, 2022b, 2022c).
- Key Challenges Hindering the Indian FinTech Sector

9 Key Challenges Hindering the Indian FinTech Sector

While India's FinTech sector has experienced remarkable growth and innovation in recent years, several key challenges continue to hinder its full potential:

Regulatory Uncertainty: Lack of clarity and consistency in regulations can create barriers, inhibit innovation, and deter investment in the FinTech space. Streamlining regulations and providing clear guidelines are crucial for fostering a conducive environment for FinTech companies to thrive (Reserve Bank of India, 2020).

Access to Capital: Despite increased investment, accessing capital remains a challenge, particularly for early-stage FinTech startups. Limited availability of venture capital funding, especially for seed and Series A stages, can impede growth and expansion. A report by the Indian government's policy think tank highlights the need for regulatory sandboxes and government support to promote FinTech innovation and address capital access issues (NITI Aayog Report, 2022).

Cybersecurity Risks: The increasing digitization of financial services has exposed FinTech companies to a wide range of cyber risks, including data breaches, financial fraud, and system vulnerabilities. Implementing robust cybersecurity measures, such as encryption, multi-factor authentication, and real-time monitoring systems, is essential to safeguard sensitive information, secure transactions, and maintain trust (Deloitte, 2021; Joshi & Singh, 2022; Bain & Company, 2022a, 2022b; KPMG, 2023).

Digital Infrastructure: While India has made strides in developing its digital infrastructure, challenges persist in rural and remote areas, including unreliable internet connectivity, limited smartphone penetration, and digital literacy gaps, hindering broader FinTech adoption (Bain & Company, 2021).

Customer Trust and Adoption: Building trust among consumers and driving adoption of FinTech services remain challenges, especially among segments with limited exposure to digital financial tools. Overcoming concerns related to security, privacy, and reliability, and providing seamless user experiences are crucial for increasing adoption (Deloitte, 2021; KPMG and NASSCOM, 2022).

Competition from Traditional Players: Traditional financial institutions are increasingly investing in digital transformation and launching their own FinTech initiatives, intensifying competition for FinTech startups and requiring them to differentiate their offerings and innovate continuously (Mehta, 2021).

Lack of Skilled Talent: FinTech companies face talent shortages, requiring investments in talent development initiatives, collaborations with educational institutions, and attractive compensation and career advancement opportunities (KPMG, 2019; PwC, 2021).

Low Financial Literacy: Limited financial literacy among consumers, particularly in rural and underserved areas, can hinder the adoption of FinTech products and services. Educating consumers, simplifying user interfaces, and providing personalized financial education and guidance can help improve financial literacy and drive adoption (Arun & Kamath, 2015; Chandran, 2011).

Addressing these challenges through comprehensive strategies tailored to India's unique circumstances is crucial for unleashing the full potential of the FinTech sector and increasing financial inclusion.

10 Conclusion

The Indian FinTech market presents significant opportunities for innovation and expansion, but it is essential to address key challenges like regulatory uncertainty, market saturation, cybersecurity threats, talent shortages, and low financial literacy (Accenture, 2020; Bain & Company, 2022a, 2022b; Deloitte, 2021; Joshi & Singh, 2022). Despite these challenges, the sector remains highly attractive due to its immense growth potential, supportive government policies, and favorable market dynamics (EY & IVCA, 2022; NITI Aayog, 2022a, 2022b). FinTech companies that can effectively navigate and overcome these challenges will be well-positioned to capitalize on opportunities and drive sustainable growth.

Governments and regulators are employing alternative methods beyond traditional regulation to attract FinTech businesses and foster competition in digital markets, such as visa schemes for talent, research and development incentives, and programs to provide financial access for entrepreneurs to grow and scale up (Ahern, 2023).

By embracing environmental, social, and governance (ESG) principles and driving innovations, partnerships, and transformations, FinTech players in India have the potential to achieve financial success while making a meaningful and lasting impact on society and the environment (KPMG & NASSCOM, 2022; OECD, 2023; PwC, 2022a, 2022b, 2022c).

References

NITI Aayog. (2021). *National health stack: Strategy overview*. https://niti.gov.in/sites/default/files/2021-09/NATIONAL-HEALTH-STACK-STRATEGY-OVERVIEW.pdf

NITI Aayog. (2022). *Catalysing FinTech innovation in India*. https://www.niti.gov.in/sites/default/files/2022-03/FinTechReport_29Mar2022.pdf

NITI Aayog. (2022). *Digital payments in India: Trends and opportunities*. https://www.niti.gov.in/sites/default/files/2022-07/Digital-Payments-in-India-Trends-and-Opportunities.pdf

Accenture. (2020). *Building a future-ready workforce for FinTech: Strategies for talent acquisition and development.*

Adithya, S. (2019, June 20). *India is quite a different FinTech market: Great for consumers and very trying for startups*. https://gomedici.com/india-is-a-different-fintech-market-great-forconsumers-and-very-trying-for-startups/

RBIC Advisory. (2022). *Digital lending: A game-changer for financial inclusion in India*. https://rbicadvisors.com/wp-content/uploads/2022/02/Digital-Lending-A-Game-Changer-for-Financial-Inclusion-in-India.pdf

Agarwal, S., & Zhang, J. (2020). FinTech, lending and payment innovation: A review. *Asia-Pacific Journal of Financial Studies, 49*(3), 353–367.

Arner, D. W., Barberis, J. N., & Buckley, R. P. (2015). The evolution of Fintech: A new post-crisis paradigm? *Available at SSRN:* https://doi.org/10.2139/ssrn.2676553

Arner, D. W., Barberis, J., Buckley, R. P., Dahdal, A. M., & Zetsche, D. A. (2022). Digital finance platforms: Toward a more resilient and sustainable financial system. *Georgetown Journal of International Affairs, 23*(2), 95–106. https://doi.org/10.1353/gia.2022.0016

Arun, T., & Kamath, R. (2015). Financial inclusion: Policies and practices. *IIMB Management Review, 27*(4), 267–287.

Bahrammirzaee, A. (2020). *A comparative survey of artificial intelligence applications in finance: Artificial neural networks, expert system and hybrid intelligent systems*. Neural computing and applications, 32(4), 1437–1480. Research Gate.

Baporikar, N. (2021). *Fintech challenges and outlook in India*. In innovative strategies for implementing FinTech in banking (pp. 136–153). IGI Global.

Centre for Finance, Technology and Entrepreneurship (CFTE). (2023). *Major players in the Indian fintech industry*. https://www.cfte.education

CFTE. (2023). *The rise of Robo-advisors in India*. https://cfte.edu.in/the-rise-of-robo-advisors-in-india/

Chandran, D. (2011). *Financial inclusion strategies for inclusive growth in India*. SSRN: https://ssrn.com/abstract=1930980

Chaudhuri, A. (2020). The impact of government initiatives on digital transformation in India. *Digital India Journal, 15*(1), 12–24.

Bain & Company. (2021). *InsurTech in India: Disrupting a trillion-dollar opportunity*. https://www.bain.com/insights/insurtech-in-india-disrupting-a-trillion-dollar-opportunity/

Bain & Company. (2022). *Cybersecurity in FinTech: Protecting digital trust*. https://www.bain.com/insights/cybersecurity-in-fintech-protecting-digital-trust/

Bain & Company. (2022). *India wealthtech report 2022.* https://www.bain.com/insights/india-wealthtech-report-2022/

Deloitte. (2021). *Bolstering cyber resilience in the FinTech sector.* https://www2.deloitte.com/content/dam/Deloitte/in/Documents/risk/in-ra-cyber-resilience-in-fintech-sector-noexp.pdf

Deloitte. (2021). *Digital lending in India: A catalyst for financial inclusion.* https://www2.deloitte.com/in/en/pages/financial-services/articles/digital-lending-in-india.html

Deloitte. (2023). *The future of Insurtech in India.* https://www2.deloitte.com/in/en/pages/financial-services/articles/the-future-of-insurtech-in-india.html

Deloitte. (2023). *The future of wealth management in India.* https://www2.deloitte.com/in/en/pages/financial-services/articles/the-future-of-wealth-management-in-india.html

Deloitte. (2023). *The Rise of ESG Lending.* https://www2.deloitte.com/us/en/pages/financial-services/articles/the-rise-of-esg-lending.html

Economic Times BFSI. (2022). *India's buy now, pay later market to touch $40 Bn by 2025.* https://bfsi.economictimes.indiatimes.com/news/fintech/indias-buy-now-pay-later-market-to-touch-40-bn-by-2025/89791825

EY. (2020). *Lending innovation in digital age.* https://www.ey.com/en_in/financial-services/lending-innovation-in-digital-age

EY. (2022). *InsurTech in India: Driving innovation and growth.* https://www.ey.com/en_in/financial-services/insurtech-in-india-driving-innovation-and-growth

Fernandez-Vazquez, S., Rosillo R., de La Fuente D., & Priore, P. (2019). *Blockchain in FinTech: A mapping study.* Sustainability (Switzerland), vol. 11, no. 22. MDPI, Nov. 01, 2019. https://doi.org/10.3390/su11226366.

Gopal, M., & Schnabl, P. (2022). *The rise of finance companies and FinTech lenders in small business lending.* The review of financial studies. 35. https://doi.org/10.1093/rfs/hhac034

Government of India. (2023). *Digital India campaign.* https://www.digitalindia.gov.in

Hill, K. (2020, July 07). *How AI is Revolutionizing the Process of Fintech Firms?* https://medium.com/towards-artificial-intelligence/how-ai-is-revolutionizing-the-process-of-fintech-firms-87e057a48d83#:~:text=AI helps Fintech companies in resolving human problems, of human intelligence at a beyond human scale

Startup India. (2023). Start-up India initiative. https://www.startupindia.gov.in

EY & IVCA. (2022). *Perspective 2025: Shaping the FinTech Decade in India.* https://www.ey.com/en_in/financial-services/perspective-2025-shaping-the-fintech-decade-in-india

Jadhav, Jaykar. (2023). *An empirical study on regulatory technology (RegTech)*. SSRN: https://ssrn.com/abstract=4483816 or https://doi.org/10.2139/ssrn.4483816

Joshi, C., & Singh, U. K. (2022). *Cybersecurity in Indian FinTech: Challenges and mitigation strategies*. International Journal of Information Security Science, *11*(1), 1–12. https://doi.org/10.37572/IJISS.2022.11.1.1

Kavuri, A. S., & Milne, A. (2018, August 07). *Fintech and the future of financial services: What are the research gaps?* https://papers.ssrn.com/sol3/papers.cfm?abstract_id=3215849

KPMG. (2020). *InsurTech in India: Disrupting the insurance landscape*. https://home.kpmg/in/en/home/insights/2020/05/insurtech-in-india.html

KPMG. (2021). *Wealthtech in India: Democratizing wealth management*. https://home.kpmg/in/en/home/insights/2021/06/wealthtech-in-india-democratizing-wealth-management.html

KPMG. (2023). *Cybersecurity in FinTech: Protecting Innovation*. https://assets.kpmg/content/dam/kpmg/xx/pdf/2023/01/cybersecurity-in-fintech.pdf

Livemint. (2023). *UPI transactions cross the 100-billion mark in FY23*. Livemint. https://www.livemint.com

Mehta, R. (2021). Digital KYC and the Future of Financial Services in India. *Indian Banking Review*, *9*(2), 29–41.

KPMG & NASSCOM. (2022). *FinTech in India: Powering mobile payments*. https://assets.kpmg/content/dam/kpmg/in/pdf/2022/05/fintech-in-india-powering-mobile-payments.pdf

National Payments Corporation of India. (2023). *Unified payment interface (UPI)*. https://www.npci.org.in/what-we-do/upi/product-overview

OECD. (2021). *Artificial Intelligence, machine learning and big data in finance: Opportunities, challenges, and implications for policy makers*. https://www.oecd.org/finance/artificial-intelligence-machine-learning-big-data-in-finance.htm

OECD. (2023). *Digital transformation of the Indian economy: towards digital inclusion and enhanced productivity*. https://www.oecd.org/economy/surveys/digital-transformation-of-the-indian-economy-2023.pdf

PricewaterhouseCoopers (PwC). (2022). *The changing face of financial services: Growth of fintech in India v2*. https://www.pwc.in/assets/pdfs/consulting/financial-services/fintech/publications/the-changing-face-of-financial-services-growth-of-fintech-in-india-v2.pdf

PricewaterhouseCoopers (PwC). (2021). *The Indian payments handbook 2021–2026*. https://www.pwc.in/assets/pdfs/consulting/financial-services/fintech/payments-transformation/the-indian-payments-handbook-2021-2026.pdf

PwC. (2021). *Digital payments in India: Trends and opportunities*. https://www.pwc.in/consulting/financial-services/fintech/dp/digital-payments-in-india.html

PwC. (2022). *Embedded finance: The next wave of opportunity*. https://www.pwc.com/gx/en/industries/financial-services/publications/embedded-finance.html

PwC. (2022). *InsurTech in India: Unlocking the next wave of growth*. https://www.pwc.in/consulting/financial-services/fintech/dp/insurtech-in-india.html

PwC. (2022). *Accelerating digital transformation in India: Building a digitally inclusive society*. https://www.pwc.in/assets/pdfs/consulting/digital-transformation/accelerating-digital-transformation-in-india.pdf

Reserve Bank of India (RBI). (2023a). *Digital payments index (RBI-DPI) for September 2021*. https://www.rbi.org.in/Scripts/BS_PressReleaseDisplay.aspx?prid=52218

Reserve Bank of India (RBI). (2023a). *Report on trend and progress of banking in India 2022–23*. https://www.rbi.org.in/Scripts/PublicationsView.aspx?id=21120

Reserve Bank of India (RBI). (2023b). Regulatory sandboxes. https://www.rbi.org.in/Scripts/PublicationReportDetails.aspx?UrlPage=&ID=1158

Sakolkar, P. C. (2023). *Impact of digital transformation on the Indian government regarding service delivery and citizen engagement*.

Satuluri, R. K. (2021). Digital transformation in Indian insurance industry. *Turkish Journal of Computer and Mathematics Education (TURCOMAT)*, *12*(4), 310–324.

Shukla, U. N., & Dubey, A. (2022). Expectations of FinTech start-ups and regulatory sandbox in India: An empirical study. *International Journal of Business Innovation and Research*, *27*(2), 242–262.

India Stack. (2023). *India stack: Transforming digital services*. https://www.indiastack.org

Ernst & Young. (2021). *Virtual collateral assessment in lending*. https://www.ey.com/en_gl/financial-services/virtual-collateral-assessment-in-lending

Ernst & Young. (2022). *WealthTech trends in India*. https://www.ey.com/en_in/financial-services/wealthtech-trends-in-india

Fintech Evolution, Opportunities, and Challenges: Perspectives from Emerging Markets

Ahmed Mohamed Habib

1 Introduction

The 2008 financial crisis produced innovation opportunities in the banking industry, where fintech gained popularity as a digitalization finance technology solution. Companies acknowledge the immense potential of robust networks. Fintech investments have significantly changed how financial service organizations adopt and accept fintech innovations (Alt et al., 2024). Fintech encompasses innovative technologies that improve and streamline financial services for individuals and companies. This technology enables payment automation and provides immediate digital access to financial resources (Thomas & Hedrick-Wong, 2019). Fintech emerged in 1856 and was initially applied to technology employed in infrastructure systems. From 2018 to 2022, there has been a shift toward consumer-oriented services, and fintech now focuses on ecosystem integration and incorporates different sectors and industries. The fintech industry has recently experienced notable progress due to the

A. M. Habib (✉)
Department of Accounting and Finance, Independent Research, Zagazig, Egypt
e-mail: dr_ahmedhabib@yahoo.com

© The Author(s), under exclusive license to Springer Nature Singapore Pte Ltd. 2025

A. S. et al. (eds.), *Trends and Challenges of Electronic Finance*,
https://doi.org/10.1007/978-981-96-3304-3_13

adoption of digitalization and the incorporation of advanced technologies (Chemmanur et al., 2020; Rafiuddin et al., 2023), as well as banks, financial institutions, and other industries, are striving to adopt fintech to provide clients with secure, rapid, and flexible services (Baba et al., 2023). The essence and evolution of fintech are discussed from a broad perspective. The latter discusses fintech opportunities and challenges, particularly in the emerging markets.

2 Fintech and How it Works

Fintech is a novel digital finance field that has become an integral part of daily life. It is a linguistic blend of 'financial' and 'technology'. Fintech encompasses any application, program, or technology that enables individuals or companies to digitally access, manage, or control financial matters. Fintech includes cutting-edge technological solutions that provide digitally enhanced services and enable widespread access to financial services at reduced cost (Tang et al., 2023). This encompasses innovative technologies that improve and streamline financial services for both individuals and companies (Milian et al., 2019). Fintech is a new technology seeking to improve and automate the delivery and use of financial services (Thomas & Hedrick-Wong, 2019). It is composed of specialized software and algorithms used on computers and smartphones. At its core, fintech helps companies, business owners, and consumers manage their financial transactions and practices better.

The various categories of financial technology applications function in distinct ways. Fintech uses mobile devices and other technical platforms to facilitate access to bank accounts, transaction notifications, and participation in financial activities. For instance, PayPal, Monzo, Cash App, Zelle, Venmo, Google Pay, and Apple Cash are examples of mobile banking and peer-to-peer (P2P) payment platforms. Fintech also includes the development and use of CR, such as Bitcoin (BTC), Ethereum (ETH), Tether (USDT), Binance Coin (BNB), and Solana (SOL). While the fintech segment may see headlines, big money still lies in the traditional global banking industry and its multi-trillion dollar market capitalization.

Fintech companies offer customers more inventive and flexible financial service solutions in exchange for fees. They offer various financial services, including digital payments, personal loans, investment management, insurance, and related services. Hence, fintech companies must be subject to government regulations to ensure compliance with the law and guarantee secure and reliable customer service. Fintech companies often collaborate with conventional financial institutions to offer supplementary services and expand their customer reach. Fintech companies typically use advanced technology to automate and streamline their financial processes. This allows them to provide expedited, user-friendly, and secure financial services.

3 Fintech Evolution

The fintech industry has recently experienced notable progress owing to the adoption of digitalization and the incorporation of advanced technologies. This progress has transformed financial service delivery to firms. As a result of modifications in business models and operations, there is an increased demand for financial firms to embrace these technologies (Jafri et al., 2024). Digital finance pertains to a diverse range of financial goods and services provided by fintech companies and their partners. These include novel methods of interacting with customers and financial operations.

Fintech dates back to the year 1856. From 1866 to 1966, fintech focused on infrastructure investments and analog financial services. Some experts call this technology 'Fintech 1.0'. Telegraphs, railroads, and steamships have enabled the first transmission of cross-border financial information. This chronology includes the first transatlantic cable in 1866 and Fedwire in the US in 1918, the first electronic fund transfer system that used telegraph and Morse codes. In the 1950s, credit cards were introduced to reduce cash-carrying. Diner's Club introduced its credit card in 1950, followed by American Express in 1958. The fintech evolution phases are summarized in Fig. 1.

From 1967 to 2008, fintech focused on financial institutions' digitalization. Some experts call this technology 'Fintech 2.0'. This period marks a shift from analog to digital, as directed by traditional financial institutions. The modern fintech era began in 1967 when Jack Kilby at Texas Instruments created the first handheld calculator, and Barclays Bank installed the first automated teller machine (ATM). The early 1970s witnessed notable movements, including the founding of the NASDAQ, the first digital stock exchange that shaped modern financial markets. The Society for Worldwide Interbank Financial Telecommunications (SWIFT) was founded in 1973 and remains the most widely used communication system for massive cross-border payments by financial institutions.

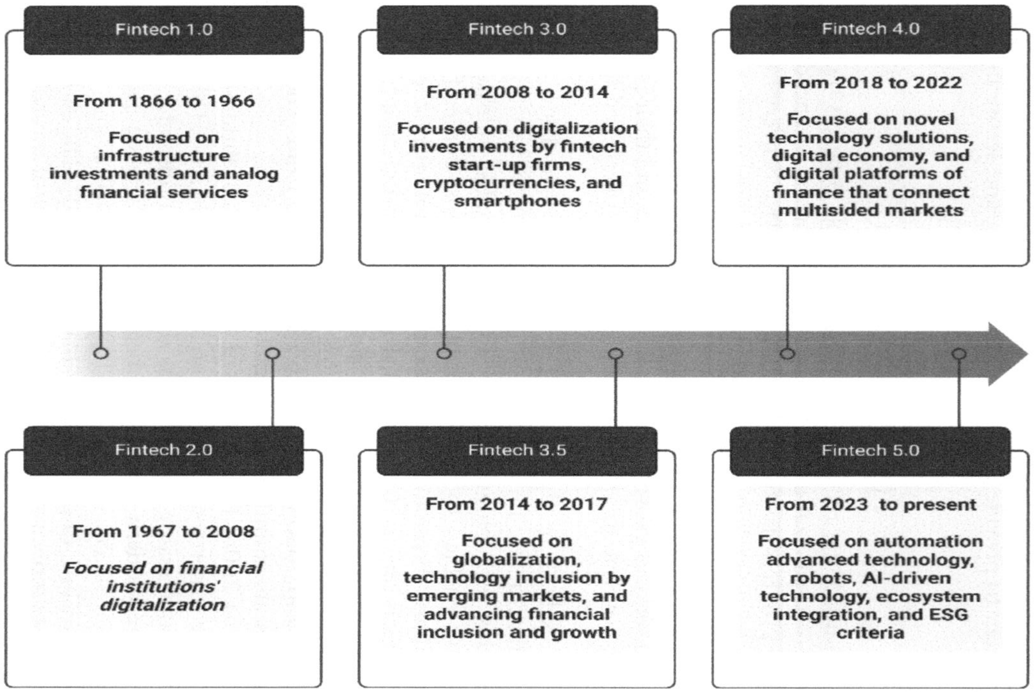

Fig. 1 Fintech phases evolution

In the 1980s, bank mainframe computers and online banking emerged and thrived in the 1990s through the internet and e-commerce. Finally, by the beginning of the twenty-first century, banks' internal procedures were digital, and this era ended with the Global Financial Crisis of 2008.

From 2008 to 2014, fintech focused on digitalization investments by fintech startup firms, cryptocurrencies, and smartphones. Some experts call this technology 'Fintech 3.0'. Many transformations in the fintech field have characterized this period. As the causes of the Global Financial Crisis, which became a broader economic disaster, became clearer, the public distrusted traditional banks. This, in addition to the fact that many financial professionals were unemployed, changed mindsets and emerged as new players, particularly fintech companies, alongside existing ones, such as banks. The 2009 release of Bitcoin v0.1 had another significant impact on the financial sector, followed by a boom in different cryptocurrencies. The mass-market spread of smartphones, which give millions of people Internet access, has also altered finance. Smartphones are also the main way consumers use the internet and financial services. Google Wallet debuted in 2011, followed by Apple Pay in 2014.

From 2014 to 2017, fintech focused on globalization. Some experts call this technology 'Fintech 3.5'. Globalization and rapid technical improvements have forced companies to be more creative (Habib & Mourad, 2023). This era witnessed a shift away from western-dominant finance and the globalization of digital banking with fintech advances. Fintech 3.5 focused on globalization, technology inclusion, and the internet by developing countries, and advancing financial inclusion and growth. China and India were more open to new solutions because they never had time to construct a Western-level physical banking infrastructure.

From 2018 to 2022 (see Fig. 2), fintech has focused on novel technology solutions, digital economy, and digital platforms of finance that connect multisided markets. Some experts call this technology 'Fintech 4.0'. Modern BC technology, ML, and AI have revolutionized how individuals engage with banks and firms, as well as developing deep insights and predictions about customer behavior to dynamically identify issues without human intervention.

From 2023 to the present, fintech has focused on automation advanced technology, robots, AI-driven technology, and ESG criteria. It also focuses on ecosystem integration, where finance interfaces with various sectors, such as healthcare, retail, transportation, and real estate. Some experts

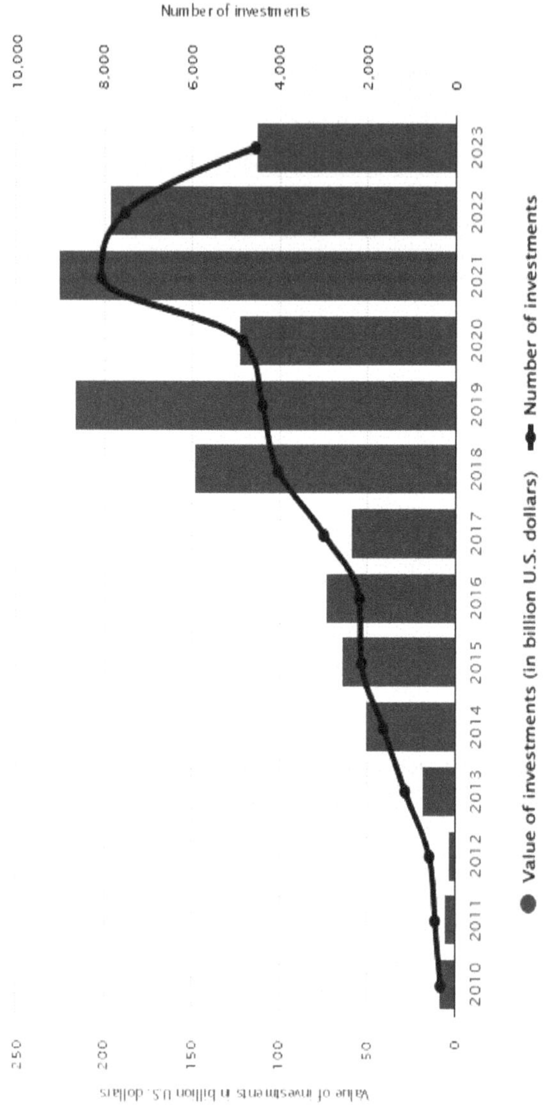

Fig. 2 Fintech investments evolution

call this technology 'Fintech 5.0'. By integrating financial services into everyday activities, the intersection of technology and finance can form a new potential for value maximization and sector collaboration enhancement. This certainly came after the challenging economic course that companies and various economies worldwide have suffered from the COVID-19 pandemic, whether microeconomic (Habib, 2024; Nuta et al., 2024; Zimon et al., 2024), or macroeconomic (Habib & Kayani, 2024; Mourad et al., 2021, 2022). Fintech 5.0 represents the paradigm shift of digital platforms using technology-driven systems to enhance operational efficiency and better manage risks.

Furthermore, it should be noted that the Americas have over 13,100 fintech startups in 2024 (Statista, 2024), establishing it as a leading area worldwide in terms of fintech startup presence. Additionally, a growing number of financial institutions are making efforts to establish connections with the fintech ecosystem through venture investments, which can stimulate innovation in global financial institutions.

Recently, with the growing use of digital technologies by consumers, fintech has helped customers overcome financial difficulties and achieve their objectives. Consumers now depend on fintech for various purposes, such as banking, budgeting, investing, and lending, owing to its practical advantages, including time savings, easier financial tracking, greater control of finances, more personalized services, and reduced fear and stress in managing their funds.

4 Islamic Fintech

Fintech uses smart technologies and other security methods to secure customer data from fraudsters. These technologies are increasing the fintech revolution and transforming Islamic fintech, which follows the Sharia law in its financial services business models. Islamic law distinguishes between halal and haram capital raising for corporations and lenders. The Islamic financial sector views money as a value measure rather than an asset. Therefore, money should not be received as income just from money, as with interest. Islamic finance is a socially and ethically appropriate investment that avoids riba or usury, which most Islamic scholars call an interest. In principle, business partners should share risks equally. Islam forbids investing in alcohol, gambling, casinos, and pork companies. Islamic fintech is a major segment of global finance that combines Sharia compliance with digital financial solutions to make

Sharia-compliant savings, investments, insurance, and mortgages accessible (Alsaghir, 2023; Muneeza & Mustapha, 2021).

Despite pandemics and geopolitical unrest, the Islamic financial and banking business has grown globally in recent years. Currently, 417 Islamic fintech companies operate internationally, indicating the ongoing development and growth of the industry. In addition, Standard & Poor's (S&P) predicted strong growth in Islamic finance in 2024 and subsequent periods. In 2021, Statista reported that global Islamic financial markets have a total asset value of 4.5 trillion US dollars. By 2027, they are expected to reach a projected total asset value of 6.67 trillion US dollars (Puri-Mirza, 2024). According to the Islamic Financial Services Board (IFSB), a significant proportion of Islamic finance assets are concentrated in Asia, the Gulf Cooperation Council (GCC), and the Middle East and North Africa (MENA).

5 Fintech Opportunities and Challenges in Emerging Markets

The current fintech industry differs. Fintech is developing, and too many changes will influence its future in the coming years. Banks have been interested in BC technology and AI since 'Fintech 4.0'. Owing to their capabilities, banks that have adopted and employed them are now challengers. Many fintech companies have developed novel fundraising methods to help startups overcome their challenges. The most significant process bypass concept is the initial coin offerings (ICOs), which issue tokens in exchange for cryptocurrencies. Many startups use these methods to finance their investments instead of inflexible and strict traditional methods (Thomas & Hedrick-Wong, 2019).

In emerging markets, fintech has caused significant shifts in the financial services sector and improved financial inclusion (Al Khub et al., 2024; Panda et al., 2023). Emerging markets offer fintech companies noteworthy opportunities because of their massive unbanked population. Traditional financial services are either unavailable or expensive in many emerging markets. Fintech can make financial services more efficient, cheaper, convenient, and accessible to large populations. It can assist many individuals previously excluded from formal banking systems to access a range of financial services, including savings accounts, loans, and insurance. This can also help improve economic growth and reduce the poverty levels in these regions (Omar & Inaba, 2020; Polloni-Silva et al., 2021).

In many emerging markets, where most people have mobile phones but no banking services, mobile payments have supplanted traditional banking. Mobile payments are a major opportunity for fintech companies in emerging markets to offer finance and insurance to these populations (Khai Nguyen & Cuong Dang, 2022). Additionally, BC technology offers another potential in emerging markets that can secure and transparent financial transactions. It is also useful in markets in which the majority distrust traditional banks. Fintech companies can employ BC technology for remittances and microfinance, thus allowing individuals and small enterprises to participate in the global economy. Finally, fintech companies can tailor their financial services to emerging market customers by using AI and ML. These technologies can analyze enormous volumes of data to identify trends and patterns, allowing fintech companies to customize products and services for each consumer (Ediagbonya & Tioluwani, 2023).

On the other hand, fintech has many prospects in emerging markets, but it must overcome various challenges in order to ensure long-term growth, especially regulatory compliance, trust, infrastructure quality, and the digital divide. Fintech companies may struggle to adapt to emerging markets under complex, changing regulations. Therefore, they must work closely with regulators to guarantee that their products and services comply with the local laws. Fintech distrust is another concern. In many emerging markets, fintech companies are less trustworthy than traditional banks. Therefore, to acquire trust, fintech organizations must prove their reliability and security to potential clients. In addition, many emerging markets are plagued by infrastructure shortages. Fintech services frequently lack crucial infrastructure, such as reliable internet access and digital identity systems. Fintech companies must work with local governments and stakeholders to establish infrastructure for their services. Finally, fintech companies in emerging markets must address the digital gaps among their populations. Certainly, mobile phones are ubiquitous in emerging markets, although some people may not have them or maybe uncomfortable using them. Therefore, fintech companies may require additional capabilities, agents, education, and awareness campaigns to reduce the digital divide among populations.

6 Conclusion

Fintech has shifted to the global financial services industry. The fintech industry has recently experienced notable progress owing to the adoption of digitalization and the incorporation of advanced technologies, such as BD, AI, ML, BI, BC technology, IoT, CR, and CBS. In this chapter, we discuss the essence and evolution of fintech, as well as its opportunities and challenges, specifically in emerging markets. Fintech encompasses innovative technologies that improve and streamline financial services for individuals and companies. This technology enables payment automation and provides immediate digital access to financial resources. Fintech investments have significantly changed how financial service organizations adopt and accept fintech innovation. Companies acknowledge the immense potential of robust networks. Fintech has developed in six phases. The first phase, from 1886 to 1966, is called 'Fintech 1.0', which focused on infrastructure investments and analog financial services. From 1967 to 2008, the second phase was called 'Fintech 2.0', which focused on financial institutions' digitalization. The third phase, from 2008 to 2014, is called 'Fintech 3.0', which focused on digitalization investments by fintech startup firms, cryptocurrencies, and smartphones. The fourth phase, from 2014 to 2017, is called 'Fintech 3.5', which focused on globalization, technology inclusion, and the internet by developing countries, and advancing financial inclusion and growth. The fifth phase, from 2018 to 2022, is called 'Fintech 4.0', which focused on novel technology solutions, digital economy, and digital platforms of finance that connect multisided markets. The sixth phase, from 2023 to the present, is called 'Fintech 5.0' and focuses on automation advanced technology, robots, AI-driven technology, ecosystem integration, and ESG criteria. Fintech now includes different sectors and industries, such as education, retail banking, fundraising and nonprofit, and investment management, to name a few. Fintech has substantial prospects for development in emerging markets. However, they also present several significant challenges. A long-term shift necessitates overcoming key challenges, such as regulatory compliance, infrastructure, trust, and the digital divide. Accordingly, it is necessary to provide reasonable and secure conditions for such technologies and address existing deficiencies and challenges through ongoing and gradual improvement processes that enhance growth and sustainability over time.

References

Al Khub, A., Saeudy, M., & Gerged, A. M. (2024). Digital Financial Inclusion in Emerging Economies: Evidence from Jordan. *Journal of Risk and Financial Management, 17*(2), 66. https://doi.org/10.3390/jrfm17020066

Alsaghir, M. (2023). Digital risks and Islamic FinTech: A road map to social justice and financial inclusion. *Journal of Islamic Accounting and Business Research*. https://doi.org/10.1108/JIABR-10-2022-0262

Alt, R., Fridgen, G., & Chang, Y. (2024). The Future of Fintech—Towards Ubiquitous Financial Services. *Electronic Markets, 34*(1), 3. https://doi.org/10.1007/s12525-023-00687-8

Baba, M. A., Haq, Z. ul, Dawood, M., & Aashish, K. (2023). FinTech Adoption of Financial Services Industry: Exploring the Impact of Creative and Innovative Leadership. *Journal of Risk and Financial Management*, *16*(10), 453. https://doi.org/10.3390/jrfm16100453

Chemmanur, T. J., Imerman, M. B., Rajaiya, H., & Yu, Q. (2020). Recent Developments in the Fintech Industry. *Journal of Financial Management, Markets and Institutions, 08*(01), 2040002. https://doi.org/10.1142/S2282717X20400022

Ediagbonya, V., & Tioluwani, C. (2023). The Role of Fintech in Driving Financial Inclusion in Developing and Emerging Markets: Issues, Challenges and Prospects. *Technological Sustainability, 2*(1), 100–119. https://doi.org/10.1108/TECHS-10-2021-0017

Habib, A. M. (2024). *Financial Development and Corporate Governance Efficiency: An Overview of MENA* (pp. 147–169). https://doi.org/10.1142/9781800614734_0006

Habib, A. M., & Kayani, U. N. (2024). Price Reaction of Global Economic Indicators: Evidence from the COVID-19 Pandemic and the Russia-Ukraine Conflict. *SN Business & Economics, 4*(19), 1–21. https://doi.org/10.1007/s43546-023-00619-w

Habib, A. M., & Mourad, N. (2023). Analyzing the Efficiency of Intellectual Capital: a New Approach Based on DEA-MPI Technology. *Benchmarking: An International Journal, ahead-of-print* (ahead-of-print). https://doi.org/10.1108/BIJ-06-2022-0384

Jafri, J. A., Mohd Amin, S. I., Abdul Rahman, A., & Mohd Nor, S. (2024). A Systematic Literature Review of the Role of Trust and Security on Fintech Adoption in Banking. *Heliyon, 10*(1), e22980. https://doi.org/10.1016/j.heliyon.2023.e22980

Khai Nguyen, Q., & Cuong Dang, V. (2022). The Effect of FinTech Development on Financial Stability in an Emerging Market: The Role of Market Discipline. *Research in Globalization, 5*, 100105. https://doi.org/10.1016/j.resglo.2022.100105

Milian, E. Z., Spinola, M. de M., & Carvalho, M. M. de. (2019). Fintechs: A Literature Review and Research Agenda. *Electronic Commerce Research and Applications*, *34*, 100833. https://doi.org/10.1016/j.elerap.2019.100833

Mourad, N., Habib, A. M., & Tharwat, A. (2021). Appraising Healthcare Systems' Efficiency in Facing COVID-19 Through Data Envelopment Analysis. *Decision Science Letters*, *10*(3), 301–310. https://doi.org/10.5267/j.dsl.2021.2.007

Mourad, N., Tharwat, A., Habib, A. M., Wafik, D., & Hamed, M. A. (2022). Appraising the Economic Efficiency of European Football Teams: Evidence from Covid-19 Crisis Using Data Envelop Analysis. *Journal of Positive School Psychology*, *6*(8), 4383–4403. https://journalppw.com/index.php/jpsp/article/view/10611

Muneeza, A., & Mustapha, Z. (2021). Islamic FinTech and Financial Inclusion. In *Islamic FinTech* (pp. 173–190). Springer International Publishing. https://doi.org/10.1007/978-3-030-45827-0_10

Nuta, A. C., Habib, A. M., Neslihanoglu, S., Dalwai, T., & Rangu, C. M. (2024). Analyzing the Market Performance of Romanian Firms: Do the COVID-19 Crisis and Classification Type Matter? *International Journal of Emerging Markets*, *ahead-of-print* (ahead-of-print), 1–32. https://doi.org/10.1108/IJOEM-05-2023-0842

Omar, M. A., & Inaba, K. (2020). Does Financial Inclusion Reduce Poverty and Income Inequality in Developing Countries? A Panel Data Analysis. *Journal of Economic Structures*, *9*(1), 37. https://doi.org/10.1186/s40008-020-00214-4

Panda, K., Sahoo, A., & Kumar, A. (2023). From the Margins to Mainstream: Fintech's Quest for Financial Inclusion in Emerging Markets. *European Economic Letters*. https://doi.org/10.52783/eel.v13i5.762

Polloni-Silva, E., da Costa, N., Moralles, H. F., & Sacomano, M. (2021). Does Financial Inclusion Diminish Poverty and Inequality? A Panel Data Analysis for Latin American Countries. *Social Indicators Research*, *158*(3), 889–925. https://doi.org/10.1007/s11205-021-02730-7

Puri-Mirza, A. (2024). *Total Value of Islamic Finance Assets Worldwide from 2012 to 2022 with a Projection for 2027*. https://www.statista.com/statistics/1090815/worldwide-value-of-islamic-finance-assets/

Rafiuddin, A., Gaytan, J. C. T., Mohnot, R., Sisodia, G. S., & Ahmed, G. (2023). Growth Evaluation of Fintech Connectedness with Innovative Thematic Indices—An Evidence Through Wavelet Analysis. *Journal of Open Innovation: Technology, Market, and Complexity*, *9*(2), 100023. https://doi.org/10.1016/j.joitmc.2023.100023

Statista. (2024). *Number of Fintechs Worldwide from 2018 to 2024, by Region*. https://www.statista.com/statistics/893954/number-fintech-startups-by-region/

Tang, X., Yao, X., Miao, Y., & Yu, L. (2023). "Cost Reduction" or "Profit Increase"?: The Impact of Fintech on the Operating Efficiency of Securities Companies from the Perspective of Absorptive Capacity. *Proceedings of the 2023 14th International Conference on E-Business, Management and Economics*, 229–236. https://doi.org/10.1145/3616712.3616781

Thomas, H., & Hedrick-Wong, Y. (2019). How Digital Finance and Fintech Can Improve Financial Inclusion. In *Inclusive Growth* (pp. 27–41). Emerald Publishing Limited. https://doi.org/10.1108/978-1-78973-779-020191004

Zimon, G., Habib, A. M., & Haluza, D. (2024). Does the Quality Management System Affect Working Capital Management Efficiency? Evidence from Polish firms. *Cogent Business & Management, 11*(1), 1–18. https://doi.org/10.1080/23311975.2023.2292787

The Role of Fintech in Financial Inclusion: A Survey of Low-Income Individuals in Kolkata

Souvik Banerjee

1 Introduction

Financial technology, commonly known as Fintech, has emerged as a transformative power in the global financial sector, particularly following the 2008 financial crisis. This technology-driven innovation is at the forefront of reshaping banking, insurance, and financial services, offering new opportunities for economic participation to those previously excluded from the financial system. In India, the Fintech revolution is not just a phenomenon of the urban elite but is increasingly seen as a pivotal tool in promoting financial inclusion among the low-income and underbanked populations (Nagaraja, 2023).

In cities like Kolkata, where a significant segment of the population lives below the poverty line, the penetration of traditional banking services is notably low. Here, Fintech has the potential to leapfrog traditional barriers to financial services, offering low-cost, scalable solutions that can be accessed via mobile phones. Recent studies indicate that nearly 80% of India's population now has access to some form of bank account, largely

S. Banerjee (✉)
Management Development Institute Murshidabad, Murshidabad, India
e-mail: souvik.2005@gmail.com

© The Author(s), under exclusive license to Springer Nature Singapore Pte Ltd. 2025

A. S. et al. (eds.), *Trends and Challenges of Electronic Finance*,
https://doi.org/10.1007/978-981-96-3304-3_14

due to the rapid adoption of mobile banking and digital payment systems (Asif et al., 2023). These technologies are integral to everyday financial activities, from transferring money to receiving government benefits, thus playing a critical role in enhancing financial inclusion.

The impact of Fintech on financial inclusion in India is profound. It extends beyond mere access to bank accounts, influencing a broader spectrum of financial behaviors including savings, loans, insurance, and investment. Fintech solutions such as Unified Payments Interface (UPI) have democratized access to financial services, creating a more inclusive financial ecosystem (Nagaraja, 2023). This is particularly significant in Kolkata, where the convergence of high mobile penetration and low financial inclusion presents a unique opportunity to harness Fintech for socio-economic upliftment.

However, the journey toward full financial inclusion through Fintech is fraught with challenges. Issues such as digital literacy, trust in digital transactions, and the regulatory environment play a crucial role in shaping the effectiveness of Fintech interventions. For instance, the work of Guild (2017) highlights the necessity of a balanced regulatory framework that supports innovation while ensuring consumer protection. This is crucial in preventing the exacerbation of existing inequalities, which can arise from unequal access to or benefits from these technologies.

Moreover, the geographical and socio-economic diversity within Kolkata calls for localized strategies to implement Fintech solutions effectively. The studies by Iwasaki (2022) point out that while digital payments and alternative finance have gained traction, their impact varies significantly across different demographic groups. The effectiveness of Fintech in promoting financial inclusion thus depends not only on technology but also on an understanding of the local context and the specific needs of targeted users.

In this light, the significance of studying the role of Fintech in financial inclusion in Kolkata cannot be overstated. It holds the key to unlocking economic opportunities for millions, contributing to the broader goals of poverty reduction and economic equity. As this study progresses, it will explore the intricate dynamics between technological advancement and financial accessibility, striving to illuminate the pathways through which Fintech can lead to more inclusive financial environments in urban India. This exploration is not only relevant to policymakers and business leaders but is essential for ensuring that the benefits of technological advancements reach all layers of society, particularly the economically marginalized communities in Kolkata.

2 Literature Review

The literature on financial technology (Fintech) and its impact on financial inclusion is vast and varied, emphasizing its transformative potential, particularly in emerging markets. This section reviews key scholarly works that investigate how Fintech has been leveraged to improve access to financial services for underserved populations, focusing on different methodologies, findings, and implications.

Bharathi S. et al. (2023) conducted a systematic literature review of 178 articles to explore the synergy between Fintech and financial inclusion. Their methodology involved a descriptive and qualitative analysis, identifying six research themes central to understanding this relationship. The findings highlight Fintech's role in democratizing financial services, providing access to the unbanked, and reducing operational costs for financial service providers. The study stresses the need for future research to focus on specific challenges and opportunities that could further accelerate financial inclusion, particularly among vulnerable populations affected by global threats. This comprehensive overview underpins much of the current understanding of Fintech's benefits and its potential to address gaps in financial service accessibility.

In another significant study, Dr. Amrik Singh and Dr. Lalit Mohan Sharma (2023) explore various Fintech mechanisms, such as mobile banking, digital payments, peer-to-peer lending, and microfinance platforms. Their research is based on a combination of case studies and secondary data analysis, which provides evidence of Fintech's success in reaching unbanked and underbanked individuals. The paper discusses both the advancements and the challenges, particularly concerning data privacy and regulatory compliance. This study is crucial as it not only presents Fintech's capabilities in enhancing financial literacy and empowering individuals but also cautions about the risks involved, thus providing a balanced perspective on Fintech's role in financial inclusion.

Hasan Babar (2023) focused on the relationship between Fintech and financial inclusion across 144 countries using data from the World Bank's 2017 Global Findex report. His study employs quantitative methods to assess how Fintech influences financial inclusion and women's economic empowerment. The results indicate a strong correlation between Fintech and increased financial inclusion, suggesting that Fintech innovations are key drivers in reducing poverty and supporting women's economic activities in low-income countries. This global perspective is invaluable for understanding the scalable impact of Fintech beyond individual national contexts.

Finally, Dr. Nagaraja K. (2023) highlights the role of Fintech in banking the unbanked in India through a variety of technological interventions like the Unified Payment Interface (UPI). His research notes the significant contributions of government initiatives that complement Fintech solutions in promoting financial inclusion. By analyzing these initiatives, the study showcases the potential of public–private partnerships in expanding financial services to the most remote areas of the country, thus ensuring that financial inclusion efforts are comprehensive and far-reaching.

These studies collectively show that while Fintech offers remarkable opportunities for enhancing financial inclusion, it also presents unique challenges that need to be addressed. The existing literature predominantly focuses on the broader impact of Fintech on financial inclusion in India and other emerging markets. However, there is a notable gap in research specifically addressing the role and effectiveness of Fintech interventions in promoting financial inclusion among low-income individuals in Kolkata. This study aims to fill this gap by conducting a survey targeting this specific demographic group, thereby providing insights into the unique challenges and opportunities faced by low-income individuals in Kolkata regarding Fintech adoption. Understanding these dynamics is crucial for tailoring Fintech solutions to the local context and maximizing their impact on financial inclusion in urban India. By addressing this gap, the research contributes to a more nuanced understanding of how Fintech can effectively serve the needs of marginalized communities in specific urban settings, ultimately advancing the broader goal of inclusive economic development.

Table 1 Details of Data Collection Source

Source	*Survey Questionnaire*
Description	Face-to-face survey administered to low-income individuals in Kolkata
Date	July to September 2023
Sample Size	500 respondents
Sampling Technique	Stratified sampling
Data Collection Method	Structured survey
Variables Measured	Demographic information, financial behaviors, perceptions of Fintech usage
Type of Questions	Close-ended

3 Research Methodology

3.1 *Research Design*

This study employed a quantitative research design to investigate the role of Fintech in financial inclusion among low-income individuals in Kolkata. A structured survey was conducted to collect data, focusing on demographic information, financial behaviors, and perceptions of Fintech usage among the target population.

3.2 *Data Collection*

The primary source of data for this study was a survey administered to low-income individuals residing in Kolkata. The survey was conducted face-to-face by trained interviewers between July and September 2023. A stratified sampling technique was employed to ensure representation from various socio-economic strata within the low-income population. The survey instrument consisted of close-ended questions to facilitate efficient data collection and analysis (refer Table 1).

3.3 *Data Analysis*

The collected survey data were analyzed using statistical software SPSS (Statistical Package for the Social Sciences). Descriptive statistics such as frequencies, percentages, mean scores, and standard deviations were computed to summarize the demographic characteristics of the sample, financial behaviors, and attitudes toward Fintech. Inferential statistical techniques, including correlation analysis and regression analysis, were employed to examine the relationships between variables and to identify significant predictors of Fintech adoption and financial inclusion among low-income individuals in Kolkata.

By employing a rigorous research design and data analysis approach, this study aimed to provide comprehensive insights into the role of Fintech in promoting financial inclusion in urban India, particularly among marginalized populations in Kolkata.

4 Results and Analysis

In this section, the results of the data analysis are presented and discussed. The analysis focused on examining the relationship between Fintech adoption and financial inclusion among low-income individuals in Kolkata.

As shown in Table 2, the sample consisted of an equal distribution of male and female respondents, with a mean age of 35.7 years. The majority of respondents resided in urban areas, with a mean monthly income of 12,000 INR. Educational and occupational distributions are detailed in subsequent tables.

As shown in Table 3, the majority of respondents reported regular savings habits and the use of formal banking services. However, a significant portion also relied on borrowing from informal sources, indicating potential gaps in access to formal credit channels.

As shown in Table 4, the majority of respondents perceived Fintech as convenient, secure, and affordable. However, trust in digital payments and familiarity with specific Fintech platforms like UPI varied among the sample.

As shown in Table 5, significant positive correlations were observed between Fintech adoption and variables such as monthly income, trust in

Table 2 Demographic Characteristics of the Sample

Demographic Variable	*Frequency (%)*
Gender (Male/Female)	250 (50%) / 250 (50%)
Age (years)	Mean: 35.7 ± 8.2
Monthly Income (INR)	Mean: 12,000 ± 3,500
Residence Type	Urban: 400 (80%), Rural: 100 (20%)

Table 3 Financial Behaviors of the Sample

Financial Behavior	*Frequency (%)*
Regular Savings	320 (64)
Borrowing from Informal Sources	180 (36)
Use of Formal Banking Services	400 (80)
Investment in Financial Assets	150 (30)
Participation in Insurance	100 (20)

Table 4 Perception of Fintech Usage

Perception	*Frequency (%)*
Fintech is Convenient	450 (90)
Fintech is Secure	380 (76)
Fintech is Affordable	420 (84)
Trust in Digital Payments	360 (72)
Familiarity with UPI	300 (60)

digital payments, and familiarity with UPI. These findings suggest that socio-economic factors and trust in digital platforms influence Fintech adoption and subsequent financial inclusion.

As shown in Table 6, regression analysis revealed that monthly income, trust in digital payments, and familiarity with UPI significantly predict Fintech adoption and financial inclusion among low-income individuals in Kolkata. Higher income levels and greater trust in digital payments are associated with increased Fintech adoption and financial inclusion.

As shown in Table 7, the chi-square test results indicate no significant association between gender and Fintech adoption among low-income individuals in Kolkata ($\chi^2 = 1.20$, $p > 0.05$).

Table 5 Correlation Analysis Results

Variables	*Fintech Adoption*	*Financial Inclusion*
Age	0.124*	0.078
Monthly Income	0.256**	0.201**
Education Level	0.097	0.065
Trust in Digital Payments	0.345**	0.278**
Familiarity with UPI	0.213**	0.187**

Table 6 Regression Analysis Results

Predictor Variables	*Fintech Adoption (β)*	*Financial Inclusion (β)*
Monthly Income	0.386**	0.301**
Trust in Digital Payments	0.267**	0.212**
Familiarity with UPI	0.189*	0.165*

Table 7 Chi-Square Test Results for Gender and Fintech Adoption

Gender	*Fintech Adoption (Yes/No)*	*Total*
Male	220/30	250
Female	210/40	250
Total	430/70	500

Table 8 ANOVA Results for Age and Fintech Adoption

Age Group	*Mean Fintech Adoption Score*
18–30	3.5
31–45	4.2
46–60	3.8
> 60	3.6

As shown in Table 8, ANOVA results suggest a significant difference in mean Fintech adoption scores across different age groups (F(3496) = 4.76, $p < 0.05$), with respondents aged 31–45 exhibiting the highest adoption rates.

Overall, the results indicate a complex interplay between socio-economic factors, perceptions of Fintech, and financial behaviors among low-income individuals in Kolkata, highlighting the multifaceted nature of financial inclusion efforts in urban India.

5 Discussion:

The findings from the data analysis shed light on several key aspects regarding the role of Fintech in promoting financial inclusion among low-income individuals in Kolkata. Comparing these findings with the literature review reveals both consistencies and disparities, contributing to a deeper understanding of the research topic and addressing the identified literature gap.

Firstly, the demographic characteristics of the sample align with existing literature highlighting the prevalence of urban residence and relatively young age among Fintech users (Table 2). This consistency corroborates findings from previous studies (Bharathi et al., 2023; Nagaraja, 2023), emphasizing the importance of targeting urban populations, especially in cities like Kolkata, where Fintech adoption is on the rise.

In terms of financial behaviors, the high utilization of formal banking services among respondents (Table 3) echoes the findings of Dr. Amrik Singh and Dr. Lalit Mohan Sharma (2023), who observed Fintech's success in reaching unbanked and underbanked individuals. However, the reliance on informal borrowing sources among a substantial portion of the sample underscores persistent gaps in access to formal credit channels, as discussed by Hasan Babar (2023).

The positive perceptions of Fintech's convenience, security, and affordability (Table 3) resonate with existing literature highlighting Fintech's potential to democratize financial services (Bharathi et al., 2023). However, the varying levels of trust in digital payments and familiarity with specific platforms like UPI underscore the importance of addressing digital literacy and awareness, as emphasized by Guild (2017) and Iwasaki (2022).

Furthermore, the correlation and regression analysis results (Tables 5 and 6) provide insights into the factors influencing Fintech adoption and financial inclusion. The significant positive correlations between monthly income, trust in digital payments, and familiarity with UPI highlight the role of socio-economic factors and trust in driving Fintech adoption, consistent with previous research (Hasan Babar, 2023). Additionally, the regression analysis reinforces these findings, indicating that higher income levels and greater trust in digital payments predict increased Fintech adoption and financial inclusion, aligning with the conclusions drawn by Dr. Nagaraja K. (2023).

The implications of these findings are multifaceted and underscore the importance of tailored interventions to enhance financial inclusion among low-income individuals in Kolkata. Firstly, the positive perceptions of Fintech's convenience and affordability suggest a fertile ground for the expansion of digital financial services in urban India. However, addressing concerns related to trust and familiarity remains crucial to ensuring widespread adoption and usage.

Moreover, the identified disparities in access to formal credit channels highlight the need for targeted initiatives to improve financial literacy and promote responsible borrowing practices among low-income populations. By bridging these gaps, Fintech has the potential to not only expand access to financial services but also empower individuals to make informed financial decisions and improve their overall financial well-being.

The findings also underscore the importance of public–private partnerships and regulatory frameworks in facilitating Fintech's role in financial inclusion. Government initiatives, such as the implementation of UPI, have played a significant role in complementing Fintech solutions and expanding financial services to remote areas (Nagaraja, 2023). However, a balanced regulatory environment is essential to ensure consumer protection and prevent the exacerbation of existing inequalities, as highlighted by Guild (2017).

Furthermore, the age disparities in Fintech adoption suggest the need for targeted outreach and education programs, particularly among older age groups. By addressing digital literacy barriers and promoting awareness of Fintech platforms, policymakers and financial institutions can maximize the reach and impact of Fintech interventions, ultimately advancing the goal of inclusive economic development.

Overall, this study contributes to a deeper understanding of the role of Fintech in promoting financial inclusion among low-income individuals in Kolkata. By examining the interplay between socio-economic factors, perceptions of Fintech, and financial behaviors, the findings offer valuable insights for policymakers, researchers, and practitioners seeking to leverage Fintech to address the unique challenges of financial inclusion in urban India. Moving forward, it is imperative to build upon these findings through continued research and targeted interventions to ensure that the benefits of Fintech are accessible to all segments of society, particularly the economically marginalized communities in Kolkata and beyond.

6 Conclusion

This study investigated the role of Fintech in promoting financial inclusion among low-income individuals in Kolkata, India. Through a quantitative research design and data analysis, several key findings emerged, shedding light on the dynamics of Fintech adoption, financial behaviors, and perceptions among the target population.

Overall, the findings suggest a positive relationship between Fintech adoption and financial inclusion, with factors such as monthly income, trust in digital payments, and familiarity with specific Fintech platforms playing significant roles. The demographic characteristics of the sample, including urban residence and relatively young age, align with existing literature on Fintech adoption patterns, emphasizing the importance of targeting urban populations for Fintech interventions.

The study also highlighted persistent gaps in access to formal credit channels among low-income individuals, indicating the need for targeted initiatives to improve financial literacy and promote responsible borrowing practices. While the majority of respondents reported regular savings habits and the use of formal banking services, a substantial portion relied on borrowing from informal sources, underscoring the importance of addressing these gaps to ensure comprehensive financial inclusion.

Moreover, the positive perceptions of Fintech's convenience, security, and affordability among respondents suggest a fertile ground for the expansion of digital financial services in urban India. However, addressing concerns related to trust and familiarity remains crucial to ensuring widespread adoption and usage.

The implications of these findings are far-reaching. By leveraging Fintech to improve financial access and literacy, policymakers and financial institutions can empower individuals to make informed financial decisions and improve their overall financial well-being. Moreover, the findings underscore the importance of public–private partnerships and regulatory frameworks in facilitating Fintech's role in financial inclusion, while also highlighting the need for targeted outreach and education programs to address age disparities in Fintech adoption.

Beyond its implications for policymakers and practitioners, this study contributes to a deeper understanding of the complex dynamics of financial inclusion in urban India. By examining the interplay between socio-economic factors, perceptions of Fintech, and financial behaviors, the study provides valuable insights for researchers seeking to advance the field of financial inclusion and digital finance.

Moving forward, it is imperative to build upon these findings through continued research and targeted interventions. By addressing the identified gaps and harnessing the potential of Fintech to empower marginalized communities, we can work toward a more inclusive and equitable financial system that benefits all segments of society. Through collaborative efforts and innovative solutions, we can unlock economic opportunities and improve the livelihoods of millions, ultimately contributing to the broader goals of poverty reduction and economic development in India and beyond.

References

Asif, M., Khan, M. N., Tiwari, S., Wani, S. K., & Alam, F. (2023). The Impact of Fintech and Digital Financial Services on Financial Inclusion in India. *Journal of Risk and Financial Management, 16*(2), 122. https://doi.org/10.3390/jrfm16020122

Babar, H. (2023). Fintech—A Solution for Financial Inclusion and Women's Economic Empowerment? *Journal of Financial Services*. https://doi.org/10.32388/afleu0

Bharathi S, V., Perdana, A., & Kulkarni, M. S. (2023). Exploring the Synergy Between Financial Technologies and Financial Inclusion: What We Know and Where We Should Be Heading? *Proceedings of the AIS, 15*(1), 104. https://doi.org/10.17705/1pais.15104

Guild, J. (2017). Fintech and the Future of Finance. *Asian Journal of Public Affairs, 10*(1), 10. https://doi.org/10.18003/AJPA.201710

Iwasaki, K. (2022). Comment on "Fintech and Financial Inclusion in Southeast Asia and India." *Asian Economic Policy Review, 17*(1), 123–145. https://doi.org/10.1111/aepr.12380

Nagaraja K, D. (2023). Role of Fintech in Financial Inclusion in India. *International Journal of Financial Management Research and Development, 5*(4), 5953. https://doi.org/10.36948/ijfmr.2023.v05i04.5953

Singh, A., & Sharma, L. M. (2023). Fintech and Financial Inclusion: Transforming Underserved Access to Financial Services. *Journal of Tourism and Hospitality Management, 5*(2), 71–85. https://doi.org/10.22271/27069583.2023.v5.i2a.71

How Can FinTech Adoption Benefit the MSME Sector in India?

Krishn A. Goyal, Teena Mertiya, Sudha Bishnoi, and Deepak Bhatia

1 Introduction

Micro, small, and medium enterprises (MSME) are paramount in driving socioeconomic advancement, job creation, and shared prosperity. Within a limited-resource predicament, it has been a major voice in enhancing the performance of entire supply chains on a local and global scale. As

K. A. Goyal
Department of Business Finance and Economics, International Affairs, Library Board, Jai Narain Vyas University, Jodhpur, India
e-mail: kag.bfe@jnvu.edu.in

T. Mertiya (✉)
Department of Economic Administration and Financial Management, Government Bangur Postgraduate College, Rajasthan, India
e-mail: teenamertiya97@gmail.com

S. Bishnoi · D. Bhatia
Department of Management Studies, Jai Narain Vyas University, Jodhpur, India
e-mail: sudh9156@gmail.com

D. Bhatia
e-mail: deepakbhatia291@gmail.com

© The Author(s), under exclusive license to Springer Nature Singapore Pte Ltd. 2025

A. S. et al. (eds.), *Trends and Challenges of Electronic Finance*,
https://doi.org/10.1007/978-981-96-3304-3_15

producers and distributors, they also contribute to the rise of larger and more mature consumer marketplaces.

The MSME division within India has been a vital component of the economy. The industry makes up for 45% of the country's industrial production and 40% of total exports, as per think tank NITI Aayog. In addition, the MSME sector accounts for nearly 30% of the nation's GDP and employed well over 110 million people in 2020. Unfortunately, India's core financial setup makes it harder for MSMEs to raise capital. Therefore, the government propelled MSMEs to the forefront of national policy. Even the Reserve Bank of India has shown sufficient devotion. So that every individual will get benefits from the financial offering.

Accordingly, the government catapulted MSMEs to the frontline of national policy by launching Make in India in 2014, Startup India in 2016. Even the Reserve Bank of India has unveiled the Trade Receivables Discounting System (TReDS), whereby the MSMEs can obtain funding by auctioning their trade receivables. In addition, public sector banks have been suggested to create at least one specialized branch within every district. Additionally, banks have been allowed to designate as specialized MSME branches if advance 60% or more to MSME (Vijayendra, 2010). All are meant to boost investment.

However, owing to higher costs, the prevailing arrangement of India's financial system makes it challenging for MSMEs to secure finance. Even after repeated government mandates to stimulate MSME funding, banks and financial institutions have been reticent about lending to them. MSMEs financing is largely done through money lenders the same has been confirmed by International Financial Corporation report, 2018. This broad foundation serves as an ideal launch pad for financial developments. It's an opportunity to fill these financial gaps with the FinTech revolution. In fact, in India, the FinTech industry is working to improve direct exposure to capital and the formal credit system across all inhabitants.

The advent of the modern techno-economic model has been a boon for the financial system, touching literally every aspect, including commerce and entertainment, through the digitalization process. With that, instruments utilized in digital technology have substantially improved the means of communicating. In India's instance, the direction of digital progression over the last few years has opened an alternative roadmap into long-term development. As illustrated by the Network Readiness Index, India's position was 67th out of 130 nations in 2021. Our main asset is electronics. In the meantime, India thrives in Internet bandwidth, active cellular broadband access, and SMS are being sent by people ages 15–69. Consequently, the country continues as one of the principal economies where its structural enablers for establishing and incubating FinTech firms have moved alongside staunchly.

Unfortunately, because of increasing dependency upon third-party lending service operators, there are already inadvertent repercussions such as immorality, impropriety toward unsuspecting clients, concerns about data security breaches, unfair corporate action, and even criminal offences. As per the RBI, during January 1, 2020–March 31, 2021, the "Sachet" portal reported about 2562 grievances against digital lending applications. Maharashtra and Karnataka states have the most unlicensed lending platforms and mobile applications (2562 Complaints, 2022). Moreover, the burgeoning proliferation of tech firms looking to aid in abetting financial products has made the governance task more onerous. Despite the proficiency of universality, anonymity, and quickness, it has grown critical to oversee current and prospective vulnerabilities in the online ecosystem without hampering innovation. Notwithstanding the reality that Aadhar is the largest global virtual identification initiative, it enables biometric 'or' demographic-based unique recognition that can be validated at any point and from any location, so it reduces duplication and counterfeit credentials. Furthermore, GST provides a comprehensive authentication infrastructure for reliable background checks on corporate executives.

Given this tendency, it is advisable to comprehend the potential of FinTech and how well it can benefit the MSME sector in India. This chapter discusses the challenges that MSMEs encounter when it comes to obtaining finance. It begins by assessing the existing credit vacuum for MSMEs and subsequently examines the supply-side, FinTech that could contribute to this imbalance. The chapter is prepared as follows. Section 2 provides an overview of the literary works concerning the subject, as well as a logical paradigm for gathering information relevant for the analysis. Section 3 outlines the research's data and methodology. Section 4 highlights the FinTech perspective in the Indian MSME sector. Section 5 explores India's FinTech Intervention Scenarios extensively. Then the last section concludes the above analysis.

2 Literature Review and Analysis of Related Work

The Micro, Small, and Medium Enterprises (MSME) sector does have fairly significant implications on economic growth. It helps nearly every industry, whether manufacturing or exports. To illustrate:

Its output adds around 40% value to the manufacturing sector and one-third to the exports. Besides, it has the second-largest employment share in India, just behind the agriculture sector. However, the nature of MSME industries is changing, forging a switch from economic to inclusivity. So, the involvement of the MSME sector within India's socioeconomic prosperity needs to be acknowledged, investigated, and promoted (Lokhande, 2011). During the past few years, India's SMEs have seen countless turning points. SME sector, the mainstay of the economy, is given special attention since India is anticipated to emerge as the world's foremost economy by 2025. Further start-ups spotted a market funding vacuum and created an easier and simpler alternative technology-driven to render SMEs to receive credit (Innovative financial solutions for MSMEs, 2018). The government has stepped up particular attention toward the growth of the small business sector using diverse initiatives. This industry is administered by the Ministry of Micro, Small, and Medium Enterprises, and is monitored by a development commissioner. Due to inherent agility, versatility, and inventive spirit, SMEs are highly keen on improving the production process, thrusting marketing tactics, and managerial competencies to prolong and shore up existing functions. The governance structure and support interventions must improve with time to support smallholder success and sustainability. So MSME department is purposefully intervening toward the regeneration of small enterprises with its service as well as branch institutes (Ligi, 2013).

Smaller firms, the core of almost every GDP, be it national or the global market, must therefore embrace change and deliver emulous goods and services (Robu, 2013). In a climate of competitive pressures, in which the players reconfigure the spirit of the system, compelling businesses to recalibrate the basics underpinning competitiveness and efficiency, holding technology as a crucial investment. Management of technology is outlined as the use of science, engineering, and managerial skills to successfully identify, pick, accumulate, build, manipulate, and empower technologies relevant to gain an edge and accomplish optimal thresholds of performance and profitability.

Some trends in the finance industry have been swayed by automation. FinTech is an example of such disintermediation. FinTech has progressed in tandem with the evolution of community choices. That's the culmination of infusing technology into daily practices. FinTech is a relatively young financial biz utilizing technology to enable users' properly regnant resources. Any such description may offer set advantages and even some shortcomings. The interpretation centers on the spirit of FinTech combining various spheres because history cannot be traced with accuracy (Schueffel, 2016). While in the contemporary era, it is normally regarded as a coupling of financial services with information technology. The digitization of finance spawned the FinTech age, and ultimately it's up to individuals to reconcile positive and negative implications (Buckley et al., 2016). Detailed picture of Philippine MSMEs provides information on the sector's fundamental features as well as major concerns influencing it, as with competitiveness, productivity, finance, and market access, things that could very well be remedied for entrepreneurs and the government (Zamora, 2010). The study briefs reflection on FinTech's guardianship to MSMEs and also the application of descriptive qualitative methods. MSMEs necessitate business operations running parallel to financial technology inside the current state of affairs. The Indonesian government has proffered encases to institutions, specifically banks to empower MSMEs by garnering capital and otherwise cumulative assets. With model's primary function is of ensuring the long-term viability of MSMEs via strengthened efficiency and effectiveness and the comfort of doing business. Also FinTech market is exploding in Indonesia— particularly among Crowdfunding & peer-to-peer lending. FinTech harnessed Indonesian capital financing to small and medium-sized businesses and offers a wide range of financial services, particularly hoping to grow. FinTech's advancement is designed toward inclusivity (Darma et al., 2020).

FinTech's role and responsibilities in the coming years are critical for any economy as could shape the banking IT ecosystem. Else non-traditional actors tend to be a danger, with varying degrees of disruption depending on the financial service. Besides restructuring of financial services has spawned a slew of new ideas, like peer-to-peer lending, pushing banks out from just the lending cycle. At the same time as lenders might expect higher returns, borrowers should expect cheaper rates. FinTechs are cutting out the intermediaries and putting more emphasis on highly valuable portions of the banking value stream (Wankhede &

Salunkhe, 2017). Multinational brands pose considerable setbacks to the Indian banks, besides there are unrealized openings that might be seized to bolster potentiality. To build a more appealing prospect, the significant loopholes underlying users' reluctant attitudes toward Online Banking should be right off the bat (Sagar, 2017). Digital technology heed among SMEs and potential clientele is redefining the mechanics of MSME financial management in the twenty-first century. By granting MSMEs rich and better information, adaptive connectivity, quicker and streamlined practices, banks can make revenue as well as strengthen their competitive positions. The MSME sector has significant potential to yield protracted commercial value well over both Latin American and Caribbean financial institutions. If somehow the regional orientation to innovation is re-calibrated, the FinTech wheel can revolutionize financial markets, MSMEs, or rather the economy itself (Hoder et al., 2016). FinTech would be an application that is supposed to be reinforced expeditiously, with rising use in small businesses. Perhaps the growth of Indonesian FinTech has been remarkable still there's lot of untapped strength (Batunanggar, 2019). Religion also has positive impact on why people choose to utilize Islamic FinTech. Perceived usefulness, perceived ease of use, and subjective norm were demonstrated to have an influence on overall intentionality, but attitude toward behavior and perceived behavioral control seemed to have no relationship. It thus underscores the primacy of partnerships between the Financial Services Authority (OJK), regulator, and Islamic FinTech entities to ameliorate awareness, offer perks, shore up data security, and incorporate religious ideals into the philosophy and practice of Islamic FinTech solutions to gain popularity among MSME players (Majid, 2021).

FinTech offers many advantages, although not without problems. Its two most prominent concerns have indeed been user and data safeguards. Since it offers services through digital arrangements, those with an internet service may leverage the power of it to steal user information. Under the worst scenario, it might jeopardize monetary sustainability if individuals are unable to discover strategies to cope. Financial interactions may actually happen beyond the restrictive legal apparatus, posing a threat to the overall structure (Value of FinTech, 2017). Assurance regarding clients' confidentiality of valuable details during banking exchanges is a significant aspect in building up financial systems. In terms of striving to improve technology penetration rates, customer delight, and quality of life, one must learn from Malaysian impulses to increase reliance on

FinTech activities. Also, youth clients have a lot of exposure to automation, which has resulted in their having a clear idea of how to utilize it. But senior customers have a harsher dilemma with admitting innovations, especially with regard to conducting financial transactions via a mobile interface (Tun-Pin et al., 2019). In terms of technology adaptability or FinTech network dexterity, MSMEs have the ability to complement. MSME can implement Technology Acceptance Model to evaluate the deciding characteristics of the tech product that may influence behavior, rather technology practices intention via perceived usefulness. Yet advocating FinTech products might be challenging given the variety of socioeconomic origins, firm size, and characteristics. Thus, it should be promoted by stressing on the positives of the use of services (Purnamasari et al., 2020).

3 Research Methodology

The descriptive research design has been followed to describe the extent to which FinTech is important in the MSME resilience in India. Secondary data sources for thorough analysis were gathered from official government publications.

4 FinTech Perspective in the Indian MSME Sector

4.1 *Present Scenario*

As per latest available data in public domain, Micro-enterprises accounts for 99% with 630.52 lakhs of total estimated MSMEs, and two years ago it stood for 47 lakh (94%) of all registered firms on the Udyam Registration platform as of October 2021, while small businesses represented 2.7 lakh (5%), and medium-sized businesses 40,062 of all registered businesses. In terms of commercial potential, this occupies a prominent hold. As of March 2019, scheduled commercial banks had outstanding loan growth of 14.08% in comparison to March 2018 (Table 1). Perhaps private sector banks have ambitiously contributed to the MSME sector (Mund, 2020). Despite progress in MSMEs' financing options, the unfilled credit gap inside the MSME sector is anticipated to be INR 25.8 trillion (USD 397 billion), that conventional banking institutions might not purvey.

Table 1 Banks' total credit allocation to MSME

Year ended	*Public sector banks*		*Private sector banks*		*Foreign banks*		*All schedule commercial banks*	
	No. of A/cs	*Amount O/s*	*No. of A/cs*	*Amount O/s*	*No. of A/cs*	*Amount O/s*	*No. of A/cs*	*Amount O/s*
March 2015	86.08 (1.37%)	852,689.27 (12.44%)	50.23 (30.15%)	281,548.83 (13.93%)	2. 84 (−3.14%)	36,787.95 (6.85%)	139.15 (10.05%)	1,171,026.05 (12.61%)
March 2016	106.82 (24.10%)	820,548.0 (−3.77%)	96.42 (91.95%)	359,085.34 (27.54%)	1.86 (−34.40%)	36,373.76 (−1.13%)	205.10 (47.40%)	1,216,007.11 (3.84%)
March 2017	111.97 (4.82%)	828,933.42 (1.02%)	119.59 (24.04%)	430,962.70 (20.02%)	2.07 (11.10%)	36,502.70 (0.35%)	233.63 (13.91%)	1,296,398.82 (6.61%)
March 2018	111.01 (−0.85%)	864,597.79 (4.30%)	148.33 (24.03%)	410,760.21 (−4.69%)	2.20 (6.21%)	48,881.34 (33.91%)	261.54 (11.95%)	1,324,239.35 (2.15%)
March 2019	112.97 (1.76%)	880,032.90 (1.76%)	205.31 (38.41%)	563,678.47 (37.23%)	2.40 (9.30%)	66,939.14 (36.94%)	320.68 (22.61%)	1,510,650.52 (14.08%)

Note YoY % growth/decline in parentheses while No. of accounts in lakhs and amount in crores
Source Report on 24th Standing Advisory Committee on MSME, FIDD, RBI Sept 2019

Strategic government measures with other assisting forces could become critical enablers for MSME, clearing the way for the rise of digital channels. On this course, the government recently created some E-portals to solve issues about financial defaulters. One of these is the Samadhaan portal (2017), it has had little effect, and thus GSTN can be merged with a portal whereby purchasers are assigned a 'timeliness rating' to mitigate the defaulting odds. In addition, banks and chosen NBFCs operate as a critical component in channeling receivables to the TReDS platform (Devarayalu, 2021). MSMEs are critical both for delivering livelihoods for thousands of families and also encouraging fundamental progress. The authorities' focus is on encouraging creativity throughout the sector to achieve the objective of having an innovation-driven society. Yet there has been little feat due to a lack of efficient oversight and strategy for detecting and nurturing innovations. On the other hand, if somehow accentuates the role of innovation, it rarely assigns priority to how this dynamic plays out in the MSMEs (Raghuvanshi et al., 2017).

4.2 *Why MSME Should Go for FinTech?*

India is making strides in digital exchanges, much like other large economies that are actively reaping the rewards of being fully automated.

Such a phenomenon is proven helpful for the MSME industry. They may gain access to a broad client base by integrating with e-commerce platforms. Overlooking the online ride is unaffordable as customers are intensely adopting digital approaches to transactions. Additionally, digitalization helps to keep track of the MSMEs' credit files, so fraud and data redundancy in payments would drop (Bhardwaj, 2020). In particular, guarantee transactional comfort to expand their potential customer market.

Henceforth after confronting hardships during the demonetization episode, the MSME sector has reared up FinTech services via mobile, point-of-sale machines, digital wallets, accounting software, FinTech SaaS, and several others. Indeed, the trend across has created a slew of possibilities for FinTech businesses. Provided the demonetization in 2016, which outlawed Rs 500 and Rs 1,000 banknotes, India had seen the unfolding of the digitized system. It was during this period that financial services picked up steam, ushering in the Unified Payment Interface (UPI). Ever since corporations have begun to develop solutions that support the nation's financial architecture.

Indeed, the Ministry of Micro, Small and Medium Enterprises has digitized all it's cleaves. Attempts are being made to propagate the message about the convenience and effectiveness of various payment systems, including BHIM UPI, and the Bharat QR code. As shown in Table 2, digital activities increased by approximately 90% during the fiscal years 2020–2021.

Furthermore, the disruptions to companies caused by COVID-19 exacerbated the credit situation. Indeed FinTech has become an integral aspect of modern firms, primarily MSMEs giving a huge opportunity for FinTech companies. Peer-to-peer lending FinTech tools have all the ability to effectively shrink this fund vacuum. There seem to be a couple of justifications for this. Firstly, FinTech lending companies are offering funds at markedly lower costs than banks as well as other typical finance houses, empowering them to reach niche clientele. Secondly, FinTech lenders embrace means to create innovative ways of credit risk analysis, like artificial intelligence and big data analytics (Ahluwalia, 2021). Despite all the necessary efforts made to strengthen the business, the financial landscape needs a lift. There are a variety of challenges that ought to be fixed for a smoother and faster loan modus operandi.

Besides, According to Instamojo's 'Indian MSME Impact Report, 2019', MSMEs hope technology will alleviate fundamental difficulties

Table 2 Digital transactions till December 2020 by the ministry of MSME or its affiliated bodies

Name of organization	*Number of transactions*					
	Total		*By digital means*		*Percentage*	
	No. of transactions	*Value in rupees (in crores)*	*No. of transactions*	*Value in rupees (in crores)*	*No. of digital transactions actions (in %)*	*Values of digital transactions (in %)*
KVIC	3,673,719	4102.92	3,202,965	4059.54	87.19	98.94
NSIC	74,534	12,918.52	69,938	12,705.74	93.83	98.35
DC office (Tool Room + DI offices + HQ)	94,856	954.74	88,450	891.61	93.24	93.39
COIR board	15,823	288.13	12,884	272.50	81.42	94.57
NIMSME	1833	9.52	1658	6.56	90.45	68.91
MGIRI	764	10.85	726	10.63	95.02	97.97
Total	3,861,529	18,284.67	3,376,621	17,946.58	90.19	92.02

Source Annual Report 2020–2021, Ministry of Micro, Small, and Medium Enterprises, Government of India

including finance, payments, and accounting. About 47% think that digital payment systems can tackle a major fraction of the difficulties, 35% switched to digital payments for its transaction convenience, 9% for the provision of data synchronization and confidentiality aspects, and 11% for consumer choice. Several MSMEs believe payment gateways are trustworthy avenues (more than 56%). But rest 44% still endorse established lines of credit over online peer-to-peer networks.

Seeing that there will surely be a lot more folks from the MSME sector engaged in FinTech. Finally when all underlying FinTech dimensions are put together will make a substantial contribution to inclusive industrial growth. That is income, investments, insurance, and institutional credits are set in motion to others; investment is feasible once income rises; insurance coverage facilitates risk and investment. The flow of credit supports performance (It's time to convert FinTech initiatives, 2021).

5 India's FinTech Interventions Scenarios

With the country intending target of a $5 trillion economy by 2024–2025, the government has to put forth enough commitment to thrive the Micro, small, and medium enterprises (MSMEs) GDP share to 50% as from given 29% (How FinTech is shaping up the MSME sector, 2021). The MSME sector including Khadi, Village, and Coir Industries has matured as a thriving yet vibrant part of the Indian economy (Elayaraja & Vijai, 2020). MSME not merely supports economic growth but also contributes to social inclusion by bridging the gap between poor and rich. They are the ones who create the most jobs and certainly contribute to industrial output and exports.

Besides, India is already among the world's tech innovation hotspots, with FinTech forging ahead with about $10 billion in investment. Mumbai and Bengaluru jointly catalog 42% are the leading FinTech hub in the country. Indeed as per the newest Global FinTech Index 2020, released by Findexable, three cities got a mention in the top 20 Global FinTech Hubs. India is home to six of the top 100 global FinTech locations. Among these cities are Bengaluru, Mumbai, New Delhi, Pune, Hyderabad, Chennai, and Ahmedabad.

At this juncture, the government is working hard to create a robust and secure technological environment, and public–private partnerships will promote financial inclusion and deliver modernized financial products to every citizen. It was seen during the pandemic time that digitalization is the most potent weapon for increasing financial inclusion. The government's concerted efforts, along with techno enhancements, have propelled India's financial inclusion but also redefined how it accesses financial services.

Here are a couple of interventions. The Karnataka Digital Economy Mission created the maiden Karnataka FinTech Task Group. Given Karnataka has been host to many of India's major FinTech start-ups, namely Razorpay, Zerodha, khatabook, and cred (Karnataka sets up a task group for FinTech growth, 2021). The Mumbai FinTech Accelerator public–private partnership, uniting the Maharashtra government, the National Payments Corporation of India (NPCI), banks, The FinTech

MeetUp, and certain other corporate groups. Its primary role is to enable FinTech start-ups and develop a pertinent culture for such businesses (Mumbai FinTech Accelerator, 2018).

BharatPe, headquartered in Delhi, was the pioneer to create an interoperable QR code that could take payments via 150+ UPI applications with no transaction costs. It is the third-largest participant in the private POS segment, with over 7 million merchants and around $300 million amount paid to them. Lendingkart Technologies Private Limited, headquartered in Ahmedabad, has created innovative solutions premised on big data analysis; assisting lenders to weigh up borrowers' credibility and deliver other associated services. These businesses are addressing concerns ranging from digital payment uptake to providing efficient neo banking services, investment opportunities, and accessible lending.

However, the capacity to establish a full end-to-end digital user experience has become a critical element of the onboarding process across FinTech lending companies, not only to ensure a smooth client service but also to reduce charges. Especially when financial data is controlled by multiple regulating parties, makes it difficult to consolidate and exchange this data with banks and financial institutions to secure credit. Therefore account aggregation mechanism (An account aggregator performs as a middleman, managing and controlling data flow) will serve a paramount purpose in providing financiers with access to credible data sources of a prospective MSME client. GST-linked data is yet another vital data aspect that equips FinTech lenders with an insight into MSME's cash flow epochs. GST data is harmonized, digitally accessible, and trustworthy; leading the MSME sector with a loan at relatively low fees.

Moreover, physical screening has been a concern in KYC practices, but the RBI's digital KYC and video KYC regulatory methodologies led FinTech platforms to design non-face-to-face client onboarding alternatives that have vastly eased procedures. The lending institution or FinTech Company does not require conducting independent KYC of the borrower. This would significantly facilitate the creation of emerging markets for credit facilities to MSME clients. To sum up, FinTech does have the potential to tweak the approach for small businesses. It can narrow a substantial chunk of the MSME finance discrepancy and can aid in credit risk management.

6 Conclusion

MSME has had a great effect on output; above all SME evolution and official intervention remain two major aspects in the emerging globe. Sad to relate enterprises face issues in accessing money, aside from the reality that they can be perceived as the spine of the state's survival and prosperity. Researchers have taken hold of multiple funding sources accessible to SMEs. This should deepen their awareness of financial tools available to them in diverse contexts and encourage constructive discourse across relevant parties (Abbasi et al., 2017). Certainly, numerous SME expansion efforts are being implemented and benefit the field, but are still inefficient in other places. In addition, commercial finance channels at each end of the spectrum remain vital. But MSMEs often have a hard time getting credit, mostly from the formal domain, as banks are reluctant to lend money to them. Dependence on the informal economy is not a sustainable substitute for the industry. Into the bargain about unregulated and disorganized MSMEs, along with government-funded groups that do funding insufficiency has been there. Deplorably borrowing is influenced by different incidents, including profitability, legal restrictions, lack of information about borrowers, organizational attributes, and the size of the company (Choudhury & Goswami, 2019).

It is very well understood that FinTech is the future of MSME. Besides, commonly acknowledged notion- FinTech business channels have the ability to bridge MSME credit gaps. Fortunately, India has experienced an astronomical surge in FinTech fundraising business over the past couple of years. Many FinTech start-ups have focused primarily on funding these pursuits, For example, 'NeoGrowth', 'Vistaar Finance', 'Capital Float', 'CoinTribe', 'SMEComer', 'Indifi Technologies'. Moreover, FinTech deployed technology to digitize traditional practices providing versatile façade. As such new financial products and smart gadgets are proving to be beneficial to MSMEs since they have increased their competitiveness and profitability. Furthermore, provides an opportunity to create an equitable financial environment that benefits all, not only the elite group.

In a broad sense, modern digital efforts have pulled venture or rather mechanisms online; harnessing modern resources to optimize workflows, bring down costs, and garner detailed insights. Since, FinTech uses virtual interfaces for marketing, sales, risk judgment, insight into business inclination, and driving growth. Thus in the foreseeable future, there is a lot of incentive to use FinTech in micro and small businesses to sustain equity, inclusion, and development in this sector.

As the FinTech contrivance alters the marketplace, giving access to inexpensive products, participants must reconsider their business model and design products for the digital realm. Thus, these findings can benefit banks and other financial institutions, conglomerates, start-ups, venture capitalists, authorities, and policymakers in reframing and pursuing their goals in the global financial landscape.

References

Abbasi, W. A., Wang, Z., & Abbasi, D. A. (2017). Potential sources of financing for Small and Medium Enterprises (SMEs) and role of government in supporting SMEs. *Journal of Small Business and Entrepreneurship Development*, *6*(1). https://doi.org/10.15640/jsbed.v5n2a4

Ahluwalia, S. M. (2021, March 30). Fintech can bridge MSME credit gap with digital data to assist risk analysis, cash flow-based lending. *The Financial Express*. https://www.financialexpress.com/industry/sme/cafe-sme/msme-fin-fintech-can-bridge-msme-credit-gap-with-digital-data-to-assist-risk-analysis-cash-flow-based-lending/2223151/

Bhardwaj. V. (2020, October 16). Digital payments: A game changer for Indian MSMEs? *India Business & Trade, an Initiative of Trade Promotion Council of India*. https://www.tpci.in/indiabusinesstrade/blogs/digital-payments-a-game-changer-for-indian-msmes/

Buckley, R., Arner, D., & Barberis, J. (2016). The evolution of Fintech: A new post-crisis paradigm? *Georgetown Journal of International Law, 47*, 1271–1319. https://doi.org/10.2139/ssrn.2676553

Batunanggar, S. (2019). *Fintech development and regulatory frameworks in Indonesia* (Indonesia; Issue 1014). Asian Development Bank. https://www.adb.org/publications/fintech-development-regulatory-frameworks-indonesia

Choudhury, M., & Goswami, C. (2019). MSME financing gaps—Review of literature for the period 2005 to 2016. *Journal of Small Business and Entrepreneurship Development*. https://doi.org/10.15640/jsbed.v7n2a5

2562 complaints against illegal digital lending apps till March '21: Govt. (2022, March 28). *Business Today*. https://www.businesstoday.in/latest/economy/story/2562-complaints-against-illegal-digital-lending-apps-till-march-21-govt-327574-2022-03-28

Devarayalu, L. K. (2021, September 21). Golden opportunity for FinTech to serve MSMEs. *The New Indian Express*. https://www.newindianexpress.com/opinions/columns/2021/sep/21/golden-opportunity-for-fintech-to-serve-msmes-2361444.html

Darma, D. C., Kadafi, M. A., & Lestari, D. (2020). FinTech and MSMEs continuity: Applied in Indonesia. *International Journal of Advanced Science and Technology, 29*(4), 4676–4685.

Elayaraja, M., & Vijai, C. (2020). *Status of micro, small and medium enterprises in India. 1*, 5–8.

How fintech is shaping up the MSME sector. (2021, February 2). *SMEcorner*. https://www.smecorner.com/how-fintech-is-shaping-up-the-msme-sector/

Hoder, F., Wagner M., Sguerra J., & Bertol, G. (2016). Harnessing the Fintech Revolution: How digital innovations are revitalizing MSME Finance in Latin America and the Caribbean. *Oliver Wyman*.

India News, The Indian Express. (2021, December 3). *It's time to convert Fintech initiatives into a revolution: PM Modi*. https://indianexpress.com/article/india/its-time-to-convert-fintech-initiatives-into-a-revolution-pm-modi-7654514/

Innovative Financial Solutions for MSMEs. (2018). ASSOCHAM.

Ligi, J. (2013). Government policy and small sectors in India. *CLEAR International Journal of Research in Commerce & Management, 4*(11), 120–121.

Karnataka sets up a task group for fintech growth. (2021, November 18). *The Times of India*. https://timesofindia.indiatimes.com/city/bengaluru/karnataka-sets-up-task-group-for-fintech-growth/articleshow/87768666.cms?from=mdr

Lokhande, M. A. (2011). Evolution of the MSMEs in India. *Journal of Social and Development Sciences, 1*(2), 79–90. https://ideas.repec.org/a/rnd/arjsds/v1y2011i2p79-90.html

Mund, C. S. (2020). Problems of MSME finance in India and role of Credit Guarantee Fund Trust for Micro and Small Enterprises (CGTMSE). *IOSR Journal of Economics and Finance, 11*(4), 6.

Mumbai FinTech Accelerator Recognises Phi Commerce Amongst Top 13 FinTech Companies. (2018, December 4). https://www.digitalterminal.in/news/mumbai-fintech-accelerator-recognises-phi-commerce-amongst-top-13-fintech-companies/14442.html

Majid, R. (2021). The role of religiosity in explaining the intention to use Islamic FinTech among MSME actors. *International Journal of Islamic Economics and Finance (IJIEF), 4*(2), 207–232. https://doi.org/10.18196/ijief.v4i2.11833

Purnamasari, P., Pramono, I. P., Haryatiningsih, R., Ismail, S. A., & Shafie, R. (2020). Technology acceptance model of financial technology in Micro, Small, and Medium Enterprises (MSME) in Indonesia. *The Journal of Asian Finance, Economics and Business, 7*(10), 981–988. https://doi.org/10.13106/jafeb.2020.vol7.no10.981

Robu, M. (2013). The dynamics and importance of SMES in economy. *The USV Annals of Economics and Public Administration*, *13*(1(17)), 84–89. https://econpapers.repec.org/article/scmusvaep/v_3a13_3ay_3a2013_3ai_3a1(17)_3ap_3a84-89.htm

Raghuvanshi, J., Ghosh, P. K., Agrawal, R., & Gupta, H. (2017). Hierarchical structure for enhancing the innovation in the MSME sector of India. *International Journal of Business Excellence, 13*, 181–198. https://doi.org/10.1504/IJBEX.2017.10007042

Sagar, D. (2017). Internet banking: Transformation from brick and mortar to click and order-Indian Journals. *ZENITH International Journal of Business Economics & Management Research*, *7*(11), 145–153. https://www.indianjournals.com/ijor.aspx?target=ijor:zijbemr&volume=7&issue=11&article=012

Schueffel, P. (2016). Taming the beast: A scientific definition of Fintech. *Journal of Innovation Management, 4*, 32–54. https://doi.org/10.2139/ssrn.3097312

Tun-Pin, C., Keng-Soon, W. C., Yen-San, Y., Pui-Yee, C., Hong-Leong, J. T., & Shwu-Shing, N. (2019). An adoption of Fintech service in Malaysia. *South East Asia Journal of Contemporary Business, Economics and Law*, *18*(5).

Vijayendra B. P. (2010, July 1). *Lending to Micro, Small & Medium Enterprises (MSME) sector*. https://rbi.org.in/scripts/NotificationUser.aspx?Id=5817&Mode=0

Value of Fintech. (2017). KPMG International.

Wankhede, M. M., & Salunkhe, S. (2017). Role of Fin Tech start ups in lending services of Indian financial sector. *SANSMARAN, 7*(1), 19–22.

Zamora, E. A. (2010). A management of technology framework for MSME success and sustainability. *Philippine Management Review, 17*, 21–51. https://www.journals.upd.edu.ph/index.php/pmr/article/view/1922

Fintech's Contribution to Supply Chain Finance Value Creation Via Banking and Financial Systems

Priya Makhija, Elizabeth Chacko, and Megha Kukreja

1 Introduction

After the financial meltdown of September 2008, when bank and financial institution loans were dramatically reduced, supply chain finance (SCF) became increasingly important. Other types of alternative finance, particularly trade credit from providers, became increasingly difficult to obtain. A credit terms extension, on the other hand, is exposed to contractual agreements, with smaller providers forced to prolong repayment schedules or forcibly delay repayment (Fabbri & Klapper, 2016). The supply chain may be put at risk or disrupted as a result of which adequate cash

P. Makhija (✉) · M. Kukreja
Center for Management Studies, Jain (Deemed to Be) University, Bangalore, India
e-mail: priya_m@cms.ac.in

M. Kukreja
e-mail: megha_k@cms.ac.in

E. Chacko
School of Business and Management, Christ University, Bangalore, India
e-mail: elizabeth.chacko@christuniversity.in

© The Author(s), under exclusive license to Springer Nature Singapore Pte Ltd. 2025

A. S. et al. (eds.), *Trends and Challenges of Electronic Finance*,
https://doi.org/10.1007/978-981-96-3304-3_16

cycle procurement and supply chain optimization are required, which SCF tries to achieve (Caniato et al., 2016).

SCF is defined as 'the use of financing and risk mitigation practices and techniques to optimise the management of the working capital and liquidity invested in supply chain processes and transactions' (GSCFF, 2021). Due to the convergence of various socioeconomic and financial elements, India's business development has accelerated in recent years and depending on the market circumstances there is always a demand for working capital. A company, large or small, will always require working capital, which is the money needed to cover day-to-day expenses not covered by fixed assets. Businesses get SME or MSME financing from commercial lenders to meet their working capital needs (Leadingkart Technologies, 2021).

A SCF has two primary viewpoints: a financial viewpoint and a supply chain viewpoint. The 'consumer self-motivated and self-approach,' which focuses mostly on converse factoring and might be considered a component of the 'finance-oriented perspective,' is another take on SCF. SCF is viewed as a set of (new) financial solutions by the finance-oriented perspective, which focuses on short-term financing, notably receivables and payables financing solutions. In this context, the role of financial institutions or banks in SCF solutions is critical. As a result, the player with more cash on hand and/or a lower financing cost has a greater demand for financing or working capital. Furthermore, SCF is not limited to solely short-term funding, and financial institutions and banks are not required to participate in SCF solutions. As a result, the 'supply chain viewpoint' of SCF has a broader picture of SCF than the 'finance-orientated approach' (Gelsomino et al., 2016). Furthermore, increased adoption of SCF in Asia-Pacific emerging economies to boost GDP, as well as a spike in the use of advanced technology such as AI and machine learning in supply chain finance, is projected to present attractive opportunities for the market (Allied Market Research, 2021).

Trade finance refers to both internal and overseas commerce transactions and is defined as 'funding for trade.' Both a vendor and a buyer of products and services are involved in a commercial contract. Mediators, such as banks and big organisations, may help facilitate these transactions. The worldwide Cash Management market was worth USD 8942.27 billion in 2019, but due to COVID-19, it fell to USD 7616.52 billion in 2020, and it is predicted to reach USD 10426.67 billion by the end of 2026, rising at a CAGR of 5.37% throughout the projected timeline (Valuates Reports, 2021).

Considering the above facts this study focuses on how emerging financial technologies (fintech) in information processing and collection—particularly through digitization, automation, and blockchain—can help these businesses gain access to capital. This paper highlights the challenges faced by supply chain finance as well as opportunities of fintech in SCF. Section 1 gives the introduction to the role of fintech in SCF and its challenges. Section 2 of the paper presents the review and analysis of previous studies conducted on the scope of supply chain finance and the role of fintech. Finally, the paper concludes that the integration of fintech through blockchain technology with SCF can boost financial intermediation and help overcome challenges by simplifying financial systems.

1.1 *Fintech in SCF*

Traditionally banks were providing SCF to only large-scale companies enjoying good credit standing, which left the SMEs struggling for SCF. With the advancement in technology, many fintech companies saw this as an opportunity and bridged this gap to support the SMEs to secure funding necessary to mitigate the risks in SCF. With the help of fintech companies are tapping new markets, researching for innovative products, and strengthening their financial positions with low-cost funding options (Rogers et al., 2016).

Companies that provide financial solutions that help businesses communicate with their suppliers. They help both of the contracting parties to boost their funds by letting the buyer to extend its payables and the seller to get payment faster. This has advantages for both parties, including increased liquidity and reduced volatility. A win-win situation for both. Fin-techs are internet companies that simplify financial systems and improve the efficiency of supply chain funding. Orbian, Prime Revenue, C2FO, Taulia, and Ariba are examples of new businesses, as are new operations created by traditional financial services organisations such as Citi Group, HSBC, BNP Paribas, and Deutsche Bank (Rogers et al., 2016).

Due to the many advantages of this underlying technology, it has been applied to other domains of business. Fintech through BCT in SCF can be applied to see these benefits. Blockchain has the potential to close the gap between trade finance demand and supply. The blockchain technology allows players to exchange information without using paper. The wise or conscience contracts are constructed using computer cards that are kept in the blockchain. It also provides information about the background of items as well as visibility into their journey through the supply chain (Rogers et al., 2016).

Blockchain technology (BCT) reasserts the value exchange mechanism and the method of information sharing via the Internet, resulting in new collaboration among SC network participants (Gomm, 2010) Verifying and preserving these old paper records of commerce is a major waste of labour and physical space (Nakamoto, 2008). Digital document management systems and entry retrieval systems, on the other hand, will help reduce workload and task difficulty while also assisting with procedural management and cost control (Montecchi et al., 2019).

The proof of work (PoW) consensus process is used by 'Bitcoin,' a global digital currency recognised in the past for its Blockchain technology (Flood & Goodenough, 2017). BCT has transformed the way individuals and organisations communicate information and transfer value via the Internet, and it has opened up new opportunities for supply chain collaboration (Fan, 2018). Based on two main baselines, a SCF application is appealing and effective for implementation: (1) Information sharing is secure, verifiable, and trustworthy in real time throughout the Blockchain, allowing all participants of the supply network to access it at any moment. (2) When particular criteria are activated by a smart con, automatic validation, and transaction execution can be accomplished (Fan, 2018).

1.2 Supply Chain Finance Challenges

Internally, a company faces the stress of product planning, development, marketing, and sales along with the pressure from the stakeholders to create innovative products catering to the requirements of the customers. On the outside, there is a pressure on the demand and supply side. Demand forecasting, price competitiveness, product quality, socially responsible initiatives, seasons, etc. to name a few. To overcome such risks and to gain a competitive advantage, it is important that companies pay close attention to the various SCF opportunities (Strom et al., 2013). At every stage in the supply chain finance is significant. Here, the role of financial intermediaries comes in place. With the advancement in the SCF industry, the SCF providers' market is no longer only big businesses with excellent credit ratings, but now small-scale enterprises (SMEs) are also in their purview of potential customers. As the scenario changes, complexities involving SCF like cross-border supply chain transactions, poor credit quality, and multidimensional supply chains, keep increasing (Beckwith, 2017; Conlon & Kasula, 2020).

2 Review of Literature

In every business, finance takes an important role which does give birth to buyer and supplier. Interest towards SCF started from 2008 onwards after the financial crisis (Vousinas, 2018). In India, Government of India (GoI) tries to increase the contribution from MSMEs but they lack sufficient credit and liquidity in working capital (S. Kumar, 2020). The scope of SCF is to manage the flow working capital among the parties involved in SCF are financial institutions, buyers, and supplier but depends highly on the market condition (Vousinas, 2018). It has also introduced inventory financing and purchase order finance to make market more sustainable (Moretto & Caniato, 2021). As per (Sharma, 2019) if compared with rest of the world Indian has adopted SCF late still the banks and other financial institutions are eager to partner with buyer and sellers for one-step solution for working capital and removing discrimination between the large firm and small vendors. As per Mckinsey report 2020 93% of the global supply chain firms are ready for the adversities and adapt the SCF for movement of more liquid funds (Botta et al., 2021).

SCF is a relief for dealer, vendor, and manufacturer by increasing the certainty of cash flows, implying automation which reduces cost of administration, and transaction uploaded in bank from parties which bank validates as per the parameters to integrate, aggregate, and transform the relation between vendor and dealer (Bank of Baroda, 2021). It also helps to remove the informal lenders and bridge the gap for lender by creating awareness of various tools to mitigate credit risk but there are still suppliers who don't have access to banking system making themselves more vulnerable (Iyer, 2021). SCF is more benefitted having a the parties through digitization and adoption of tools like fin- tech and AI which has reduced the cost for companies to manage working capital (Caniato et al., 2016). The benefit of SCF for MSMEs is having platform like Trade Receivable Discounting System (TReDS) through which instant credit from banks can be availed and it can also monitor the transaction of borrowers and lenders (Iyer, 2021).

Banks as a mediator gives diverse ways for buyers and suppliers to transact through various modes like:- Bank end to end taking care of delivery of funds, or bank collaborating with fintech and ERPs known as platform partners to deliver the funds (Botta et al., 2021). Banks as acting agent for SCF are a relief for dealer, vendor, and manufacturer by increasing the certainty of cash flows, implying automation which reduces cost of administration, and transaction uploaded in bank from parties which bank validates as per the parameters to integrate, aggregate, and transform the relation between vendor and dealer (Bank of Baroda, 2021). Fintech with the growth of technology has revolutionised and brought interaction between the buyer and supplier making it more transparent and flexible (S. Kumar, 2020). The innovation in fintech has applied technology as invoice discounting, early cycle discounting, securitisation of SCF, and usage of blockchain for enabling transparency in this platform (S. Kumar, 2020). Blockchain has helped the mediator of the bank with security and credibility of the trading parties which provides smooth flow in supply chain finances (Zhanga et al., 2021).

By integrating BCT in SCF, every supplier will be a participant in the blockchain and can independently verify and process transactions. Information regarding supplier evaluation, credit rating, and invoice status is transferred securely among all the participants on the blockchain, thereby giving real-time data access to them (Omran et al., 2017). The results of a BCT-driven SCF study through quantitative analysis revealed that it creates value to all its participants by providing key resources to its customers (Wang et al., 2021).

Cost-effective commodities resolution, which makes the accounts payable investment product more desirable, to cost-effective selection process via a shared trusted KYC registry are just a few of the benefits of a BCT implementation in SCF. Additional factors include expedited invoicing clearance, accurate rights of possession, and billing legality, as well as faster but less cost cash transfers (Hofman et al., 2018).

The challenges of transparency and the verifiable uniqueness of invoices can also be addressed by blockchain technology. Commercial banks and funding organisations can quickly search a relational ledger for duplicate invoices on an irreversible blockchain-based network. Companies related to the invoice can confirm that it is genuine, and banking institutions can be confident that it has not been formerly funded. To avoid duplicate financing on the same invoice, each invoice transmitted over the network is hashed, transcoded, and assigned a special identification. Even if the provider tries to resell the same ticket across the network, invoicing will remain the same, and the private blockchain will display all parties a previous financing incident. As a result, the likelihood of injury is minimised (Lawlor, 2016).

SCF being a tool used globally is still to be instilled in the Indian market and needs acceptability. The industry-wise study is yet to be conducted to have proper output of the technique. Before implementation, the study on the awareness of the technique and perception of buyers and suppliers need to be studied regarding SCF and the financing institutions.

2.1 Analysis

Trade finance is transitioning from a conventional paper-based manual model to a digitally computerised form these days. Manual operations are largely replaced with electronic transactions to achieve this. The supply chain financing ecosystem includes financial institutes, anchoring enterprises, transmission and distribution industries, and freight forwarders. Microfinance companies are the primary source of funding in the ecosystem. The immutability of distributed ledger technology ensures the accountability and authenticity of distribution network information while allowing multiple several users to access relatively similar datasets. As a result of improved visibility into industrial networks and access to accessible supplier information, supply chain risk can be effectively managed (Lin, 2020).

SCF has an impact on businesses in three areas: volume, cost, and duration. The solutions will have an impact on one or more of the dimensions, with some solutions having a higher impact than others (Pfohl & Gomm, 2009), lowering the cost of funding. It makes it easier to provide funding at a lesser cost to SC partners, who aren't usually eligible for lower-cost capital. As a result, financial service companies are able to issue credit at reduced interest rates. Supply chain finance not only allows for lower financing costs, but it also aids in the reduction of overall supply chain costs, such as the cost of goods (Babich & Kouvelis, 2018; Hui & Yun-lin, 2015; J. Zhang & Zheng, 2017).

Lack of training in Supply Chain Finance has been identified as a stumbling block for SCF management. Lack of automated processes, expertise and knowledge, and a skilled labour have all been recognised as major barriers to implementing technology-driven SCF solutions. So instead of actively controlling their supply network to realise major economic gains, businesses prefer to take a prudent approach to addressing their working capital (Zekhnini et al., 2020).

Blockchain, a sort of smart contracts, is a decentralised database system that stores and shares a constantly-growing list of data entries across network users. A blockchain not only allows novel information to be added to the database, but it also ensures that everyone on the network has access to the same data, resulting in a distributed linked data that is impervious to alteration (Muzammal et al., 2018). In order to effectively manage the value chain, players can use blockchain technology to keep track of costs, dates, geographies, reliability, authentication, and other pertinent data. The availability of this relevant data within blockchain can assist organisations in improving resource supplier authenticity, reducing deceptive and grey market losses, attracting people and adherence over offsite quality control, and feasibly elevating their position as a dependable manufacturing leader (Laaper & Fitzgerald, 2021).

Blockchain technology can improve supply chain operations by offering transparency, analytical expression, info authentication, contractual execution, and network durability. Blockchain technology can help supply chains become more reliable, transparent, secure, efficient, ethical, and resilient. The integration of supply chains and finance can be made easier with blockchain technology (Babich & Hilary, 2020).

3 Conclusion

The worldwide supply chain financing (SCF) business has a lot of untapped potential. Nearly 80% of qualifying assets do not benefit from enhanced working-capital financing, and the remaining one-fifth of assets are frequently funded incorrectly. Supply chain finance promotes a sustainable environment when it is correctly implemented: it allows corporate purchasers to secure inventory by extending payment terms, and it gives suppliers more assurance on forward orders. Banks and non-bank SCF providers deliver consistent, short-duration (and thus lower-risk) transaction volumes that are generally recurrent, while also providing a channel for larger offerings including foreign currency, payment processing, and structured finance. SCF frequently used to focus on larger, better-funded international organisations and their supply chains, while smaller and less well-funded businesses suffer access restrictions. Many accelerators, including digital delivery, finance innovation, industry utilities, blockchain, and API technologies, have the potential to make SCF more affordable and accessible, but progress has been gradual. COVID-19 & its impact have accelerated digital adoption and reconfiguration of trade and supply chains, for example, to strengthen resilience and diversify sourcing, as of 2020.

Blockchain Technology holds the potential to improve supply chain visibility and deliver a slew of other advantages such as improved material supply chain accountability to meet enterprise supplier quality guidelines, reducing the fabrication and fraudulent sourcing risks, improvising visibility and compliance, and reducing paperwork and administrative expenditures. However, it also has certain limitations such as it requires a complete redesigning of the system, tagging of all the steps digitally for the proper flow of information; cybersecurity breach concerns and moves to a decentralised network, which necessitates user and operator investment (Laaper & Fitzgerald, 2021).

Customers, suppliers, funders, and other peer-to-peer members are the participants in SCF Blockchain technology. Each participant represents a node with equal authority and responsibility for the same task. All of these transactions are securely captured and transmitted to all sensor nodes, who all retain the same data (A. Kumar & Chowdhury, 2020). It can be considerably easier to track products as they move around the supply chain, as well as offer a history of what happened during that journey, whether with the object itself or its surroundings, with visible, trustworthy, and auditable data through blockchain and Smart Contracts (Lyons & Courcelas, 2019).

Using blockchain technology to construct an enormous information platform that includes all nodes in the modern enterprise would not only increase the bond of trust between the businesses in the chain but also save cost by increasing the credit standard and performance of core businesses maintaining the integrity of working capital in the distribution chain (Liu, 2021; Q. B. Zhang, 2018).

Online integration via BCT connects all participants in the SCF's interaction and transaction behaviour, making the transaction process appear more pleasant, boosting the comfort of financial intermediation, and enabling society to transact in a comparatively elevated, content manner (Liu, 2021; Yi et al., 2020). In many ways, the flexibility and stability of cloud technology for supply chain finance assist SMEs in overcoming financing challenges while also delivering a minimal cost, moderate risk, elevated opacity, and more favourable outcomes ecosystem for SMEs.(Liu, 2021; Sun et al., 2021).

It is beneficial to strengthen the integration of blockchain technology with Internet Finance, as well as fully exploit the good benefits of Internet Finance, by implementing risk avoidance measures in four areas. Growing technological R&D, better legal structures, harmonised industry best practices, and the development of certain skills are all concerns that must be addressed (Liu, 2021; C. H. Zhang & Wang, 2021). A modern funding economic model based on digital smart contracts is investigated, as well as the impact of blockchain smart contracts on the banking industry (Cao, 2021).

As the world struggles to meet the SDGs and firms scramble to mend supply networks affected by the COVID-19 pandemic, banking institutions can help address the financial gap. Credit guarantees are being used in part by development banks around the world to help SME financing while allowing private lenders to establish, execute, and retrieve on debt. By providing money, reducing risks, and increasing financier capacity, microfinance institutions might possibly contribute in encouraging SCF activities (Chhabra et al., 2021).

References

Allied Market Research. (2021). *Supply Chain Finance Market*. Retrieved August 14, 2021, from Allied Market Research website: https://www.alliedmarketresearch.com/supply-chain-finance-market-A08187

Babich, V., & Hilary, G. (2020). Distributed ledgers and operations: What operations management researchers should know about blockchain technology. *Manufacturing and Service Operations Management, 22*(2), 223–240. https://doi.org/10.1287/MSOM.2018.0752

Babich, V., & Kouvelis, P. (2018). Introduction to the special issue on research at the Interface of Finance, Operations, and Risk Management (iFORM): Recent contributions and future directions. *Manufacturing & Service Operations Management*, *20*(1), 1–18. https://doi.org/10.1287/MSOM.2018.0706

Bank of Baroda. (2021, June 17). *Supply chain finance: Channel financing solutions in India*. Retrieved August 9, 2021, from bankofbaroda website: https://www.bankofbaroda.in/supply-chain-finance.htm

Beckwith, T. (2017, October 27). *Supply chain finance for SMEs—The hidden opportunity*. Retrieved September 13, 2021, from BCS consulting website: https://www.bcsconsulting.com/blog/supply-chain-finance-smes-hidden-opportunity/

Botta, A., Höll, R., Jain, R., Shah, N., & Tan, L. H. (2021). *Supply-chain finance: A case of convergent evolution?* Retrieved August 9, 2021, from McKinsey Global Payments Report website: https://www.mckinsey.com/~/media/mckinsey/industries/financialservices/ourinsights/acceleratingwindsofchangeinglobalpayments/chapter-3-supply-chain-finance-a-case-of-convergent-evolution.pdf

Caniato, F., Gelsomino, L. M., Perego, A., & Ronchi, S. (2016). Does finance solve the supply chain financing problem? *Supply Chain Management: An International Journal, 21*(5), 534–549. https://doi.org/10.1108/SCM-11-2015-0436

Cao, L. (2021). Blockchain smart contract and banking business development. *FinTech Time, 1*, 40–43.

Chhabra, P., Wilson, J. M., Degenhart, E., & Martinez, P. (2021, February). *Supply chain financing: An effective way for development banks to support small entrepreneurs.* Retrieved September 13, 2021, from World Bank Blogs website: https://blogs.worldbank.org/psd/supply-chain-financing-effective-way-development-banks-support-small-entrepreneurs

Conlon, N., & Kasula, M. (2020, September 3). *Supply chain financing: Forging stronger links.* Retrieved September 13, 2021, from Financialservice Blog website: https://financialservicesblog.accenture.com/growth-markets/supply-chain-financing-forging-stronger-links

Fabbri, D., & Klapper, L. F. (2016). Bargaining power and trade credit. *Journal of Corporate Finance, 41*, 66–80. https://doi.org/10.1016/J.JCORPFIN.2016.07.001

Fan, X. (2018). Scalable practical byzantine fault tolerance with short-lived signature schemes. In A. J. Onut, G. Jourdan, D. C. Petriu, & W. Chen (Eds.), *CASCON '18: Proceedings of the 28th Annual International Conference on Computer Science and Software Engineering* (pp. 245–256). Markham, Ontario, Canada: ACM. Retrieved from https://doi.org/10.5555/3291291.3291316

Flood, M. D., & Goodenough, O. R. (2017). *Contract as automaton: The computational representation of financial agreements.* Retrieved from https://www.financialresearch.gov/working-papers/files/OFRwp-2015-04_Contract-as-Automaton-The-Computational-Representation-of-Financial-Agreements.pdf

Gelsomino, L. M., Mangiaracina, R., Perego, A., & Tumino, A. (2016). Supply chain finance: A literature review. *International Journal of Physical Distribution and Logistics Management, 46*(4), 348–366. https://doi.org/10.1108/IJPDLM-08-2014-0173

Gomm, M. L. (2010). Supply chain finance: Applying finance theory to supply chain management to enhance finance in supply chains. *International Journal of Logistics Research and Applications, 13*(2), 133–142. https://doi.org/10.1080/13675560903555167

GSCFF. (2021). *Global supply chain finance forum—Home of supply chain finance terminology*. Retrieved August 13, 2021, from supplychainfinanceforum.org website: http://supplychainfinanceforum.org/

Hofmann, E., Strewe, U. M., & Bosia, N. (2018). *Concept—Where are the opportunities of blockchain-driven supply chain finance?* 51–75. https://doi.org/10.1007/978-3-319-62371-9_5

Hui, Y., & Yun-lin, M. (2015). The supply chain finance model—Based on the order-to-factoring mode. *Systems Engineering—Theory & Practice, 35*(7), 1733–1743. Retrieved from http://www.sysengi.com/EN/abstract/abstract110973.shtml?utm_source=TrendMD&utm_medium=cpc&utm_campaign=Systems_Engineering_-_Theory_%2526_Practice_TrendMD_0

Iyer, R. (2021, May 31). *MSME: How supply chain financing can resolve capital issues for MSMEs—The Economic Times. ET*. https://economictimes.indiatimes.com/small-biz/sme-sector/how-supply-chain-financing-can-resolve-capital-issues-for-msmes/articleshow/83106050.cms?from=mdr

Kumar, A., & Chowdhury, S. G. (2020). Transforming supply chain finance with blockchain. In *Infosysbpm*. https://www.infosysbpm.com/offerings/business-transformation-services/insights/documents/transforming-supply-chain-finance-with-blockchain.pdf

Kumar, S. (2020). *Unlocking credit for MSMEs: Innovations in supply chain finance*. Retrieved August 9, 2021, from PwC website: https://www.pwc.in/consulting/financial-services/fintech/fintech-insights/unlocking-credit-for-msmes-innovations-in-supply-chain-finance.html

Laaper, S., & Fitzgerald, J. (2021). *Using blockchain to drive supply chain transparency and innovation*. Retrieved August 12, 2021, from DeloitteStratOp website: https://www2.deloitte.com/us/en/pages/operations/articles/blockchain-supply-chain-innovation.html

Lawlor, C. (2016). Tokenization of invoices: A blockchain technology supply chain finance use-case—Commercial Finance Association Blog.

Leadingkart Technologies. (2021). *Supply chain finance—Invoice Bill Discounting & Finance Solutions in India*. Retrieved August 13, 2021, from Leadingkart website: https://www.lendingkart.com/supply-chain-finance/

Lin, A. (2020, March 4). *How blockchain-based supply chain finance helps solve financing pressures*. Retrieved August 12, 2021, from Assuredam website: https://assuredam.com/2020/03/supply-chain-finance-helps-solve-current-financing-pressures/

Liu, Z. (2021). Literature review of supply chain finance based on blockchain perspective. *Open Journal of Business and Management, 9*, 419–429. https://doi.org/10.4236/ojbm.2021.91022

Lyons, T., & Courcelas, L. (2019). *Blockchain in trade finance and supply chain.*

Montecchi, M., Plangger, K., & Etter, M. (2019). It's real, trust me! Establishing supply chain provenance using blockchain. *Business Horizons, 62*(3), 283–293. https://doi.org/10.1016/J.BUSHOR.2019.01.008

Moretto, A., & Caniato, F. (2021). Can supply chain finance help mitigate the financial disruption brought by Covid-19? *Journal of Purchasing and Supply Management*, 100713. https://doi.org/10.1016/J.PURSUP.2021.100713

Muzammal, M., Qu, Q., & Nasrulin, B. (2018). A blockchain database application platform. *ArXiv*. Retrieved from https://github.com/ChainSQL/chainsqld

Nakamoto, S. (2008). *Bitcoin: A peer-to-peer electronic cash system.*

Omran, Y., Henke, M., Heines, R., & Hofmann, E. (2017). *Blockchain-driven supply chain finance: Towards a conceptual framework from a buyer perspective.*

Pfohl, H.-C., & Gomm, M. (2009). Supply chain finance: Optimizing financial flows in supply chains. *Logistics Research, 1*(3), 149–161. https://doi.org/10.1007/S12159-009-0020-Y

Rogers, D., Leuschner, R., & Choi, T. Y. (2016, June 22). *The rise of FinTech in supply chains.* Retrieved August 13, 2021, from HBR website: https://hbr.org/2016/06/the-rise-of-fintech-in-supply-chains

Sharma, N. (2019, January 8). *The role of technology in supply chain finance.* Retrieved August 9, 2021, from Credable website: https://www.credable.in/business-insights/the role of technology-in-supply-chain-finance/

Strom, M., Levi, D. S., Vassiliadis, C. G., Bijsterbosch, J.-W., Diks, E., & Kyratzoglou, I. M. (2013). *Supply chain and risk management.* Retrieved September 13, 2021, from PwC website: https://www.pwc.com/gx/en/operations-consulting-services/pdf/pwc-supply-chain-and-risk-management.pdf

Sun, H., Zhou, Z. Y., & Fu, T. S. (2021). Research on financing of small and medium sized enterprises under the background of "Blockchain + Supply Chain Finance." *Modern Business, 3*, 48–50. https://doi.org/10.4236/AJIBM.2014.49051

Valuates Reports. (2021, February 8). Trade finance market size is projected to reach USD 10426.67 billion by 2026 at CAGR 5.37%.

Vousinas, G. L. (2018). *Supply chain finance revisited: A critical review with future prospects.* SSRN. Retrieved from https://doi.org/10.2139/ssrn.3286977

Wang, L., Luo, X. R., Lee, F., & Benitez, J. (2021). Value creation in blockchain-driven supply chain finance. *Information & Management*, 103510. https://doi.org/10.1016/J.IM.2021.103510

Yi, Z. L., Zhang, H. F., & Gong, Z. H. (2020). Innovation and discussion on the application of blockchain technology under the supply chain financial mode. *Management & Technology of SME, 4*, 44–47. https://doi.org/10.4236/EPE.2013.54B142

Zekhnini, K., Cherrafi, A., Bouhaddou, I., Benghabrit, Y., & Garza-Reyes, J. A. (2020). Supply chain management 4.0: A literature review and research framework. *Benchmarking: An International Journal*, *28*(2), 465–501. https://doi.org/10.1108/BIJ-04-2020-0156

Zhang, C. H., & Wang, X. (2021). Risk prevention of internet finance under blockchain technology. *China Economic & Trade Herald*. https://doi.org/10.4236/OJBM.2021.91022

Zhang, J., & Zheng, J. (2017). Analysis on the interest coordination mechanism in cross-border e-commerce subject. *International Journal of New Developments in Engineering and Society*, *1*(3), 133–135. https://doi.org/10.25236/IJNDES.17340

Zhang, Q. B. (2018). Analysis of the optimization effect of blockchain technology on supply chain finance. *Hebei Enterprises, 8*, 119–120. https://doi.org/10.4236/OJBM.2021.91022

Zhanga, T., Li, J., & Xinbo, J. (2021). Analysis of supply chain finance based on blockchain. In *International Conference on Identification, Information and Knowledge in the Internet of Things,2020*, 1–6. Procedia Computer Science. https://doi.org/10.1016/j.procs.2021.04.025

Evolution, Growth, and Future of Electronic Finance and FinTech in the GCC and MENA

Arindam Banerjee

1 Introduction

The development of technology has revolutionized the way people interact with each other. Gone are the days when people mostly met in person and physical presence was necessary for carrying out monetary transactions. In modern times, technology enhancements, coupled with Internet penetration, have facilitated businesses to operate beyond the realms of physical boundaries. The advent of electronic finance (e-finance) redefined finance functions across all verticals of financial services resulting in improved industry performance and better bottom-line outcomes. Franklin et al. (2002) defined e-finance as a financial and economic service that uses electronic communication and accounting, using technology as a financial tool such as e-commerce. Unlike traditional financial markets that use physical currency as a medium of exchange, the electronic industry replaced traditional currency with digital currency, also known as electronic or e-money. In the last decade, the rapid development of technology largely replaced physical debit and credit cards with

A. Banerjee (✉)
SP Jain School of Global Management, Dubai, UAE
e-mail: arin_006@yahoo.com

© The Author(s), under exclusive license to Springer Nature Singapore Pte Ltd. 2025

A. S. et al. (eds.), *Trends and Challenges of Electronic Finance*,
https://doi.org/10.1007/978-981-96-3304-3_17

smartphones-based applications. Today, a prepaid card is a classic example of a cashier and digital devices occupy an important part of digital overall e-finance ecosystem. They are considered to be more secure, and in addition to simple payments and receipts, they can be used for all online transactions.[1] Over the period of time, modes of financial transactions have gradually evolved into applications such as Apple Pay, Samsung Pay, Android Pay, and Alipay that use smartphone and electronic payment systems. Transactions carried out using these platforms resulted in more efficient of transactions and better consumers' satisfaction. At the same time, financial transactions, carried out electronically, could be easily tracked (resulting in better transparency) with faster turnaround time, an example being less queueing time at banks for deposits or withdrawals Shahrokhi (2008).

The FinTech industry in the Gulf Cooperation Council (GCC) region appears to be well-positioned for a time of substantial expansion, as the environment for FinTech growth in the GCC region is favorable. The GCC countries are progressively transitioning toward becoming developed markets in terms of financial inclusion, while over 22% of the GCC's population still lacks access to banking services, in contrast to around 60% in North Africa. Regional governments are cognizant of the magnitude of the rapid expansion of FinTech and are actively striving to implement regulatory measures that will foster the expansion of the market. International corporations are also capitalizing on the opportunities presented by the GCC FinTech market. The regional electronic banking market is positioned for substantial expansion, which can occur through two potential avenues. The FinTech market, encompassing different features such as electronic wallets, near-field communication, blockchain, and virtual reality, is still in its early stages of development. The future trajectory of the GCC FinTech market remains uncertain and will be determined over time.

2 Literature Review

In recent decades, the global financial system has witnessed a revolution in financial technology. Technology can improve financial services through cost reduction, better decision-making, faster implementation,

[1] Lo, Stephanie, and Christina J. Wang, "Bitcoin as Money? Current Policy Perspectives," Federal Reserve Bank of Boston, September 2014.

and better access to information, Lu et al. (2020). Technology has rapidly developed and influenced traditional financial services by providing value-added services. With the help of digital payments, digital currency, digital loan, wealth management services, financial technology (FinTech), artificial intelligence, data analysis, cloud and blockchain management, and other services, the financial services sector has redesigned itself to become more transparent, efficient, and financially inclusive, Nacera (2021). Over the years, e-finance achieved better and faster business by focusing on certain key growth incentives. E-finance has a strong influence in improving a country's overall economic growth. According to research conducted by Jungmittag (2004) and Sassi and Mohamed (2013), financial and technological improvements generally promote financial growth. The MENA countries (Middle East and North America), in particular, achieved significant economic growth leveraging its growth in e-finance sector. E-finance plays a critical role in various other ways. First, e-finance reduces communication costs involved in financial transactions, thereby reducing asymmetric data and marginal production costs, Franklin et al. (2002) and Meijers (2014). As argued by Shahrokhi (2008), traditional means of accessing capital not only consume more time, but also take time to upgrade and modernize legacy banking systems. In contrast, e-finance reduces global transaction time and provides better access to global financial markets. Finally, e-finance eases access restrictions by creating a financial environment with regulatory constraints in place. Thus, e-finance not only supports business growth by fostering competitive markets but also facilitates overall market growth.

2.1 The Evolution of Electronic Finance

The end of the 18th and the beginning of the nineteenth centuries were characterized by the rapid development of electricity and the railways. The last decade of the twentieth century was marked by industrial prosperity, that witnessed significant advances in the development of technology and innovation across all industries. According to some, this prosperity led to a new era of advanced business intelligence and digital transformation in every sphere of life. This period also witnessed economies of scale and improved computing and communication capabilities. As a result, usage of computers became a universal phenomenon. Commercial organizations started using computers to manage internal and external operations and non-commercial entities started connecting to the Internet and other networks to bring in better productivity at work place. This growth led to further boost in online commerce and led to the universal usage of electronic exchange of money. The new form of "currency" that gained popularity around the world became popular as "e-money." The term referred to prepaid currency in the real and virtual world where the goal was to primarily improve the functionality of existing payments systems.[2]

There is no universal definition of electronic money. In 1998, the ECB defined electronic money electronic commerce with monetary value as a technical tool that can be widely used to make payments to entities other than the electronic money issuer. The tool works as a prepaid carrier's tool without having to enter bank accounts in transactions.[3] Online banking emerged in the mid-1990s with Security First Network Bank (SFNB), following a unique venture in the United States in 1995. Since then, it has grown rapidly in many countries around the world. According to a study by Lyu and Zhao (2019), online spending involves three stages including exchange, growth, and development. The growth of Internet marketing has surged over the last couple of decades. This fact was observed in a study by Hou et al. (2016) who opined digital inclusion as a long-term process. Aided by digitization, growth of online finance has rapidly developed. Studies across the globe have shown that online finance centers around four primary pillars, namely ecology, care, technology, and needs. Internet finance platforms innovate products and services by segmenting product groups around a target, including new concepts, e.g. loan lines, repayment procedures, interest rates, product risk, and risk management to support online financial transactions of products and services by meeting these sets of particular consumer needs. The same conclusions were found in a study by Lin et al. (2015), that found out that electronic finance led to more satisfied consumers with new and innovative products. Additionally, it is found that online finance is helpful in identifying large data files and electronic documents pertaining to social issues, past inquiries, information exchange, and consumer credit. Further, online finance brings in more effective supervision of financial transaction. Internet finance improves the legal awareness of the industry,

[2] Boshkov, T., Radjenovic, Z., Davcev, L., Digital Innovations in the World of Finance, SocioBrains, issue 52, December 2018.

[3] ECB (1998).

enhancing the overall security systems and regulations as well as encouraging firms for operating legally and combat illegal transactions. It has been highlighted in the research of Al Ahbabi and Nobanee (2019) that continuous improvements in the e-finance sector complement traditional finance through system integration. In years to come, traditional financial institutions and Internet finance will potentially present a trend of continuous development through gradual convergence. With financial technology development, the borderline between the two will likely dilute in years to come as well as service innovation and products will take the center stage.

2.2 *Financial Technology (FinTech)*

The Financial Standards Board (FSB) defines FinTech as a technology that enables financial services innovation that can result in new business models, applications, processes, or products that have a relevant material impact on financial markets, institutions, and the provision of financial services. According to Leong and Sung (2018), FinTech is seen as any innovative idea that can improve financial service processes by designing technology solutions to different business situations, and ideas that can potentially lead to new business models. Additionally, according to Zavolokina et al. (2016), the term FinTech can be defined as the use of information technology in the areas of finance, financial innovation, and digital innovation, in addition to start-ups (financial services). Sahay (2020) defined FinTech as a technologically driven innovation in financial services that can result in new business models, applications, processes, or products with a relevant material impact. In short, FinTech is a field in the financial industry that uses technology to improve financial activities, Schueffel (2017).

In the past few years, advances in technology and digitization have brought a fundamental transformation in the financial industry and advances in financial technology (FinTech). The history of technological innovation in the financial sector began with the emergence of controls as a means of payment. Bank of America produced the first credit card (1958), and in 1967, ATMs appeared to be helping to process financial transactions, followed by the issuance of debit card as a transaction instrument. Supported by the development of the Internet, the 1990s witnessed the launch of the Internet banking. In 2000, FinTech's advances in mobile payments and crowdfunding were introduced, thus ensuring that FinTech is a fast-growing industry, Ashta and Biot-Paquerot (2018). Developments in e-finance and mobile technologies for financial companies drove FinTech innovations until the global financial crisis in 2008. These developments were characterized by the integration of financial innovation, Internet technologies, social networking services, social media, artificial intelligence, and big data analytics, Suryono et al. (2020).

FinTechs provide many services to its sub-industries. FinTech innovations affect many different aspects of financial services. Some service offerings target consumers as businesses, while others connect consumers and businesses by facilitating transactions between the two parties. Although FinTech ecosystem analysis is part of the general ecosystem, Sweid and Moftah (2020), FinTech as a whole can help drive the dynamics of competition and cooperation, Lee and Shin (2018). According to Leong and Sung (2018), FinTech classifies applications into four main operational business processes, namely payments, consulting, financing, and compliance. While Lee and Shin (2018) categorizes FinTech into six business models, namely insurance services, crowdfunding, payments, loans, asset management, and capital markets.

3 FinTech in the MENA Region

The MENA region is home to a population of close to 450 million people. Out of this, almost 50% is aged below 25 years.[4] A sizeable portion of this relatively young population presents an exciting and dynamic business environment of early innovation adopters. The region additionally presents potential business appeal due to its geographical advantage. FinTech regulatory systems began taking shape in the Gulf nations in 2017. From that point onward, the region has turned into a major attraction for FinTech development.[5] Among the MENA countries, Bahrain and the UAE provide a perfect entry point for investments in

[4] Veera Mendonca, et al., "MENA Generation 2030: Investing in children and youth today to secure a prosperous region tomorrow," UNICEF (April 1, 2019), https://www.unicef.org/mena/media/4141/file.

[5] When we use the term "Gulf region," we are referring to members of the Gulf Cooperation Council (GCC). It is important to point out that even though the focus of this paper is on the UAE and Bahrain, we provide some analysis on regional trends. In this paper, we cite several reports that have provided analysis on the Middle East and North Africa (MENA) region and the GCC. The MENA region, as defined by the World Bank, includes Algeria, Bahrain, Djibouti, Egypt, Iran, Iraq, Jordan, Kuwait, Lebanon,

the electronic finance sector, especially in the FinTech. By having its base in one country, FinTechs create potential opportunities to enter other emerging markets across the Middle East, Africa, and South Asia. Those extended markets total a market value of around $8 trillion with home to 3 billion individuals, 70% of whom have restricted or no access to advanced financial services.[6,7] While at present, the FinTech investments across the Middle East address just 1% of worldwide FinTech investments, the region is developing at a compounded annual growth rate (CAGR) of 30%. By the end of 2022, it is anticipated that the region would be a hub for nearly 500 FinTech organizations with more than $2 billion investment, a giant leap when contrasted with merely 30 FinTechs companies that brought around $80 million in 2017 (Chart 1).

The significant infiltration of mobile phones and web accessibility in the region has driven the surge in e-finance usage and adaptability in the MENA region. The Middle East boasted of 100% mobile infiltration in 2020, while smartphone penetration recorded almost 60%. In 2020, Bahrain, UAE, and Qatar were among the most infiltrated markets globally. Saudi Arabia and Kuwait were estimated to join the three nations in establishing 5G networks in years to follow.[8] However, the recent Covid-19 pandemic severely affected financial systems around the world and created one of the most complex challenges for the financial sector worldwide, including the provision of digital financial services and the growth of financial technology markets. Recent evidence suggests that the social and economic shocks associated with the global pandemic have severely disrupted some FinTech sectors (World Bank and CCAF, 2020), created opportunities for others, and created a state of shock for others.

The FinTech sector in the region has attracted many start-ups, largely due to the enhanced speed and low transaction costs that FinTech has

Libya, Morocco, Oman, Qatar, Saudi Arabia, Syria, Tunisia, United Arab Emirates, West Bank, and Gaza.

6 "DIFC home to first, innovative Equity Crowdfunding platform in the region, as Eureeca.com begins DFSA regulated activity," Dubai International Financial Centre (November 6, 2016), https://www.difc.ae/newsroom/news/difc-home-first-innovative-equity-crowdfunding-platform-region-eureecacombegins-dfsa-regulated-activity/.

7 "A Roadmap for FinTech Firms Entering Fast-Growing Emerging Markets: Featuring case studies and market analysis," LendIt FinTech (2019), http://pages.lendit.com/2019-roadmap-for-fintech-firms-difcwhite-paper.html.

8 Huawei is involved in 5G rollouts in the UAE, Bahrain, Qatar, Saudi Arabia, and Kuwait.

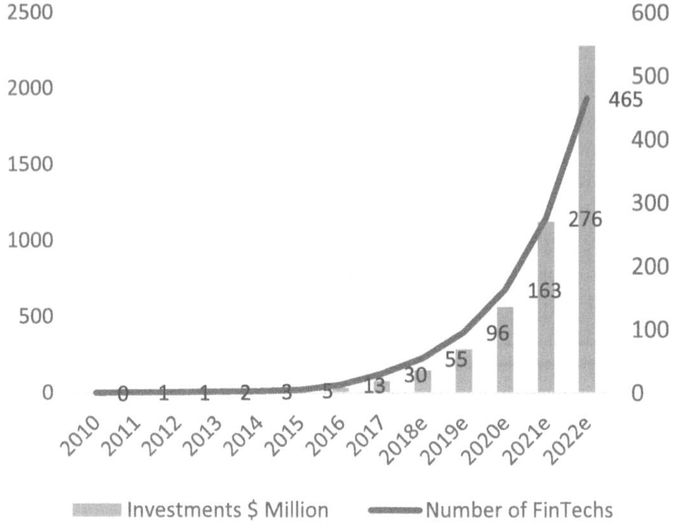

Chart 1 Venture capital investment into Middle East FinTech Companies (Source: Author complied)

brought into the financial sector. In its early days, developments and investments in FinTech in the MENA have never been very promising when compared with other emerging and developing markets. When compared with global FinTech investments, MENA regions merely made up somewhere around 1% of worldwide FinTech investment.[9] According to the findings of a research conducted by Lu et al (2020), a significant reduction in the cost of computers, storage, and equipment facilitates relatively lower cost of processing and analysis of large amounts of data and thus improving the access to financial services for the larger consumer base. This wave of FinTech growth globally snowballed into MENA and the region witnessed tremendous FinTech growth in a short span of time. A significant part of the regional FinTech investment has been in the more vibrant areas of FinTech sector. Specifically, new businesses

[9] Nada Al Rifai, "Middle East FinTech investments make up just 1% of global total—Bahrain Fintech Bay CEO," Zawya (March 3, 2019), https://www.zawya.com/mena/en/business/story/Middle_East_fintech_investments_make_up_just_1_of_global_total__Bahrain_Fintech_Bay_CEO-ZAWYA20190304025937/.

were more focused toward services such as payments and remittances, web-based trading, InsurTech, RegTech, crowdfunding, computerized banking, blockchain, and cryptocurrency-related activities. Among all the areas, the major concentration of FinTech investments remains in the payments space making up for approximately 85% of FinTech firms in the MENA that work in the remittances, transfers, and payments sector.[10] As a result, over the years, most of investment in the region has moved into the payment space, and the region continues to remain a major attractor for payments-related activities. The UAE, in specific, has been a key driver in remittances, largely due to its significant expatriate population making up for approximately 90% of the country's total population.[11] In 2017, expat remittances from the UAE added up to $44.5 billion, 70% of which was moved through money exchange firms and the rest through banks. The main recipients of this money were India, Pakistan, and the Philippines.[12]

4 Results

The Gulf Cooperation Council (GCC) region appears to be primed for a period of substantial FinTech expansion, and the conditions are favorable for FinTech expansion in the GCC. Despite the large influx of smartphones, the unbanked population in the region still remains high. Regional governments saw the potential and implemented legislation to encourage the growth of the FinTech business. International corporations have also begun to show a strong interest in the region, as evidenced by Western Union's recent acquisition of a small portion of STC. This acquisition is likely to stimulate further investment and accelerate market growth. However, there is still debate about what exactly the market looks like. The present smartphone penetration in GCC is 96%, above the global average of 58%. However, FinTech did not develop at the same pace. The global share of mobile payments in the GCC is growing, but

[10] Bahrain FinTech Ecosystem Report 2018," Bahrain FinTech Bay (July 2018), https://www.bahrainfintechbay.com/FinTech-ecosystem-report.

[11] The vast majority of the expat population are contracted workers from overseas including laborers and domestic staff.

[12] "Expat remittances in UAE surge to $44.5bn in 2017," TradeArabia (March 12, 2018), http://www.tradearabia.com/news/BANK_337764.html.

still lags far behind other regions like the Asia Pacific. The GCC countries are progressively transitioning toward developed markets in terms of financial inclusion, with around 22% of the GCC's population still lacking access to banking services, in contrast to around 60% in North Africa.[13] This phenomenon was especially evident during the Covid-19 crisis, when physical monetary transactions faced severe challenges. In a 2021 PwC survey of more than 1,000 respondents in the United Arab Emirates, Saudi Arabia, and Egypt, 53% of the surveyed sample admitted to the use of smartphone payments for online deliveries during the pandemic. In addition, more than 90% of this sample said that they would continue to make smartphone payments even after the crisis subsided.[14]

5 Conclusions

Regional governments understand the extent of rapid FinTech growth and are working to introduce regulations that will facilitate market growth. Saudi Arabia, for example, aims to reach the target of 70% of electronic payments by 2030. The government is taking several steps to make this goal achievable, in particular the national QR code for land payments. In 2019, Saudi Payments that represents the regulator, the Saudi Monetary Authority (SAMA) signed a memorandum of understanding of this impact with twelve parties (nine banks and three FinTech companies). Another significant development was unveiled in January 2021, announcing that SAMA intends to live with the open banking initiative in the first half of 2022. This move is expected to bring an increase in various services in the field of FinTech, creating more competition and consumer choice.[15] Bahrain is also very active in this regard, introducing regulations on regulatory sandboxes, open banks, crypto assets, Robo-advisory, and payment services.[16]

International companies are also tapping the potential of the GCC FinTech market. In October 2021, Western Union announced the completion of its purchase of 15% minority stake in STC payments

[13] Camarate, J., Mir. J. E., and Khadige, A., Why FinTech is on the brink of rapid expansion in the GCC, Gulf Business, February 20, 2021.

[14] Digital Trust Insights 2022—Middle East findings, PWC.

[15] Hamid, T., and Azim, N. A., Can Saudi Arabia become the region's FinTech frontrunner? 10th June, 2021 Wamda.

[16] Bahrain "set to become FinTech hub," 13th June, 2021 Gulf Daily News.

totaling $1.3 billion (a 10% stake of $133.3 million and another 5% of $66.67 million if STC pay obtains a digital banking license). The transaction could benefit the Saudi authorities in their desire to increase the value of the national FinTech market by 2023 to $33 billion. In particular, the "payments and currency exchange" segment will further strengthen and will represent 41% of the total Saudi FinTech market in 2019.[17] As STC pay becomes the first FinTech unicorn (worth more than $1 billion) in the Middle East, a major acquisition of minority stakes represents a symbolic divide in the development of the regional FinTech market and potentially draws attention to it with even more international investors looking for opportunities in new areas. The agreement will even allow STC customers to shift their focus toward global expansion. Although both parties have been involved in the strategic partnership since October 2018, Western Union's newly acquired formal stake will strengthen its incentive to support this expansion. As a result, 4.5 million computer-based customers have access to cross-border financial services. For example, they can send e-wallet transfers to other customers in Africa, Asia, Europe, and Latin America through Western Union partners or through an extensive network of money transaction agents. Given that the e-finance market is such an important part of the overall FinTech atmosphere, this groundbreaking transaction offers a good opportunity to assess the current situation in the region and consider its future direction.[18] Significant expansion of the regional electronic finance market is possible in two distinct ways. The market containing numerous FinTech components, including electronic wallets, near-field communication, blockchain, and virtual reality, is still in its infancy. The first option is that the regional e-wallet market will follow the same consolidation trend that other mature markets have witnessed. Several e-wallets have been closed in the United States in recent years, including Citi Pay, Wells Fargo Wallet, Chase Pay, and Capital One. Many banks have succumbed to tough competition from popular digital wallets, such as Apple Pay or Google Pay. Today, in Europe, pure payment players such as Worldline, Worldpay, and Ingenico have achieved a number of goals in recent years that have helped them increase transactions and expand their service offerings. In

[17] Western Union Expands Global Ecosystem with Completion of Investment into STC Bank, BusinessWire.

[18] Western Union Expands Global Ecosystem with Completion of Investment into STC Bank, Yahoo finance.

the GCC region itself, consolidation will largely stem from a lack of relevant capabilities, such as cutting-edge technologies and company-wide R&D platforms. The market containing numerous FinTech components, including electronic wallets, near-field communication, blockchain, and virtual reality, is still in its infancy. In addition, although traditional banks are becoming more resilient to data analysis, many prefer to invest in compliance, although data and open APIs are likely to be at the top of the open banking agenda.[19]

Another possible market direction is that small e-wallet start-ups will have their hands full with product innovations outside the area of payments. Suitable examples can be found from all over the world. Paytm, a popular e-slot in India, offers gaming services through the Paytm First Games brand with more than half a million active users every day. E-wallets also have opportunities to expand through resources such as business loyalty programs, customized financial advice, or planning tools. Time will reveal precisely what direction the FinTech market in the GCC will progress. However, after Western Union paid for its investment in STC, rapid growth is surely to follow.[20]

References

Al Ahbabi, A. R., & Nobanee, H. (2019, October 19). *Conceptual building of sustainable financial management & sustainable financial growth*. Available at SSRN: https://ssrn.com/abstract=3472313

Ashta, A., & Biot-Paquerot, G. (2018). FinTech evolution: Strategic value management issues in a fast changing industry. *Strategic Change, 27*, 301–311.

Franklin, A., Andrews, J., & Strahan, P. (2002). E-Finance: An introduction. *Journal of Financial Services Research, 22*(1–2), 5–27.

Hou, X., Gao, Z., & Wang, Q. (2016). Internet finance development and banking market discipline: Evidence from China. *Journal of Financial Stability, 22*, 88–100. https://www.sciencedirect.com/science/article/pii/S1572308916000024

Jungmittag, A. (2004). Innovations, technological specialisation and economic growth in the EU. *International Economics and Economic Policy, 1*, 247–273. https://doi.org/10.1007/s10368-004-0018-5

[19] Cole, W., Mobile wallet use projected to surge, Paymentsdive, 27th July, 2021.

[20] Buhejji, D., From pearl trade to e-wallets: The rise of digital payments in the GCC, Wamda, 23rd December, 2020.

Lee, I., & Shin, Y. (2018). Fintech: Ecosystem, business models, investment decisions, and challenges. *Business Horizons, 61*, 35–46. https://doi.org/10.1016/j.bushor.2017.09.003

Leong, K., & Sung, A. (2018, April). FinTech (Financial Technology): What is it and how to use technologies to create business value in Fintech a way? *International Journal of Innovation, Management and Technology, 9*(2).

Lin, Z., Whinston, A. B., & Fan, S. (2015). Harnessing Internet finance with innovative cyber credit management. *Financial Innovation, 1*(1), 5. https://doi.org/10.1186/s40854-015-0004-7

Lu, H., Bingzhong, W., Qing, W., & Jing, Y. (2020, September). Fintech and the future of financial service: A literature review and research agenda. *China Accounting and Finance Review, 22*(3), 107–132.

Lyu, X., & Zhao, J. (2019). Compressed sensing and its applications in risk assessment for internet supply chain finance under big data. *IEEE Access, 7*, 53182–53187. https://ieeexplore.ieee.org/stamp/stamp.jsp?arnumber=8693964

Meijers, H. (2014). Does the internet generate economic growth, international trade, or both? *International Economics and Economic Policy, 11*(1–2), 137–63.

Nacera, B. (2021). Covid-19 pandemic and financial technology: Analysis the state of funding in MENA region. *Journal of Contemporary Economic Studies, 6*(2), 569–588.

Sahay, R. U. (2020). *The promise of Fintech: Financial inclusion in the post COVID-19* (Era Departmental Paper Series (29)). https://www.imf.org/en/Publications/Departmental-Papers-PolicyPapers/Issues/2020/06/29/The-Promise-of-Fintech-Financial-Inclusion-in-the Post-COVID-19-Era-48623

Sassi, S., & Mohamed, G. (2013). Financial development, ICT diffusion and economic growth: Lessons from MENA region. *Telecommunications Policy, 37*(4–5), 252–61.

Schueffel, P. (2017). Taming the beast: A scientific definition of FinTech. *Innovation Management, 4*, 32–54.

Shahrokhi, M. (2008). E-Finance: Status, innovations, resources and future challenges. *Managerial Finance, 34*(6), 365–98.

Sweid, N., & Moftah, B. (2020, April). Fintech in MENA an overview 2020. Venture. Global.

Suryono, R. R., Budi, I., & Purwandari, B. (2020). Challenges and trends of financial technology (Fintech): A systematic literature review. *Information, 11*(590).

The World Bank, & CCAF. (2020). *The global Covid-19 FinTech regulatory rapid assessment study*. World Bank and the Cambridge Centre for Alternative Finance at the University of Cambridge Judge Business School. Retrieved

8 15, 2021, from UK. https://www.jbs.cam.ac.uk/wp-content/uploads/2020/10/2020-ccaf-report-fintech-regulatory-rapid-assessment.pdf

Zavolokina, L., Dolata, M., & Schwabe, G. (2016). *FinTech—What's in a name?* In Proceedings of the Thirty Seventh International Conference on Information Systems, 11–14, pp. 469–490. Dublin, Ireland.

Fintechs as an Enabler of Financial Inclusion: An Empirical Analysis in the Landscape of African Economies

Rachida El Yamani and Fadwa Betane

1 Introduction

The first step toward an inclusive financial system is having access to a current account, which enables the ability to make deposits, send, and receive payments. The World Bank Group is still working to guarantee that every adult, wherever in the world, has a current account since it is a gateway to additional financial services. The World Bank reports that throughout the past ten years, there has been a notable advancement in financial inclusion (FI): between 2011 and 2017, 1.2 billion adults globally were able to open a current account, increasing the global rate of account ownership to 69%. Currently, digital financial services, including those accessed through mobile devices, are accessible in over 80 countries

R. El Yamani (✉)
Faculty of Law, Economic and Social Sciences, Mohammedia, Hassan II University, Casablanca, Morocco
e-mail: rachida.elyamani@univh2c.ma

F. Betane
Faculty of Law, Economic and Social Sciences, Sale, Mohammed V University of Rabat, Rabat, Morocco
e-mail: fadwa_betane@um5.ac.ma

© The Author(s), under exclusive license to Springer Nature Singapore Pte Ltd. 2025

A. S. et al. (eds.), *Trends and Challenges of Electronic Finance*,
https://doi.org/10.1007/978-981-96-3304-3_18

and are commonly utilized in several of them. With the use of a mobile phone or other digital device, millions of underprivileged individuals who were previously underprivileged or excluded and who only had access to cash transactions can now obtain formal financial services.

The necessity of increasing digital FI has been emphasized by the Covid-19 pandemic. In order to ensure that service providers can continue to operate profitably, it is necessary to provide more cheap dematerialized services. This will enable individuals who are presently unbanked or underserved to take advantage of a variety of formal financial services that are affordable and customized to their needs.

With the increasing number of people owning mobile phones and having access to the internet, fintechs open a lot of new options in this context. FI, a term that covers a far wider range of financial products, services, and providers, has replaced microcredit as the primary means of funding for the underprivileged. One significant technological advancement that is transforming the banking and financial industries is fintechs. They are launching fresh business concepts as well as cutting-edge financial products and services that are affordable and easily accessible. To the detriment of the products offered by established financial firms, consumers are adopting these solutions more frequently, which has prompted further mergers.

A number of studies carried out by various global organizations about the link between fintechs and FI have indicated that fintechs, significantly, contribute to the advancement of FI. The role of fintechs in FI has been studied by international institutions like the International Monetary Fund (IMF) (2020), which has found that fintechs, such as digital banking and mobile payments, significantly promote FI by making financial services more accessible and reducing transaction costs. Furthermore, the World Bank (2021) highlights fintech's potential to improve FI by making services more accessible, affordable, and efficient, particularly during the Covid-19 crisis.

Digital financial services, such as cross-border remittances and mobile money, have made it possible for governments to safely and swiftly communicate with people that are at risk. By the end of 2021, 68% of the world's population owned a smartphone. Preliminary data from IDC's Worldwide Quarterly Mobile Phone Tracker indicates that after two years of volatility, the global market is starting to show hopeful signs of recovery, growing 7.8% in the first quarter of 2024 compared with the same period the previous year. The first step toward universal FI is this worldwide mobile inclusion. The proliferation of powerful and reasonably priced mobile technology is leading to the development and implementation of novel mobile-based financial services. Mobile technology is now being used to alleviate common issues in developing nations, such as the lack of access to banking services in rural areas. For those who are underbanked or unbanked, digital financial services have revolutionized their situation by enabling them to participate in and have access to an inclusive digital economy. Furthermore, there has been a significant shift in consumer behavior due to the Covid-19 pandemic and the associated health precautions. African economies are enacting reforms in reaction to the crisis in order to create a more robust and inclusive economic model and increase FI through fintechs. Therefore, FI has drawn more attention from policymakers in numerous African nations. Allen et al. (2014) state that new financial services have made finance more accessible in a number of African countries. Evans (2018) comes to the conclusion that mobile phones, Internet, and FI have increased because they have made it simpler for people to access fundamental financial services.

This study aims to contribute to the existing literature on the role of fintechs in promoting FI, by offering new research perspectives and concrete recommendations for fostering FI in African countries, and using dynamic panel, which is able to capture the short- and long-term effects. By highlighting the implications of mobile penetration, the use of Internet, and the granting credit on the promotion of FI in Africa, furthermore, the goal of this research is to contribute to policy discussions and encourage initiatives aimed at utilizing fintechs to advance an equitable financial system in Africa.

There is a lack of research in the literature, especially in Africa, on fintechs and FI. The majority of related research gives little attention to fintechs' contribution to the development of an inclusive financial system, preferring to concentrate more on the factors that influence FI or analyzing the causal relationship between fintechs and FI with regard to income inequality or even gender. In reality, it has been determined that the primary source of inadequate policy advice in the expansion of fintechs, despite saturation levels in developed countries, is the absence of reliable empirical studies using novel modeling methodologies. This study closes this gap through examining the impact of fintechs on FI, which measured by the Financial Inclusion Index (FII) introduced by Sarma (2008), for a panel data of 9 African nations between 2004 and

2022, using dynamic panel ARDL, that allows for the short- and long-term estimation of coefficients for a group of countries, with results that may be interpreted as a general conclusion that applies to other countries.

2 Literature Review

Any economic system's ultimate goal is to ensure the well-being of the people, and one of the factors that makes this goal achievable is the growth of a strong and inclusive financial sector. However, without the use of fintechs, it is becoming increasingly difficult to develop an inclusive financial sector in today's technology and artificial intelligence-driven global economy.

2.1 Introduction to Key Concepts

The technological innovation is fundamentally dependent on process innovation in banking sector (Campanella et al., 2017). Process innovation refers to the invention of working methods or techniques used in banks' production processes with the use of sophisticated software and computerized systems, which increase productivity, decrease labor costs, and save time. For example, the use of mobile applications and digital financial management tools ensures effective and efficient management of transactions, making it possible to expedite payment processing, provide online banking, establish electronic contact channels with customers, and make it easier for customers to access and use financial services. Hence the emergence of the concepts of Financial technologies known as "fintechs" in 1971 and Financial inclusion (FI).

On the one hand, despite the fact that fintechs have received extensive coverage in information and communication media (Milian et al., 2019). They are frequently confused with financial innovation without being able to provide a clear and consistent definition of the concept in scientific literature. However, other authors attempt to define fintechs without being able to provide a single, cohesive definition; instead, they provide characteristics of fintechs. For example, fintechs are defined by Puschmann (2017) as the process of developing innovative financial products and technologies, institutions, markets, and then making them widely known. Furthermore, fintechs are described by Lee and Shin (2018) as an "ecosystem" consisting of five major participants (Fintech Startups; Government; Technology; Financial Customers; Developers; and

Traditional Financial Institutions). These participants support economic growth, innovation, collaboration, and competitiveness in the financial sector and benefit consumers in the sector.

On the other hand, in the early 2000s, the term "financial inclusion" gained popularity. In 2005, the Reserve Bank of India (RBI) made a noteworthy initial statement, emphasizing the importance of providing financial services to all groups of society, particularly the underserved and unserved population. In order to guarantee comprehensive access for the unbanked, the United Nations Capital Development Fund (UNCDF) also adopted and expanded this concept at around the same time. The UNCDF focused on offering a wide range of financial services beyond microcredit, such as savings, credit, insurance, and payment services. As defined by World Bank, FI is the term used to describe the availability of practical and reasonably priced financial products and services to individuals and enterprises that satisfy their requirements for credit, insurance, payments, transactions, and savings in an ethical and sustainable way. FI has attracted the interest of several authors who have attempted to define it and study its determinants and effects. In fact, researchers cannot agree around a common definition of FI. In this regard, Sarma's (2008) definition emphasizes the availability, accessibility, and affordability of financial services. Furthermore, the author believes that utilization is a crucial component of FI. However, Fungáčová and Weill (2015) consider it in the context of utilization rather than the caliber of services supplied.

2.2 *Theoretical Frameworks*

It is imperative to address several significant obstacles in order to guarantee the success and enduring influence of FI. Technological innovation is the first one of these. Fintechs, or digital technologies, have a lot of promise to expand financial services accessibility in underserved or rural locations. While cutting expenses, solutions like crowdfunding and mobile banking can greatly simplify the management of credit and savings.

Researchers have mobilized a variety of theories to explain the relationship between fintechs and FI, including the Technology Acceptance Model (TAM), the Financial Intermediation Theory (FIT), the Disruptive Innovation Theory (DIT), and other theories. The Technology Acceptance Model (TAM) by Davis et al. (1989) was employed to clarify how people adopt and utilize technology. According to the model, an individual's intention to utilize technology is largely influenced by their perception of its usefulness and simplicity of use. This model can be used in the fintechs context to comprehend how these attitudes affect the use of fintechs services, which can promote FI.

The Financial Intermediation Theory (FIT), developed by Merton and Bodie (1995) argues that financial intermediation plays an essential role in reducing transaction costs and information asymmetries, thereby facilitating a more efficient allocation of resources. Fintechs, as a contemporary method of financial intermediation, promotes FI by offering financial services that are more affordable, accessible, and efficient.

According to the Disruptive Innovation Theory (DIT) by Christensen (2013), required market-leading companies and products are eventually replaced by disruptive innovations that generate new markets and value networks. Fintechs are a disruptive innovation that improves FI by offering financial services to marginalized groups.

2.3 Empirical Literature Review

The creation of databases such as the World Bank's Global Findex database and the IMF's Financial Access Survey (FAS) has made it possible to create and employ more multidimensional composite measures of FI that account for a variety of household and firm access and use factors (Demirgüç-Kunt & Klapper, 2012; Sarma, 2008). These measures have opened the way for exploring the determinants of FI (Asuming et al., 2019; El Yamani, 2024; Kumar, 2013; Sanderson et al., 2018) as well as the development of its macroeconomic impact analyses (Sahay et al., 2015; Rastogi & Ragabiruntha, 2018; Duvendack & Mader, 2020).

Regarding the relationship between fintechs and FI, several studies, conducted by some international institutions, confirmed that fintechs play a significant role in FI. The International Monetary Fund (IMF) (2020) has examined the role of fintechs in FI. Their analysis indicates that fintech innovations, such as digital banking and mobile payments, can significantly reduce transaction costs and increase access to financial services for underserved populations. The IMF highlights the potential of fintechs to enhance FI by making financial services more accessible, affordable, and efficient. Furthermore, the World Bank (2021), in its report, discusses how fintechs have shown promise in enhancing FI, especially during the Covid-19 crisis. Digital financial services, including mobile money and cross-border remittances, have allowed governments to reach vulnerable populations quickly and securely. This has helped in providing financial services to those without traditional bank accounts, thereby promoting FI globally. Mohammad Asif et al. (2023) have analyzed the impact of digital financial services and fintechs on FI in India. Using regression and correlation analyses, the authors found that fintech businesses significantly contributed to FI, particularly for the middle class. This study emphasized how fintechs may help underbanked people access more financial services.

Concerning FI in African economies, FI has drawn more attention in African policy circles in recent years. According to Allen et al. (2014), in several African nations, new financial services have improved access to financing and assisted in resolving infrastructure issues. Zins and Weill (2016) examined, in 37 African nations, several factors that influence FI, and found that being older, male, wealthier, and better educated is associated with greater FI in African countries. According to Chikalipah's (2017) analysis of the factors influencing FI in Sub-Saharan Africa, the primary obstacle to FI in this region is illiteracy. In his analysis of the link between mobile phones, Internet, and FI in Africa between 2000 and 2016, Evans (2018) concludes that these technologies have made it easier for people to obtain basic financial services, which have raised the level of financial inclusion. Furthermore, El Yamani (2024) demonstrates that financial innovation can improve FI in African countries.

3 Background

Over the last few decades, the FI of individuals has improved steadily thanks to the new approach adopted by the banking sector and their regulatory authorities. According to the World Bank, "Covid-19 has reinforced the need for greater digital FI". This implies the introduction of lower-cost dematerialized services to provide unbanked or underprivileged groups with a variety of formal financial services that are accessible and suited to their needs. The Covid-19 pandemic and the corresponding health measures have drastically changed consumer behavior while ensuring that the providers' operations remain profitable. In response to this crisis, the economies of the African continent are implementing reforms to build a resilient and more inclusive economic model in order to improve FI through fintechs. The European Investment Bank claims that even with the advancements made since 2011, a significant percentage of Sub-Saharan Africa's population is still unbanked. Bank account ownership has grown more quickly than the use of financial services, despite the region having the highest mobile payment adoption rate globally. Although there are still gaps, North Africa has made notable progress in achieving FI. There is room for advancement and development given the increasing popularity of remote banking services, digital payment methods, and mobile banking. Nevertheless, this region has not yet experienced the same level of success with mobile payment schemes as Sub-Saharan Africa. This highlights the importance of pursuing the potential of fintechs to promote wider and more effective FI across the African continent.

Some African countries have already found ways to make FI a reality. For example, South Africa and Uganda have been ranked among the top five most inclusive countries according to the latest report from the Brookings Financial and Digital Inclusion Project (FDIP). Other countries scored high on individual measures. Rwanda, also, scored high on the regulatory environment. Uganda's move to alter a significant section of legislation controlling financial institutions is partly responsible for its high rating. The amendment, among other things, permits some financial institutions to implement Islamic banking methods, which expand their customer base by appealing to a sizable religious population.

As part of a comprehensive plan to increase national connectivity, Rwanda has drawn significant investment in mobile banking platforms from both public and commercial entities. Like Sub-Saharan Africa nations, the mobile telephony market in Morocco is among the most developed in North Africa. At the beginning of 2022, there were 48.55 million mobile connections in Morocco (or subscribers), i.e. 1 connection per user. This number represents an increase of 6.3% between 2021 and 2022, or 2.9 million new connections year-on-year. The number of mobile connections in Morocco rose to more than 49.47 million (137.61% of the population) at the start of 2021. According to the National Telecommunications Regulatory Agency (NTRA), the continued expansion of 4G networks across the country has helped to have a positive impact on Morocco's online ecosystem, with mobile data usage up 26.66% year-on-year at the end of March 2021 (or more than 4.5 million). As a facilitator of fintechs in Morocco, Bank Al Maghrib (BAM) has been active since 2018 on a digital plan, which is becoming intrinsic to financial and socio-economic development, which involves both mastering new technologies in this area and the inevitable evolution of legislation. BAM has now committed to implementing the regulatory Sandbox, which is a test environment designed to oversee the small-scale and willing consumer investigation of novel fintech products.

4 Methodology

This paper aims to investigate the fintechs's impact on FI in the African economies. We test the two following major hypotheses in accordance with the research goal and in response to the insights obtained from the literature review:

H_1: Fintechs may have an impact on financial inclusion in African economies in the short term;

H_2: Fintechs might affect financial inclusion in African economies in the long term.

4.1 Model Specification

This study will focus on a panel of nine African economies to examine the relationship between fintechs and FI using an empirical methodology based on the AutoRegressive Distributed Lag (ARDL) approach for panel data from 2004 to 2022.

- The dependent variable:

Financial Inclusion (FI): Previous research has been able to distinguish between two groups by measuring FI. The first category is Sarma's (2008), which is based on an index that can be calculated on two or even three dimensions depending on the availability of data.

The second group mostly relied on research conducted in individual countries or on special measures of FI, such as the number of banking offices, automated teller machines, and individual bank accounts (Ahamed & Mallick, 2019; Allen et al., 2014; Emara & El Said, 2021).

In order to quantify FI in our study, we drew inspiration from Sarma's (2008) methodology and computed a tridimensional synthetic index of financial inclusion (FII) made from the following dimensions:

Dimension 1: By referring to Sarma's (2008) research, the amount of bank penetration is determined by counting the number of adults with bank accounts in a certain point of sale, divided by the population's size.

Dimension 2: Drawing from Sarma's (2008) work, this dimension measures the accessibility of banking services as indicated by the number of banking branches for 100,000 residents and the number of Automated Teller Machine (ATMs) for 100,000 adults.
Dimension 3: This dimension refers to the use of the banking system; it's based on two basic services, credit and deposit, which are measured, respectively, by the outstanding deposits with commercial banks and loans from commercial banks relative to the country's gross domestic product.

- The main explanatory variable:

Based on the research of Otekunrin et al. (2021), three indicators are used to measure fintechs:

Domestic credit to private sector (CPS) by banks refers to the financial resources provided to the private sector by other depository corporations (deposit taking corporations other than central banks) in the form of trade credits, loans, purchases of nonequity securities, and other accounts receivable that create a claim to repayment.

Individuals using the Internet (% of population) (NET): Those who have used the Internet within the last three months, regardless of location, are considered Internet users. A computer, smartphone, PDA, game console, digital TV, etc. can all be used to access the Internet.

Mobile phone users (MOB): is the proportion of the total population that use digital financial services.

- The control variable:

The secondary school enrolment rate (LITER), which measures the financial education, will be added as a control variable. For instance, it aims to accelerate financial education policies in order to facilitate the use of fintechs and the transition to an inclusive digital finance.

Thus, the model will be specified using the following equation, Eq. (1):

$$\mathrm{FII}_{it} = \beta_0 + \beta_1 \mathrm{CPS}_{it} + \beta_2 \mathrm{NET}_{it} + \beta_3 \mathrm{MOB}_{it} + \beta_4\, \mathrm{LITER}_{it} + \varepsilon_{it} \quad (1)$$

Table 1 Data source

Variable	*Description*	*Source*
FII	Financial inclusion index	The International Monetary Fund
NET	Individuals using the Internet (% of population)	The World Bank Indicators
CPS	Credit provided to the private sector	
MOB	The percentage of the whole population that uses mobile phones	
LITER	The secondary school enrolment rate	

Source Authors

Where FII is the financial inclusion index is used to measure FI; for the three variables that measure fintechs are: credit to private sector (CPS); individuals using the Internet (% of population) (NET); mobile phone users as a proportion of the total population (MOB), and the secondary school enrolment rate (LITER) as a control variable.

The constant term and the parameters that require estimation are indicated by β_0 and β_k (1, 2, 3, 4), respectively. The error term ε_{it} is assumed to be independently and identically distributed (i.i.d).

4.2 Sample and Data Source

The research methodology used in this study is correlational, and it covers a 19-year period (from 2004 to 2022). The choice of this time frame was made based on the availability of data, particularly those used to calculate the FII, which are published by the IMF starting in 2004. The sample for this study consists of 9 African countries[1] for which data are available. Additionally, the study makes use of secondary data from the IMF (for FI indicators) and World Bank Indicators (for other variables) (refer Table 1).

4.3 Estimation Approach

Two estimation techniques are commonly applied to dynamic panel data model estimation. Three estimation methods are often used to estimate dynamic panel data models: the Mean Group (MG) developed by Pesaran

[1] Algeria; Ghana; Guinea; Madagascar; Mauritius; Morocco; Rwanda; South Africa; Uganda.

and Smith (1995) and the Pooled Mean Group (PMG) and Dynamic Fixed Effect DFE introduced by Pesaran et al. (1999) to address the bias in dynamic panels due to hétérogène slopes. Furthermore, by averaging the long-term parameters of each individual AutoRegressif Distributed Lags (ARDL) model, these estimators yield the long-term parameters of the panel.

It is important to note that these estimation techniques are dependent on the following conditions: the temporal dimension T, which must be greater than the number of individuals N; the inequality of the model's examined coefficients in the individual dimension (heterogeneous échantillon); the independence between transversal cuts; the dependent variable's integration order, which must be 1, while the independent variables' integration order must be a mixture of 0 and 1; and the existence of cointegration between the explicative and explaining variables. Since our study satisfies each of these requirements, using these estimations to produce our results is appropriate.

The model to be estimated is written as follows:

$$\begin{aligned}\Delta \mathrm{FII}_{it} = \alpha_i &+ \sum_{i=1}^{p} \beta_0 \Delta \mathrm{FII}_{i(t-1)} + \sum_{i=0}^{q} \beta_1 \Delta \mathrm{CPS}_{i(t-1)} \\ &+ \sum_{i=0}^{r} \beta_2 \Delta \mathrm{NET}_{i(t-l)} + \sum_{i=0}^{m} \beta_3 \Delta \mathrm{MOB}_{i(t-l)} + \sum_{i=0}^{n} \beta_4 \Delta \mathrm{LITER}_{i(t-1)} \\ &+ \delta_0 \mathrm{FII}_{(t-1)} + \delta_1 \mathrm{CPS}_{i(t-1)} + \delta_2 \mathrm{NET}_{i(t-1)} + \delta_3 \mathrm{MOB}_{i(t-1)} \\ &+ \delta_4 \mathrm{LITER}_{i(t-1)} + \varepsilon_{it} \qquad (2)\end{aligned}$$

With $i = 1,..., 9$ and $t = 1,..., 19$ represent the individual and temporal dimensions, respectively. $\mathrm{FII}_{\mathrm{it}}$ stands for the FI composite index and is a model-dependent variable. The model's independent variables are $\mathrm{CPS}_{\mathrm{it}}$, $\mathrm{MOB}_{\mathrm{it}}$, and $\mathrm{NET}_{\mathrm{it}}$, whereas the control variable is LITER.

Additionally, (Δ) denotes the first difference operator, and (ε) denotes the error term. The coefficients β_0 to β_4 represent the short-term relation, whereas the coefficients δ_0 to δ_4 represent the long-term relation. The numbers of lags are represented by p, q, r, m, and n.

Table 2 Descriptive statistics

Variable	*Mean*	*Std. dev*	*Min*	*Max*
FII	0.2044	0.1777	0.0123	0.6146
CPS	40.1971	40.3407	2.6598	142.4
NET	24.5647	24.2094	0.4308	90.42
MOB	78.6358	45.2480	1.5613	168.9
LITER	59.2729	28.43569	14.9520	111.8

5 Results and Discussion

The purpose of this section is to present and interpret the results of our empirical study. We used the software packages Eviews 13 and Stata version 17 to perform the tests required to study the relationship between fintechs and FI using a panel data of 9 African countries for the period from 2004 to 2022.

5.1 Descriptive Analysis

Table 2 shows the descriptive statistics for the variables studied, with a large difference between the minimum and maximum values of the variables. The synthetic index of FI reaches a maximum value of 0.61, which is a very high level of FI among the countries studied, for some countries, this level is very low, the minimum value of 0.01 is close to 0. Moreover, this index is less volatile (with a standard deviation of 0.17) than the variables studied, namely credit provided to the private sector, Internet, mobile telephony, and financial education, which have very high standard deviations indicating high volatility.

5.2 Correlation Matrix Analysis

The correlation matrix between the variables shows a strong positive correlation between the financial inclusion index and credit provided to the private sector, the Internet, and mobile telephony, with correlation coefficients of 83%, 70%, and 71%, respectively. This indicates that there is a significant relationship between the fintech variables and FI (refer Table 3).

Table 3 Correlation matrix

	FII	*CPS*	*NET*	*MOB*	*LITER*
FII	1.0000				
CPS	0.8321 0.0000	1.0000			
NET	0.7008 0.0000	0.5781 0.0000	1.0000		
MOB	0.7150 0.0000	0.6241 0.0001	0.8607 0.0000	1.0000	
LITER	0.8106 0.0000	0.7225 0.0000	0.7260 0.0000	0.8100 0.0000	1.0000

5.3 *Regression Analysis*

To estimate the modele's parameters, we used the logarithm of the variables, which firstly homogenizes our database, secondly improves the precision of the estimates, and facilitates the interpretation of the results, as well as reduces the differences in magnitude between the observations, and finally allows us to obtain measures of elasticity that are more representative of economic reality.

- Swamy homogeneity test

The first thing to check when examining a sample of panel data is whether the data-generating process is homogeneous or heterogeneous in terms of slope. We test the slope homogeneity hypothesis using the test developed by Swamy (1970) (see Table 4).

Table 4 Swamy test results

Log (FII)	*Coefficient*	*Std. err*	*P > |z|*
Log (CPS)	0.6251	0.3495	0.074
Log (NET)	0.0731	0.0643	0.256
Log (MOB)	0.1322	0.0698	0.059
Log (LITER)	0.0923	0.1822	0.612
Constant	−4.7765	1.0394	0.000
Chi2(40) = 4062.67			
Prob > Chi2 = 0.0000			

Table 5 Results of inter-individual dependency tests

Test	*Statistic*	*P-value*
LM	43.3	0.1879
LM adj*	0.1323	0.8947
LM CD*	−1.093	0.2744

The results of our model do not support the hypothesis of parameter constancy (Chi2 probability is less than 5%), which indicates that our sample is heterogeneous in term of slope. We should therefore use heterogeneous panel techniques.

- Panel inter-individual dependency test

The inter-individual dependency test is based on three tests: the Lagrange Multiplier by Breusch-Pagan (1980), CD by Pesaran (2004), and LM adj by Pesaran et al. (2004). These tests were used in this study, and Table 5 shows the test results.

The results reveal the existence of inter-individual independence in the panel data model (p-value > 5%). These results show that shocks, which can occur in any variable of a country, cannot affect the variable of another country, which verifies the condition of inter-individual independence.

- Unit root tests

The results of the inter-individual dependence test indicate an absence of inter-individual dependence. Consequently, the appropriate unit root tests are those of the first generation. In this study, we used the Im et al. (2003) unit root tests.

The results indicate, in Table 6, that the variables studied have a mixed level of integration between (0) and (1), which is an essential condition for using dynamic ARDL modeling.

- Selecting the optimum lag

Table 7 shows the optimal lag for each variable.

Table 6 Results of the unit root test

Im–Pesaran–Shin			
Variables	*In level*	*In first difference*	*Level of integration*
Log (FII)	0.1620	0.0000***	I (1)
Log (CPS)	0.8916	0.0000***	I (1)
Log (NET)	0.0794	0.0000***	I (1)
Log (MOB)	0.0000***	–	I (0)
Log (LITER)	0.0045***	–	I (0)

Note *** Significant at the 1% level

Table 7 Optimal lag

Variables	*Optimal lag*
Log (FII)	1
Log (CPS)	0
Log (NET)	0
Log (MOB)	0
Log (LITER)	0

- The test of the long-term relationship

To check whether there is a long-term relationship between fintechs and FI, we used the panel cointegration tests proposed by Pedroni (2004) and Westerlund (2007) in Table 8.

Table 8 The results of the long-term relationship test

	Pedroni (2004) Stat	*Westerlund (2007) Stat*
Modified Phillips–Perron	1.5394*	0.1341
Phillips–Perron	−8.9056***	
Augmented Dickey–Fuller	−6.1323***	

Note *** Significant at 1%; *significant at 10%

According to the results of Pedroni's test (2004), the p-values of the PP and ADF statistics are less than 0.01 and that of MPP is less than 0.1, so the hypothesis of no long-term relationship is rejected. Therefore, a long-term relationship is conceivable between fintechs and FI.

- Estimation of the ARDL model

Three estimation methods are commonly used for estimating dynamic panel data models: Mean Group (MG), Pooled Mean Group (PMG), and Dynamic Fixed Effect DFE.

We used the three estimators PMG, DFE, and MG. Consequently, we applied a robustness test to arbitrate between the three and choose the most efficient estimator for this model.

Table 9 shows the estimation results for the ARDL model.

According to the results of the Hausman test (Table 9), the most efficient and appropriate estimators for our model are the PMG estimators.

Table 9 Model estimations and Hausman-test results

	Pooled Mean Group (PMG)	*Mean Group (MG)*	*Dynamic fixed effect (DFE)*
Variables	Coefficient	Coefficient	Coefficient
D (logFII)			
Long run equation			
Log (CPS)	0.1047*	219.5	0.1369
Log (NET)	0.1918***	−60.68	0.1979***
Log (MOB)	0.1986***	24.41	0.2472**
Log (LITER)	0.3689**	−99.56	0.4618
Short run equation			
COINTEQ 01	−0.3410**	−0.7315***	−0.2331***
Log (CPS)	0.3122*	−0.0106	0.2397***
Log (NET)	−0.0230	−0.0856	0.0048
Log (MOB)	−0.0743	0.0393	0.0594
Log (LITER)	−0.1783	−0.0481	−0.1228
Const	−0.7010**	−2.804	−0.4661
Hausman test			
(PMG) > (MG): Prob (Chi2) = 0.90			
(PMG) > (DFE): Prob (Chi2) = 1			

Note ***Significant at 1%; significant at 5% and *significant at 10%

Table 10 The transversal section's dependence tests

Test	*Statistic*	*Prob*
Breusch-Pagan LM	46.95	0.1046
Pesaran scaled LM	1.2906	0.1968
Bias-corrected scaled LM	1.0259	0.3049
Pesaran CD	−0.0792	0.9368

Thus, before discussing the model results, we will perform a cross-section dependence test (Table 10).

We find that the observations in the different cross-sections are independent in terms of residuals, so we can validate the PMG model.

5.4 *Discussion*

Based on the results of the ARDL model using panel data and the PMG estimators, the variables, in particular the variables of interest that measure fintechs including credit provided to the private sector (CPS), the Internet (NET) and mobile telephony (MOB), have a positive and significant impact on financial inclusion (FII) in the long term, respectively at the 10% level for CPS and at the 1% level for NET and MOB. However, the control variable, the secondary school enrolment ratio (LITER), has a negative and significant impact on FI in the long term. Indeed, fintechs have a positive and significant effect on long-term FI in African nations and more specifically in the two Sub-Saharan and North African regions studied. This result shows the contribution of fintechs in improving the level of FI in African economies. Indeed, an increase of 1 unit of credit granted to the private sector will improve financial inclusion by 0.10% points over the long term. These results are in line with those found by Otekunrin et al. (2021) who demonstrated how bank credit extended to the private sector plays a crucial role in advancing the FI process.

Furthermore, in the long term, the development of financial inclusion is a result of the increase in Internet and mobile telephony, so that a 1 unit improvement in Internet and mobile telephony increases the banked population formally by 0.19 and 0.20 percentage points with a significance level of 1%. This result is clearly in line with several studies that analyze the impact of Internet and mobile money (Loukoianova et al., 2018). The degree of mobile penetration and FI both within and between nations is strongly correlated, and there is also evidence of a positive correlation between mobile money usage and FI for households and businesses. It is common for households with mobile money accounts to be banked and to send and receive money. Consequently, in nations where the majority of people possess mobile phones but are not banked, mobile technology holds significant promise for expanding the reach of the official banking system.

On the other hand, in the long term, the secondary school enrolment rate has a negative effect on FI, when the secondary school enrolment rate increases by 1 unit, the level of FI decreases by 0.37% points with a significance level of 5%. However, the relationship between these two variables is complex and confusing. Given the extremely high unemployment rate in Africa, this result can be explained by the fact that more young people attending school delay their economic engagement, temporarily reducing the demand for financial services. In addition, financial systems in Africa may not be sufficiently developed to meet the specific financial needs of students and young graduates.

In the short term, we found an insignificant impact of fintechs on FI. The reason for this erroneous outcome is the late adoption of digital financial services by financial institutions in African nations. In contrast, credit extended to the private sector continues to have a short-term and positive effect on the degree of FI.

Moreover, the unfavorable ecosystem of African countries may also explain the insignificant impact of fintechs on FI in the short term, as financial infrastructures are often undeveloped in these countries and providers face high costs to overcome information asymmetry. This can be improved by developing full access to formal credit registries and credit bureaus that are fully integrated into the financial landscape, to which banks and microcredit institutions would regularly report data on their portfolios and customers, ensuring the necessary information sharing between actors.

In summary, our results suggest that all the variables that explain fintechs have a positive effect on the level of FI in the long term, however, their impact remains insignificant in the short term. This can be explained by the obstacles facing financial services in Africa, in particular the late adoption of digital financial services and the telecommunications infrastructure, which remains undeveloped.

6 Conclusion and Policy Implications

It is increasingly clear that the use of digital financial services has the potential to rapidly advance FI. The promotion of digital solutions, in turn, makes it possible to design and deliver financial services and products securely and cost-effectively, and thus to establish business models that can sustainably serve financially unserved or underserved households and small and medium-sized companies.

Payments are usually the starting point in the use of financial services by excluded people, for example through the receipt of remittances or social benefits. Today, we can take advantage of payment solutions that enable our economies to emerge stronger from this health crisis and establish a post-Covid-19 future. To support this opportunity, three main factors are essential: e-commerce, contactless and digital.

Thus, the health crisis has highlighted the fact that not everyone has the same level of access to new technologies and the necessary digital tools, widening the gap between developed and developing countries. The abandonment of cash disproportionately affects unbanked citizens. Retailers who do not have access to digital payments are losing out even more as distance purchases increase. The time has come to design systems where all merchants and consumers, regardless of their income or level of education, will have access to financial services. The limitations of payment infrastructures or prices must not be used as an excuse. Governments must put in place strategies to accelerate the level of FI and to reduce financial exclusion and the gaps between the population. This strategy must necessarily be designed for people on low incomes, excluded women, young people in need of funds, and so on.

With regard to the effect of fintechs on FI in the landscape of African economies, the following conclusions can be drawn. In the long term, fintechs have a significant and positive impact on the IF. In fact, all of the independent variables used to measure fintechs have a positive and significant impact on the FI. First, the credit provided to the private sector is a crucial component in advancing the financial inclusion process. Second, in countries where a significant proportion of the population is still excluded, mobile technology has enormous potential to expand access to formal financial services. Third, the positive and significant impact of the Internet on the IF demonstrates that Internet access promotes access to digital financial services in Africa, it represents one of the main indicators supporting the IF process in African countries.

However, the control variable of our study (education) has a negative effect on FI, this result is invalid, therefore it is essential to implement financial and digital education to accompany the emergence of fintechs, prevent information asymmetry at the consumer level, and avoid any rejection of innovative financial solutions.

Fintechs, nevertheless, have no immediate effect on FI, which can be attributed to the financial institutions in the area adopting digital financial services later than others. Lastly, although only temporarily, fintechs are boosting FI in African nations.

Indeed, Demir et al. (2022) suggest that appropriate consumer protection laws and a focus on financial education should be implemented in order to foster a climate that is supportive of fintechs and FI, which is proving to be a barrier for low-income households, particularly in developing countries. In fact, literacy and financial education are essential elements in fostering FI. When individuals are informed and educated about basic financial concepts, they are better prepared to make informed decisions about their finances, including the use of financial products and services, so it is crucial that financial institutions and service providers take these disparities into account and offer tailored solutions. In addition to financial services, they should also offer non-financial services aimed at strengthening customers' financial knowledge. This can include training programmes on budget management, savings, investment, responsible use of credit, etc. In short, literacy and financial education are key elements in promoting long-term FI. The combination of accessible financial services and appropriate financial education can help to strengthen the confidence and financial autonomy of individuals, promoting their active and informed participation in the financial system.

Furthermore, the regulatory environment has presented barriers to the adoption of new digital financial services in African countries, both for new businesses and for existing financial institutions. These barriers have particularly affected non-bank financial institutions such as telecom operator-led models.

However, in recent years, regulation has evolved in some countries in the region, such as Morocco, with the creation of payment institution status. This new status complements the banking offering of credit institutions and aims to encourage the development of digital financial services. The long-term objective is to reduce cash transactions, which are still widespread in the region. Regulations continue to evolve to support the development of digital financial services in African countries, but further efforts are needed to overcome these obstacles and create a regulatory environment conducive to the widespread adoption of these services across the continent.

In conclusion, it is vital that state authorities strengthen the supply of financial services and reduce the barriers to accessing these services, in order to encourage the public's access to the formal financial system in Africa and to advance digital FI.

References

Ahamed, M. M., & Mallick, S. K. (2019). Is financial inclusion good for bank stability? International evidence. *Journal of Economic Behavior & Organization, 157*, 403–427. https://doi.org/10.1016/j.jebo.2017.07.027

Allen, F., Carletti, E., Cull, R., Qian, J. Q., Senbet, L., & Valenzuela, P. (2014). The African financial development and financial inclusion gaps. *Journal of African Economies, 23*(5), 614–642. https://doi.org/10.1093/jae/eju015

Asif, M., Khan, M. N., Tiwari, S., Wani, S. K., & Alam, F. (2023). The impact of fintech and digital financial services on financial inclusion in India. *Journal of Risk and Financial Management, 16*(2), 122. https://doi.org/10.3390/jrfm16020122. Empirical literature review.

Asuming, P. O., Osei-Agyei, L. G., & Mohammed, J. I. (2019). Financial inclusion in sub-Saharan Africa: Recent trends and determinants. *Journal of African Business, 20*(1), 112–134. https://doi.org/10.1080/15228916.2018.1484209

Breusch, T. S., & Pagan, A. R. (1980). The Lagrange multiplier test and its applications to model specification in econometrics. *The Review of Economic Studies, 47*(1), 239–253. https://doi.org/10.2307/2297111

Campanella, F., Della Peruta, M. R., & Del Giudice, M. (2017). The effects of technological innovation on the banking sector. *Journal of the Knowledge Economy, 8*, 356–368. https://doi.org/10.1007/s13132-015-0326-8

Chikalipah, S. (2017). What determines financial inclusion in sub-Saharan Africa? *African Journal of Economic and Management Studies, 8*(1), 8–18. https://doi.org/10.1108/AJEMS-01-2016-0007

Christensen, C. M. (2013). *The innovator's dilemma: When new technologies cause great firms to fail*. Harvard Business Review Press.

Davis, F. D., Bagozzi, R. P., & Warshaw, P. R. (1989). User acceptance of computer technology: A comparison of two theoretical models. *Management Science, 35*(8), 982–1003. https://doi.org/10.1287/mnsc.35.8.982

Demir, A., Pesqué-Cela, V., Altunbas, Y., & Murinde, V. (2022). Fintech, financial inclusion and income inequality: A quantile regression approach. *The*

European Journal of Finance, 28(1), 86–107. https://doi.org/10.1080/1351847X.2020.1772335

Demirgüç-Kunt, A., & Klapper, L. F. (2012). *Measuring financial inclusion: The global findex database* (World bank policy research working paper (6025)). Available at SSRN: https://ssrn.com/abstract=2043012

Duvendack, M., & Mader, P. (2020). Impact of financial inclusion in low-and middle-income countries: A systematic review of reviews. *Journal of Economic Surveys, 34*(3), 594–629. https://doi.org/10.1111/joes.12367

El Yamani, R. (2024). Determinants of financial inclusion: Evidence from the MENA region. In *Handbook of banking and finance in the MENA region* (pp. 381–403). https://doi.org/10.1142/9781800614734_0015

Emara, N., & El Said, A. (2021). Financial inclusion and economic growth: The role of governance in selected MENA countries. *International Review of Economics & Finance, 75*, 34–54. https://doi.org/10.1016/j.iref.2021.03.014

Evans, O. (2018). Connecting the poor: The internet, mobile phones and financial inclusion in Africa. *Digital Policy, Regulation and Governance, 20*(6), 568–581. https://doi.org/10.1108/DPRG-04-2018-0018

Fungáčová, Z., & Weill, L. (2015). Understanding financial inclusion in China. *China Economic.* https://doi.org/10.1016/j.chieco.2014.12.004

Im, K. S., Pesaran, M. H., & Shin, Y. (2003). Testing for unit roots in heterogeneous panels. *Journal of Econometrics, 115*(1), 53–74. https://doi.org/10.1016/S0304-4076(03)00092-7

International Monetary Fund (IMF). (2020). *Annual report 2020.* https://www.imf.org/external/pubs/ft/ar/2020/eng/downloads/imf-annual-report-2020.pdf

Kumar, N. (2013). Financial inclusion and its determinants: Evidence from India. *Journal of Financial Economic Policy, 5*(1), 4–19. https://doi.org/10.1108/17576381311317754

Lee, I., & Shin, Y. J. (2018). Fintech: Ecosystem, business models, investment decisions, and challenges. *Business Horizons, 61*(1), 35–46. https://doi.org/10.1016/j.bushor.2017.09.003

Merton, R. C., & Bodie, Z. (1995). A conceptual framework for analyzing the financial system. The global financial system : A functional perspective, 3–31. https://un.uobasrah.edu.iq/lectures/1782.pdf

Milian, E. Z., Spinola, M. D. M., & de Carvalho, M. M. (2019). Fintechs : A literature review and research agenda. *Electronic Commerce Research and Applications, 34*, 100833. https://doi.org/10.1016/j.elerap.2019.100833

Loukoianova, M. E., Yang, Y., Guo, M. S., Hunter, M. L., Jahan, M. S., Jamaludin, M. F., & Wu, M. Y. (2018). Financial Inclusion in Asia-Pacific. *International Monetary Fund.*

Otekunrin, A. O., Chinoda, T., & Matowanyika, K. (2021). The nexus between economic growth, financial development, financial inclusion and financial innovation in Africa.

Pedroni, P. (2004). Panel cointegration: Asymptotic and finite sample properties of pooled time series tests with an application to the PPP hypothesis. *Econometric Theory, 20*(3), 597–625. https://doi.org/10.1017/S0266466604203073

Pesaran, M. H. (2004). General diagnostic tests for cross-section dependence in panels. *Cambridge Working Papers. Economics, 1240*(1), 1.

Pesaran, M. H., Schuermann, T., & Weiner, S. M. (2004). Modeling regional interdependencies using a global error-correcting macroeconometric model. *Journal of Business & Economic Statistics, 22*(2), 129–162. https://doi.org/10.1198/073500104000000019

Pesaran, H., Shin, Y., & Smith, R. (1999). Pooled mean group estimation of dynamic heterogeneous panels. *Journal of the American Statistical Association, 94*, 621–634. https://doi.org/10.1080/01621459.1999.10474156

Pesaran, M. H., & Smith, R. (1995). Estimating long-run relationships from dynamic heterogeneous panels. *Journal of Econometrics, 68*, 79–113. https://doi.org/10.1016/0304-4076(94)01644-F

Puschmann, T. (2017). Fintech. *Business & Information Systems Engineering, 59*, 69–76. https://doi.org/10.1007/s12599-017-0464-6

Rachida, E. L. Y. (2023). Does Financial innovation improve financial inclusion in African countries. *Journal of Sustainable Development and Green Technology, 1*(1), 8–18. https://doi.org/10.54216/JSDGT.010101

Rastogi, S., & Ragabiruntha, E. (2018). Financial inclusion and socioeconomic development: Gaps and solution. *International Journal of Social Economics, 45*(7), 1122–1140. https://doi.org/10.1108/IJSE-08-2017-0324

Sahay, M. R., Cihak, M., N'Diaye, M. P., Barajas, M. A., Mitra, M. S., Kyobe, M. A., Mooi, M., & Yousefi, M. R. (2015). Financial inclusion: can it meet multiple macroeconomic goals? *International Monetary Fund.*

Sanderson, A., Mutandwa, L., & Le Roux, P. (2018). A review of determinants of financial inclusion. *International Journal of Economics and Financial Issues, 8*(3), 1. ISSN: 2146-4138 at available at http: www.econjournals.com

Sarma, M. (2008). *Index of financial inclusion (No. 215)* (Working Paper). https://hdl.handle.net/10419/176233

Swamy, P. (1970). Efficient inference in a random coefficient regression model. *Econometrica, 38*, 311–32. https://doi.org/10.2307/1913012

Westerlund, J. (2007). Testing for error correction in panel data. *Oxford Bulletin of Economics and Statistics, 69*(6), 709–748. https://doi.org/10.1111/j.1468-0084.2007.00477.x

World Bank. (2021). *Annual report 2021.* https://thedocs.worldbank.org/en/doc/cd05d27f0203b90751fcfe7145cd5a3d-0330122021/original/EDS05-Annual-Report-2021-English-Summary.pdf

Zins, A., & Weill, L. (2016). The determinants of financial inclusion in Africa. *Review of Development Finance,* 6(1), 46–57. https://hdl.handle.net/10520/EJC193922

Fintech Adoption and Sustainable Supply Chain Performance in GCC Markets

Faisal Khan, Shatha Hussain, and Muhammad Ikhlaas Gurrib

1 Introduction

The Gulf Cooperation Council (GCC) was founded in 1981 and comprises six (6) countries including the United Arab Emirates (UAE), the Kingdom of Bahrain, the Kingdom of Saudi Arabia, the Sultanate of Oman, the State of Qatar, and the State of Kuwait.[1] The GCC regions have been witnessing a significant emergence in Fintech adoption more recently. Numerous factors might be adding to this trend in GCC countries including advancements in technology, supportive government policies, and shifts in consumer behaviors (AbuRaya et al., 2021). For instance, the governments across GCC regions have been proactively

[1] https://www.gcc-sg.org/en-us/AboutGCC/MemberStates/Pages/Home.aspx.

F. Khan (✉) · S. Hussain
College of Business, City University Ajman, Ajman, UAE
e-mail: f.khan@cu.ac.ae

S. Hussain
e-mail: s.hussain@cu.ac.ae

M. I. Gurrib
School of Management, Canadian University Dubai, Dubai, UAE
e-mail: ikhlaas@cud.ac.ae

© The Author(s), under exclusive license to Springer Nature Singapore Pte Ltd. 2025

A. S. et al. (eds.), *Trends and Challenges of Electronic Finance*,
https://doi.org/10.1007/978-981-96-3304-3_19

assisting the Fintech sectors through financial incentives and regulatory sandboxes to raise innovation and competition within the financial services industry. Furthermore, the rapid digital technology advancements and rise in the penetration of smartphones have made financial technology more appealing to a tech-savvy population and more accessible which in turn requires convenience and efficiency in financial transactions (Deloitte, 2023; PwC, 2023).

Simultaneously, an increasing prominence is observed on sustainable business practices across sectors within these regions. This transition is led by growing concerns regarding climate degradation, depletion of resources, and social responsibility. More and more business enterprises are integrating environmental, societal, and governance (ESG) criteria into their business model to boost their sustainability. For instance, many enterprises in GCC regions are adopting green energy solutions, fair labor practices, and waste management practices. These trends are supported by both consumer preferences and governmental policies that favor firms that demonstrate genuine commitments to sustainability and reducing carbon footprints (Arab News, 2023; Gulf Business, 2023).

2 Fintech Adoption in GCC Markets

Financial technology, commonly "Fintech", comprises a wide range of technological innovations aimed to improve and automate the delivery and use of financial services. Moreover, Fintech is applied to help enterprises, entrepreneurs, and consumers manage their financial operations, processes, and lives in a better manner. There might be several drivers for the firms to adopt Fintech; however, in the GCC markets, the following factors could be attributed in this regard:

2.1 GCC Governments Initiatives

The governments across the GCC countries have identified and realized the importance of Fintech as the main economic development and financial inclusion driver. Consequently, they announced to implement initiatives and regulatory frameworks which could encourage Fintech innovation and entrepreneurship such as the launching of Bahrain Fintech Bay by the Central Bank of Bahrain (CBB) which is dedicated to Fintech development and fostering collaboration and innovation in this sector (Central Bank of Bahrain, 2023). The CBB is considered the pioneering institution that introduced the Fintech hub in 2018. This initiative has provided a solid platform for financial institutions, new startups, and tech-based enterprises to apply Fintech solutions. This platform (Fintech Bay) offers many resources such as co-working spaces, access to mentors and investors, and accelerator programs which make it a major player in the region's Fintech ecosystem (Central Bank of Bahrain, 2023).

The UAE has developed the "Dubai International Financial Centre (DIFC)" a Fintech hive that is the largest Fintech hub in the region and provides a platform for throwing start-up ideas, facilitates funding, and collaborates with established financial institutions. In addition, the Abu Dhabi Global Market has also launched the RegLab which is a regulatory sandbox and allows tech firms to test innovative products in a controlled setting. All these measures are part of the UAE's broader vision to diversify its economy and minimize its dependence on oil by fostering a knowledge-based economy (Abu Dhabi Global Market, 2023; Dubai International Financial Centre, 2023).

In Saudi Arabia, the Saudi Central Bank (formerly known as Saudi Arabian Monetary Authority (SAMA)) promotes the Fintech initiatives. This organization, in 2018, has developed a regulatory sandbox that enabled local and foreign Fintech firms to test new digital solutions in an active market setting under the regulator's supervision. These initiatives help the Saudi government realize its Vision 2030 which aims to transform the country into a leading hub for innovation and technology (Saudi Central Bank, 2023).

The Qatar Fintech hub was established by the Qatar Financial Centre (QFC) which offers a collaborative workplace, access to financial institutions, a network of investors, and accelerator programs. The QFC also provides a regulator sandbox that allows Fintech organizations to develop and test their products with regulatory oversight that in turn ensures compliance and fosters innovation (Qatar Financial Centre, 2023).

Finally, in Oman, the Central Bank of Oman (CBO) launched a regulatory sandbox in the year 2020. The purpose of this is to encourage the development of innovative financial products and services. These measures by the Oman government serve the purpose of attracting Fintech startups and facilitating the development of the digital economy in the country (Central Bank of Oman, 2023).

All these initiatives across the GCC countries exhibit the commitment of respective governments to leverage Fintech as a major player in economic diversification and financial inclusion. Hence, by developing supportive ecosystems, innovative hubs, and regulatory sandboxes, the GCC countries are positioning themselves as leaders in the global Fintech landscape.

2.2 *Technological Infrastructure in GCC Countries*

The countries in the GCC group have been boasting advanced technological infrastructure such as robust Internet connectivity and smartphone penetration rates. This environment favors facilitating the adoption of Fintech solutions including digital banking, mobile payments, and robo-advisors (Telecommunications Regulatory Authority, UAE, 2022). Among the key determinants of the rapid adoption of Fintech solutions in the regions is the high rate of smartphone penetration. As per the statistics provided by the Telecommunications Regulatory Authority (TRA) in UAE, the country has one of the highest smartphone penetration rates universally, i.e. 99% of the UAE population owns a smartphone (Telecommunications Regulatory Authority, UAE, 2022). Similarly, this ratio is also very high across the other countries in the GCC, i.e. smartphone is used for interpersonal communication, commerce and trade, and financial transactions. This extensive access to smartphones warrants that a large segment of the population can easily adopt and use mobile-based financial services.

Additionally, in the GCC regions, people also have access to robust Internet connectivity. These countries have heavily invested in their digital infrastructures, consequently, this allowed them to have access not only to speedy Internet but also enjoy a seamless operation of online services. For example, the UAE has been ranked among the top nations in the world for Internet speed and quality, providing a strong foundation for digital innovation (Telecommunications Regulatory Authority, UAE, 2022). A fast and reliable Internet connection is important for the effective functioning of Fintech applications and enables real-time transactions and access to financial services. Hence, this combination of high smartphone penetration and robust Internet connectivity has drastically facilitated the adoption of Fintech solutions in the GCC countries.

In GCC regions, the mobile payment platforms have observed considerable rise due to the convenience and speed they offer to the consumer. Consumers using smartphones can not only transfer money but also make payments for various utilities and expenditures along with managing their accounts (using apps such as Apply Pay, STC Pay, and Samsung Pay).

Similarly, conventional banks have now been transformed into digital banks that offer mobile banking services throughout GCC countries (Emirates NBD, 2020). Robo-advisors (automatic investment services such as Sarwa) are becoming increasingly popular in GCC countries and use algorithms that provide personalized investment portfolio management and advice at a lower cost as compared to traditional financial advisors. They offer easy access to a diversified investment portfolio in UAE that appeals the younger investors who prefer digital solutions (Sarwa, 2021). The main determinants of Fintech adoption in the GCC countries are the advanced information technology infrastructure, robust Internet connectivity, and smartphone penetration. Such an environment enables the integration of digital banking, robo-advisors, and mobile payments in the daily lives of customers and meets the demands of a tech-savvy population. Hence, with the further advancement in these technologies, the growth of the Fintech sector is more evident in these regions (Aldaarmi, 2024).

2.3 Changing Consumer Preferences

The millennials (born from 1981 to 1996) and digital natives or generation "Z" (born 1997 onward) being a major portion of GCC markets have transformed the financial services landscape. This generation has grown up along with technology and anticipates accessible, convenient, and personalized financial services that may align with their digital preferences. These shifts in the demographics of the regions drive the significant rise in Fintech solutions in the regions. They feel convenient with digital wallets, mobile banking apps, and online investments that permit these generations to manage their finances painlessly. According to another survey conducted in the context of MENA (Middle East and North Africa region) countries, 57% of consumers in these regions prefer using Fintech services (Ernst & Young, 2021). These senses indicate the growth and acceptance of digital solutions among the masses of these countries due to the following benefits:

First, the convenience with which Fintech offers 24/7 access to financial services (such as mobile banking and digital wallets allow for money transfer, bill payments, and access to account management) and hence, eliminates the need to physically visit the bank's branch (Pazarbasioglu et al., 2020). Second, the ease of access to Fintech services from anywhere using multiple options makes them further user-friendly and accessible.

Third, customization as per the preferences of consumers as these platforms allow the consumers to make necessary settings as per their needs and even the intelligent system itself memorizes all these patterns (Aïmeur et al., 2008; Khan et al., 2024).

In GCC countries, financial institutions are responding to these shifts by venturing with Fintech firms and investing in digital transformation. Conventional banks, to meet the demands of their customers, are either developing their own Fintech solutions or they are collaborating with new startups to meet these demands. For instance, in the UAE, banks have adopted digitalization via Liv., a digital bank initiative targeting millennials and young talents (Emirates NBD, 2020). Moreover, the governments across GCC countries have actively supported the adoption of Fintech by companies through favorable regulatory environments and frameworks specifically designed to assist startups. In this regard, the government of Bahrain has established Fintech Bay, and the government of Saudi has launched the Fintch Saudi, both aimed at fostering a conducive environment for Fintech evolution in these countries (Bahrain FinTech Bay, 2021; Fintech Saudi, 2021).

3 Sustainable Supply Chain Performance in GCC Markets

The sustainability of business firms operating in GCC countries has become an increasingly significant concern mainly due to the following factors:

3.1 Environmental Concerns

The major environmental concerns in the GCC countries that are becoming threats to the sustainability of business firms include scarcity of water reserves, desertification, and high levels of air pollution. These concerns are further exacerbated by the harsh climate conditions prevailing in these regions. To elaborate on these issues further, the scarcity of water is the most pressing challenge among all three in the GCC countries. The levels of freshwater availability and its consumption are extremely low and high, respectively. According to the World Bank's survey, the level of freshwater availability per capita in GCC regions is the lowest in the world (World Bank, 2017). The second important challenge is desertification which poses a significant threat. Desertification leads to the degradation of arable land and loss of biodiversity. This process is mainly driven by deforestation, unsustainable agriculture practices, and overgrazing. Thirdly, air pollution which is mainly caused by industrial emissions, dust storms, and vehicular exhaust poses the third crucial threat to the sustainability of businesses in GCC countries. In addition, rapid urbanization and other industrial activities have further elevated the level of air pollution in GCC countries. In most of the regions in GCC, these air pollutions have become hazardous to the health of the population, and livelihood is not recommended there (as per the report issued by WHO in 2016).

Consequently, to overcome these environmental challenges and climate change risks, the businesses operating in the GCC countries are inclined to adopt sustainable practices. For example, businesses are investing in renewable energy sources including wind power and solar, etc. to minimize reliance on fossil fuels. The Masdar City of UAE is a classical instance, designed in a manner to be zero-waste urban development power and zero-carbon entirely by renewable energy (Masdar, 2024). Furthermore, companies are applying water conservation measures such as advanced irrigation techniques and wastewater recycling to address water scarcity. The Saline Water Conversion Corporation has started energy-efficient desalination technologies that ominously mitigate the carbon footprint of water production (SWCC, 2021). Saudi Aramco is yet another example that has initiated the "Green Saudi" project aiming to plant ten billion trees in the whole country to restore degraded lands and enhance carbon sequestration (Ministry of Economy and Planning, 2023). Similarly, the UAE's Emirates Global Aluminium has applied emission control technologies to reduce industrial emissions and enhance air quality (Emirates Global Aluminium, 2020). Thus, businesses might play a significant role in minimizing the effects and promoting a more sustainable future by following these sustainable principles.

3.2 Regulatory Pressures

Governments in the GCC regions are keen to implement regulations to promote sustainability across various sectors. For example, the government of UAE has set "UAE Vision 2021" and the Saudi government has set "Saudi Vision 2030". Both of these visions have the core objectives of achieving a diversifying economy, promoting renewable energy sources, and reducing reliance on fossil fuel, which stem from their main vision about sustainability (GCC Secretariat General, 2021). More specifically, the UAE Vision 2021 is focused on producing a sustainable environment and infrastructure by bringing investments in renewable energy, increasing its efficiency, and minimizing carbon emissions. For this purpose, the UAE government has initiated several important projects, including the "Mohammed bin Rashid Al Maktoum Solar Park" (with an expected capacity of generating 5000 megawatts of solar power by 2030) and targets a mix of clean energy sources to meet 50% of the UAE's energy needs (UAE Government, 2021; Ministry of Energy & Infrastructure, 2022). Likewise, the Saudi Vision of 2030 focuses on sustainability as a major component of the state's economic transformation plan. It further aims to diversify the economy and reduce dependence on oil by investing in different industries such as technology, tourism, and renewable energy (Government of Saudi Arabia, 2016). In this regard, the NEOM megacity project is aimed at implementing renewable energy and serves as a model for sustainable urban development (NEOM, 2022). In addition to these, the Saudi Vision 2030 also aims to achieve a major reduction in carbon emissions, pollution, and preservation of marine and terrestrial environments (Saudi Green Initiative, 2021).

These initiatives by the GCC states reflect their proactive approaches to sustainability and carry effects beyond environmental benefits such as enhancing the global competitiveness of GCC businesses. The business entities having operations in these regions are incentivized to innovate and adopt sustainable practices. These measures ultimately lead to efficiencies in operations, savings in costs, and improvement in market positioning. This is why Saudi Aramco's efforts in carbon management and emissions reduction have positioned this company as a leader in sustainability across all the oil and gas firms in Saudi Arabia (Saudi Aramco, 2023).

3.3 Stakeholder Expectations

The stakeholders including consumers and investors are exerting immense pressure on businesses to follow corporate social responsibility (CSR) and sustainability practices in the GCC countries. This increasing trend is led by the growing awareness of social and environmental issues besides the recognition that sustainable practices may bring long-term business advantages (Tsai & Kuan-Jung, 2017). More recently, a drastic shift has been observed in consumer behavior showing a tendency for firms more responsibly concerned about their sustainability. In this connection, the existing studies have shown that a significant majority of consumers desire to pay a premium for products and services from companies that are committed to positive social and environmental impact (Wekesa, 2024). This tendency has been observed mainly in the young generations who are willing to do business with companies that are more socially responsible and sustainable (Jones, 2023). In addition, they are also focused on integrating environmental, societal, and governance (ESG) aspects of their decision-making (BlackRock, 2021). As a consequence of all these, the firms in the GCC regions are facing huge pressures to exhibit their commitment to these areas to enhance stakeholders' trust and also maintain their brand reputation (Alshukri et al., 2024).

Furthermore, in the GCC countries, the regulatory authorities have made it mandatory for firms to report their compliance with sustainability and international trends. For instance, the UAE and Saudi governments have initiated policies that require firms to disclose their performance and sustainability practices (GCC Secretariat General, 2021). The regulations are in place to ensure transparency and accountability, and that these businesses indeed contribute to the overall sustainability goals. By integrating sustainability goals into their operations, businesses can benefit from increased customer loyalty and improved brand reputation which gives them a competitive advantage (add citation). Thus, through alignment of the business strategies with the stakeholders' expectations (customers' demands and regulatory requirements), firms may improve their brand reputation, attract investments, and achieve longer-run success in a rapidly changing business environment (Tsai & Kuan-Jung, 2017).

4 Interplay Between Fintech Adoption and Sustainable Supply Chain Performance

The convergence of Fintech adoption and sustainable supply chain practices offers unique opportunities for businesses in the GCC markets:

4.1 *Fintech-Enabled Supply Chain Financing*

Fintech platforms offer innovative financing resolutions that might support sustainable supply chain practices (Bal & Pawlicka, 2021; Boute et al., 2022; Tsai & Kuan-Jung, 2017). For instance, supply chain finance platforms enable suppliers to access liquidity by monetizing their receivables, thereby improving cash flows and supporting investment in sustainability initiatives (Bal & Pawlicka, 2021). Through the adoption of automation and advanced data analytics, these platforms could streamline the financing process, reducing the time and cost associated with traditional methods (Boute et al., 2022). This level of efficiency facilitates the suppliers, especially small and medium-sized businesses (SMEs) in securing their funds quickly and economically (Tsai & Kuan-Jung, 2017). They also concluded that the transparency provided by online supply chain financing platforms improves risk management and trust among supply chain participants. Real-time data sharing facilitates better credit evaluation and decision-making, guaranteeing that financing is provided to reliable partners committed to sustainable practices (Boute et al., 2022; Tsai & Kuan-Jung, 2017). Due to the improvement in financial stability, suppliers are empowered to invest in renewable energy sources, eco-friendly technologies, and green finance initiatives which help them align their operations with sustainability goals (Bal & Pawlicka, 2021; Tsai & Kuan-Jung, 2017).

Furthermore, the encompassing quality of Fintech platforms makes it convenient to access capital and authorizes a large scale of suppliers to engage in sustainable supply chains (Shabir, 2024). Hence, all the previously underserved suppliers can now access financial support through these alternative funding sources outside the conventional banking structure (Tsai & Kuan-Jung, 2017). This inclusive access promotes a more sustainable and resilient supply chain ecosystem, as a different array of suppliers might contribute to advantage from sustainable practices. Thus, Fintech platforms not only enrich supply chain liquidity and efficiency but also contribute a significant role in promoting sustainability.

4.2 Blockchain for Supply Chain Transparency

Blockchain technology possesses the ability to improve the supply chains concerning transparency and traceability and hence, it supports sustainability goals. Furthermore, using blockchain technology, firms can trace the provenance of raw materials, keep an eye on the environmental effects throughout the supply chain, and conform to sustainability standards (Queiroz et al., 2020). Blockchain platforms provide an immutable and decentralized ledger system that records each transaction transparently which is useful for supply chain management and enables real-time tracking of the goods from their origin to the destination of the consumer. This surely enhances the trust and confidence of the consumers in the product of the firm as they can have access to each record related to their products on the blockchain (Saberi et al., 2019). Moreover, this technology can provide an unalterable record of transactions and hence, the reliability, integrity, and security of data on this platform are very high. These features indeed guarantee compliance with sustainable standards and allow for independent verification of environmental, social, and governance (ESG) claims (Kouhizadeh & Sarkis, 2018).

Besides ensuring traceability, blockchain technology could even streamline supply chain operations by minimizing the requirement for intermediaries and relaxing administrative processes. "Smart" contracts are self-operating agreements with terms written directly into code and can automate various supply chain functions including payments, order processing, and inventory management. This automation not only minimizes the costs but also reduces the risk of human errors and fraud (Treiblmaier, 2018). Furthermore, blockchain may contribute significantly to sustainability by enabling more efficient resource management. Such firms might utilize this technology to manage and track the carbon footprint of their products throughout the supply chain. This assists in identifying areas where emissions might be abridged and, hence, adds to the overall efforts of sustainability (Saberi et al., 2019). Similarly, Walmart is quoted as a successful case that implemented the blockchain system for their tracking of the project from their place of origin to destination, thereby improving food security (Kamath, 2018)

4.3 *Data Analytics for Sustainability Insights*

Data analytics and AI being solutions provided under Fintech give valuable insights into supply chain sustainability performance. Firms may optimize opportunities to improve their supply chain operations for greater sustainability if they analyze data on resource usage, carbon emissions, and social impact (Bracarense et al., 2022). The integration of these technologies has enabled the firms to make data-driven decision-making that in turn increases efficiency, minimizes the environmental footprints, and guarantees compliance with sustainable standards. The functions of data analytics are systematic computational analysis of data for uncovering patterns, correlations, and insights. These data analytics when applied to supply chain management may give a comprehensive picture of different sustainability measures including waste generation, energy consumption, and greenhouse gas emission. Through constant monitoring of these measures, firms may identify inefficiencies in the areas where sustainability practices might be applied. For instance, Choi et al. (2016) concluded that advanced analytics might reveal trends in energy usage and enable firms to adjust their operations to reduce consumption during peak periods.

Machine learning algorithms which are a sub-domain under artificial intelligence (AI) may increase the forecasting ability of data analytics. AI might analyze historical data to predict future trends and recognize potential hazards in the supply chain that in turn enable sustainability initiatives as it permits firms to forecast and reduce environmental and social effects before their incurrence. For instance, AI might forecast supply chain disruption due to regulatory changes and natural disasters which allows firms to develop contingency plans that reduce their environmental effects (Wang et al., 2016). Furthermore, AI-based data analytics also facilitate the application of circular economy principles in supply chain management. Through data analysis on product life cycle, firms may construct processes that enhance resource efficiency and reduce waste including identifying opportunities for recycling, designing products for longer life spans, and reusing materials. For instance, these practices may not merely contribute to sustainability but also help achieve economic benefits by minimizing material costs and improving operational efficiency (Genovese et al., 2017). The literature has exhibited the practical advantages of integrating data analytics and AI into supply chain management for sustainability. For instance, to track and minimize the carbon footprint in the entire supply chain, the Unilever Company uses an advanced data analytics system. Through extracting data from different sources, they can identify hotspots of carbon emission and apply targeted strategies to minimize its level, such as optimizing transportation routes and improving energy efficiency in production processes (Bracarense et al., 2022). More so, artificial intelligence and data analytics could increase transparency and accountability in the supply chain. These features further increase the trust of the customers in the company's reputation and provide a competitive advantage in the market (Dubey et al., 2019).

5 Challenges and Opportunities

The integration between Fintech and sustainable supply chain performance gives several benefits; however, this integration also poses some significant challenges:

5.1 Data Privacy and Security

Fintech solutions deal with the collection and processing of sensitive data which raises concerns regarding data security and privacy. The volume of data and its exchange increase substantially with the increase of Fintech applications in the organization. This data comprises not merely the financial transactions but also the data regarding resource usage, carbon emissions, and social effect metrics. This requires robust cyber security mechanisms to secure the data against data breaches and guarantee compliance with data protection regulations due to the sensitive nature of data (Huang & Rust, 2018). In addition, the adoption of comprehensive cyber security measures by the business to secure data privacy is also required such as encryption of data while transferring so that the data might not be readable during the transmission. Similarly, the application of multi-factor authentication may enhance security by including an extra layer of verification before handing over access to sensitive data (Shackelford, 2016). These businesses are also required to conduct vulnerability and penetration tests to identify and address potential security weaknesses. Along with these measures, businesses may adopt intrusion detection systems including intrusion detection and prevention systems, which can help in identifying and mitigating potential cyber threats in real time (Cavusoglu et al., 2004).

Collecting and managing customers' data requires compliance with existing protection regulations and law requires firms to ensure explicit consent from the data respondents and transparency in this regard before and after the collection of data (Voigt & Von dem Bussche, 2017). In addition, firms are highly encouraged to avoid the collection of unnecessary and irrelevant data. The regular audit may help firms in compliance with these regulatory requirements and further improvements (Tankard, 2016).

Despite all these issues and challenges, the integration of Fintech with a sustainable supply chain might raise various opportunities. For instance, this integration brings more transparency and high efficiency to the operations of the firm. Similarly, this brings insights that drive sustainable practices, improve resource management, and reduce waste. More so, features such as the ability to track and verify sustainable measures may increase corporate social responsibility measures, build consumer trust, and provide a competitive advantage (Saberi et al., 2019). In addition, the traceability and accountability of the supply chain could also be enhanced through blockchain. The high level of transparency is especially prized in sectors where ethical sourcing and sustainability are critical concerns (Kamath, 2018).

5.2 *Integration and Interoperability*

The integration of a Fintech solution with a supply chain management system is a complex and challenging process. Enterprises are required to ensure compatibility between various platforms and technologies so that data exchange and collaboration across the supply chain take place smoothly. This integration needs smart planning, a clear understanding of the systems involved, and a robust technological framework of all the systems involved in the process (Tallon et al., 2019). Similarly, another major challenge might be the compatibility of the systems and software involved in this integration as most of them are heterogeneous. For instance, supply chain management is usually developed on a wide array of legacy systems such as enterprise resource planning applications to which the other proprietary technologies may not be compatible and could not be integrated with modern Fintech software. Consequently, this particular challenge would lead to the trapping of information in one system and could not be accessible or utilizable by others (Gunasekaran et al., 2017). Addressing these challenges requires businesses to focus on investing in integration platforms and middleware (an intermediary layer) and adoption of APIs (application programming interfaces) which will help integrate and enhance the interoperability among these disparate systems (Korpela et al., 2017).

However, the technological aspect is one side of the story, businesses are also faced with organizational challenges linked to the integration of Fintech into their supply chain management (Francisco & Swanson, 2018). For instance, the resistance from the existing employees toward the automation of systems requires their counseling, orientation, and training regarding these systems. Hence, to smoothly complete this transition, effective change management strategies are important to overcome all these challenges and align all the stakeholders with the integration goals (AlMashari, 2001). For this purpose, a thorough evaluation of the existing system must be conducted to identify the gaps for improvement and the development of a clear roadmap for successful integration. The management responsible for integration may collaborate with technology consultants, vendors, and other relevant stakeholders to get the required expertise and resources for the effective implementation of Fintech solutions (Tallon et al., 2019). However, this integration should be long-lasting and accommodative to any future extension along with the emergence of Fintech technologies (Treiblmaier, 2018).

5.3 *Regulatory Compliance*

The GCC markets are still in their evolutionary phases concerning the regulatory frameworks governing Fintech and sustainability; hence, businesses need to navigate regulatory uncertainty to ensure compliance with them as they may vary across regions (Restoy, 2019). Moreover, the regulatory environment for Fintech and sustainability solutions is constantly developing in the GCC regions and presents challenges as well as opportunities for businesses that want to implement Fintech solutions. The governments across the GCC countries are proactively developing frameworks that enable innovation along with financial stability and consumer protection (Zalan & Toufaily, 2017). For example, the UAE government has initiated several steps to nurture Fintech development, such as regulatory sandboxes that allow for the testing of new technologies under regulatory supervision. In addition, the Dubai Financial Services Authority (DFSA) and the Abu Dhabi Global Market (ADGM) have been predominantly proactive in this connection. Likewise, the Saudi Vision of 2030 embraces provisions for enhancing the regulatory framework to support Fintech adoption (Chueca Vergara & Ferruz Agudo, 2021).

Yet another challenge encountered by businesses in GCC countries is the regulatory risk inherited by them due to the rapidly evolving sectors. As these regulatory changes take place so rapidly, they complicate compliance with differing regulations across these regions. For instance, the General Data Protection Regulations (GDPR) of the EU can inflict strict requirements on firms that are functioning within or interacting with firms operating in the EU. Hence, governments across the GCC countries are also introducing their data protection regulations that may differ in scope and enforcement from the GDPR, adding to the complication (Voigt & Von dem Bussche, 2017).

Effective compliance strategies are crucial to managing regulatory uncertainties and businesses are required to conduct frequent compliance audits and risk assessments to detect any gaps to ensure adherence to standards (Ji et al, 2017). Leveraging solutions based on regulatory technologies (RegTechs) could streamline these processes by automating monitoring and reporting, managing workflows, tracking regulatory changes, and generating compliance reports, hence, reducing administrative burdens on business (Arner et al., 2017). Compliance with regulations poses both challenges and opportunities for this business. For instance, businesses that strictly adhere to regulatory compliances earn a reputation in the market, win the trust of the customers, provide a competitive advantage, and position themselves as market leaders (Restoy, 2019). Moreover, regulatory frameworks that complement Fintech and sustainability might drive innovation and open new business opportunities. For example, regulatory sandboxes deliver a safe environment for analyzing new Fintech solutions that allow businesses to innovate without the risk of non-compliance. Consequently, it leads to the evolution of state-of-the-art technologies that increase supply chain efficiency, transparency, and sustainability (Zalan & Toufaily, 2017).

6 Conclusion

Businesses operating in the GCC regions stand at a critical juncture, where they are facing environmental constraints as well as technological advancements that shape their future trajectory. The emergence of Fintech and cutting-edge technologies is upending the businesses in GCC countries. The significance of Fintech technology for sustainable supply chain performance has been confirmed by various research studies. Moreover, Fintech is particularly interesting to emerging markets such as GCC since it helps them grow. The purpose of this chapter was to reveal the relationship between Fintech adoption and sustainable supply chain performance in the context of the GCC. In this regard, various research studies have been quoted and it can be claimed that the acceptance of Fintech is what drives the expansion of GCC firms. In addition, Fintech significantly improves organizational sustainability. There could be many reasons for adopting Fintech by these firms such as all documentation and data being securely saved along with the chain, digital ledger solutions like blockchain can assist automate antiquated procedures, saving billions of hours of paperwork every year, and lower human error. To leverage these advanced technologies and dynamic landscape, both businesses and policymakers need to collaborate and innovate to address environmental challenges, foster economic growth, and enhance financial inclusion. Moreover, the governments across GCC regions may chart a path toward prosperity, reliance, and a more inclusive future. Nevertheless, the research presents fresh insights for theory and practice as well as certain issues that must be resolved by policymakers. The research primarily focuses on GCC markets to address the need for Fintech which may be extended to other regions of the world by taking the other aspects of technologies such as artificial intelligence to identify organizational performance and sustainability. Future studies are advised to be conducted in other regions of the world on comparative basis. Similarly, these studies might also consider the other important aspects of technology including artificial intelligence to evaluate this relationship.

References

Abu Dhabi Global Market. (2023). About ADGM. https://www.adgm.com/about-adgm

AbuRaya, R., Abdulla, Y., Kumaraswamy, S., & Ebrahim, R. (2021, December). FinTech global outlook and the Bahraini landscape: empirical exploratory analysis and documentary evidence. In *2021 International Conference on Decision Aid Sciences and Application (DASA)* (pp. 1007–1015). IEEE.

Aïmeur, E., Brassard, G., Fernandez, J. M., & Mani Onana, F. S. (2008). Alambic: A privacy-preserving recommender system for electronic commerce. *International Journal of Information Security, 7*(5), 307–334.

Aldaarmi, A. A. (2024). Fintech Service Quality of Saudi Banks: Digital Transformation and Awareness in Satisfaction, Re-Use Intentions, and the Sustainable Performance of Firms. *Sustainability, 16*(6), 2261.

AlMashari, M. (2001). Process orientation through Enterprise Resource Planning (ERP): A review of critical issues. *Knowledge and Process Management, 8*(3), 175–185.

Alshukri, T., Ojekemi, O. S., Öz, T., & Alzubi, A. (2024). The interplay of corporate social responsibility, innovation capability, organizational learning, and sustainable value creation: Does stakeholder engagement matter? *Sustainability, 16*(13), 5511. https://doi.org/10.3390/su16135511

Arab News. (2023). Sustainability initiatives in the GCC: Trends and impacts. Retrieved from Arab News.

Arner, D. W., Barberis, J., & Buckley, R. P. (2017). FinTech, RegTech, and the reconceptualization of financial regulation. *Northwestern Journal of International Law & Business, 37*(3), 371–413.

Bahrain FinTech Bay. (2021). About us. https://www.bahrainfintechbay.com/about

Bal, M., & Pawlicka, K. (2021). Supply chain finance and challenges of modern supply chains. *LogForum, 17*(1), 71–82.

BlackRock, Inc. (2021). 2021 Annual Report. https://s24.q4cdn.com/856567660/files/doc_financials/2021/ar/online/pdfs/BlackRock_2021_AR_Complete_040822.pdf

Boute, R. N., Gijsbrechts, J., & Van Mieghem, J. A. (2022). Digital lean operations: Smart automation and artificial intelligence in financial services. *Innovative Technology at the Interface of Finance and Operations, I*, 175–188.

Bracarense, N., Bawack, R. E., Fosso Wamba, S., & Carillo, K. D. A. (2022). Artificial intelligence and sustainability: A bibliometric analysis and future research directions. *Pacific Asia Journal of the Association for Information Systems, 14*(2), 136–159.

Cavusoglu, H., Mishra, B., & Raghunathan, S. (2004). A model for evaluating IT security investments. *Communications of the ACM, 47*(7), 87–92.

Central Bank of Bahrain. (2023). Bahrain fintech bay. Retrieved from https://www.cbb.gov.bh/fintech/

Central Bank of Oman. (2023). About us. https://www.cbo.gov.om/Pages/AboutCBO.aspx

Choi, T. M., Cheng, T. C. E., & Zhao, X. (2016). Multi-methodological research in operations management. *Production and Operations Management, 25*(3), 379–389.

Chueca Vergara, C., & Ferruz Agudo, L. (2021). Fintech and sustainability: Do they affect each other? *Sustainability, 13*(13), 7012.

Deloitte. (2023). Fintech in the GCC: Catalysts and growth opportunities. *Retrieved from Deloitte.*

Dubai International Financial Centre. (2023). DIFC business innovation. https://www.difc.com/business/establish-abusiness#innovation

Dubey, R., Gunasekaran, A., & Childe, S. J. (2019). Big data analytics capability in supply chain agility: The moderating effect of organizational flexibility. *Management Decision, 57*(8), 2092–2112.

Emirates NBD. (2020). About us. https://www.emiratesnbd.com/en/about-us/

Ernst & Young. (2021). Global FinTech Adoption Index 2021. Retrieved from https://www.ey.com/en_gl/financial-services/global-fintech-adoption-index

Fintech Saudi. (2021). Fintech Saudi annual report 2020/2021. https://fintechsaudi.com/wpcontent/uploads/2021/09/FintechSaudi_AnnualReport_20_21E1.pdf

Francisco, K., & Swanson, D. (2018). The supply chain has no clothes: Technology adoption of blockchain for supply chain transparency. *Logistics, 2*(1), 2.

Genovese, A., Acquaye, A. A., Figueroa, A., & Koh, S. C. L. (2017). Sustainable supply chain management and the transition towards a circular economy: Evidence and some applications. *Omega, 66*, 344–357.

Government of Saudi Arabia. (2016). Saudi Vision 2030. https://www.vision2030.gov.sa/en

Gulf Business. (2023). The rise of sustainable business practices in the GCC. *Retrieved from Gulf Business*.

Gulf Cooperation Council Secretariat General. (2021). Economic integration in the GCC: Progress and challenges. https://www.gcc-sg.org/en/publications/economic-integration-2021.pdf

Gunasekaran, A., Papadopoulos, T., Dubey, R., Wamba, S. F., Childe, S. J., Hazen, B., & Akter, S. (2017). Big data and predictive analytics for supply chain and organizational performance. *Journal of Business Research, 70*, 308–317.

Huang, M. H., & Rust, R. T. (2018). Artificial intelligence in service. *Journal of Service Research, 21*(2), 155–172.

Ji, Y., Rozenbaum, O., & Welch, K. (2017). Corporate culture and financial reporting risk: Looking through the glassdoor. Available at SSRN 2945745.

Jones, G. (2023). Deeply responsible business: A global history of values-driven leadership. Harvard University Press.

Kamath, R. (2018). Food traceability on blockchain: Walmart's pork and mango pilots with IBM. *The Journal of the British Blockchain Association, 1*(1), 3712.

Khan, H. R., Kazmi, M., Lubaba, Khalid, M. H. B., Alam, U., Arshad, K., ... & Qazi, S. A. (2024). A low-cost energy monitoring system with universal compatibility and real-time visualization for enhanced accessibility and power savings. *Sustainability, 16*(10), 4137.

Kouhizadeh, M., & Sarkis, J. (2018). Blockchain practices, potentials, and perspectives in greening supply chains. *Sustainability, 10*(10), 3652.

Korpela, K., Hallikas, J., & Dahlberg, T. (2017). Digital supply chain transformation toward blockchain integration. In *Proceedings of the 50th Hawaii International Conference on System Sciences (HICSS 2017)*,(pp. 4182–4191). https://doi.org/10.24251/HICSS.2017.506

Masdar. (2024). Green finance report: Allocation and impact report 2023. https://masdar.ae/en/thought-leader-reports/greenfinance/green-finance-report-2023

Ministry of Energy and Infrastructure. (2022). State of energy report 2022/2023. https://www.moei.gov.ae/en/mediacenter/news/8/11/2023/second-emirates-energy-forum-pushes-energy-transition-and-decarbonization-agenda-ahead-of-cop28

Ministry of Economy and Planning. (2023). State of the Saudi economy annual report 2022. https://mep.gov.sa/files/en/KnowledgeBase/EconomicReports/Documents/State%20of%20the%20Economy%202022%20EN.pdf

NEOM. (2022). Social responsibility report 2022. https://www.neom.com/content/dam/neom/files/sr-annual-report-2022-digitalen.pdf

Pazarbasioglu, C., Mora, A. G., Uttamchandani, M., Natarajan, H., Feyen, E., & Saal, M. (2020). Digital financial services. *World Bank, 54.*

PwC. (2023). GCC fintech report: The rise of financial technology in the gulf cooperation council. *Retrieved from PwC.*

Qatar Financial Centre. (2023). About QFC. https://www.qfc.qa/en/about-qfc

Queiroz, M. M., Telles, R., & Bonilla, S. H. (2020). Blockchain and supply chain management integration: A systematic review of the literature. *Supply Chain Management: An International Journal, 25*(2), 241–254.

Restoy, F. (2019). Regulating fintech: What is going on, and where are the challenges? *Bank for International Settlements*, 1–7.

Saberi, S., Kouhizadeh, M., Sarkis, J., & Shen, L. (2019). Blockchain technology and its relationships to sustainable supply chain management. *International Journal of Production Research, 57*(7), 2117–2135.

Saline Water Conversion Corporation. (2021). Sustainability report 2021. https://www.swcc.gov.sa/uploads/SustainabilityReport2021%28English%29.pdf

Sarwa. (2021). Annual report 2021. https://www.sarwa.co/annual-report-2021

Saudi Aramco. (2023). Annual report 2022. https://www.aramco.com/-/media/publications/corporate-reports/annualreports/saudi-aramco-ara-2022-english.pdf

Saudi Central Bank. (2023). About SAMA. https://www.sama.gov.sa/en-US/About/Pages/default.aspx

Saudi Green Initiative. (2021). About Saudi Green Initiative. https://www.sgi.gov.sa/about-sgi/

Shabir, G. (2024). AI-Driven fintech: Revolutionizing payments and supply chain dynamics.

Shackelford, S. J. (2016). Protecting intellectual property and privacy in the digital age: The use of national cybersecurity strategies. *Chapman Law Review, 19*, 445–474.

Tallon, P. P., Queiroz, M., Coltman, T., & Sharma, R. (2019). Information technology and the search for organizational agility: A systematic review with future research possibilities. *The Journal of Strategic Information Systems, 28*(2), 218–237.

Tankard, C. (2016). What the GDPR means for businesses. *Network Security, 2016*(6), 5–8.

Telecommunications Regulatory Authority. (2022). About TRA. https://www.tra.gov.ae/en/about-tra.aspx

Treiblmaier, H. (2018). The impact of the blockchain on the supply chain: A theory-based research framework and a call for action. *Supply Chain Management: An International Journal, 23*(6), 545–559.

Tsai, C. H., & Kuan-Jung, P. (2017). The FinTech revolution and financial regulation: The case of online supply-chain financing. *Asian Journal of Law and Society, 4*(1), 109–132.

UAE Government. (2021). Vision 2021. https://u.ae/en/about-the-uae/strategies-initiatives-and-awards/strategies-plans-andvisions/strategies-plans-and-visions-untill-2021/vision-2021

Voigt, P., & Von dem Bussche, A. (2017). *The EU General Data Protection Regulation (GDPR). A Practical Guide* (1st Ed., 10 (3152676), 10–5555). Springer International Publishing.

Wang, G., Gunasekaran, A., Ngai, E. W., & Papadopoulos, T. (2016). Big data analytics in logistics and supply chain management: Certain investigations for research and applications. *International Journal of Production Economics, 176*, 98–110.

Wekesa, J. (2024). Impact of CSR (Corporate Social Responsibility) on consumer behavior. *International Journal of Marketing Strategies, 6*(2), 35–45.

World Bank. (2017). World development report 2017: Governance and the law. https://www.worldbank.org/en/publication/wdr2017

Zalan, T., & Toufaily, E. (2017). The promise of fintech in emerging markets: Not as disruptive. *Contemporary Economics, 11*(4), 415–430.

Smart Money, Smarter Marketing: Fintech's AI Evolution on Social Platforms

Mahalakshmi S., Bharath H., Kavitha Desai, and Narayani Ramachandran

1 Introduction

FinTech is a fairly straightforward and evident mix of both the domain ("financial") and the technology ("technology"), much like other related compound names like "BioTech." Since the founding of the first bank in 1472 and the subsequent establishment of numerous additional enterprises, including investment firms, insurance firms, and real estate advisors, the banking sector has expanded over several centuries (Puschmann & Alt, 2016, p. 9). Since they help businesses in a main market conduct their operations, financial corporations are frequently

Mahalakshmi S. · Bharath H.
Jain Deemed-to-Be University, Bengaluru, India
e-mail: dr.mahalakshmibharath@cms.ac.in

Bharath H.
e-mail: bharath.h@cms.ac.in

K. Desai (✉) · N. Ramachandran
SVKM's NMIMS School of Business Management, Bengaluru, India
e-mail: Kavitha.desai@nmims.ed

N. Ramachandran
e-mail: narayani.ramachandran@nmims.edu

© The Author(s), under exclusive license to Springer Nature Singapore Pte Ltd. 2025

A. S. et al. (eds.), *Trends and Challenges of Electronic Finance*,
https://doi.org/10.1007/978-981-96-3304-3_20

referred to as service providers. Over time, they have also shaped a secondary market where financial service providers operate (Zhu et al., 2004). The outcome was "a vast web of connections that are more intricate, mutual, and nonlinear than conventional manufacturing and retailing sectors." In order to manage financial processes, technologies—the second component of the FinTech term—have become essential. Technology is a way to arrange things, coordinate procedures, and complete jobs more quickly, according to Bouwman et al. (2005). Both analog and digital technologies, which have proliferated in the financial sector, are recognized under this broad term. Research from the past on the development of FinTech indicates that the term FinTech itself is not as old as financial technologies. Banks and trade organizations employed physical materials, such as paper or coins, to store information and value in the early days of their technology applications. Because these documents and values could only be transported physically, markets were mainly restricted to a localized area. Information and communication technology advancements brought to this transition. Specifically, information could be isolated from the material representation and transferred more quickly across longer distances thanks to the invention of the optical and then electrical telegraphs. In modern civilizations, the telegraph was acknowledged as a component of industrialization, with profound economic ramifications. They persisted until the middle of the twentieth century and can be viewed as a second wave of financial innovations (Malone et al., 1987).

1.1 Fintech and its Rapid Growth in the Present Day

The financial industry has witnessed a dramatic shift in recent years due to the phenomenal expansion of fintech. Global digitization, shifting consumer behaviors, legislative changes, and technology improvements are some of the main drivers of this expansion. Financial services have undergone a transformation thanks to cutting-edge technologies like mobile computing, blockchain, artificial intelligence (AI), and machine learning. These services are now more streamlined, individualized, and easily accessible (Marinč, 2013). The rapid use of fintech services like mobile payments, peer-to-peer lending, robo-advisors, and digital wallets is being driven by consumer demand, particularly among millennials and Gen Z, for convenient and digital financial solutions.

Fintech growth has been further boosted by regulatory changes that have fostered competition and innovation, especially with regard to open banking efforts. The financial sector has experienced a notable surge in digital transformation due to the COVID-19 epidemic, which forced individuals and organizations to adjust to remote and contactless transactions. Prominent fintech domains such as digital payments, online lending, wealth management, insurtech, and regtech are experiencing exponential growth. At the forefront of the industry, companies like Ant Financial, Square, and Stripe are showcasing its potential through their creative thinking and quick growth rates (Marjanovic & Murthy, 2015). However, issues including cybersecurity threats and regulatory compliance confront the fintech sector. Keeping up with the ever-changing and complex regulatory environment is still a big challenge, and the rise in digital transactions makes fintech companies easy targets for cyberattacks, thus strong security is required. Fintech has a bright future ahead of it despite these obstacles. It is anticipated that ongoing developments in AI and big data analytics would increase financial services' efficiency and level of personalization. Furthermore, emerging nations with strong mobile penetration rates and a demand for financial inclusion are likely to see an increase in the number of fintech companies expanding there. A stronger partnership between fintech companies and conventional financial institutions will also support long-term innovation and growth by fusing technology advancement with well established regulatory expertise and trust (Mention, 2019).

1.2 The Intersection of AI and Fintech: A New Paradigm

The financial sector is undergoing a significant transformation as a result of the convergence of fintech and artificial intelligence (AI), which offers previously unheard-of chances for disruption and innovation. With the ability to analyze data more quickly, assess risk more accurately, and provide more individualized client experiences, artificial intelligence (AI) technologies like machine learning, natural language processing, and predictive analytics are radically changing the traditional financial services landscape. Through the use of non-traditional data sources, AI-driven algorithms in lending are revolutionizing credit scoring and increasing access to financial services for previously disadvantaged populations. Wealth management is being revolutionized by AI-powered robo-advisors that provide low-cost, automated investing advice based on each client's goals and risk tolerance (Nosova et al., 2021).

There are certain difficulties and factors to take into account because of this mutually beneficial link between fintech and AI. To enable the equitable and responsible application of AI in financial decision-making, ethical issues pertaining to data privacy, algorithmic bias, and transparency must be carefully considered. In order to strike a balance between promoting innovation and defending the interests of consumers, regulatory frameworks must change to meet the complexities and hazards involved with AI-driven fintech solutions (Ferraro et al., 2022). Furthermore, because of the speed at which technology is developing, professionals must continue their education and training in order to acquire the skills necessary to successfully navigate this new environment.

Notwithstanding these difficulties, fintech and AI integration has a lot of potential to influence the direction of finance in the future. Fintech organizations can now deliver more customized products and services, increase operational efficiency, and reduce risks thanks to AI's real-time analysis of massive volumes of data. Additionally, chatbots and virtual assistants driven by AI are improving customer service and engagement by offering prompt assistance and tailored recommendations. AI's influence on fintech is anticipated to grow as it develops further, spurring more innovation and change throughout the financial sector. To fully use AI in fintech while resolving ethical, legal, and societal issues, cooperation among stakeholders—including regulators, business leaders, and technological specialists—will be essential (Nosova et al., 2021).

1.3 Social Media as a Marketing Platform for Fintech

Social media has become an essential marketing tool, providing unmatched chances for customer acquisition, brand promotion, and engagement. Social media offers finance companies a broad global reach and accurate targeting capabilities, thanks to the billions of active users across numerous platforms such as Facebook, Instagram, LinkedIn, Twitter, and TikTok. Because of their wide audience, fintech companies can build their reputation and brand awareness and become reliable sources of financial services and information. Furthermore, fintech firms may directly contact with clients, swiftly respond to requests, and successfully handle difficulties thanks to social media platforms' ability to promote real-time interaction and feedback. Social media's conversational style encourages real connections with clients, which increases advocacy and consumer loyalty. Furthermore, fintech companies have access to unique ways to exhibit their products and services through the visual and interactive capabilities of platforms such as Instagram and TikTok, which make complicated financial ideas more approachable and captivating for customers (Chan et al., 2022).

By offering insightful data on the demographics, habits, and preferences of the target audience, social media analytics solutions help fintech marketers reach a wider audience and increase their efficacy. Fintech marketers can effectively allocate resources, improve content, and fine-tune their campaigns for maximum impact and return on investment with this data-driven approach. Additionally, influencer marketing's surge on social media offers financial companies new ways to work with reliable people and groups to increase their visibility and credibility with target customers. The significance of social media as a fintech marketing platform is anticipated to increase as it continues to develop new features and trends. Fintech organizations may remain relevant, adaptable, and nimble in a world that is becoming more digital and networked by using social media into their marketing plan. In the digital era, fintech companies may successfully express their value offer, increase client engagement, and drive business growth by utilizing social media (Oh et al., 2024).

Moreover, fintech companies may promptly address customer requests, resolve complaints, and obtain vital insights to enhance their offerings by leveraging social media channels, which offer instantaneous user feedback. Since trust and credibility are so important in the financial industry, social media's real-time nature encourages a sense of community. A skillfully designed campaign can quickly raise brand awareness thanks to social media's viral potential. An organization's reputation can be greatly enhanced and new clients can be drawn in by user-generated content, reviews, and testimonials posted on social media. Fintech companies can also carefully monitor the campaign performance with the use of social media analytics tools, which offer data-driven insights that can guide future marketing initiatives (Chan et al., 2022).

2 The Rise of AI in Fintech

2.1 Historical Context and Evolution of AI in the Financial Sector

The financial sector has experienced a fundamental transformation in the last several decades due to the considerable evolution of artificial intelligence (AI) integration. Early on, in the 1960s and 1970s, financial institutions used statistical models and simple computer algorithms to automate repetitive processes like transaction processing and basic risk assessment. By showcasing the promise of computing power in financial processes, these early systems set the stage for more sophisticated applications.

Developments in neural networks and early artificial intelligence algorithms led to significant progress in the 1980s and 1990s. New capabilities in fields like identifying fraudulent activity and market forecasting were made possible by these technologies, which allowed for more advanced predictive analytics. By processing and analyzing enormous datasets, these technologies have made it possible for financial organizations to provide more accurate and dependable insights than they could have using more conventional approaches (Bag et al., 2020). The emergence of sophisticated artificial intelligence (AI) technologies like deep learning and natural language processing (NLP) has changed the financial environment even further in recent years. Artificial intelligence (AI)-powered chatbots and robo-advisors have transformed customer service by offering individualized financial guidance and assistance with exceptional efficiency and precision. Financial services are now more widely available to a wider audience thanks to these instruments, which have opened up access to them. Furthermore, by decreasing bias and promoting financial inclusion, AI-powered systems for credit scoring have increased the reliability of credit assessments (Bag et al., 2020).

2.2 Key AI Technologies Transforming Fintech: Machine Learning, Natural Language Processing, Predictive Analytics, and Automation

Predictive analytics, automation, machine learning, natural language processing (NLP), and other cutting-edge AI technologies are transforming the financial industry. Through the use of sophisticated recommendation engines and large dataset analysis capabilities, machine learning helps financial institutions improve fraud detection, credit scoring, and tailored client experiences. Ever-more precise and effective financial solutions are guaranteed by its capacity to learn from fresh data. Machines that can comprehend and react to human language, thanks to natural language processing (NLP), are revolutionizing consumer interactions. Artificial intelligence-driven chatbots and virtual assistants lower operating expenses and increase customer satisfaction by providing real-time customer service, answering questions, and providing tailored financial advice (Bredt, 2019).

Fintech organizations can use predictive analytics to analyze past data and forecast future trends and behaviors. Enabling accurate market projections, identifying investment opportunities, and assessing credit risk are critical functions of risk management. Financial institutions are able to reduce risks and make better decisions as a result. Artificial intelligence (AI) enables automation to simplify a wide range of financial operations, including transaction processing, compliance, and reporting. Financial professionals can concentrate on more important work thanks to robotic process automation (RPA), which automates repetitive, rule-based processes and decreases human error. When combined, these AI technologies in fintech spur innovation, boost customer satisfaction, and boost operational effectiveness, changing the financial environment to be more easily accessible, more efficient, and more focused on the needs of the consumer (Brandl & Hornuf, 2020).

2.3 *Benefits of AI for Fintech Companies: Efficiency, Accuracy, and Cost-Effectiveness*

Fintech organizations' operations are greatly improved by AI due to its increased accuracy, cost-effectiveness, and efficiency. Financial professionals can concentrate on higher-value work by using AI to automate repetitive chores and streamline processes. This speeds up service delivery while also boosting productivity. Through the analysis of large datasets to find patterns and abnormalities, machine learning algorithms improve the accuracy of crucial financial operations including risk assessment, credit scoring, and fraud detection. This reduces the possibility of mistakes that could cost money and promotes more accurate decision-making (Bredt, 2019).

Through the elimination of the necessity for heavy manual work, AI also promotes cost-effectiveness in the financial industry. Operational expenses are reduced via automated operations, such as transaction processing and customer question answering. AI-driven chatbots and robo-advisors also provide real-time, tailored financial advice and customer help at a fraction of the cost of keeping up big customer service personnel. With the help of these technologies, fintech organizations may extend their operations without incurring corresponding increases in costs, all while providing prompt and efficient client service. Fintech companies can now function more effectively, make more accurate judgments, and cut expenses thanks to artificial intelligence (AI). This promotes innovation, enhances client satisfaction, and helps them keep a competitive edge in the quickly changing financial industry (Choi & Ozkan, 2019).

3 AI-Driven Marketing Strategies in Fintech

3.1 Personalization and Customer Segmentation

Fintech companies are embracing revolutionary methods to customize services based on user preferences and behaviors, such as customer segmentation and AI-driven personalization. Customized financial advice, product suggestions, and focused marketing campaigns are made possible by personalization, which uses advanced algorithms to examine enormous volumes of customer data. Through the provision of relevant recommendations that are in line with each client's particular financial goals and situation, this dynamic approach increases customer happiness and cultivates loyalty (Akter et al., 2023).

At the same time, consumer segmentation entails grouping customers into discrete categories according to common traits including purchasing habits, investing inclinations, and demographics. Making use of artificial intelligence (AI), this procedure gets more sophisticated as algorithms identify subtle patterns in large datasets, enabling accurate and efficient segmentation. As a result, fintech businesses may create services and targeted tactics that are suited to the unique requirements of each group, maximizing resource allocation and increasing conversion rates (Akter et al., 2023).

3.2 *Utilizing AI to Create Personalized Financial Products and Services*

Creative fintech businesses are utilizing artificial intelligence (AI) to create customized financial services and products that meet each client's unique requirements and preferences. To provide useful insights and recommendations, artificial intelligence (AI) algorithms examine enormous volumes of data, including financial transactions, spending patterns, investing activities, and life goals. Fintech companies can provide individualized investment portfolios based on AI that are catered to the risk tolerance, financial goals, and time horizon of each customer. These portfolios are dynamically updated in response to shifting market conditions and personal preferences, efficiently controlling risk and optimizing returns. Furthermore, lenders can assess borrowers' creditworthiness more precisely thanks to AI-driven credit scoring models, which results in more equitable loan terms and better credit availability for marginalized communities (Patial, 2023).

Additionally, AI-driven chatbots and virtual assistants improve consumer engagement and happiness by offering real-time, tailored financial advice and support. These virtual assistants help with financial planning, investment advice, and account balance inquiries by using natural language processing (NLP) and machine learning algorithms to comprehend client queries and offer pertinent answers. Fintech organizations can achieve competitive advantage in the market by incorporating artificial intelligence (AI) into their operations. This allows them to provide highly customized financial solutions that cater to the individual demands of each customer, thereby increasing customer happiness and loyalty and eventually driving business growth (Patial, 2023).

3.3 *Predictive Analytics in Fintech*

In the fintech industry, predictive analytics is essential because it uses both historical and current data to predict future patterns and events. This helps with strategic planning and decision-making, making it more informed. Predictive analytics is employed in the fintech industry for a number of purposes, including risk management, fraud detection, client segmentation, and customized suggestions.

Predictive analytics models are used in risk management to evaluate historical data and find patterns and trends that help financial organizations anticipate default risks and evaluate creditworthiness more precisely. In the end, this lowers the possibility of defaults and minimizes financial losses by empowering lenders to make better informed judgments when authorizing loans or setting credit limits. Similar to this, by spotting unusual patterns or behaviors that diverge from typical transactional activity, predictive analytics plays a crucial role in the detection of fraud. Fintech companies may stop illegal transactions and lessen financial losses for both themselves and their clients by identifying fraudulent activity in real time (Bolger & Wright, 1994).

By segmenting their customer base according to their habits, tastes, and traits, fintech organizations may use predictive analytics to create more individualized product suggestions and marketing campaigns that are more precisely targeted. By providing individualized offerings that suit each client's wants and preferences, this improves customer engagement and happiness. In the quickly changing financial world, predictive analytics helps fintech companies stay ahead of the curve and remain competitive by enabling them to foresee and respond to risks, client behaviors, and market changes more efficiently (Broby, 2022).

3.4 Chabot's and Virtual Assistants

The financial sector is undergoing a change thanks to chatbots and virtual assistants, which offer effective and customized client support. Natural language processing (NLP) and machine learning techniques are used by these AI-powered applications to comprehend user requests and provide pertinent and correct information in real time. In order to help clients with a variety of tasks, chatbots and virtual assistants are used in fintech across several touchpoints, such as websites, mobile apps, and messaging platforms. They can offer consumers individualized financial advice based on their own preferences and financial objectives in addition to assisting with account balance checks, money transfers, bill payment, and more (Stellar Market Research (2020).

The ability to provide clients with 24/7 access to help and information—without having to wait for business hours or talk with a human agent—is one of the main benefits of chatbots and virtual assistants in the finance industry. By offering prompt support and cutting down on response times, this improves customer happiness and loyalty. Because chatbots and virtual assistants can handle a lot of requests at once, fintech organizations can operate more efficiently and have less customer service teams. This improves the customer experience overall by ensuring correct and consistent responses in all customer encounters while also cutting costs (Patial, 2023).

4 Social Media Platforms as Catalysts for Fintech Marketing

4.1 *The Role of Social Media in Modern Marketing in Fintech*

Social media now forms a vital part of contemporary fintech marketing strategy, providing a dynamic platform for lead generation, brand growth, and consumer involvement. Fintech companies use social media platforms like Instagram, LinkedIn, Twitter, Facebook, and LinkedIn to engage with their target audience, offer insightful material, and create deep connections. Building a brand is one of social media's most important functions in fintech marketing. Fintech companies may boost exposure, define their brand identity, and raise brand recognition by making a big social media presence. Fintech companies may establish themselves as respected thought leaders and authorities in the financial field by using compelling content, such as industry insights, success stories, and instructive pieces (Shahbaznezhad et al., 2021).

Social media gives fintech companies instantaneous access to their audience, allowing for two-way dialogue and client feedback. In addition to improving customer relations, this engagement offers insightful information about the wants, preferences, and pain points of the target market that can help with product development and marketing tactics. Social networking is an effective technique for fintech lead generation and customer acquisition. Fintech organizations may efficiently reach potential customers and generate conversions through influencer collaborations, sponsored content, and targeted advertising campaigns (Patial, 2023).

4.2 *Key Social Media Platforms Used by Fintech Companies*

Fintech businesses use a wide range of social media channels to interact with their target market and build their brand awareness. Facebook's large user base and flexible advertising opportunities make it a platform that stands apart. Fintech companies may reach particular demographics with tailored content and adverts, increasing brand recognition and customer acquisition. Fintech organizations find Twitter to be an excellent real-time communication tool since it allows them to disseminate industry developments, participate in conversations, and offer timely customer service. Its brief structure makes for fast exchanges and encourages participation from the community (Chaklader et al., 2023).

As a professional networking tool, LinkedIn is especially important for business-to-business fintech companies. They can demonstrate thought leadership, establish valuable relationships with business people, and produce leads by focusing their outreach. Because of Instagram's visually immersive structure, financial companies may promote their brand identity, publish visually appealing material, and establish a more personal connection with their audience on this network. User-generated material, success stories, and behind-the-scenes looks can all help humanize the business and build stronger relationships with fans (Shahbaznezhad et al., 2021).

4.3 *AI Tools and Algorithms Used for Social Media Marketing in Fintech Solutions*

Social media marketing strategy optimization is becoming more and more dependent on AI-powered tools and algorithms in the ever-changing fintech scene. With the use of Natural Language Processing (NLP) algorithms, financial companies can now better target their messaging to resonate with their target audience by analyzing social media interactions and harvesting insightful data. Fintech businesses are better able to provide relevant and captivating content that encourages meaningful interactions and fosters brand loyalty by analyzing customer sentiment and spotting emerging trends. Using past data, predictive analytics algorithms project future social media trends and user behavior. Fintech organizations may develop more focused and successful marketing efforts by anticipating client requirements and preferences through the analysis of historical performance metrics and user engagement patterns. By taking a proactive stance, fintech companies may remain ahead of the curve, adjust to shifting market conditions, and keep a competitive advantage in the quickly changing social media scene (Belanche et al., 2019).

Recommendation engines make use of machine learning to make content or product recommendations related to finance that are based on user preferences and actions. Fintech organizations may increase engagement and conversion rates by using algorithms to evaluate user data and interactions to provide personalized suggestions that speak to each user individually. In addition to improving the user experience, this degree of customization boosts client loyalty and pleasure. Fintech organizations may monitor brand mentions, discover trends, and assess customer sentiment using visual data by using image recognition algorithms, which automatically classify visual information published on social media. Fintech companies may use this feature to properly respond to client feedback and issues and stay informed about how their brand is perceived online.

Artificial intelligence (AI)-driven social media listening solutions monitor industry trends, competitor activity, and brand mentions in real time, offering insightful data to guide marketing plans and preserve a competitive advantage. Fintech organizations may promote innovation in their marketing activities, find growth opportunities, and reduce risks by keeping an eye on industry trends and social media debates. In order for fintech companies to effectively use social media marketing, engagement, meaningful connections with their audience, and eventually business success in a highly competitive industry, artificial intelligence (AI) technologies and algorithms are essential (Bredt, 2019).

5 Ethical and Regulatory Considerations

5.1 Ethical Implications of Using AI in Fintech Marketing

In order to guarantee ethical and just procedures, there are important ethical questions raised by the fintech industry's use of AI in marketing. The risk of algorithmic bias, in which AI systems unintentionally reinforce or worsen preexisting prejudices in the data they are trained on, is one of the main causes for concern. Certain demographic groups may be disproportionately affected by discriminatory consequences as a result, such as biased targeting or pricing policies. Since AI-powered predictive analytics systems frequently rely on enormous volumes of personal data to produce insights and predictions, their application in marketing may give rise to privacy problems. To safeguard consumer privacy rights and uphold confidence, fintech companies should place a high priority on consent and transparency in their data collecting and usage procedures (Kumar, 2023).

The openness and accountability of AI systems in marketing are issues that need to be addressed. It could become more difficult to comprehend how judgments are made or to hold people accountable for any mistakes or unethical behavior that occur as AI algorithms grow more complicated and opaque. AI-driven automation also runs the danger of creating job displacement or escalating socioeconomic inequality by prioritizing some industries or skill sets over others. When implementing AI-driven marketing strategies, fintech companies need to think about how these strategies will affect society as a whole and take proactive steps to minimize any negative effects (Kumar, 2023).

5.2 *Data Privacy and Security Concerns*

The convergence of artificial intelligence and fintech marketing presents important data privacy and security issues that require serious consideration and strong protections. Given that artificial intelligence (AI) depends heavily on user data for analysis and personalization, protecting the security and privacy of this data is critical to upholding regulatory compliance and consumer confidence. Potentially harmful actors could gain access to private financial information due to illegal access or data breaches. This is one of the main causes for concern. To guard against such attacks and reduce the chance of data breaches, fintech companies need to have strict security measures in place, like encryption, access controls, and frequent security audits (Nurmara et al., 2023).

Before collecting and using user personal data for marketing reasons, fintech companies are required to get explicit agreement from consumers and maintain transparency regarding the use of this data. Furthermore, businesses need to provide consumers easy ways to withdraw from data collecting and customized marketing campaigns, should they so desire. Algorithmic bias has the potential to produce biased results in marketing strategies. To ensure fair and equitable treatment of all consumers, regardless of criteria like ethnicity, gender, or socioeconomic background, fintech companies must thoroughly assess and reduce bias in their AI algorithms (Nurmara et al., 2023).

5.3 Regulatory Frameworks and Compliance Issues in Fintech Marketing

Fintech companies that market must navigate regulatory frameworks and compliance challenges. Important data protection regulations such as the California Consumer Privacy Act (CCPA) in the US and the General Data Protection Regulation (GDPR) in Europe mandate that fintech companies maintain open and honest data gathering procedures, obtain user consent, and have strong data protection mechanisms in place. In order to prevent fraud and illegal actions, compliance with financial regulations, such as those pertaining to know your customer (KYC) and anti-money laundering (AML), guarantees comprehensive client identification verification and transaction monitoring. Fintech marketing also needs to follow the rules established by regulatory authorities for advertising, making sure that messages are truthful, transparent, and fair, and that financial goods and services are accurately represented. As AI-powered personalization, transparent, guaranteeing user privacy and trust (AlBenJasim, et al., 2023).

In order to ensure that communications are truthful, transparent, and free from deception, as well as that financial goods and services are accurately represented, fintech marketing must also conform to the criteria for advertising established by regulatory organizations. In order to ensure that algorithmic decision-making is impartial and respects user privacy, regulators are pressing for openness in the use of AI-driven personalization. Furthermore, consumers must be educated about the financial products and services they use since fair marketing practices are required by consumer protection regulations (AlBenJasim et al., 2023).

Fintech companies must set up thorough compliance systems, keep up with legislative revisions, and use best practices for data protection, transparency, and ethical marketing in order to meet these regulatory obligations. Following these principles not only helps steer clear of legal issues but also increases reputation and confidence among clients (Didenko, 2020).

6 Future Trends and Innovations in Fintech Marketing

Fintech marketing is going to see significant changes in the coming years due to a number of new developments and trends that take advantage of cutting-edge technology and changing consumer preferences. The growing application of machine learning (ML) and artificial intelligence (AI) to improve predictive analytics and personalization is one noteworthy development. Fintech firms will be able to provide highly customized experiences by utilizing AI-powered tools. These tools will allow them to offer financial goods and services that are specific to each user's needs, preferences, and behavior. The increasing significance of multichannel marketing techniques is another noteworthy development. Fintech companies aim to offer a unified and smooth client experience by integrating many digital platforms such as websites, mobile apps, and social media accounts. By ensuring consistent message and user interaction across all touchpoints, this strategy enhances customer retention and happiness (Liu et al., 2024).

Fintech marketing is poised for a change thanks to block chain technology, which will increase transaction security and transparency. Decentralized applications (dApps) and smart contracts can improve client confidence and expedite business procedures for fintech organizations. The way consumers interact with financial services is changing due to the emergence of voice search and conversational AI. Chatbots and voice-activated assistants will advance in sophistication, allowing users to conduct transactions, get advice, and manage their accounts with basic vocal instructions (Sulistiani, 2021).

Another fascinating trend in fintech marketing is the application of virtual reality (VR) and augmented reality (AR). Customers can have immersive experiences from these technologies, such as interactive lectures on utilizing fintech goods or virtual financial planning sessions. Fintech marketing techniques will be influenced by the focus on sustainability and social responsibility. To draw in customers who care about social issues, businesses will emphasize their dedication to moral behavior, environmental projects, and community involvement more and more (Sulistiani, 2021).

Advanced customization, seamless omnichannel experiences, improved security and transparency via blockchain, conversational AI integration, immersive AR and VR experiences, and an emphasis on sustainability and social responsibility will all be hallmarks of fintech marketing in the future. These developments will help fintech businesses stay competitive in a sector that is changing quickly while also allowing them to innovate and engage customers more successfully (Bajwa et al., 2022).

7 Conclusion

AI's incorporation into fintech marketing on social media represents a revolutionary change in the way financial services interact and provide for their clients. Fintech organizations may offer highly tailored and effective marketing tactics by utilizing powerful AI technologies such as machine learning algorithms, natural language processing, and image identification. These techniques are covered in detail throughout this chapter. Along with improving client targeting and segmentation, these technologies also promote real-time engagement and deeper connections through customized interactions. Fintech organizations can create a smooth and captivating user experience by customizing product suggestions, optimizing content distribution, and precisely predicting consumer behavior using AI-driven marketing. Marketing initiatives are guaranteed to be both targeted and flexible in response to shifting customer demands and market dynamics when large volumes of data can be analyzed in real time. The financial industry is fiercely competitive, and maintaining customer loyalty and happiness at this level of personalization and responsiveness is critical.

But the ethical questions and difficulties with regulatory compliance that were raised emphasize how important it is to use AI responsibly. Retaining consumer confidence and complying with legal requirements depend on preserving openness, reducing biases, and protecting data privacy. To make sure that their AI-driven marketing tactics are both efficient and equitable, fintech companies need to carefully negotiate these obstacles by putting in place strong compliance systems and ethical guidelines. Future developments in fintech marketing point to a scene that will likely be even more inventive and dynamic. Greater security and transparency in transactions and consumer interactions are promised by the use of blockchain technology. Consumer interactions with financial services will change as conversational AI and voice-activated assistants proliferate, providing more user-friendly and accessible interfaces. Marketing techniques will also be impacted by the growing significance of sustainability and social responsibility, as businesses emphasize their dedication to moral behavior and community involvement in an effort to draw in socially conscious customers.

In conclusion, AI is at the forefront of enabling better, more successful marketing strategies in the fintech sector, and the road toward "Smart Money, Smarter Marketing" is only getting started. Fintech companies may improve their marketing efficacy, cultivate stronger client relationships, and support a more open, inclusive, and consumer-focused financial ecosystem by carefully and strategically utilizing these innovations.

References

Akter, S., Hossain, M. A., Sajib, S., Sultana, S., Rahman, M., Vrontis, D., & McCarthy, G. (2023). A framework for AI-Powered service innovation capability: Review and agenda for future research. *Technovation, 125*, 102768. https://doi.org/10.1016/j.technovation.2023.102768

AlBenJasim, S., Dargahi, T., Takruri, H., & Al-Zaidi, R. (2023). Fintech cybersecurity challenges and regulations: Bahrain case study. *Journal of Computer Information Systems*, 1–17. https://doi.org/10.1080/08874417.2023.2251455

Almansour, M. (2023). Artificial Intelligence and resource optimization: A study of fintech start-ups. *Resources Policy, 80*, 103250. https://doi.org/10.1016/j.resourpol.2022.103250

Bag, S., Yadav, G., Wood, L. C., Dhamija, P., & Joshi, S. (2020). Industry 4.0 and the circular economy: Resource melioration in logistics. *Resources Policy, 68*, 101776. https://doi.org/10.1016/j.resourpol.2020.101776

Bajwa, I. A., Ur Rehman, S., Iqbal, A., Anwer, Z., Ashiq, M., & Khan, M. A. (2022). Past, present and future of fintech research: A bibliometric analysis. *SAGE Open, 12*(4), 215824402211312. https://doi.org/10.1177/21582440221131242

Belanche, D., Casaló, L. V., & Flavián, C. (2019). Artificial Intelligence in Fintech: Understanding robo-advisors adoption among customers. *Industrial Management & Data Systems, 119*(7), 1411–1430. https://doi.org/10.1108/imds-08-2018-0368

Bolger, F., & Wright, G. (1994). Assessing the quality of expert judgment. *Decision Support Systems, 11*(1), 1–24. https://doi.org/10.1016/0167-9236(94)90061-2

Bouwman, H., van den Hooff, B., van de Wijngaert, L., & Dijk, J. (2005). Information and communication technology in organizations: Adoption. *Implementation, Use and Effects*. https://doi.org/10.4135/9781446211519

Brandl, B., & Hornuf, L. (2020). Where did fintechs come from, and where do they go? The transformation of the financial industry in Germany after digitalization. *Frontiers in Artificial Intelligence, 3*. https://doi.org/10.3389/frai.2020.00008

Bredt, S. (2019). Artificial Intelligence (AI) in the financial sector—potential and public strategies. *Frontiers in Artificial Intelligence, 2*. https://doi.org/10.3389/frai.2019.00016

Broby, D. (2022). The use of predictive analytics in finance. *The Journal of Finance and Data Science, 8*, 145–161. https://doi.org/10.1016/j.jfds.2022.05.003

Chaklader, B., Gupta, B. B., & Panigrahi, P. K. (2023). Analyzing the progress of fintech-companies and their integration with new technologies for innovation and entrepreneurship. *Journal of Business Research, 161*, 113847. https://doi.org/10.1016/j.jbusres.2023.113847

Chan, R., Troshani, I., Rao Hill, S., & Hoffmann, A. (2022). Towards an understanding of consumers' fintech adoption: The case of open banking. *International Journal of Bank Marketing, 40*(4), 886–917. https://doi.org/10.1108/ijbm-08-2021-0397

Choi, J. J., & Ozkan, B. (2019). Innovation and disruption: Industry practices and conceptual bases. *Disruptive Innovation in Business and Finance in the Digital World*, 3–13. https://doi.org/10.1108/s1569-376720190000020003

Didenko, A. (2020). Cybersecurity regulation in Singapore's financial sector: Protecting fintech 'ants' in a jungle full of 'elephants.' *SSRN Electronic Journal*. https://doi.org/10.2139/ssrn.3679678

Ferraro, G., Ramponi, A., & Scarlatti, S. (2022). Fintech meets industry 4.0: A systematic literature review of recent developments and future trends. *Technology Analysis & Strategic Management*, 1–17. https://doi.org/10.1080/09537325.2022.2117025

Kumar, D. (2023). Ethical and legal challenges of AI in marketing: An exploration of solutions. *SSRN Electronic Journal*. https://doi.org/10.2139/ssrn.4396132

Liu, Q., Chan, K.-C., & Chimhundu, R. (2024). Fintech research: Systematic mapping, classification, and future directions. *Financial Innovation, 10*(1). https://doi.org/10.1186/s40854-023-00524-z

Malone, T. W., Yates, J., & Benjamin, R. I. (1987). Electronic markets and electronic hierarchies. *Communications of the ACM, 30*(6), 484–497. https://doi.org/10.1145/214762.214766

Marinč, M. (2013). Banks and information technology: Marketability vs. relationships. *Electronic Commerce Research, 13*(1), 71–101. https://doi.org/10.1007/s10660-013-9107-2

Marjanovic, O., & Murthy, V. (2015). From product-centric to customer-centric services in a financial institution—Exploring the organizational challenges of the transition process. *Information Systems Frontiers, 18*(3), 479–497. https://doi.org/10.1007/s10796-015-9606-x

Mention, A.-L. (2019). The future of fintech. *Research-Technology Management, 62*(4), 59–63. https://doi.org/10.1080/08956308.2019.1613123

Nosova, S., Norkina, A., Makar, S., & Fadeicheva, G. (2021). Digital transformation as a new paradigm of economic policy. *Procedia Computer Science, 190*, 657–665. https://doi.org/10.1016/j.procs.2021.06.077

Nurmara, M. A., Hakim, M. N., Ardy, O. H., Jeffrey, R., Setiono, V. A., Kanigoro, B., & Irwansyah, E. (2023). A review of security in financial technology. *Procedia Computer Science, 227*, 958–965. https://doi.org/10.1016/j.procs.2023.10.603

Oh, S., Chung, G., & Cho, K. (2024). New sustainable fintech business models created by open application technology: A case study of Korea's open banking application platform. *Sustainability, 16*(16), 1–20. https://doi.org/10.20944/preprints202405.0416.v1

Patial, A. (2023). *AI-Powered banking: From customer service to risk management*. https://doi.org/10.31219/osf.io/tmvns

Puschmann, T., & Alt, R. (2016). Sharing economy. *Business & Information Systems Engineering, 58*(1), 93–99. https://doi.org/10.1007/s12599-015-0420-2

Shahbaznezhad, H., Dolan, R., & Rashidirad, M. (2021). The role of social media content format and platform in users' engagement behavior. *Journal of Interactive Marketing, 53*, 47–65. https://doi.org/10.1016/j.intmar.2020.05.001

Stellar Market Research. (2020a, April 21). *Shell*. https://www.stellarmr.com/report/AI-in-Fintech-Market/1564

Sulistiani, I. (2021). Systematic literature review: Bankruptcy prediction menggunakan teknik machine learning Dan Deep Learning. *INTECH, 2*(1), 13–18. https://doi.org/10.54895/intech.v2i1.824

Zhu, K., Kraemer, K. L., & Dedrick, J. (2004). Information technology payoff in E-Business environments: An international perspective on value creation of e-business in the financial services industry. *Journal of Management Information Systems, 21*(1), 17–54. https://doi.org/10.1080/07421222.2004.11045797

Cryptocurrency, Blockchain and Artificial Intelligence

Recent Trends in the Development of Artificial Intelligence Among Banking Sectors in India

Sumi A. M, Asha Devi. J, and K. S. Chandrasekar

1 Introduction

Artificial intelligence (AI) is estimated to be a 450 billion opportunity for banks; it will increase their knowledge of working in the banking sector. Very competitive, more effective, and efficient AI could be an ample opportunity for banks and other companies. Based on this the objectives of this are to analyse the importance of Artificial Intelligence in the banking sector in India and to investigate the changes that occurred in the banking sector due to the emergence of AI, the field of science that deals with rivalling the capabilities of modern computer systems to resolve issues using human-like complex powers of reasoning, learning, and self-correction. Applying artificial intelligence in diverse fields is far-reaching, and recent developments in both hardware and software technologies have increased the capabilities of artificial intelligence systems. The application of artificial intelligence is wide-ranging.

S. A. M (✉) · A. Devi. J · K. S. Chandrasekar
Institute of Management in Kerala, University of Kerala, Thiruvananthapuram, Kerala, India
e-mail: sumiam777@gmail.com

K. S. Chandrasekar
e-mail: kscnair@gmail.com

© The Author(s), under exclusive license to Springer Nature Singapore Pte Ltd. 2025

A. S. et al. (eds.), *Trends and Challenges of Electronic Finance*,
https://doi.org/10.1007/978-981-96-3304-3_21

It is applied in optical communication, network planning, programming, transportation networks, and medical science, to name a few.

There are four types of AI: Artificial Intelligence Platforms: This will provide the platform for developing an application from scratch. Many built-in algorithms are provided in this. The yawn and drop facility makes it comfortable to use. Chatbots: This software choice gives the result that a human or individual is doing in a discussion. Deep Learning Software: It includes speech, image distinction, etc. Machine Learning Software: Machine learning is the method that will cause the computer to learn via data (Alzaidi, 2018).

Technological adaptation in the banking sector has been gradual compared to technological adoption in other sectors; one of the crucial regions is the high dependence of the banking industry on human involvement. Most of the procedures were hanging on employed human aids. They adopted technological inventions in everyday banking operations, which efficiently improved their performance. Artificial intelligence in the banking sector can make operations more impactful and hassle-free. Some of the areas in the banking industry where one can successfully apply artificial intelligence are listed below:

Tailored Financial Services: Artificial intelligence can analyse stock markets and provide recommendations for individual customer financial goals.

Underwriting: Automating this process is possible using artificial intelligence services that use unstructured information in decision-making.

Voice-Aided Banking: Vocabulary processing operating artificial intelligence can lower human error and enhance efficiency.

Data-Driven Loaning Decisions: Artificial intelligence systems' assistance in analysing vast chunks of data and performing calculation and prediction capabilities can aid in developing strategies in the financial loaning department for better returns.

The Digitalization of Branches: The lengthy banking process can be replaced by the complete digitization of records by generating a comprehensive platform using artificial intelligence in the industry, which tries to examine more valuable ways of getting banking to the customers. Research from insider intelligence has come out with specific findings that say that the potential cost saves banks from artificial applications.

Intelligence application is estimated to be around 450 billion, and it is going to replace the front and middle office, accounting for 460 billion. These opportunities are driven by technological advancement, increased profitability, competition, and regulations. Now, this is a significant development. The future of the banking industry will be minor manual and more based on artificial intelligence. Banks won't hire people but will use artificial intelligence to serve customers and get better work done (Table 1).

1.1 Evolution of the Indian Banking Sector

The last six decades have viewed the macroeconomic expansion of India. The monetary, external, and banking policies have undergone several changes with the help of new technologies. The structural and technological transformations in the Indian financial system, particularly in the banking system, have affected the evaluation of Indian Banking in distinct ways (Kumar and Prakash, 2019). After India's independence, the implementation of banking reforms changed the functioning of commercial banks (Meghani, 2020).

1.2 Six Key Areas of Artificial Intelligence in Banking

Financial institutions like banking are the lifeline of any current economy. It is one of the critical financial pillars of the financial industry, which plays a vital role in the functioning of an economy. It is significant for a nation's economic growth that its financing necessities of commerce, enterprise, and farming are met with a higher degree of responsibility and accountability (Alzaidi, 2018). Therefore, the evolution of a country is integrally correlated with the expansion of banking (Fig. 1). Today, most banks in India (80%) are admiringly familiar with AI's potential benefits. The six key areas in which AI can be applied in the banking sector are as follows: They are,

- Process Optimization

It aims at lowering operational costs and driving profitability and involves both front-end and back-end activities such as,

Table 1 Evolution of the Indian banking system

1921	*1935*	*1936–1955*	*1956–2000*	*2000 onwards*	*2020 Onwards*
Closed market	RBI was established as the central bank of the country	Imperial Bank expanded its network to 480 branches	Nationalization of 14 large commercial banks in 1969 & six more banks in 1980	In 2003, Kotak Mahindra Finance Ltd received a banking license from RBI and became the first NBFC to be converted into a bank	As per Union Budget 2021–22, the government will disinvest IDBI Bank and privatize two public sector banks
State-owned Imperial Bank of India was the only bank existing	Quasi central banking role of Imperial Bank came to an end	In order to increase penetration in rural areas, Imperial Bank was converted into State Bank of India	Entry of private players such as ICICI intensifying the competition	In 2009, the Government removed the Banking Cash Transaction Tax which was introduced in 2005	According to the RBI, India's foreign exchange reserves reached US$ 580.3 billion, as of March 5, 2021
			Gradual technology upgradation in PSU banks		The Finance Ministry announced to infuse Rs. 14,500 crore in banks that are under the RBI's prompt corrective action framework

Source Indian Bank's association, BMI

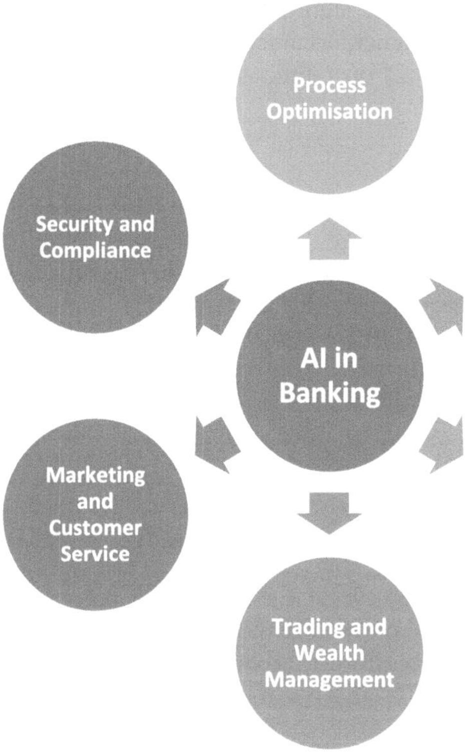

Fig. 1 Six keys of AI in the banking sector (Source: Kamila [2022])

Claims processing uses AI's natural language processing to analyse large volumes of data about policyholders, their habits, etc., to offer more customized products in real time.

A mortgage is a natural language processing that can automatically read and comprehend records that concern loan or mortgage processing.

Custom-built customer service can use intelligent chatbots to streamline tedious customer service processes, automatically solve simple customer requests, and prioritize other tickets based on sentiments for an outing to the right team.

Operational cost reduction AI algorithms handle large quantities of data, thus increasing the efficiency, accuracy, and speed of mathematical calculations resulting in reduced operating costs.

- Credit Decisioning

Credit scoring through AI banks can capture data by analysing mobile phone activities, social media usage, etc., to capture a more accurate assessment of creditworthiness. This will result in faster and cheaper credit scoring and quality loan assessments that are accessible to many people. It can also use Credit risk in AI to analyse financial and non-financial data using trained machine learning algorithms to predict credit default more accurately than traditional methods.

- Fraud and Money Laundering

Appliance learning algorithms can interpret thousands of data pinpoints in real time and flag any suspicious or dishonest transactions. Thus, by stopping many illegal clients, AI can detect anomalies in spending behaviours. Thus, preventing thefts, machine learning-driven fraud analytics can process customer account transactional and even geospatial data to spot patterns that seem unrelated and go unnoticed by human data analytics.

AI can also uncover money laundering activities by analysing the wire transfer, the details about the money being moved, the source destination and the nature of the wire transfer, and the relationships of the sender to the bank.

- Trading and Wealth Management

Trading: Banking industries widely use machine learning algorithms to improvise new trading and investment strategies (Wittmann and Lutfiju, 2021). By harnessing the predictive authority of data, AI trading helps funds spot recent trends and potentially profitable trades above the human scope of understanding. It also helps spot new signals of price movements to make more rapid trading decisions.

Robo advisors: Power tools of Artificial Intelligence can assist traders in facilitating the account beginning process and advise them on scaling their portfolios. It comprises creating a financial plan suggesting scheduled protection needs, home purchases, retirements, estate planning, etc.

Trade channel optimization: AI can optimize trade according to price and from which channel to process the payment more quickly.

Stock markets: The AI system provides a faster analysis of structured and unstructured data related to stock markets, leading to quick decision-making.

- Marketing and customer services

Operating different AI solutions, such as event extractions, transcribing, sentiment analysis, keyword matching, etc., can answer queries such as how to keep clients happy. What are people saying? And who is interested in products?

- Security and Compliance

AI can help find security breaches, such as analysing documentation for account registration, detecting issues within accounts, and more.

AI-based solutions can correspondingly scrutinize and investigate millions of strings in the regulatory range, including commentary, lawful documents, guidance, and legal cases, to spot applicable requirements much faster and enable compliance.

1.3 Digital Lending Market Scenario

The digital effect in the Indian banking sector has grown quickly due to the rising digital imprint (Meena and Parimalarani, 2020). In FY19, India's digital lending stood at US$ 110 billion. By 2023, digital lending to micro, small, and medium enterprises (MSMEs) in India is envisioned to acquire US$ 100 billion. In December 2020, the Digital Lenders' Association issued a revised code of conduct for digital lending in response to the RBI's cautionary message. Mobile banking allows customers to avail themselves of banking assistance when shifting via their cell phones. The development of mobile banking could seriously influence the banking sector. Mobile banking is exceptionally critical for countries like India as it swears to supply a chance to provide banking facilities to a formerly under-banked market. RBI has accepted several steps to allow roaming charges, which form a necessary part of mobile banking; the central bank keeps removing the dealing limit of Rs.50,000 (US$ 745.82) and permitted banks to fix their boundaries. In February 2021, Unified Payments Interface (UPI) documented 2.29 billion transactions worth Rs.4.25 lakh crore (US$ 57.68 billion). On November 6, 2020, WhatsApp activated the UPI payments service in India by accepting the National Payments Corporation of India (NPCI) permission to 'Go Live' on UPI in a graded way.

1.4 Strategy of AI in Banking in India

The banking sector in India is now increasingly adopting AI. According to a collaborative study accomplished by the National Business Research Institute and Narrative Science, about 32% of financial service providers in India are already using AI technologies such as predictive analytics and voice recognition. Other banks such as SBI, Bank of Baroda, HDFC, ICICI, Yes Bank, and others are already deploying AI to streamline their everyday processes. According to a recent report, 83% of Indian bankers—higher than the global average of 79%—believe AI will work alongside humans in the next two years (Suresh and Rani, 2020). However, the report also noted that 77% of Indian bankers agreed to develop and implement AI tools effectively in banking services. It can further enhance the adoption of AI in the Indian banking and finance industry by addressing the following challenges (Kaur et al., 2020):

- Trained Employees: The unavailability of professionals with the requisite data science skills means that only a small number of good data scientists are available in the country to work on AI. In addition to the scarcity of trained human resources, the existing workforce in banks is not familiar with the latest tools and applications. The financial services industry needs to work with Indian universities to develop skilled data scientists and in-house training programs to implement AI technologies for banking functions successfully. In India, HDFC Bank has launched a program in partnership with engineering and MBA colleges to educate students on emerging banking technologies.

- Standardization of data: Independent banks and other financial organizations are in the process of developing internal practices by using XBRL and different data standards. Data standards would expedite the mainstream adoption of AI in the financial sector. Non-uniform digitization of data will lead to issues with the interoperability of the individual services and their usability. It will also improve regulatory compliance and adaptability to changing requirements.
- Enforcement approaches: The lack of harmonization in enforcement approaches across different countries and regulators creates challenges for financial firms employing AI solutions. Differing enforcement approaches make it hard for firms to adopt practical global standards and quantify their risk of rolling out AI innovations internationally.
- Capacity of User: Articulating requests that are comprehensible to AI is a challenge. The vast diversity compounds the problem among customers who use banking services and their differing levels of digital literacy. A financial/banking service is effective only when the data provided by a customer is valid and can be comprehended by the AI systems in use. The AI systems can then recognize their queries and adequately respond to them.
- Multiple languages: Given the multiplicity of languages in India, the most effective AI-enabled communication services will reach most Indians in their first/preferred languages. However, this is a challenge due to the limited machine-readable corpus of vernacular languages used to train natural language processing and generation algorithms. Presently, there are wide gaps between AI operating in English or bilingual mode and AI processing and comprehending local languages. An effective AI-based communication platform intending to provide banking or financial services must understand the consumer's spoken language and respond to the same vocabulary.
- Data protection and privacy: AI systems require vast amounts of training data as inputs. Consumer data is continuously collected by tracking online and offline consumer behaviour, stored and merged with other data sources to generate big datasets and extract further consumer information through profiling. Recording the online actions of individuals can create massive databases. These datasets typically contain information about an individual's transactions, email, video, search queries, health records, and social

networking interactions. Often, loopholes and unprotected servers result in unauthorized access to this data. According to a report by the Data Security Council of India, India faced the second-highest number of cyber-attacks between 2016 and 2018.

2 Literature Review

O. Kaya (2019), in his study, defines that AI can revolutionize several aspects of our everyday life. Especially in the U.S. and China, AI has attracted significant investments in recent years and is increasingly being implemented. In Europe, the image is partially mixed, with a pair of nations retaining an active AI landscape while others languish. European policymakers bear trained steps to improve AI activity in Europe by standing familiar with its potential. AI also has the potential to fundamentally change aspects of financial services. To date, though, routine in banking has been modest. Looking ahead, regulatory standards near data privacy and the highly controlled character of banking might assemble barriers to AI undertaking.

Donepudi (2017), in this investigation defines Machine Learning and Artificial Intelligence applications in the monetary sector. Their enormous leverage has been harnessed in these organizations to offer industry solutions in front-end and back-end methodologies to develop efficiency and enhance the client experience. This paper focuses on machine learning and artificial intelligence applications, assesses their utility in diverse banking industry functional areas, and structures how these organizations effectively use computational intelligence to improve their business. While traditional banking organizations are quickly catching up with computational intelligence technologies with outcomes like Chatbots, fintech companies, which embraced AI long ago, play a critical role through innovation and contribute substantially to financial intelligence (Sandu and Gide, 2019).

AA, Alzaidi (2018), can mention from this investigation that technological transformation in the banking sector of the Middle East has been pushed at a broadly gradual pace than in different global markets. With time, there has been a shift in attitude towards technological tools, and now, banking professionals aim to work hand in hand with technological developments. Artificial intelligence transformation in the banking sector is far from reaching a comprehensive maturity level within the industry.

Still, artificial intelligence in the banking industry has become a trendsetter. The findings of the quantitative analysis conducted for this study were comparable to the results of the secondary literature analysed. Thus, it can be inferred that applying Artificial Intelligence in the banking sector of the Middle East can significantly boost local banks' performance.

3 Research Methodology

Data for the current examination have been accumulated from a secondary source. This study mainly considers secondary data to analyse the recent trends in the development of the artificial intelligence market in India. It is second-hand information. These data were collected from secondary sources. Collected the secondary data needed for the study from the organization's records and journals and from the organization's website, which includes social surveys, health data, agricultural statistics, energy expenditure statistics, population censuses, import/export data production statistics, etc.

4 Results

AI is not the future of banking; it is the present. As more data becomes available, new technologies like quantum edge and cloud computing will continue transforming the market. Success requires a holistic transformation spanning multiple layers of the organization and the need to put together people, processes, and data and work collaboratively. For banks, ensuring the adoption of AI technologies across the enterprise is no longer a choice but a strategic imperative. The banking industry has adopted superior artificial intelligence (AI) technology. The penetration of AI technology in this industry has significantly increased with the advent of the Internet, online banking, and self-service branch networks.

Despite the variety of problems addressed in AI research, several essential features emerge that seem familiar to all divisions of the field, which include,

- The benefit of computers is that they can do logic, design recognition, learning, or some other layout of inference.
- An emphasis on troubles that do not answer to algorithmic solutions. It underlies the backing of heuristic tracking as an AI problem-solving technique.

- A reference with problem-solving operating unclear, missing, or poorly explained data and figurative formalisms allows programmers to balance these issues.
- Reasoning regarding the compelling qualitative characteristics of a problem.
- Try to haggle with problems of semantic meaning and syntactic form.
- The benefit of extensive quantities of domain-specific learning in solving problems.

AI technology has triggered a significant digital disruption that has affected the entire banking sector in the twenty-first century. This is primarily because AI solutions can help banking institutions innovate, make more informed decisions, and solve complex problems more efficiently and effectively. Furthermore, it can use predictive analytics, neural networks, machine learning, and other AI technologies to enable banks to make more accurate predictions and respond to emerging issues promptly and appropriately (Kochhar et al., 2019). Therefore, AI is a technology that can help banks to stay ahead of market competition. However, many pitfalls must be addressed to ensure that the opportunities fronted by AI are optimally exploited. Notable ones include privacy violations, job loss, data availability and quality, and strategic AI-business alignment concerns (Perez and Martin, 2018). While a vast body of knowledge pertains to AI opportunities and challenges in banking, existing studies are mainly descriptive and based on secondary data sources. Therefore, future studies should employ thorough empirical investigation techniques to deliver concrete evidence concerning AI opportunities and challenges in the banking sector.

Global financial bodies and panels view technologies such as AI as enablers in the expansion and customization of financial services. In 2017, the Financial Stability Board (FSB), an international body that monitors and makes recommendations about the global financial system, set out different applications of AI in the financial sector, such as in the verticals of portfolio management, client due diligence, credit scoring, and regulatory compliance. The FSB also outlined possible benefits for retail customers and small and medium-sized enterprises (SMEs) and efficiency gains in back-office procedures carried out by banks. In a 2018 report, the Basel Committee on Banking Supervision (BCBS)—a committee of banking supervisory authorities and the primary global standard-setter for the prudential regulation of banks—boosted banks to harness arising technologies such as AI to increase their efficiency in responding to fintech-related risks. The Committee then commenced discussions with regulators and the industry on risk management and AI systems, including through a workshop hosted by its Supervision and Implementation Group (SIG) in Tokyo in October 2019. In the past two decades, India's digital banking (including retail banking) and the finance sector have witnessed immense growth. Increased digital payments across sectors and industries have primarily driven this transformation. The country's established financial institutions are now deploying fintech to provide end-users with agile, efficient, and differentiated experiences along the complete value chain of financial services.

The rise in fintech use will bring financial innovations and transform India's financial landscape in two primary ways: (i) consumers will have a more extensive set of options at competitive prices, and (ii) lower operational costs can improve efficiency at financial institutions. The Government of India's 'Digi Dhan Mission' recognizes that financial inclusion remains one of India's foremost challenges and that digital payments promise access to formal financial services and benefits, especially to those who continue to be excluded. AI measures are being employed to catch fraudulent accounts and enhance efficiency (Singh, 2020; Singh and Agarwal, 2019). Today, in India, the states are already at the vanguard of the fintech wheel. In recent years, the accumulation of mobile technology in India has contributed to the remarkable growth of India's fintech sector. The sector has leveraged the changing shopper choices that have arisen from this growth in digitization to develop an array of innovative services and products for the changing economy. These include internet and mobile banking, as well as various payment apps. This evolution in business procedures has led to increased partnerships between technology developers, banks, and financial institutions using such technologies. Banks can mine the dealing financial data induced by the proliferation of digital earnings and banking to adequately monitor, predict, and respond to consumer behaviour. The rising demand for online banking and financial information offerings has created opportunities for AI implementation in India's retail banking, financial, and investment services sectors. In 2019, an inter-ministerial panel on fintech suggested a comprehensive legal framework to protect consumers of digital services. The board also recommended increasing the levels of automation using AI, cognitive analytics, and ML in their backend processes. The Central Bank of India (RBI) established an Inter-Regulatory Working Group to study India's fintech and digital banking issues.

The Working Group set out to comprehend the crucial creations in the fintech initiative and how diverse actors in the financial sectors were using new techniques, outcomes, and technologies. Released in February 2018, the Group's report categorizes the use of AI and robotics in data analytics and risk management as one of the significant fintech innovations. The report states that the digital transformation of the banking and financial sector would ride on three pillars: blockchain, AI, and the Internet of Things (IoT). The report also stated that the banking sector will expand beyond apps, websites, and physical branches when devices connect and use self-learning and evolving AI. The contributions to AI, ML, and data science in banking started at IDRBT (Institute for Development & Research in Banking Technology) in 2005 under the aegis of the Centre of Excellence in Analytics. The Centre is involved in advanced research, training, teaching, developing POCs, and guiding Indian banks' AI journey in several areas. These areas include segmentation of customers, NPA prediction, credit scoring, market basket analysis (cross-sell/upsell), fraud detection, sentiment analysis, analytics for credit recovery, and big data analytics. Over 1000 executives from the IT and business segments of public and private sector banks have already been trained in these areas. The hallmark of these customized training programs has been the rigorous hands-on component of state-of-the-art commercial and open-source tools. In the use of AI in banking, AI is demonstrating a massive impact on the banking sector, impacting the working of organizations at three fundamental levels:

- The processes they adopt.
- The products and services they sell.
- The user experiences they offer to their customers and employees.

Globally, banks are already starting to adopt AI at a massive scale. According to a UBS Evidence Lab report23, 75% of respondents at banks with over USD 100 billion in assets say they are implementing AI strategies, compared to 46% at banks with less than USD 100 billion in assets.

5 Conclusion

The across-the-board adoption of artificial intelligence (AI) in the banking sector is evident from its current implementation across various facets of banking operations. AI technologies drive a significant digital disruption in the industry, including machine learning, predictive analytics, and robotics, which enable banks to innovate, make informed decisions, and enhance operational efficiency. From process optimization to personalized customer experiences, AI is reshaping how banks operate, sell products and services, and interact with customers and employees. Banks must ensure a holistic transformation encompassing people, processes, and data to adopt AI technologies effectively. Collaboration between financial institutions, technology developers, and regulators is essential to address these challenges and maximize the potential benefits of AI in the banking sector. As AI continues to develop and shape the fate of banking, rigorous empirical research and strategic planning will be vital to navigating this transformative journey successfully.

In recent years, the banking sector in India has increasingly embraced artificial intelligence (AI) to enhance the customer experience, streamline operations, and mitigate risks. One notable trend is the implementation of AI-driven solutions to improve customer satisfaction by offering round-the-clock assistance and helping banks reduce operational costs by automating routine tasks. Moreover, AI is being used for scam detection and subsequent actions, leveraging machine learning algorithms to diagnose vast volumes of transaction data in real time and identify suspicious activities, safeguarding customers' financial assets and maintaining trust in the banking system.

References

Alzaidi, A. A. (2018). Impact of artificial intelligence on the performance of the banking industry in the middle east. *International Journal of Computer Science and Network Security, 18*(10), 140–148.

Caron, M. S. (2019). The transformative effect of AI on the banking industry. *Banking & Finance Law Review, 34*(2), 169–214.

Donepudi, P. K. (2017). AI and machine learning in banking: A systematic literature review. *Asian Journal of Applied Science and Engineering, 6*(3), 157–162.

Kaur, D., Sahdev, S. L., Sharma, D., & Siddiqui, L. (2020). Banking 4.0: 'The influence of artificial intelligence on the banking industry & how

AI is changing the face of modern-day banks'. *International Journal of Management, 11*(6).
Kaya, O., Schildbach, J., AG, D. B., & Schneider, S. (2019). Artificial intelligence in banking. *Artificial Intelligence*.
Kochhar, K., Purohit, H., & Chutani, R. (2019). The rise of artificial intelligence in the banking sector. In *The 5th International Conference on Educational Research and Practice (ICERP) 2019* (p. 127).
Kumar, K., & Prakash, A. (2019). Developing a framework for assessing the sustainable banking performance of the Indian banking sector. *Social Responsibility Journal*.
Meena, M. M. R., & Parimalarani, G. (2020). Impact of digital transformation on employment in the banking sector. *International Journal of Scientific & Technology Research, 9*(1), 4912–4916.
Meghani, K. (2020). Use of artificial intelligence and blockchain in banking sector: A study of scheduled commercial banks in India. Use of artificial intelligence and blockchain in banking sector: A study of scheduled commercial banks in India. *Kishore Meghani Indian Journal of Applied Research, 10*(8).
Perez, C., & Martin, F. (2018). Digitalization and artificial intelligence: The new face of the retail banking sector. Evidence from France and Spain. Virtuous circles between innovations, job quality and employment in Europe? Case study evidence from the manufacturing sector, private and public service sector, 178.
Sandu, N., & Gide, E. (2019, September). Adoption of AI-Chatbots to enhance the student learning experience in higher education in India. In *2019 18th International Conference on Information Technology Based Higher Education and Training (ITHET)* (pp. 1–5). IEEE.
Singh, K. (2020). Banks banking on AI. *International Journal of Advanced Research in Management and Social Sciences, 9*(9), 1–11.
Smith, A., & Nobanee, H. (2020). Artificial intelligence: In banking a mini-review. Available at SSRN 3539171.
Singh, S., & Agarwal, L. (2019). Pros and cons of artificial intelligence in the banking sector of India. BICON-2019, 63.
Suresh, A., & Rani, N. J. (2020). Role of Artificial Intelligence (AI) in the Indian Banking scenario. *Journal of Information Technology & Economic Development, 11*(2).
Wittmann, X., & Lutfiju, F. (2021, June). Adopting AI in the banking sector–The wealth management perspective. In *International Conference on Society 5.0* (pp. 151–162). Springer, Cham.

Website

Kamila. (2022). What is Artificial Intelligence: Definition & Sub-fields of AI. *Software Testing Help*. Available at www.softwaretestinghelp.com/what-is-artificial-intelligence. Accessed on 24 May 2024.

Bibliometric Analysis on Digital Financial Inclusion Through Blockchain Technology Crowdfunding

Aanchal Nigam Verma, *Farhina Sardar Khan*, *and Syed Shahid Mazhar*

1 Introduction

Technology when it got merged with Finance, a new finnovational activity came into trend and launched in the early 1990s. With the advent of disruptive financial services, the market scenario changed its facets and then emerged **"FinTech"**. This paved a new path for a revolutionary adaptation on the part of the service customers. In the words of (Schindler, 2017), those innovations having capability to affect financial services deeply may have the potential to make people ready for adaptability. Such kind of finnovation that ultimately has proven to be a game changer in the coming future is Blockchain Technology (BCT).

A. N. Verma (✉) · F. S. Khan
Lucknow Public College of Professional Studies, Lucknow, UP, India
e-mail: aanchalnigam.lpcps@gmail.com

F. S. Khan
e-mail: farhina@iul.ac.in

S. S. Mazhar
Integral University, Lucknow, UP, India
e-mail: ssmazhar@iul.ac.in

© The Author(s), under exclusive license to Springer Nature Singapore Pte Ltd. 2025

A. S. et al. (eds.), *Trends and Challenges of Electronic Finance*,
https://doi.org/10.1007/978-981-96-3304-3_22

There is an intense hike in the usage of mobile and internet to use the financial services, thereby strengthening the new technologies like BCT, cryptocurrency, etc. (Niforos, 2017a, b).

The prioritization of BCT can only be possible by means of information related to the execution of this innovative system globally. Especially in a country like India, where three-fourth of the population is rural, it is necessary to ascertain the urgent requirement of such innovative aspects to be implemented so as to give access, reduce cost and minimize risk and make the financial services available to an extent (Schuetz & Venkatesh, 2020).

Reports that got updated and approved from Securities Exchange Board of India (SEBI) on 17th August 2021 have asked for a centralized depository to create a system for secured digitized distributed ledger technology or BCT so that proper recording and monitoring can be implemented efficiently. A few discussions nowadays are coming up with the idea of raising funds through digital financial platforms. Multiple startups are being launched as the source of funds by identifying the correct solution. These could be an ample finnovational strategy to overcome the loopholes in the traditional banking services (Cai, 2018).

At global level, it has also been researched that climatic disasters impact adversely around 375 million people annually and this vulnerability gets intense in poor developing countries. So studies are being made to understand the financial inclusion with climate finance and green investment to benefit these people as well as set up an innovative trend (Thomason et al., 2018).

Few studies have been executed to learn the correlation between poverty and DFI, to understand the immediate impact over farmers in China through usage of data surveyed over 1900 households of rural areas. As a result, it has been found out that almost 35.63% of farmers have an accessibility to enable financial services that ultimately lessen the risk and vulnerability effects (*Shen* et al., n.d.)

There has been a tremendous development in terms of the literary work that has been conducted and reviewed to help researchers to understand the efficacies as well as scandals related on the part of financial technology. COVID-19 has also impacted the Indian Financial Inclusion to an extent (Wójcik, 2021).

The objective of this study is to provide a review of literature with the help of content analysis and citation analysis methodologies in bibliometric analysis. The blockchain development which is related to society, economy, policy-related factors, and technological clinches may be solved with the conceptual framework that has been provided for benefiting at global level.

Further sections in this study have been started with review of literatures, methodologies adopted to perform bibliometric analysis for systematic literature review, keyword and co-authorship analysis along with cluster mapping, then some discussions over the variations of crowd-funding and BCT with crowdfunding and finally conclusive notion with future research and its practical implications.

2 Literature Review

The study has been done on Asian crowdfunding platforms which included Indonesia, China, Malaysia, Philippines, Thailand and Singapore mentioning the procedures and earnings. It explained how the Islamic crowdfunding platform has different elements in terms of execution (Wahjono et al., 2016).

The literature has been reviewed on the basis of bibliometric analysis that has been performed with the help of different tools to get an idea about the collaboration of citations and the number of key terms that are being interrelated with the topic (Mondal et al., 2017).

The reasons due to which Fintech products are achieving edge over traditional services are its innovation and the way it serves the consumers. DFIs gained a lot of impact and enhanced the quality resulting in increment of customers (Ravikumar, 2019).

As per the reports of Alliance for Financial Inclusion (AFI), on the basis of accessibility, usability and quality, dimensions are categorized for financial inclusion. Comprehensive analysis about the strategies of DFIs in India helped the policymakers to create a place for financial technology. All the documentations will help in supporting financial growth of technological advancement. It will impact the overall incredibility of structures (AFI, 2018).

A comparative analysis has been performed to analyze crowdfunding with the already available financial institutional services provided to customers for getting a gist of regulatory framework that has been followed for years (Kolesnikov, 2020).

There are so many psychological factors that have direct impact over investors decision, talking in relatedness with crowdfunding. To understand this by testing hypotheses established in the research work, 215 projects from Chinese Equity crowdfunding, data collected and further implemented. It has also been found that the support provided by the lead investors gets little or no affect over the decision-making criteria. He also discussed about the funding target and fundraising amount. (*Understand Ing China's Fintech Sector: Development, Impacts and Risks Xiuping Hua, Yiping Huang*, 2021) Indian Global platforms, if compared with China, could show a broad picture.

A research has been executed to have a gist about the small medium enterprises in China. New third board market listing had been examined from 2011 to 2018 from Perking University so as to examine its impact over DFIs. The outcome of this study showed a positive impact of DFIs over the sustainable growth that can be adopted by the developing countries like India for further growth of financial technology. This stream of research study will show a new phase of time (Wang & He, 2020).

Empirical research work has also been done for ranging counterparty risk on different parameters that are related with the operational and investing purposes. Automated approach has been followed to check the trustworthiness of NBFIs networking system through crypto payments. It followed both the traditional as well as fintech companies' activities (Venegas, 2020).

The framework of BCT development includes society, economy and finance, policy, technology and business. Discussion went on about ICT evolutionary movements related to three levels, i.e., on-disk, on-line, on-chain (Rupino et al., 2021).

Financial inclusion is supported by fintech in terms of policy implication, pitfalls and potential benefits. Many direct and indirect risks were found out regarding financial exclusion. There are some factors correlated with machine learning and artificial intelligence. Study has been directed toward the post-pandemic trends and trust lacking factors (Chacko & Baag, 2021).

3 Methodology for Bibliometric Analysis

Various government policies like Pradhan Mantri Jan Dhan Yojna (PMJDY) helped a lot in supporting the regime of financial inclusion in our country. To support growth of emerging or undeveloped economies, it is of great importance to provide them the opportunities for working toward reducing such gaps by means of technological advancement (Chacko & Baag, 2021).

Due to the identical advancement facility that has been provided to the people, digital financial inclusion has gone a step ahead and it will be surely accomplished in the coming future (Arner et al., 2020).

Authors argued about the role of crowdfunding, a fintech phenomenon in financial inclusion to benefit people who are not having access toward the borrowing facilities and developing a framework to make them available with the profitable returns also. The models, ecosystem and benefits and risks are being discussed in the study. (Jenik et al., 2017b) It has been found that government intervention and changing economical conditions are responsible factors for the development of digital financial inclusion. Also, it has been observed that in rural areas, education is just a formality and it merely impacts the awareness about the usage of the new technology (Liu et al., 2021).

The initiation of bibliometric analysis in the field of research was done by Pritchard (1969). Bibliometric analysis facilitates a comprehensive understanding of a research area and the mapping of its boundaries and the identification of influential authors and new directions for future research (Donthu et al., 2020; Leung et al., 2017; Xu et al., 2018). This technique has been employed by scholars across multiple domains, such as manufacturing (Caviggioli & Ughetto, 2019), arts-based management (Ferreira, 2018), marketing (Gurzki & Woisetschl¨ager, 2017), social media or networks (Leung et al., 2017; Shiau et al., 2017), finance (Corbet et al.,2018) as well as technology and innovation (Li et al., 2018a; van Oorschot et al., 2018).

Secondly, the researchers followed systematic literature review to analyze the BCT and crowdfunding relationship by clustering the items that are essential to find the base foundation. As per Figs. 1 and 2, out of 310 research papers obtained from the Dimensions, a website with having open access for journals/articles, to have the association links of 68 items has been undertaken with 10 clusters. 277 links are there with linkage strength of 388 showing the positive relationship among "Digital Financial Infusion" AND "Blockchain" OR "Crowdfunding" (Boolean Operators "AND", "OR" used). The analysis has been executed on the basis of research information system files. Output came with 66 occurrences in research studies of financial inclusion with 66 link strengths portraying positive networks with 33 links altogether making people aware about this financial technology with the work that has been performed by 67 authors after implementing filtration regarding the relevance of the subject matter.

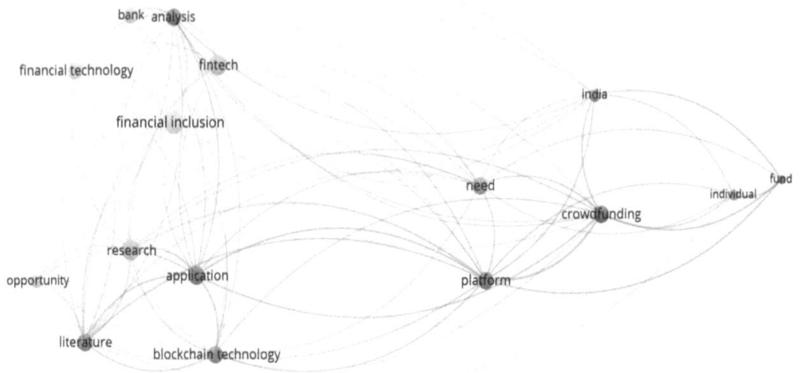

Fig. 1 Keyword analysis (Source: VOSviewer)

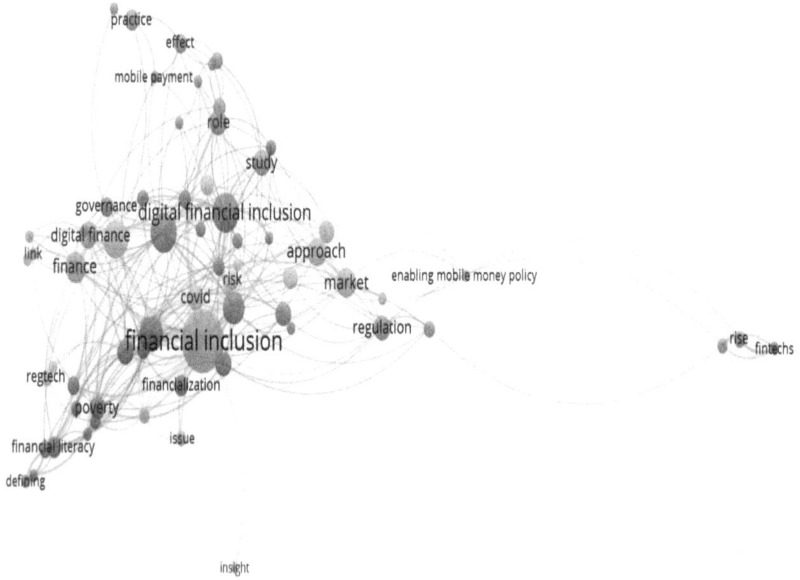

Fig. 2 Cluster mapping for keyword analysis to show the link strengths (Source: VOSviewer)

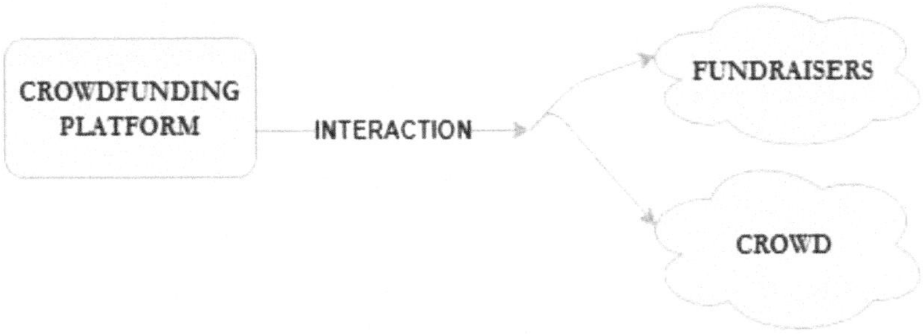

Fig. 3 Interactions with customers (Source: Author's Self-creation)

4 Crowdfunding Variants

The term "crowdfunding" can be defined as an accumulation of funds to make it available for those who want small amounts for projects, joint ventures or supporting society by means of raising funds from small investors through online modes or social networking sites. (Sarkar, 2014) It has also been mentioned by researchers that the usage of these digital financial technology platforms will be helpful in reaching out to the excluded people from financial access and make them understand the usage and variations to hold profit and avail services (Muneeza et al., 2018).

In a report on the basis of interview in UK, people are supporting crowdfunding platforms because of social and community causes and entrepreneurs are searching for such opportunities as well to help people.[1]

This is a matter of fact with India also. Fundraising capability of the investors cannot be judged on the basis of the causes that give rise to the initiation of such crowdfunding companies. Financial Inclusion is getting strength in the form of its digital model.

4.1 *Kinds of Crowdfunding*

(a) **Equity Crowdfunding**—Equity funding aims at helping those startups/business ideas that will flourish in the coming days tremendously and will provide a handful of returns in terms of

[1] https://www.nesta.org.uk/report/crowdfunding-good-causes/.

profit. Equity investors are very optimistic toward the term "liquidity". They are the risk takers and ultimate profit makers unlike banking institutions.[2]

As per SEBI rules, equity crowdfunding is considered to be illegal and unauthorized to be performed in India.

(b) **Donation/Social Lending Crowdfunding**—Basically, donation-based crowdfunding is a creation of pool for accumulating monetary funds without any intention of getting back return or profit (Baber, 2019).
(c) **Peer-to-Peer Crowdfunding**—It's about matching the profiles of lenders/investors with borrowers/issuers in need so as to provide unsecured loans and the rate of interest is fixed by fundraising platforms.[3]
(d) **Reward Crowdfunding**—This type of crowdfunding model represents co-creators or customers/users instead of investors as here project founders are the main parties to get benefits through rewards for various projects (Frydrych et al., 2014).

5 Factual Comparison among Indian Crowdfunding Platforms

The researcher tried to include all those crowdfunding platforms that are not mentioned in some of the research works in order to give a fresh review over such companies/startups (Table 1).

6 BCT in Crowdfunding

To understand the two financial innovation techniques, namely BCT and Crowdfunding, and research that is conducted eventually to see through the scenario of financial technology, a bibliometric analysis was being performed. With the help of research databases, 402 papers were searched to find the correlational facets of BCT and crowdfunding between the

[2] https://www.fundable.com/crowdfunding101/types-ofcrowdfunding.

[3] https://taxguru.in/sebi/crowdfunding-india.html.

Table 1 Crowdfunding platforms with reviews over companies/startups in researches

Crowdfunding Platforms	*Foundation*	*Objectives*	*Category*	*Charges*	*Fund raised (till now)*
Crowdera	2009	Social Causes	Donation Based	0%	**Rs.1400 Crores plus**
Gofundme	2010	Healthcare, Social causes	Debt & Donation Based	0%	**Rs.900 Crores plus**
LetsVenture	2013	Business, Start-ups	Donation Based	10%	**Rs.50 Crores plus**
Dream Wallets	2015, Rajasthan	Creativity, Passion	Reward Based	0%	**Rs.10 Crores plus**
Fueladream	2016, Bengaluru	Ideas, Charity, Causes, Event	Debt & Donation Based	3%	**Rs.50 Crores plus**

timeline 2010 and 2018 which helped a lot to grab the development on that particular terminology. With the help of HistCite™, a bibliographical map had been created efficiently by the researcher in his study (Cai, 2018).

Researchers tried to understand the implication of BCT in equity crowdfunding for the reason to provide voting rights to crowdfunders, efficient cost cutting, give full support to marketers to have an insight of the market and facilitate circulation of securities (Zhu & Zhou, 2016).

Through the discussion over Islamic crowdfunding platforms and ways of performances, a conclusive matter as an outcome toward BCT usage in crowdfunding has been examined. It will ultimately expand the growth of financial inclusion and also provide solutions (Muneeza et al., 2018).

BCT, in terms of smart contract crowdfunding platforms, is being studied and explored in order to safeguard the interest of funders. It has been a problem that is related to security matter in which phishing, spamming, etc. occurred due to which funders feel it difficult to find the one who is actually in need and fraudulent practices took place in the name of financial help. Discussion about permissioned and consortium blockchain nodes for distributing funds keeping in mind the security aspect has been done. Keep-It-All (KIA), Structured Goal Scheme (SGS) and All or Nothing (AON) schemes are mentioned to understand variations in crowdfunding platforms (Ashari et al., 2020)

On the basis of the bibliometrical analysis, with *Boolean Operators (AND)*, the terms.

"Crowdfunding" and "Blockchain Technology" are searched through Dimensions in which a collection of 6640 articles were there during the period 2013 to 2022, out of which 2381 open access journal papers are taken into consideration and included in this study through inclusion criteria and 89 closed one. As per the analysis of the author, 218 items formed 78 clusters of authors and co-authors with 357 links and 397 total link strength and the maximum citation link strength went to 80 citations with 56 clusters (yellow) showing the positive and followed with 73 citations of another author with 13 clusters, proving the positive interrelation of blockchain and crowdfunding together as shown in Fig. 4. The below tabular chart shows number of publications in graphical chart also (Fig. 5). Maximum number of papers published in open access domain in the year 2021 with 2074 papers (Table 2).

The above chart (Fig. 6) has been presented here in order to get a gist about the different streams which has mentioned Blockchain (BCT and Crowdfunding). All these are open access journals. The highest number of publications has been done in the area of commerce, management, tourism and services, i.e., 696 papers.

7 Conclusion, Implications and Limitations

The study has enabled potential fundraisers and companies adopting BCT methodologies for solutions and to work over the crowdfunding aspects correlated with it. Also bibliometric analysis has not been done before to grab an idea about the research conducted in the fields of BCT and crowdfunding. The objective of the author was to throw light over the research done in the area of BCT and crowdfunding by means of review of literature to analyze the growth of the Indian market to accept BCT crowdfunding and how much crowdfunding platforms are getting fame in terms of donations and moral responsibility that has been fulfilled by the people. The comparison among the various crowdfunding platforms and its implacability with BCT will enable the entrepreneurs to work ahead and grab opportunities to benefit the business set-ups as well as the society as a whole.

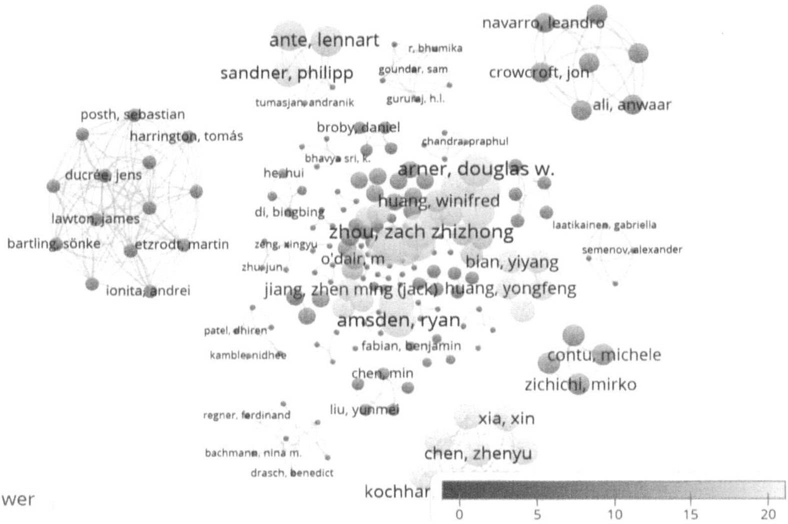

Fig. 4 Network clusters shown here through citation analysis (Source: VOSviewer)

Here, the author tried to pay attention over the connectivity among the terminologies BCT, crowdfunding and DFIs by means of reviewing literatures systematically. Theoretical implications will provide a strong base to the upcoming empirical studies that could be performed with a central idea of quantitatively judging the parameters. Bibliometrical analysis has presented the till date studies with variations. The financial policymakers of the companies need to understand the whole procedure of this innovative fintech sector so as to inculcate Blockchain in Crowdfunding with ease of accessibility and operations to be executed with full security. If outcome needs to be discussed here about the platforms availability, more focus needs to be given over the satisfactory levels of funders to successfully adopt BCT in crowdfunding in India.

Future research studies can be conducted to compare the BCT and Crowdfunding considering factors like social, psychological, etc. in terms of consumer awareness. Bibliometric analysis can be performed further in order to get an idea about the citations related with financial technology and consumer preferences patterns efficiently. There are still some unturned stones regarding exploration in terms of empirical studies with

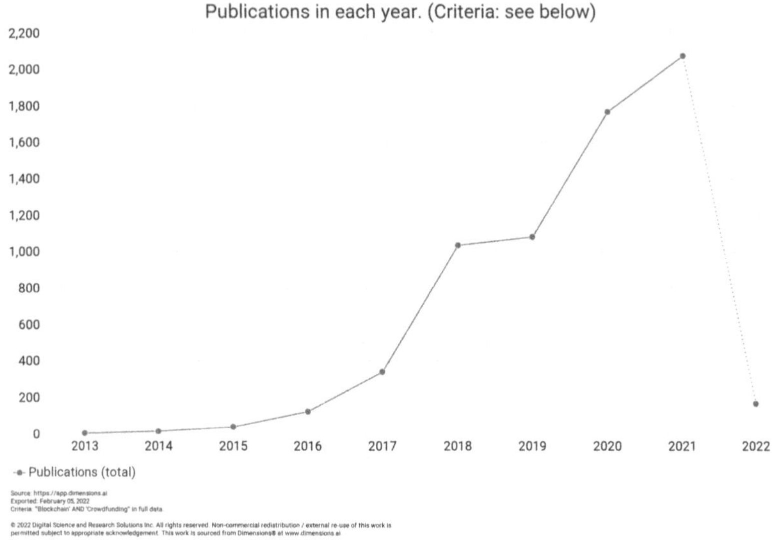

Fig. 5 Chart showing publications per year in the category of BCT and crowdfunding from 2013 to 2022 (Source: Dimensions web platform, open access)

Table 2 Tabular form to show the number of publications

Category	*Publications (total)*
2013.00	2.00
2014.00	12.00
2015.00	36.00
2016.00	121.00
2017.00	339.00
2018.00	1034.00
2019.00	1080.00
2020.00	1767.00
2021.00	2074.00
2022.00	165.00

numbers. Many empirical studies may be done along with this qualitative database.

This study aims at performing systematic literature review with the help of bibliometric analysis and meta-analysis to have a gist about BCT and

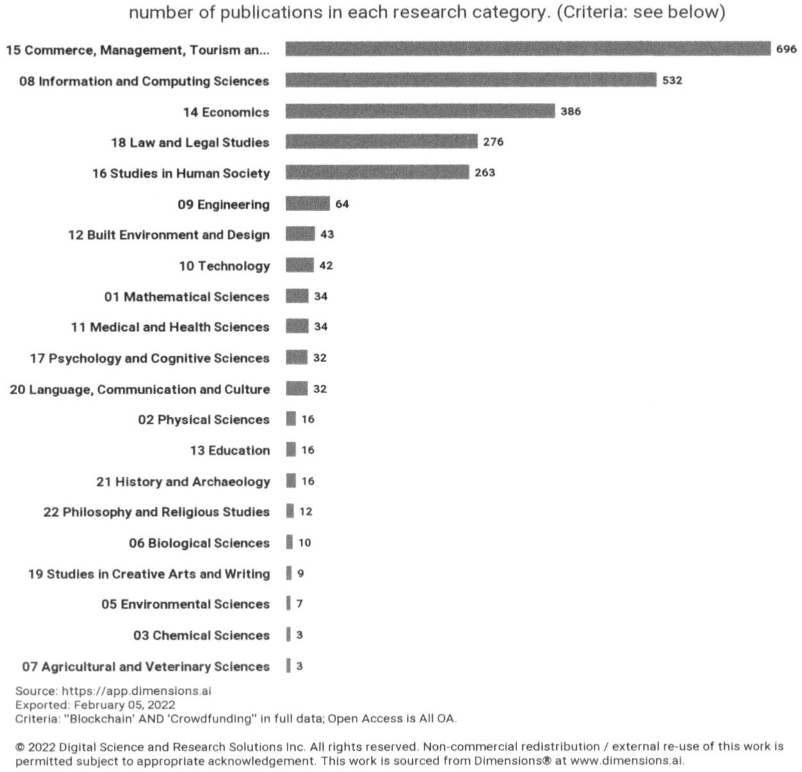

Fig. 6 Number of publications in each arena of research (Source: Dimensions, open access)

crowdfunding together in India and its takeaways. Due to shortage of time, few aspects are not unveiled for analysis and therefore the outcome needs to be more elaborative. This paper covered only BCT and crowdfunding along with its impact over financial inclusion. Empirical study could be performed to compare the available variations. Factual comparison that has been included in this review paper can be extended further with consumer satisfaction, base, pros and cons, etc.

References

Arner, D. W., Buckley, R. P., & Zetzsche, D. A. (2018). Fintech for financial inclusion: A framework for digital financial transformation. *UNSW Law Research Paper*, (18–87).

Arner, D. W., Buckley, R. P., Zetzsche, D. A., & Veidt, R. (2019). Sustainability, FinTech and financial inclusion. *European Business Organization Law Review, 21*(1), 7–35.

Ashari, F., Catonsukmoro, T., Bad, W. M., & Sfenranto, W. (2020). Smart contract and blockchain for crowdfunding platform. *International Journal of Advanced Trends in Computer Science and Engineering, 9*(3), 3036–3041.

Baber, H. (2019). Subjective norms and intention- A study of crowdfunding in India. *Research in World Economy, 10*(3), 136–146.

Cai, C. W. (2018). Disruption of financial intermediation by FinTech: A review on crowdfunding and blockchain. *Accounting and Finance, 58*(4), 965–992.

Chacko, K. T., & Baag, P. K. (2021). Financial inclusion in India: An approach through FinTech as a solution.

Frydrych, D., Bock, A. J., Kinder, T., & Koeck, B. (2014). Exploring entrepreneurial legitimacy in reward-based crowdfunding. *Venture Capital, 16*(3), 247–269.

Hua, X., & Huang, Y. (2021). Understanding China's fintech sector: Development, impacts and risks. *The European Journal of Finance, 27*(4–5), 321–333.

Jenik, I., Lyman, T., & Nava, A. (2017). *Crowdfunding and financial inclusion* (CGAP (Consultative Group to Assist the Poor) working paper, 41).

Jenik, I., Timothy, L., & Nava, A. (2017b). Crowdfunding and financial inclusion. In *Cgap (Working Paper)* (Issue March).

Kessler, M. M. (1963). Bibliographic coupling between scientifc papers. *American Documentation, 14*(1), 10–25.

Kraus, S., Li, H., Kang, Q., Westhead, P., & Tiberius, V. (2020). The sharing economy: A bibliometric analysis of the state-of-the-art. *International Journal of Entrepreneurial Behavior & Research., 26*(8), 1769–1786.

Kraus, S., Breier, M., & Dasí-Rodríguez, S. (2020). The art of crafting a systematic literature review in entrepreneurship research. *International Entrepreneurship and Management Journal, 16*(3), 1023–1042.

Kolesnikov, Y. A. (2020). Features of state regulation of crowdfunding as a new institution of the financial market. *Public Policy & Administration/Viesoji Politika ir Administravimas, 19*(4), 9–20.

Leela, V. (2016). Crowdfunding: A study of risk factors. *South Asian Journal of Management, 23*(3), 170.

Liu, G., Huang, Y., & Huang, Z. (2021). Determinants and mechanisms of digital financial inclusion development: Based on urban-rural differences. *Agronomy, 11*(9), 1833.

Likens, S. (2019, May 16). How artificial intelligence is already disrupting financial services. *Barron's Online*.

Mondal, S., Bandyopadhyay, A. K., & Roy, B. K. (2017). Bibliometric analysis of doctoral dissertations in political science: A study of the University of Burdwan. *International Research: Journal of Library & Information Science, 7*(3), 594.

Muneeza, A., Arshad, N. A., & Arifin, A. T. (2018). The application of blockchain technology in crowdfunding: Towards financial inclusion via technology. *International journal of management and applied research, 5*(2), 82–98.

Niforos, M. (2017a). Blockchain in financial services in emerging markets, part I: Current trends.

Niforos, M. (2017b). Blockchain in financial services in emerging markets, part I.

Pritchard, A. (1969). Statistical bibliography or bibliometrics. *Journal of Documentation, 25*, 348.

Ravikumar, T. (2019). Digital financial inclusion: A payoff of financial technology and digital finance uprising in India. *International Journal of Scientific & Technology Research, 8*(11), 3434–3438.

Rupino, P., Soja, P., Themistocleous, M., Rupino, P., & Soja, P. (2021). Blockchain for development: A guiding framework. *Information Technology for Development, 27*(3), 417–438.

Small, H. (1973). Co-citation in the scientific literature: A new measure of the relationship between two documents. *Journal of the American Society for Information Science, 24*(4), 265–269.

Sarkar, A. (2014). *Crowdfunding in India : Major roadblocks and the*. 1–10. http://fortune.com/2014/04/17/why-investors-are-pouring-millions-into-crowdfunding/

Schindler, J. (2017). FinTech and financial innovation: Drivers and depth. *Finance and Economics Discussion Series, 2017* (081).

Schuetz, S., & Venkatesh, V. (2020). Blockchain, adoption, and financial inclusion in India: Research opportunities. *International Journal of Information Management, 52*.

Thomason, J., Ahmad, M., Bronder, P., Hoyt, E., Pocock, S., Bouteloupe, J., Donaghy, K., Huysman, D., Willenberg, T., Joakim, B., Joseph, L., Martin, D., & Shrier, D. (2018). Blockchain—Powering and empowering the poor in developing countries. In *Transforming climate finance and green investment with blockchains* (pp. 137–152). Academic Press.

Venegas, P. (2020, July). trustable risk scoring for non-bank gateways in blockchain and DLT financial networks. In *International Conference on Complex Systems* (pp. 165–178). Springer.

Wang, X., & He, G. (2020). Digital financial inclusion and farmers' vulnerability to poverty: Evidence from rural China. *Sustainability, 12*(4), 1668.
Wójcik, D. (2021). Financial geography II: The impacts of FinTech–Financial sector and centres, regulation and stability, inclusion and governance. *Progress in Human Geography, 45*(4), 878–889.
Zhu, H., & Zhou, Z. Z. (2016). Analysis and outlook of applications of blockchain technology to equity crowdfunding in China. *Financial Innovation, 2*(1), 1–11.
Zupic, I., & Čater, T. (2015). Bibliometric methods in management and organization. *Organizational Research Methods, 18*(3), 429–472.

Websites/Blogs

List of Crowdfunding Websites in India—TechAccent. (n.d.). Retrieved September 1, 2021, from https://www.techaccent.com/list-of-crowdfunding-websites-in-india/
LetsVenture Launches Plus Investment Platform For HNIs, Family Offices. (n.d.). Retrieved September 1, 2021, from https://inc42.com/buzz/letsventure-launches-plus-investment-platform-for-hnis-family-offices/
LetsVenture | Tracxn. (n.d.). Retrieved September 1, 2021, from https://tracxn.com/d/companies/letsventure.com
How crowdfunding works | Xero US. (n.d.). Retrieved August 25, 2021, from https://www.xero.com/us/guides/financing-your-business/how-crowdfunding-works/
Fundable.com. (2015). *Types of crowdfunding*. Fundable. https://www.fundable.com/crowdfunding101/types-of-crowdfunding
Crowdera Foundation. (n.d.). Retrieved September 1, 2021, from https://gocrowdera.com/crowderafoundation
Catapooolt- India's Largest Crowdfunding Platform. (n.d.). Retrieved September 1, 2021, from https://www.catapooolt.com/howitworks
Fueladream : Best Crowdfunding Platform in India | Crowdfunding in India | Online fundraising website | Online Crowdfunding Platform | largest crowdfunding platform in India | crowdfund innovations & pre-order unique products. (n.d.). Retrieved September 1, 2021, from https://www.fueladream.com/
Dream Wallets—Tech Stack, Apps, Patents & Trademarks. (n.d.). Retrieved September 1, 2021, from https://www.crunchbase.com/organization/dream-wallets/technology

Cryptocurrency Conundrum: Understanding the Dynamics of Indian Consumer Intentions using an Extended UTAUT Model

Shrinivas K, Shivam Sharma, Ananda S, and Raghavendra Prasanna Kumar

1 Introduction

The 2008 financial crisis and the bail-out of banks by the government really highlighted the cracks in the current financial system and solidified the need for a truly global digital currency which could be spent and earned by people without a third party (usually these banks). This

S. K · R. P. Kumar (✉)
School of Business and Management, CHRIST Deemed to Be University, Bangalore, India
e-mail: raghuhbk1988@gmail.com

S. K
e-mail: shrinivas@christuniversity.in

S. Sharma
Marketing and Sales Manager, RP3, Bangalore, India

A. S
College of Banking and Financial Studies, Muscat, Oman

© The Author(s), under exclusive license to Springer Nature Singapore Pte Ltd. 2025

A. S. et al. (eds.), *Trends and Challenges of Electronic Finance*,
https://doi.org/10.1007/978-981-96-3304-3_23

led to Bitcoin, which has since its inception in January 2009, gone on to touch great heights and come down equally fast—giving it the reputation of a highly volatile asset class. However, proponents of cryptocurrencies would prefer viewing them as a new form of money rather than investing in them. We have had cryptocurrency companies in India which have been working hard to get this to Indians, but they found their big break after the demonetization of 2016, which increased interest in cryptocurrencies. From then on—notwithstanding the unending legal roadblocks—cryptocurrencies in India have gone through a whole era. Yet, these companies are still not sure on where to concentrate their efforts to increase cryptocurrency adoption. This is more or less what the paper aims to address.

Bitcoin started off with a published paper by a person whose real identity is unknown (he/she calls him/herself Satoshi Nakamoto) and details the structure of this cryptocurrency. This paper essentially put together various existing computer concepts like linked lists, hashing algorithms, distributed computing, peer-to-peer protocols, digital signatures, and Byzantine fault tolerance—concepts that had been matured and explored enough but never thought of together—and created the first ever cryptocurrency: Bitcoin.

1.1 Bitcoin in a Nutshell

Bitcoin is a cryptocurrency that consists of users (with their private and public keys), transactions (propagated across the network), and miners who validate transactions and constantly add them to the blockchain, which is a public ledger of all the transactions that ever took place. By validating transactions and adding them to the blockchain, a new cryptocurrency is brought into circulation, which is capped at 21 million (in the case of Bitcoin).

However, this structure of Bitcoin has several limitations as well, which are very well understood as of today and which subsequently led to the creation of newer cryptocurrencies with novel solutions to the issues. For example, one flaw of Bitcoins can be their lack of true anonymity. While Bitcoin is "pseudonymous" (i.e., on the one hand everyone knows all the transactions that have ever happened, however on the other hand there is no way to link the identity of the person who is doing these transactions), it is not difficult to trace transactions or public addresses to individuals. The solution to this problem was brought by Monero, a

Table 1 Leading cryptocurrencies of today

Rank	*Name*	*Market Cap ($ Billions)*	*Price ($)*	*Circulating Supply ($ billions)*
1	Bitcoin	155.62	8563.95	27.8
2	Ethereum	17.77	162.48	11.71
3	Ripple	9.89	0.23	1.77
4	Bitcoin Cash	5.94	325.84	3.07
5	Bitcoin SV	5.01	275.12	2.7

Source www.coinmarketcap.com

privacy-focused cryptocurrency which introduced the concept of "Ring Signatures" that ensures true anonymity at a fundamental level. Several other cryptocurrencies have their own features, but we shall restrict our focus to Bitcoins only.

1.2 Cryptocurrencies and Governments

Globally, there are 3000 + cryptocurrencies in circulation, with the market leaders (as per Market Capitalization) being Bitcoin, Ethereum, Ripple, Bitcoin Cash, and Bitcoin SV (the last two being forks of Bitcoin). The present market scenario is summarized in Table 1.

In the past year, approximately 280,000 to 380,000 Bitcoin transactions took place every day amounting to $50 billion. (These are confirmed transactions as analyzed from the public blockchain which is around 232 GB in size.) These facts have contributed to governments and big banking corporations warming up to the concept of cryptocurrency. Figure 1 plots the market cap and price per unit (both in USD) of Bitcoin, and Table 2 summarizes the stance of various countries on cryptocurrencies.

1.3 The UTAUT Model

While performing literature review of an article titled "Variables Influencing Cryptocurrency Use: A Technology Acceptance Model in Spain" (Arias-Oliva et al., 2019), the author was introduced to the field of modeling and analyzing factors that lead to adoption of technologies.

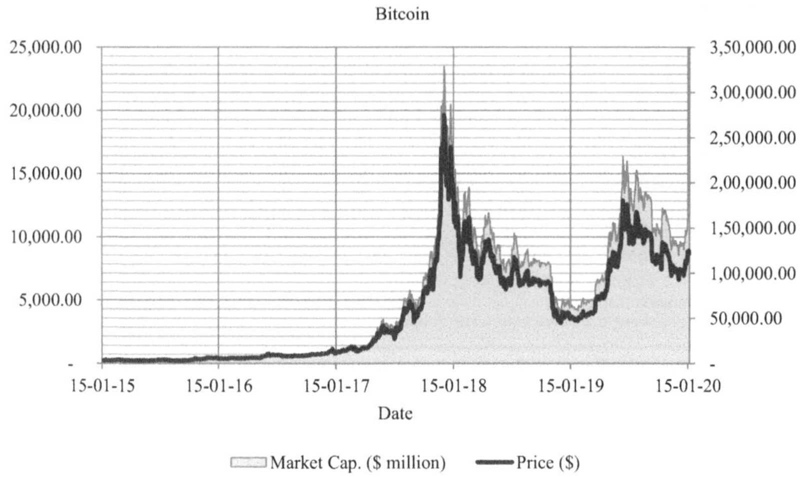

Fig. 1 Bitcoin price and market cap

This is an area that has been of wide interest especially since the IT boom. Multi-national corporations and their clients have been performing studies to understand the perception of present employees to technology in the workplace and whether they "truly" migrated to the new setup or still operate with the "old" mentality. These studies can be compared to the motion studies of the early twentieth century which was to improve the efficiency and worker satisfaction (for example, the Hawthorne Study).

Through this research, they were able to find out what are the key elements that influence the perception of the employees toward new technology and then work on that to ensure that the new technology is being utilized and the benefits are being passed as we move in the value chain. It helped them understand the drivers of acceptance to plan the next logical step (i.e., more training, or marketing it better, etc.) to achieve the objective of successful deployment of the technology.

The Unified Theory of Acceptance and Use of Technology (UTAUT) model is a new model that takes the best from eight common models used to study acceptance and use of technology and comes up with a new structure that better explains the dependent variable being studied. This new structure has a higher R-squared value and is commonly used

Table 2 Stance of different countries on cryptocurrencies

Stance	*Countries*
Complete Ban	Bolivia
	Morocco
	Nepal
	Pakistan
	Vietnam
Banned locally*	Qatar
*Citizens can engage in crypto outside country borders	Bahrain
Indirect Restriction: Local Financial Institutions Banned from Dealing in Crypto	Bangladesh
	Iran
	Thailand
	Lithuania
	Lesotho
	China
	Cambodia
Cryptocurrency Friendly Regulations**	Spain
	Belarus
	The Cayman Islands
**To invite investment in the country	Luxembourg
Developing National Cryptocurrency	Marshall Islands
	Venezuela
	The EECB# States
	#Eastern Caribbean Central Bank
	Lithuania
Size of Market Insignificant for Govt. Intervention	Belgium
	South Africa
	United Kingdom

Source An analysis of the cryptocurrency industry, Ryan Farrell

today in areas of understanding adoption and acceptance of technology (Venkatesh et al., 2012).

1.4 Literature Review

According to two decisions made by the Commodity Futures Trading Commission, virtual currencies are commodities covered by the Commodity Exchange Act (Lim et al., 2016). In the event that it has developed into a "strong currency," what are the managerial implications? Moreover, generally speaking, we anticipate that CCs that exhibit club convergence patterns, like Bitcoin (Sahoo, 2020), and that are “near stock” (Sahoo et al., 2019), would behave similarly to the market (near stock) and to each other (club dynamics). Given that some have proposed using CCs as a hedge investment, it’s critical to comprehend how they respond in times of crisis.

Since Nakamoto (2008)created Bitcoin, the exponential expansion of cryptocurrencies has drawn the interest of investors, speculators, regulators, and researchers. In actuality, a significant amount of research has been focused on the pricing mechanisms of cryptocurrency markets (Balcilar et al., 2017; Blau, 2017; Cheah & Fry, 2015; Cheung et al., 2015; Urquhart, 2016, 2017); the drivers of volatility (Bouri et al., 2018a, 2018b; Katsiampa, 2017); and the diversification potential of cryptocurrencies (Brière et al., 2015; Dyhrberg, 2016).

In order to facilitate near real-time transactions, accurate data collection, and more efficient payment procedures, crypto-assets are being incorporated into financial services applications more and more. Nonetheless, a major obstacle to putting these assets into practice is the absence of legal clarity (Dutch Banking Association, 2020). According to a few recent research (Cheah & Fry, 2015; Kristoufek, 2015; Malladi & Dheeriya, 2021), market sentiment and memory may be somewhat responsible for the volatility of CCs. In these situations, one semi-important factor influencing CC prices is their “memory” of shocks. But for risk-averse investors, Bitcoin might be a useful tool for hedging against market-specific risk and guarding against unfavorable market shocks. According to Grima et al. (2021), the volatility of major financial markets, particularly the CBOE Volatility Index (VIX), has been influenced by new COVID-19 cases and deaths.

2 Research Methods

Internationally, there has been sizable activity in academia circles related to cryptocurrencies (especially in subjects like economics, finance, mathematical modeling, quantitative techniques of analysis, cryptography, computer science, and several others), but there is a lack of research done on the reasons, or the qualitative factors that determine why individuals use cryptocurrencies. This trend is mirrored in India where most of the academic work on this topic has been limited to the analyses of price, price movements, and similar efforts or to present an understanding of the technology. Hence, the objective of this study is to clearly find out the factors responsible for cryptocurrency usage in India.

2.1 Scope and Methodology

The scope of this study is limited to people in India who have conducted transactions (that is, ever bought or sold) in cryptocurrencies or dealt with cryptocurrencies in any manner. The study is limited to analyze of the participant's responses pertaining to their subjective and qualitative understanding and feelings regarding cryptocurrencies. The methodology followed was to collect primary data by distributing surveys (electronically through Google Forms) and then doing analyses on the data so collected.

The survey was divided into five sections with the first section asking if the respondent was familiar with cryptocurrencies (out of 136 participants, 104 said they were familiar with cryptocurrencies thus we only analyzed their responses). To get respondents we combed social media websites like Twitter, with search on hashtags (such as "#IndiaWantsCrypto", "#BitcoinIndia", "#CryptoIndia", and "#RBIvsCRYPTO") and on Facebook with posts on groups ("Bitcoin Meetups—India", created on March 26, 2017, with 1588 members who are mostly Indian; "Blockchained India", created on March 11, 2017, with 6835 members who are again, mostly Indian; and, "Ethereum Developers Sharing Knowledge", created on March 4, 2018, with 172 members which belong to varied nationalities) and one Telegram group ("Crypto India Community" with 2689 members). We also contacted founders of blockchain/cryptocurrency companies which were based out of India and send them survey links.

The UTAUT model presented by Venkatesh et al. was modified with a cryptocurrency focus and six variables were narrowed down with two to three questions in each. The rest of the questions aimed to get an understanding of the respondents' perception of cryptocurrency.

2.2 Mathematical and Statistical Tools Used

The analysis was divided into three parts: refining the model, performing regression analysis, and analyzing the non-model responses. For the first part, we relied on the results of a factor analysis done in SPSS. Various tests of validity were checked inside of factor analysis itself (for

Table 3 Initial correlation matrix

Correlation Matrix[a]

	EE1	*EE2*	*TA1*	*TA2*	*SI1*	*SI2*	*IU1*	*IU2*	*IU3*	*FC1*
EE1	1	**0.778**	0.658	0.525	0.079	0.631	0.513	0.687	0.248	0.747
EE2	**0.778**	1	0.683	0.419	0.016	0.522	0.478	0.542	0.352	0.782
TA1	0.658	0.683	1	**0.647**	0.269	0.681	0.566	0.557	0.371	0.551
TA2	0.525	0.419	**0.647**	1	0.391	0.531	0.526	0.673	0.683	0.389
SI1	0.079	0.016	0.269	0.391	1	**0.298**	0.225	0.322	0.419	0.008
SI2	0.631	0.522	0.681	0.531	**0.298**	1	0.528	0.848	0.346	0.44
IU1	0.513	0.478	0.566	0.526	0.225	0.528	1	**0.556**	**0.482**	0.56
IU2	0.687	0.542	0.557	0.673	0.322	0.848	**0.556**	1	**0.398**	0.468
IU3	0.248	0.352	0.371	0.683	0.419	0.346	**0.482**	**0.398**	1	0.329
FC1	0.747	0.782	0.551	0.389	0.008	0.44	0.56	0.468	0.329	1

a. Determinant = 0.000
Source Factor analysis

example the correlation matrix, the KMO test, Bartlett's test, total variance explained, rotated component matrix, average variance extracted, and HTMT Ratios). For the second part, we relied on the results of a partial least square regression done on SmartPLS. For the third part, we performed simple slice-and-dice functions in MS Excel.

3 Results and Discussion

3.1 *Factor Analysis*

3.1.1 Correlation Matrices

To start off our analysis, we coded our questions with reference to the constructs and then using factor analysis in SPSS, found out the correlation matrix. We then refined it by removing items that are loaded too heavily or too lightly, which increased out determinant value to 0.003 (which is above the threshold of 0.00001, indicating the absence of multicollinearity in our data). (These matrices can be found in Tables 3 and 4.)

3.1.2 KMO Test and Bartlett's Test of Sphericity

In our factor analysis, we checked the option of obtaining the Kaiser–Meyer–Olkin Measure of Sampling Adequacy and Bartlett's Test of

Table 4 Refined correlation matrix

Correlation Matrix[a]

	EE1	*EE2*	*TA1*	*TA2*	*IU1*	*IU2*	*IU3*	*FC1*
EE1	1	**0.778**	0.658	0.525	0.513	0.687	0.248	0.747
EE2	**0.778**	1	0.683	0.419	0.478	0.542	0.352	0.782
TA1	0.658	0.683	1	**0.647**	0.566	0.557	0.371	0.551
TA2	0.525	0.419	**0.647**	1	0.526	0.673	0.683	0.389
IU1	0.513	0.478	0.566	0.526	1	**0.556**	**0.482**	0.56
IU2	0.687	0.542	0.557	0.673	**0.556**	1	**0.398**	0.468
IU3	0.248	0.352	0.371	0.683	**0.482**	**0.398**	1	0.329
FC1	0.747	0.782	0.551	0.389	0.56	0.468	0.329	1

a. Determinant = 0.003
Source Factor analysis

Table 5 KMO measure and Bartlett's test

KMO and Bartlett's Test		
Kaiser–Meyer–Olkin Measure of Sampling Adequacy		0.773
Bartlett's Test of Sphericity	Approx. Chi-Square	585.981
	df	28
	Sig	0

Sphericity to see how suitable our data is for structure detection. As the KMO measure is greater than 0.5 and the significance of Bartlett's Test of Sphericity less than 0.05 (refer Table 5), we can say with confidence that we can detect a structure in our data. (The null hypothesis for Bartlett's Test of Sphericity is that data is unsuitable to detect a structure. This is rejected as significance is less than 0.05.)

3.1.3 Total Variance Explained and Rotated Component Matrix

To decide the number of factor solutions, we chose those many which explained more than 85% of the variance in all variables. From Table 6, it is clear that four components would satisfy this condition. So now that we know that a structure can be found in the data and that we have four-factor variables, we can go ahead and arrange the variables (i.e., the questions) into suitable constructs (i.e., the factor solutions) to arrive at a refined version of our model. For this purpose, we refer to the rotated component matrix and find out which variables load onto which factor solution (Table 7).

Table 6 Total variance explained of the different factor solutions

Total Variance Explained

Component	*Initial Eigenvalues*			*Extraction Sums of Squared Loadings*			*Rotation Sums of Squared Loadings*		
	Total	*% of Variance*	*Cumulative %*	*Total*	*% of Variance*	*Cumulative %*	*Total*	*% of Variance*	*Cumulative %*
1	**4.828**	**60.355**	**60.355**	4.828	60.355	60.355	2.643	33.039	33.039
2	**1.132**	**14.149**	**74.504**	1.132	14.149	74.504	1.918	23.97	57.008
3	**0.611**	**7.632**	**82.136**	0.611	7.632	82.136	1.493	18.664	75.672
4	**0.5**	**6.255**	**88.39**	0.5	6.255	88.39	1.017	12.718	88.39
5	**0.437**	**5.46**	**93.85**						
6	**0.233**	**2.91**	**96.76**						
7	**0.152**	**1.896**	**98.656**						
8	**0.108**	**1.344**	**100**						

Extraction Method: Principal component analysis
Source Factor analysis

Table 7 Which factors load on which component

Rotated Component Matrix[a]

	Component			
	1	*2*	*3*	*4*
EE1	**0.749**	0.544	0.003	0.159
EE2	**0.893**	0.255	0.175	0.085
TA1	**0.559**	0.552	0.265	0.133
TA2	0.176	**0.676**	**0.638**	0.119
IU1	0.299	0.29	0.264	**0.856**
IU2	0.28	**0.827**	0.144	0.277
IU3	0.144	0.134	**0.935**	0.199
FC1	**0.868**	0.093	0.145	0.322

Extraction Method: Principal component analysis
Rotation Method: Varimax with kaiser normalization
a. Rotation converged in 5 iterations
Source Factor analysis

The threshold to select a variable for a factor solution was if the matrix value was greater than 0.6. (For TA1, since the matrix value was less than 0.6, we chose that factor solution in which the matrix value was the maximum.) So now our refined construct has begun to take shape. As of now, there are four constructs in our data, namely (EE1, EE2, TA1, FC1), (TA2, IU2), (IU3), and (IU1). We check this data for construct validity. If the data satisfies the conditions for construct validity, then we shall build new constructs based on the new clubbing of items.

3.1.4 Construct Validity

Construct validity has two parts to it: convergent validity and divergent validity. To check for convergent validity, we find out the average variance extracted, i.e., the average variance extracted (AVE) from each of the constructs. It should be greater than or equal to 0.5. We also find out the composite reliability (a.k.a. CR, a measure of internal consistency, which tells us how consistent the items are in a particular construct). This should be greater than 0.7.

The calculation of AVE and CR for one construct is presented below in Table 8. The values of other constructs are then displayed in Table 9. To calculate the AVE and CR, we take λ (which is nothing but the rotated component matrix score of one item that loads on a construct), λ^2 and ε (which is nothing but $1-\lambda^2$) and their sums.

The formulae are presented below:

$$CR = \frac{(Sum of \lambda)^2}{(Sum of \lambda)^2 + (Sum of \varepsilon)}$$

Table 8 Calculation of AVE and CR for component 1

	λ	λ^2	ε
EE1	0.749	0.56	0.44
EE2	0.893	0.797	0.203
TA1	0.559	0.313	0.687
FC1	0.868	0.753	0.247
Sum	3.068	2.423	1.577

AVE = 2.423 / 4 = 0.6058
CR = (3.068^2) / $(3.068^2 + 1.577)$ = 0.8566
Source Author's calculation

Table 9 AVE and CR of each component

Component	*AVE*	*CR*
1	0.6058	0.8566
2	0.5705	0.7245
3	0.6406	0.7749
4	0.7327	0.7327

Source Author's calculation

$$AVE = \frac{Sum of \lambda^2}{n}$$

(where n is the number of variables loading on that factor).

As you can see from Table 9, convergent validity is proven. For divergent validity, we calculate the Heterotrait-Monotrait Ratio. This tells us whether the items of a construct explain only what they are supposed to and nothing else. If the HTMT conditions are not satisfied, then this means that the items explain more than what they are supposed to, hence we can never really be sure of the structural paths we obtain in our regression analysis (i.e., we can never really be sure whether the relationships are true or not). Henseler et al. (2015) in "A New Criterion for Assessing Discriminant Validity in Variance-based Structural Equation Modeling" proved that the HTMT Ratio is superior to all other methods of divergent validity. The HTMT values are presented in Table 10 where we can see that all values, except the correlation between the same constructs, are less than 0.9 which implies that we have divergent validity as well.

Table 10 HTMT values of different constructs

HTMT Value Matrix

	C_1	C_2	C_3	C_4
C_1	1	0.6574	0.3689	0.6013
C_2	0.6574	1	0.5912	0.5913
C_3	0.3689	0.5912	1	0.4823
C_4	0.6013	0.5913	0.4823	1

Source Author's calculation

The HTMT values of all constructs are in the below table. Notice how all of them are below 0.9 which means that our data has divergent validity

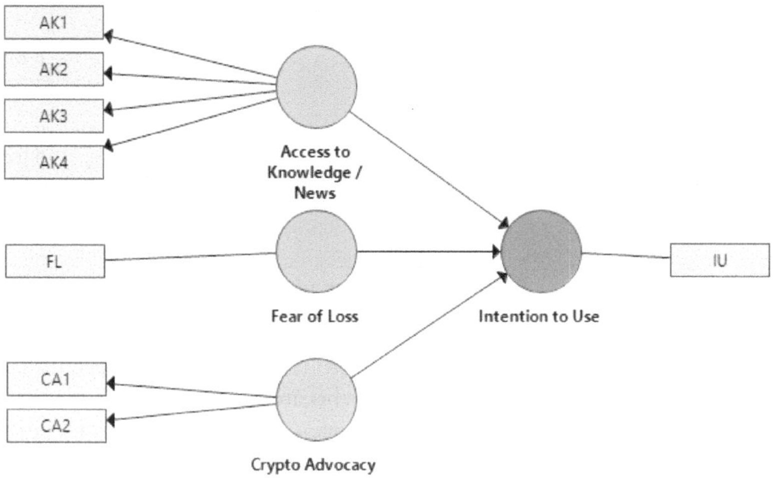

Fig. 2 Refined model

The refined model is presented in Fig. 2 on which we have performed the partial least square regression analysis.

3.2 Regression Analysis

Since linear regression is not applicable over here (since each final dependent variable is loaded upon by three independent variables which are *themselves* loaded upon by other variables), we use partial least square regression which is used in such scenarios. Since we had only 104 observations, we bootstrapped the data with 5000 resamples before performing the regression analysis. The results of the regression analysis are presented in Table 11.

The R-squared value of 0.8125 indicates that our model fits well with the data. The most important factor that influences the intention to use cryptocurrency (approx. 40%) is the access to knowledge/news about cryptocurrencies. The implications of this are presented in the next section.

Table 11 Partial least square regression results

Construct	R^2	*Direct Effect*	*p-value*
Intention to Use (IU)	0.8125		
Access to Knowledge/News (AK)		0.3876	0
Crypto Advocacy (CA)		0.2089	0.044
Fear of Loss (FL)		0.2161	0.0079

3.3 Analysis of Non-model Questions

A rather expected but disappointing result, 92.31% were men. This solidifies a prevalent belief that when it comes to tech, especially emerging tech like cryptocurrencies, it is usually men who are involved in this space.

85.58% of the participants were between the ages of 18–24. This is understandable, as the older people view cryptocurrencies as either a very risky investment avenue or they are against the concept of cryptocurrencies but are for the concept of blockchain and those technologies. This finding is again confirmed when we see that a majority (i.e., 69.23%) of respondents feel it is a medium of exchange, as opposed to an investment vehicle.

A very important fact here, which can also predict the outcome of our regression analysis, is that 80.77% of the respondents were familiar with cryptography or computer science. This validates the outcome of our regression analysis which says access to knowledge is the most important factor in predicting intention to use cryptocurrencies. Thus, individuals who have traditionally had good access to knowledge (a young person with knowledge about cryptography and computers must have grown in a household that has a computer/can afford one; hence his access to knowledge is high).

Then, analyzing the responses of the data pertaining to educational qualifications, we see that individuals who use cryptocurrency are committed to educating themselves. This trend is seen as the young people who use cryptocurrencies mostly attend colleges/high-schools and the older ones usually hold a post-graduate or master's degree.

We had established that crypto advocacy i.e., advocating for the cause of cryptocurrencies among social circles is the second most important factor that predicts intention to use cryptocurrency. Our analysis of the responses to people attending cryptocurrency meetups or being part of social media groups tells us that less than half of the people are in a crypto group or attend meetups and that only a quarter do both. This implies the presence of a massive opportunity of people to spread information and knowledge about cryptocurrencies.

We also asked the respondents to tell us which of the following day-to-day transactions (buying a cup of coffee, receiving your take-home pay, paying taxes, pay monthly utility (water, gas, electricity), buying plane tickets, making an international payment, and saving for a life goal) and which one were they most likely to use cryptocurrencies for. The results are in Fig. 3.

In conclusion, through our analysis we have found out the two types of cryptocurrency users: the first, tend to be school/college-going men who are relatively well off and have an interest in computer science. This individual resonates with the original motive of Bitcoin and believes in cryptocurrencies being a medium of exchange. In fact, answers to

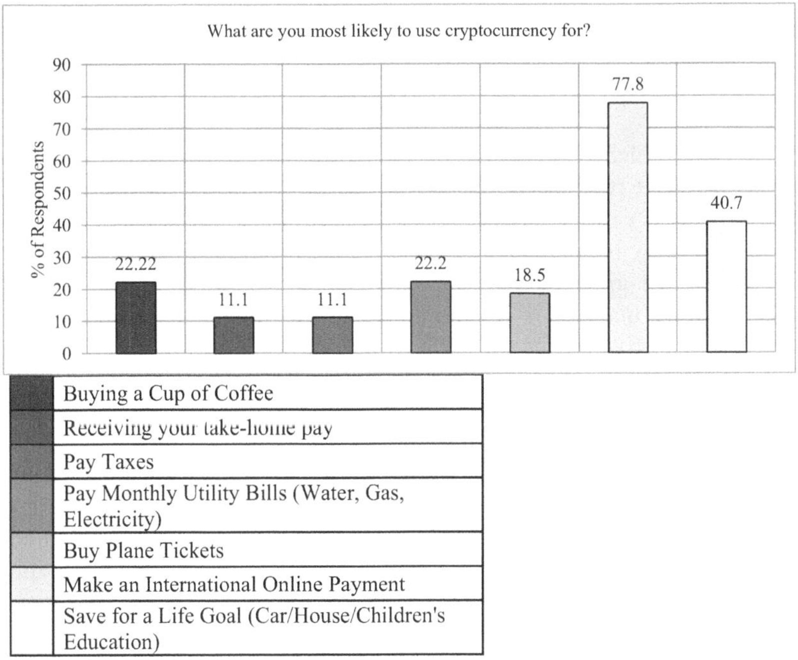

Fig. 3 Cryptocurrency usage

the question "Will cryptocurrencies ever replace the current financial structure of the world?" are an average of 2.96 on 5 because of the disproportionate representation of young people in our survey. The same can be said about the answer to the question "How likely are you to recommend using cryptocurrencies to someone you know?" which is 6.27 on 10.

The second type of users are older individuals with advanced degrees in computer science/related fields and are more for the underlying technology of cryptocurrency (i.e., the blockchain) and its applications rather than actual usage of cryptocurrencies. These individuals also want more regulation in the cryptocurrency space.

4 Conclusion

The objective of this study was to find out which factors influence the intention of Indian's consumers' intention to use cryptocurrencies and the results of our analysis point to three main factors which explained below.

4.1 Access to Knowledge/News

This factor, which is the most important one in predicting intention to use, consists of two parts, first is the ease of learning. Having learning material that is easily accessible is not enough, individuals must also have the opportunity to interact with other experienced individuals to resolve any doubts or give them more clarity. This is a tough ask since the basic learning material is itself unavailable. So individuals interested in increasing cryptocurrency adoption must focus on putting out content in different languages so it is accessible and explain the concepts of cryptocurrencies. (On YouTube India, most videos are watched in Hindi followed by Telugu and *then* English, so more content must be produced in vernacular.) The second, which is well covered, is the news components where happenings in the cryptocurrency space including new regulations, coins, technological developments, etc. are documented and presented. Currently, we have several good outlets (CryptoKanoon, CoinTelegraph, and the like) which ensure that the crypto community is well-informed so this should be worried about.

4.2 Crypto Advocacy

Trailing closely the first factor, crypto advocacy is another important factor which is pertaining to individuals who are already a part of the cryptocurrency ecosystem. To increase adoption among non-users, it is imperative to have present users "endorse" cryptocurrencies by means of spreading information, having discussions and taking part actively in the crypto communities. The barrier to entry should be further made lower.

4.3 Fear of Loss

While this factor can easily be clubbed in any of the above two factors (and one can argue that a fear of loss is automatically addressed with proper knowledge about the technology), the fact is that individuals who are acquainted with the concepts of computer science and understand the intricacies of cryptocurrencies more than the average person, these individuals *also* have a fear of "losing their money forever." This fear is valid as in a society where any transaction can be reversed if it really has to, the concept of a transaction that is completely irreversible does bring with it a certain amount of hesitance. This fear must be understood and kept in mind when formulating programs or strategies to increase cryptocurrency adoption among individuals.

4.4 Scope for Future Research

Historically, whenever we have had new technologies, the studies concerned with investigating user adoption and user behavior could to a large extent be applied to populations much different from that of the population in the study. We have seen this: with computers, smartphones, and smartwatches the adoption process and user reaction—with its minor changes—can be said to be same throughout geographics. However, when it comes to cryptocurrencies, the scenario can't be more different.

This can be understood from the following distinction. While other technologies have focused on providing a simpler means of performing activity, or a novel storage method, or anything else: they can be summarized to be *related only with the data*. However, when it comes to cryptocurrencies, they are *directly related to individuals' money*, and people are naturally more attached (and with good reason) to their wealth, their ways to earning it, storing it, and using it. Hence, to understand cryptocurrency use we cannot generalize the findings: we must work with the different groups of individuals and cultures to understand the unique perspectives to money and the factors which contribute to it. The same way reception medical advances cannot be generalized (we must see the limitations that culture imposes. A classic example is delivering children: while most mothers don't mind common day methods and procedures some strictly adhere to the traditional methods); the same way we cannot generalize cryptocurrency affects.

Coming to the Indian perspective, few areas ripe for research include studying the consumer habits not only pertaining to cryptocurrency, but also digital payments (since parallels can be drawn) and understanding how so many Indian's have come to adopt digital payments like UPI, Paytm, etc. This might give cryptocurrency firms a better idea as to how understand and position themselves in the Indian market.

Another area of research can be to study the transactions of cryptocurrencies happening *in* the country, to understand the movements and cycles of the Indian cryptocurrency and how they can be compared to that in other countries. Most importantly, research must be done to contribute to the lobbying efforts of various individuals and organizations that are tirelessly working to show the government the immense value cryptocurrencies shall unlock. This should be the main focus.

4.5 *Conclusion*

In conclusion, we can say that the cryptocurrency industry in India is at its infancy, and any steps taken now will have a long-term impact going forward. Few of these steps as outlined above are increasing the access and availability of correct knowledge of cryptocurrencies to the Indian public, the majority of which do not converse or consume content in English. After this, effort must be put to increase diversity in the cryptocurrency, this shall help get all sections of society involved which is important as cryptocurrencies are for anyone who uses money. Finally, we must focus on lobbying our government and getting them on-board. Cryptocurrencies have massive potential to disrupt the rural livelihood and make lives easier for almost everyone.

As we have seen with cell phones, while the Western world had a multi-step transition from the pager to the current smartphone, India leap-frogged directly from trunk calls to smartphones and that too successfully. Similarly, we should keep this leap-frogging potential in mind and be inspired by a future where Indians have adopted cryptocurrencies and made lives easier for 1.32 billion people.

References

Allen, S. (2015, March). Russian ministry of finance to pass anti-bitcoin law this year. Retrieved from https://cointelegraph.com/news/113766/russian-ministry-of-finance-antiBitcoin-law-will-finally-be-passed-this-year

Arias-Oliva, M., Pelegrín-Borondo, J., & Matías-Clavero, G. (2019). Variables influencing cryptocurrency use: A technology acceptance model in Spain. *Frontiers in Psychology, 10*(MAR), 1–13. https://doi.org/10.3389/fpsyg.2019.00475

Balcilar, M., Bouri, E., Gupta, R., & Roubaud, D. (2017). Can volume predict bitcoin returns and volatility? A quantiles-based approach. *Economic Modelling, 64*, 74–81.

Blau, B. M. (2017). Price dynamics and speculative trading in bitcoin. *Research in International Business and Finance, 41*, 493–499.

Bouri, E., Das, M., Gupta, R., & Roubaud, D. (2018). Spillovers between bitcoin and other assets during bear and bull markets. *Applied Economics, 50*(55), 5935–5949.

Bouri, E., Gupta, R., Lahiani, A., & Shahbaz, M. (2018). Testing for asymmetric nonlinear short- and long-run relationships between bitcoin, aggregate commodity and gold prices. *Resources Policy, 57*, 224–235.https://doi.org/10.1016/j.resourpol.2018.03.008

Brière, M., Oosterlinck, K., & Szafarz, A. (2015). Virtual currency, tangible return: Portfolio diversification with bitcoin. *Journal of Asset Management, 16*(6), 365–373.

Cheah, E. T., & Fry, J. (2015). Speculative bubbles in bitcoin markets? An empirical investigation into the fundamental value of bitcoin. *Economic Letters, 130*, 32–36.

Cheung, A., Roca, E., & Su, J. J. (2015). Crypto-currency bubbles: An application of the Phillips–Shi–Yu (2013) methodology on Mt. *Gox Bitcoin Prices. Applied Economics, 47*(23), 2348–2358.

Cryptocurrency Market. (n.d.). Retrieved from https://www.marketsandmarkets.com/Market-Reports/cryptocurrency-market-158061641.html

Cryptocurrency Statistics. (n.d.). Retrieved from https://leftronic.com/cryptocurrency-statistics/

Dutch Banking Association (2020) Crypto-assets in Dutch perspective, opportunities for a Dutch crypto-asset ecosystem https://www.nvb.nl/media/3560/nvb-crypo-assets_eng.pdf Accessed 18 Feb 2021.

Dyhrberg, A. H. (2016). Hedging capabilities of Bitcoin. Is it the virtual gold? *Finance Research Letters, 16*, 139–144.

EViews Help. (n.d.). Creating a factor object. Retrieved from https://www.eviews.com/help/helpintro.html#page/content%2Ffactanal-Creating_a_Factor_Object.html%23

Grima, S., Özdemir, L., Özen, E., & Romānova, I. (2021). The interactions between COVID-19 cases in the USA, the VIX index and major stock markets. *International Journal of Financial Studies, 9*(2), 26.

Henseler, J., Ringle, C., & Sarstedt, M. (2015). A new criterion for assessing discriminant validity in variance-based structural equation modeling. *Journal of the Academy of Marketing Science., 43*, 115–135. https://doi.org/10.1007/s11747-014-0403-8

Katsiampa, P. (2017). Volatility estimation for Bitcoin: A comparison of GARCH models. *Economic Letters, 158*, 3–6.

Kristoufek, L. (2015). Grandpa, grandpa, tell me the one about bitcoin being a safe haven: New evidence from the COVID-19 pandemic. *Frontiers in Physics, 8*, 296.

Lim, B., Hsu, E. T., Chen, P., & Levy, A. J. (2016). In two recent orders, CFTC holds that Bitcoins are commodities. *Intellectual Property & Technology Law Journal, 28*(3), 19.

Malladi, R. K., & Dheeriya, P. L. (2021). Time series analysis of cryptocurrency returns and volatilities. *Journal of Economics and Finance, 45*(1), 75–94.

Notice Number of Daily Cryptocurrency Transactions By Type 2019. (n.d.). Retrieved from https://www.statista.com/statistics/730838/number-of-daily-cryptocurrency-transactions-by-type/

Regulation of Cryptocurrency Around The World. (n.d.). Retrieved from https://www.loc.gov/law/help/cryptocurrency

Sahoo, P. K. (2020). Convergence patterns in cryptocurrency markets: Evidence from club convergence. *Global Economy Journal, 20*(04), 1–10.

Sahoo, P. K., Sethi, D., & Acharya, D. (2019). Is bitcoin a near stock? Linear and non-linear causal evidence from a price–volume relationship. *International Journal of Managerial Finance, 15*(4), 533–545.

Urquhart, A. (2016). The inefficiency of bitcoin. *Economic Letters, 148*, 80–82.

Urquhart, A. (2017). Price clustering in bitcoin. *Economic Letters, 159*, 145–148.

Venkatesh, V., Thong, J., & Xu, X. (2012). Consumer acceptance and use of information technology: Extending the unified theory of acceptance and use of technology. *MIS Quarterly, 36*, 157–178. https://doi.org/10.2307/41410412

Impact of AI on Accounting Practices in Saudi Arabia

Azeem Ahmad Khan, Seraj Bahrawe, and Sarfaraz Javed

1 Introduction

According to a study, professionals are increasingly utilizing automation to enhance the efficacy and effectiveness of their routine weekly tasks. Accounting information systems began to supplant paper journals and ledgers with computer-based forms when computers were first introduced. Eventually, these technologies evolved into computer-based forms. In the majority of instances, accounting databases are transformed into vast warehouses that only contain a restricted quantity of information on accounting operations and fail to meet the requirements of decision-making authorities. This is the case in the vast preponderance of instances.

A. A. Khan · S. Bahrawe
Department of Accounting, College of Business, Al-Baha University, Al-Baha, Kingdom of Saudi Arabia
e-mail: a.khan@bu.edu.sa

S. Bahrawe
e-mail: sbahrawi@bu.edu.sa

S. Javed (✉)
Department of Accounting and Finance Faculty of Business, Sohar University, Sohar, Sultanate of Oman
e-mail: sjaved@su.edu.om

© The Author(s), under exclusive license to Springer Nature Singapore Pte Ltd. 2025

A. S. et al. (eds.), *Trends and Challenges of Electronic Finance*,
https://doi.org/10.1007/978-981-96-3304-3_24

To solve conventional system issues, AI creates sentient computers that behave like humans. This is done to create a more favorable environment. Due to the occurrence of unforeseen events, certain corporate organizations are unable to effectively manage complex events in their process management software. This poses an issue for numerous of these organizations. The function of artificial intelligence systems is to assume the responsibility of making systematic decisions on behalf of individuals, thereby significantly improving the quality of business judgments. It is essential for the profession to address fundamental commercial challenges and implement new technology approaches in order to achieve this advancement.

Shukla and Jaiswal (2013) define artificial intelligence (AI) as the study and development of intelligent computer systems. The term "artificial intelligence" is employed to denote the development of intelligent computer systems. According to Carol and O'Leary (2017), artificial intelligence (AI) is a powerful technology that has the potential to more effectively address human and corporate issues than humans. The application necessitates that the user select an option from a predetermined list of options, with the selection being made in accordance with a series of logical procedures, as per Ahmadi et al. (2019). The user is obligated to make the selection. Essentially, artificial intelligence is the process by which a computer is capable of performing operations that are typically conducted by the human brain (Kumar & Thakur 2012). In the paper he published in 2017, Greenman contends that the advancement of AI significantly facilitates the development of professionals like accounting professional and auditing. Computers and software have replaced paper and pencil in accounting (Greenman, 2017). Particularly in accounting, AI has advanced significantly in recent years. The most significant applications of artificial intelligence in accounting have been the auditing and reporting of financial transactions over the course of more than 25 years.

2 Literature Review and Analysis of Related Work

2.1 AI

AI can be defined as a machine that simulates a human and learns by observation (Morgan & Mates, 2021). Machine learning (ML), on the other hand, is the capacity to learn to accomplish jobs in the same manner that humans do, such as statistical programmers. Big data, which concentrates on the volume, velocity, and diversity of data collected, is used to train machines to learn and subsequently develop correct ML models. According to this, AI is an extension of ML, and extensive data analysis is a precursor and foundation for ML and AI (Chandra, 2023). AI refers to computerized systems that collect data in order to complete the tasks of intelligent humans and enhance their chances of accomplishment. A machine with strong AI has consciousness and a cognitive system, as well as intelligence in more than one domain. Weak AI (Narrow AI) is task-specific (autonomous vehicles are a perfect illustration of Narrow AI).

According to Rosenberg (2016), based on the Constellation study, looking at investment in all areas of the market, there would be an investment in AI of more than 100 billion euros per year in 2025, compared to only 2 billion in 2015. AI is a branch of computer science that aims to create computer systems that can intelligently replicate human-like behavior. A machine performing a task, compared to a human, is considered intelligent. In the commercial setting, AI, particularly ML, can be defined as the constantly decreasing cost of forecasting (Merilehto 2024). Because the concept of AI varies by respondent, it is usually referred to as intelligent code rather than AI. The demand for AI research is motivated by two factors: (i) giving novices to the field with knowledge of the essential arrangement of the AI literature Patel-Schneider and Sebastiani (2003), and Zanuttini (2003) and (ii) increased desire for AI, which has resulted in considerable investments in AI infrastructures and increased interest in the subject.

2.2 AI Functioning in Accountancy

AI, big data, and cloud have become the key components of the Industry 4.0 era over the past years. According to Greenman (2017), an emerging trend has reduced the demand for some jobs and significantly highlighted the possibility of changing business structures. According to PwC's Global Industry 4.0 Survey (2016), efforts to migrate to Industry 4.0 will have significant positive effects on a variety of fronts, including lowering expenses, enhanced productivity, and increased profit. AI capabilities like Deep Learning (DL) and Robotic Process Automation (RPA), for instance, will significantly boost computer processing capacity. A task that once required much time can now be finished quickly (Frey & Osborne, 2017).

The PwC Global Industry 4.0 Survey. Two thousand sixteen reports that these new technologies have already influenced many different industries. The Fourth Industrial Revolution resulted in the application of information technology in production as well as services in the private sector, according to Piccarozzi et al.'s (2018) analysis of management literature on the subject of Industry 4.0. Nevertheless, this same study found that when technology develops, some jobs are lost while others are created (Robson, 1992). It suggests that AI would improve the efficiency of accounting services by lessening the strict, time-consuming, and arduous nature of the field.

2.3 AI in Saudi Arabia

Modern marketing technologies make artificial intelligence very essential for business growth. Companies from Saudi Arabia are facing marketing-related issues. AI simplifies data storage. Marketing-related issues are troubling Saudi Arabian companies. Artificial intelligence facilitates data storage. Structurally related and very important are knowledge management, decision support, artificial intelligence, and data warehouses. Enabling numerous corporate operations, including marketing activities, artificial intelligence has the capacity to improve business performance and boost effective corporate management (Nemati et al., 2002).

2.4 AI Adoption in Accounting Practices

Financial institutions are also implementing comparable strategies to assess the financial requirements and creditworthiness of their consumers. This has led to an additional rise in customer satisfaction, as the accessibility of financial products, such as loans that can be repaid in a matter of minutes, has been simplified. In addition to contributing to an overall improvement in the trustworthiness of financial institutions, these initiatives have also led to a decrease in the percentage of defaults. Artificial intelligence (AI) technology is being increasingly integrated into the financial sector of the Kingdom of Saudi Arabia. In contrast, the financial institutions of the nation are encountering substantial challenges in the implementation of their concepts.

Artificial intelligence technologies have the potential to revolutionize the financial sector by improving the overall client experience, reducing expenditures, and increasing efficiency. This could be accomplished through a variety of methods. In contrast, they introduce new risks and disadvantages that require a comprehensive analysis. Artificial intelligence's capacity to manage immense quantities of data and provide insights that humans would be unable to discern is one of its most significant benefits to the financial industry. This data facilitates the training of machine learning algorithms, which will subsequently be capable of predicting future actions. Another advantage of artificial intelligence is its ability to automate processes and activities that are repetitive or regular. Two examples of technology that fall into this category are chatbots and robo-advisors. These technologies have the ability to promptly and precisely respond to client requests, thereby enabling humans to concentrate on more difficult duties (Mishra & Guru Sant, 2021).

Furthermore, artificial intelligence-based technologies facilitate the identification of fraudulent activities and the management of risks (Fares et al., 2022). Artificial intelligence influencing data analysis and customer experience real-time analysis of massive data sets by artificial intelligence is revolutionizing to allow speedier identification of harmful behavior. This quick identification is very important for financial companies as it directly relates to preserving reputation and minimizing prospective damages. The interrelated nature of these components highlights the requirement of efficient artificial intelligence implementations. By permitting unique interactions made possible by virtual assistants and chatbots, artificial intelligence is also enhancing consumer experiences. These technologies might provide recommendations precisely suited to individual preferences, therefore enhancing degrees of enjoyment and loyalty.

2.5 *The Financial Industry AI Integration in KSA*

Automating repetitive tasks, improving efficiency, and providing better knowledge of consumer behavior, artificial intelligence is radically altering the global banking industry. This tendency is particularly evident in the Kingdom of Saudi Arabia (KSA), as the banking sector fast adopts artificial intelligence technologies. This shift catches a more widespread global movement toward integration of financial technologies.

Focusing on how AI, along with blockchain technology, cloud computing, and data security, is being introduced into Islamic banking, a 2022 study by Swain and Gochhait examined how Middle Eastern financial institutions are being impacted. Based on their literature review, cloud computing has seen substantial growth—especially during the epidemic—because of its high data security features throughout collection, storage, and analysis. The article addressed how cloud computing may enhance the infrastructure of Islamic financial institutions.

Moreover, Saudi banks are increasingly using AI-driven technologies to improve the quality of their offerings. The Saudi National Bank (SNB) has put up artificial intelligence-powered chatbots for 24/7 customer support and fraud detection systems that review user transactions. These advances reveal a growing ambition to integrate artificial intelligence in ways that increase operational efficiency and customer satisfaction. 2020 study on the use of natural language processing and machine learning to improve customer experiences, streamline processes, and boost risk management in financial institutions by AlQudah and Shaalan exposed. Still, the industry faces challenges as Al-Ghamdi and Al-Shehri (2020) have shown: a lack of AI professionals is a key impediment to effective AI adoption.

2.6 Challenges in AI Acceptance Applied in Systems of Accounting

Saudi Arabia's quick development of artificial intelligence in the financial sector raises certain problems that want attention. Since artificial intelligence cannot be generally accepted in the financial industry, one of the main problems is the shortage of qualified professionals in this field. AlBarrak et al. (2020) noted that correctly combining these technologies largely requires AI expertise deficient in availability. This scenario is aggravated by the increased need for artificial intelligence skills in sectors like energy and healthcare.

Ourdani and Chrayah (2022) underline, however, significant challenges to the expansion of big data projects, including budgetary constraints and technological knowledge, stressing the promise of big data analytics to offer value, maximize resources, and stop public financial misbehavior.

Including artificial intelligence raises various challenges for Saudi financial institutions, among which the substantial outlay for the necessary infrastructure. Making the required considerable hardware, software, and other resource investments Alotaibi and Alshehri (2023) said would be challenging for smaller universities. Moreover, aggravating these costs is maintenance for artificial intelligence systems.

Still another major issue is data accessibility and quality. Many financial firms fight with fragmented data and organizational silos, which hinder the collection of high-quality data needed for training artificial intelligence algorithms (Kshetri, 2021). Moreover in demand are legal solutions ensuring ethical use of artificial intelligence. Openness in artificial intelligence applications and well-defined policies create regulatory challenges that must be addressed if responsible AI deployment in the banking sector is to be encouraged.

2.7 Empirical Reviews

Muhammad and associates looked at how artificial intelligence may affect accounting moving forward in 2020. The research aims to look at how artificial intelligence-based technologies affect accounting, address the issue of how they have altered the surroundings of accounting practitioners, and provide relevant advice to legislative authorities. The study consists on the conclusions of a qualitative document analysis on artificial intelligence used in the area of accounting. The research claims that an artificial intelligence-based automated solution may handle the main problems that practicing accountants deal with. Accountants have to adjust to the always shifting corporate environment as well as the use of information technology in order to prevent this result. It has been argued that accountants and accounting companies should be continually informed of continuous artificial intelligence innovations in their sector if they are to increase the efficacy and performance of their operations. Eventually, by focusing accountants on data-driven, analytics-based judgments rather than current arduous procedures, this would result in a drop in the accounting expenditures of the organization and raise the value of the accounting field. Das (2021) studied how artificial intelligence affected banking. AITO may enable accountants to evaluate their companies, increase their efficiency, and provide additional insight. The aim of the research is to examine, using artificial intelligence, accounting process performance, and utilizing secondary data. The study stresses how strongly the use of artificial intelligence affects the management of accounting tasks. The research argues that in the fundamental ideas of artificial intelligence, accountants should thrive by means of enhancing their style of excellence and converting into complete specialists, thus minimizing certain accounting charges. This is the situation should experts in accounting, auditing, and artificial intelligence fail to coordinate and collaborate to guarantee the continuation of their respective fields.

In their 2018 study, Zehong and Zheng said that greater value expert judgment produced by massive data mining and analysis replaces challenging core accounting chores by artificial intelligence systems. Their general acceptance clarifies the reason for the slow declining need for accountants. For accountants, quitting their positions so becomes difficult.

From the previous review of literature, the researchers formulated the objectives of this study.

1. To assess the present state of AI adoption in AP in Saudi Arabia.
2. To examine the challenges encountered in the integration of AI in AP in the Saudi Arabian
3. To assess the impact of AI on the accuracy of financial reporting, fraud detection, and financial decision-making in Saudi Arabia.

In order to achieve the above objectives, the researchers formulated the few hypotheses for the study.

$H0_1$: There is no significant impact of the adoption of AI in AP on financial decision-making processes.

$H0_2$: Challenges encountered in the integration of AI do not significantly impact financial decision-making processes.

$H0_3$: Financial reporting and fraud detection using AI do not have a significant impact on financial decision-making processes.

3 Research Methodology

3.1 *Conceptual Framework*

Figure 1 presents the conceptual framework of this chapter.

3.2 *Research Design and Methodology*

Descriptive survey research techniques were used in this paper. Mostly used in scientific research, this method involves observing and evaluating data from individuals without compromising data quality. Descriptive survey research addresses questions of what, when, and how certain traits of a group, community, or population evolve by methods of

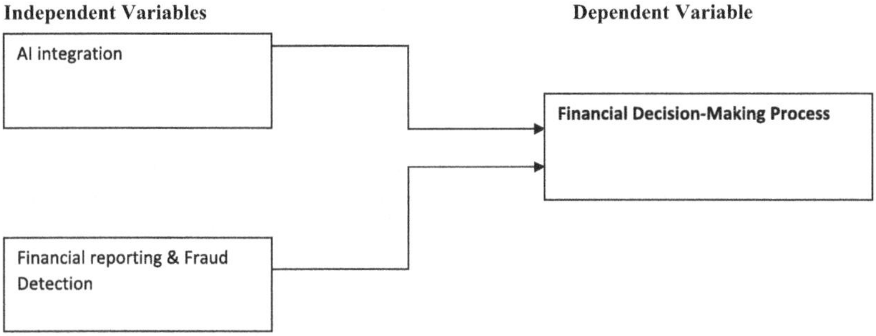

Fig. 1 Conceptual framework

information collecting, therefore helping to determine the properties of a population. Most of this research comprises Saudi Arabian financial analysts, accountants, and IT professionals. Methodologies for intentional sampling enabled the selection of 150 total respondents.

Method of research: Approach of data gathering a questionnaire consisted of three sections that served to compile the primary information. The first section addressed the socio-demographic characteristics of the respondents. The second section included statistics about AP Saudi Arabia's current embrace of artificial intelligence. The first section addressed how artificial intelligence affects financial reporting, fraud detection, and financial decision-making in Saudi Arabia; the third section compiled data on the challenges of adding artificial intelligence into accounting techniques, quite fervently then agree (5), disagree (1). On the five-point Likert scale, there was very great variation of responses. This study used strategies of purposive sampling.

The validity of the research instrument evaluates the features under study. The research supervisor checked it before the participants received their study tool. Analysis of the obtained questionnaire data was done using SPSS version 23.0. The socio-demographic features of the respondents were investigated using descriptive statistics; three hypotheses were tested using multiple regression analysis and Pearson correlation.

4 Results

4.1 Data Analysis

Table 1 shows that the sample's gender distribution shows a male dominance with 62.0% males and 38.0% females, raising concerns about potential gender bias and its impact on the generalizability of the findings, especially regarding technology adoption and workplace challenges. The age distribution indicates that 70% of respondents are young adults between 18 and 35 years, reflecting the growing participation of younger professionals in accounting, IT, and finance. However, the limited representation of those under 18 and over 35 may neglect the insights of more experienced professionals on AI integration.

Educationally, the majority of respondents hold bachelor's degrees (46.7%) or professional qualifications (39.3%), indicating a well-qualified sample likely to provide informed opinions on AI adoption. Nonetheless, the small number of respondents with diplomas (5.3%) or postgraduate degrees (8.7%) suggests the need for a more balanced representation across different education levels to capture a broader range of perspectives.

Table 1
Socio-Demographic characteristics of respondents

Gender of Respondents	*Frequency*	*Percent*
Male	93	62.0
Female	57	38.0
Age		
Less than 18 years	22	14.7
18–25 years	50	33.3
26–35 years	55	36.7
36–45 years	23	15.3
Education		
Diploma	8	5.3
Professional	59	39.3
Bachelor's	70	46.7
Postgraduate	13	8.7
Area of Specialization		
Accounting	61	40.7
Information Technology	52	34.7
Finance	37	24.7
Total	**150**	**100.0**

In terms of specialization, the majority are in accounting (40.7%), followed by information technology (34.7%), and finance (24.7%). This distribution, while aligned with the study's focus, may skew findings toward accounting-related issues, potentially overlooking crucial technological and financial insights necessary for a comprehensive understanding of AI adoption in these fields.

From Fig. 2, the level of familiarity with AI in AP was high, as 62.7% of the respondents claimed that they were familiar with AI in accounting processes, while 37.3% claimed that they were not familiar with it. This implies that most of the respondents are familiar with AI in accounting processes in Saudi Arabia.

Figure 3 shows that 35.3% of the respondents claimed that their organization currently makes use of AI in their accounting processes, while 64.7% claimed that their organization does not make use of AI in its accounting processes. This implies that the majority of organizations in Saudi Arabia have not integrated AI into their accounting processes.

Based on the challenges encountered in AI integration in accounting practices, the tendency of losing jobs had the highest mean score (X = 1.97, SD = 0.90), followed by AI integration into existing accounting systems and procedures being a daunting task with mean (X = 1.89, SD = 0.82) and knowledge gap of skills in AI among accounting professionals (X = 1.58, SD = 1.14) (refer Table 2). This implies that the top three challenges encountered in AI integration in AP are the tendency

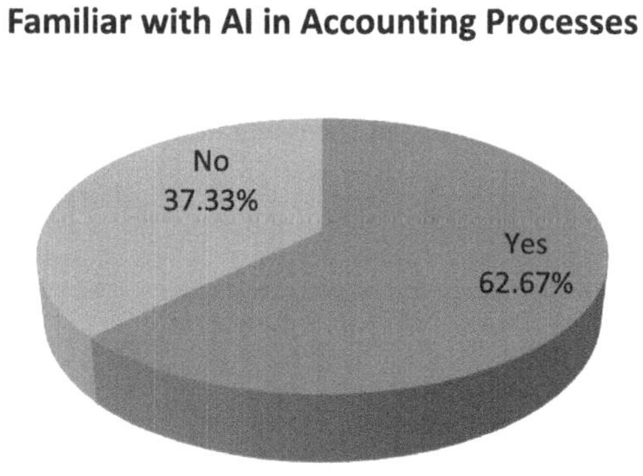

Fig. 2 Familiarity with AI in accounting practices

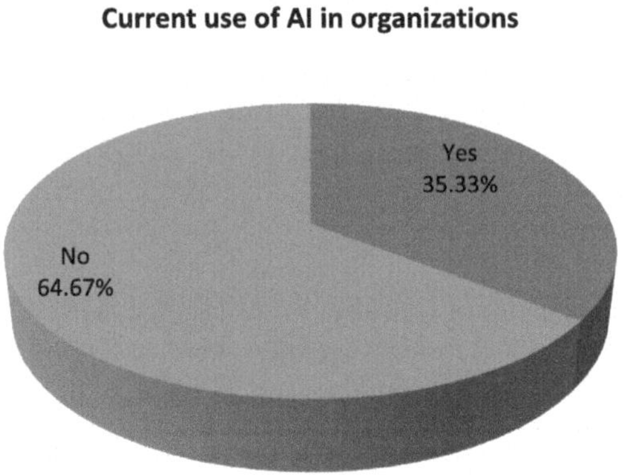

Fig. 3 Use of AI in accounting processes

to lose jobs, AI integration into existing accounting systems and procedures being a daunting task and the knowledge gap of skills in AI among accounting professionals.

***$H0_1$*: There is no significant relationship between the adoption of AI in AP and financial decision-making processes.**

Hypothesis one was tested using Pearson correlation (refer Table 3). The result revealed a positive significant correlation between the adoption of AI and the financial decision-making process ($r = 0.839$, $p <$

Table 2 Challenges encountered in the integration of AI

ITEMS	*Mean*	*Standard Deviation*
Data protection, security, and privacy concerns are some of the significant challenges encountered in the adoption of AI in accounting practices	1.52	0.61
There is a knowledge gap in skills in AI among accounting professionals	1.58	1.14
Integrating AI into existing accounting systems and procedures can be a daunting task	1.89	0.82
Integrating AI into AP might make professionals in the field lose their jobs	1.97	0.90

0.05). This implies that the adoption of AI in the accounting process will improve the financial decision-making process in Saudi Arabia.

$H0_2$: **Challenges encountered in the integration of AI do not significantly impact financial decision-making processes. Hypothesis two was tested using Multiple Regression Analysis.**

The result showed that challenges encountered in the integration of AI (data protection, knowledge gap, AI integration being a daunting task, and loss of jobs) significantly impacted financial decision-making processes ($R^2 = 0.280$, F (4, 149) = 14.093; $p < 0.05$) (refer Table 4). This implies that challenges encountered in the integration of AI (data protection, knowledge gap, AI integration being a daunting task, and loss of jobs) jointly accounted for about 28.0% of the variance observable in financial decision-making processes in Saudi Arabia (refer Table 5). The result of the coefficient of multiple determination for the model showed that data protection and loss of jobs were positively significant ($\beta = 0.456$, $t = 5.799$; $p < 0.05$) and ($\beta = 0.012$, $t = 0.152$; $p < 0.05$) while knowledge gap and AI integration being a daunting task were not significant (refer Table 6).

$H0_3$: Quality Financial reporting and fraud detection using AI do not have a significant impact on financial decision-making processes. Hypothesis three was tested using Multiple Regression Analysis.

Table 3 Pearson correlations of adoption of AI and financial

		Financial Decision-Making	*Adoption of AI*
Financial decision-making	Pearson Correlation	1	0.839**
	Sig. (two-tailed)		0.000
	N	150	150
Adoption of AI	Pearson Correlation	0.839**	1
	Sig. (two-tailed)	0.000	
	N	150	150

**Correlation is significant at the 0.01 level (two-tailed)

R (0.492): The correlation coefficient (refer Table 7) indicates a moderately positive relationship between the predictors (financial reports, fraud detection) and the dependent variable (financial decision-making). *R* Square (0.242): This indicates that approximately 24.2% of the variance

Table 4 Model summary loss of jobs, knowledge gap, data protection, AI integration

Model	*R*	*R Square*	*Adjusted R Square*	*Std. Error of the Estimate*
1	0.529[a]	0.280	0.260	0.607

[a]Predictors: (Constant), loss of jobs, knowledge gap, data protection, AI integration

Table 5 ANOVA (financial decision-making, loss of jobs, knowledge gap, data protection, AI integration)

Model		*Sum of Squares*	*df*	*Mean Square*	*F*	*Sig*
1	Regression	20.755	4	5.189	14.093	0.000[b]
	Residual	53.385	145	0.368		
	Total	74.140	149			

[a]Dependent Variable: Financial decision-making
[b]Predictors: (Constant), loss of jobs, knowledge gap, data protection, AI integration

Table 6 Coefficients (financial decision-making, loss of jobs, knowledge gap, data protection, AI integration)

Model		*Unstandardized Coefficients*		*Standardized Coefficients*		
		B	*Std. Error*	*Beta*	*t*	*Sig.*
1	(Constant)	0.829	0.177		4.699	0.000
	Data protection	0.528	0.091	0.456	5.799	0.000
	Knowledge gap	−0.021	0.044	−0.034	−0.477	0.634
	AI integration	0.107	0.072	0.125	1.497	0.137
	Loss of jobs	0.009	0.061	0.012	0.152	0.029

[a]Dependent Variable: Financial decision-making

in financial decision-making can be explained by the predictors. Adjusted R Square (0.232): This value adjusts the R Square for the number of predictors in the model, slightly lower than the R Square, which accounts for the degree of freedom. It suggests a relatively moderate fit of the model. Std. Error of the Estimate (0.618): This value measures the accuracy of predictions. A lower standard error indicates more precise predictions.

The sum of squares (Regression: 17.943, Residual: 56.197, Total: 74.140): These values measure the variation explained by the model and the residual error not explained by the model. df (Degrees of Freedom: Regression: 2, Residual: 147, Total: 149): These values indicate the number of independent pieces of information involved in estimating parameters and assessing the model (refer Table 8).

Mean Square (Regression: 8.971, Residual: 0.382): Mean squares are obtained by dividing the sum of squares by the corresponding degrees of freedom. F (23.468): This is the F-statistic, which tests if the overall regression model is a good fit for the data. Sig. (0.000): The p-value is less than 0.05, indicating that the regression model significantly predicts the dependent variable.

Table 9 provides the coefficients of the regression equation and their significance. (Constant: $B = 1.011$, Std. Error = 0.174, $t = 5.799$, Sig.

Table 7 Model summary financial reports, fraud detection

Model	*R*	*R Square*	*Adjusted R Square*	*Std. Error of the Estimate*
1	0.492[a]	0.242	0.232	0.618

[a]Predictors: (Constant), financial reports, fraud detection

Table 8 ANOVA (financial decision-making, financial reports, and fraud detection)

Model		*Sum of Squares*	*df*	*Mean square*	*F*	*Sig*
1	Regression	17.943	2	8.971	23.468	0.000[b]
	Residual	56.197	147	0.382		
	Total	74.140	149			

[a]Dependent variable: financial decision-making
b. Predictors: (Constant), financial reports, fraud detection

Table 9 Coefficients (financial decision-making, financial reports, and fraud detection)

Model		*Unstandardized Coefficients*		*Standardized Coefficients*	*t*	*Sig.*
		B	*Std. Error*	*Beta*		
1	(Constant)	1.011	0.174		5.799	0.000
	Fraud detection	0.567	0.083	0.490	6.820	0.000
	Financial reports	−0.029	0.050	−0.041	−0.570	0.569

[a]Dependent variable: Financial decision-making

= 0.000): The constant term of the regression equation is significant, indicating that the baseline level of financial decision-making (when other factors are zero) is 1.011. Fraud detection (B = 0.567, Std. Error = 0.083, Beta = 0.490, t = 6.820, Sig. = 0.000): The coefficient for fraud detection is significant. It suggests that an increase in fraud detection by one unit leads to an increase in financial decision-making by 0.567 units. The high t-value and low p-value indicate strong evidence against the null hypothesis, affirming the predictor's significance. Financial reports (B = – 0.029, Std. Error = 0.050, Beta = – 0.041, t = – 0.570, Sig. = 0.569): The coefficient for financial reports is not significant, as indicated by the high p-value. This suggests that changes in financial reports do not significantly impact financial decision-making in the model.

5 Conclusion

5.1 Conclusions and Implications

The ANOVA analysis reveals that the combination of financial reporting and fraud detection greatly affects financial decision-making. Among these variables, only fraud detection has a significant positive effect; so, it is rather important to improve fraud detection if one wants to improve financial choices. On the other hand, financial data expose no statistically significant impact. This outcome underlines the requirement of robust fraud detection systems in developing financial decisions; the influence of financial reporting is somewhat less.

The paper also highlighted many challenges like job displacement risk, difficulty modifying present systems, and lack of AI awareness among accounting professionals in incorporating artificial intelligence into accounting. These findings support the findings of Zehong and Zheng (2018), who saw a decline in demand for accountants brought on by artificial intelligence's growing impact on the industry, therefore casting doubts on work security. Likewise, Greenman (2017) suggested that this inclination would lead demand for certain roles to drop and organizational structures to change.

Furthermore, the studies revealed a strong positive association between the adoption of artificial intelligence and financial decision-making practices, suggesting that incorporation of AI might help Saudi Arabia to make better decisions. The challenges of artificial intelligence integration include data security, knowledge gaps, and employment losses also profoundly affect these operations. Moreover greatly affecting the variety in financial decision-making in Saudi Arabia is the use of artificial intelligence for fraud detection and financial reporting accuracy assurance.

Apart from simplifying accounting tasks, artificial intelligence makes a big difference in the discipline. Artificial intelligence systems will most likely acquire ever more complex decision-making duty for various services as they develop more sophisticated, maybe replacing people in certain sectors. Still, extremely human traits such as imagination, empathy, and leadership cannot be replaced by artificial intelligence.

5.2 Recommendations

Artificial intelligence might transform accounting by means of enhanced accuracy, productivity, and decision-making. Effective use of artificial intelligence, however, depends on large investment, extensive training, a willingness to embrace new technologies, and the development of properly defined regulatory frameworks. The given recommendtion will help professional of accounting section in Saudi Arabia.

If the Saudi government seeks to simplify challenging accounting tasks, artificial intelligence technology should be first focus for investment. This investment will enable accountants to focus on more strategic operations from human mistake, decrease human error, and improve financial reporting accuracy and efficiency. Very important are training and development programs giving accountants the capabilities to integrate artificial intelligence into their jobs. This would ensure effective use of artificial intelligence technology by motivating professionalism and innovation in the sector.

Companies and accountants should be willing to use artificial intelligence to increase production and save costs. AI speeding operations and enhancing services like real-time financial analysis, predictive analytics, and fraud detection follow from more customer delight and competitiveness. Strong legislative mechanisms covering ethical usage of artificial intelligence in accounting should be developed by policymakers. Emphasizing data privacy, security, and transparency, these models should help to build trust among interested parties and assure ethical artificial intelligence use. Advancement of artificial intelligence in accounting relies on collaboration among technical enterprises, accounting firms, and academic organizations. The field will be progressed much further by means of AI-driven tools and methods created via cooperative research. Constant research will also help to identify and fix any artificial intelligence integration issues.

References

Ahmadi, M., Jafarzadeh-Ghoushchi, S., Taghizadeh, R., & Sharifi, A. (2019). Presentation of a new hybrid approach for forecasting economic growth using artificial intelligence approaches. *Neural Computing and Applications, 31*(12), 8661–8680.

Albarrak, M. A., Altwaijri, N. T., & Alghamdi, S. A. (2020). AI in the financial sector: A review of Saudi Arabia. In *Proceedings of the 2020 IEEE/ACS 17th International Conference on Computer Systems and Applications (AICCSA)*, Antalya, Turkey, 2–5 November 2020 (pp. 1–6).

Al-Ghamdi, R. A., & Al-Shehri, M. T. (2020). The role of AI in enhancing the quality of financial services: The case of Saudi Arabia. *Journal of Financial Services Marketing, 25*, 1–12.

Alotaibi, N. S., & Alshehri, A. H. (2023). Prospects and obstacles in using AI in Saudi Arabian higher education institutions—The potential of AI-based learning outcomes. *Sustainability, 15*, 10723.

Carol, E. B., & O'Leary, D. (2017). Introduction to artificial intelligence and export system; 2013. *Retrieved on, 6*(10).

Chandra, V. S. (2023). Role of artificial intelligence in indian agriculture: A review. *Agricultural Reviews, 44*(4), 558–562.

Das, P. K. (2021). Impact of AI on accounting. *Sumerianz Journal of Economics and Finance, 4*(1), 17–24.

Fares, O. H., Butt, I., & Lee, S. H. M. (2022). Utilization of AI in the banking sector: A systematic literature review. *Journal of Financial Services Marketing*, 1–18.

Frey, C. B., & Osborne, M. A. (2017). The future of employment: How susceptible are jobs to computerisation? *Technological Forecasting and Social Change, 114*, 254–280.

Greenman, C. (2017). Exploring the impact of AI on the accounting profession. *Journal of Research in Business, Economics and Management, 8*(3), 1451.

Kshetri, N. (2021). The role of AI in promoting financial inclusion in developing countries. *Journal of Global Information Technology Management, 24*, 1–6.

Kumar, K., & Thakur, G. S. M. (2012). Advanced applications of neural networks and artificial intelligence: A review. *International journal of information technology and computer science, 4*(6), 57–68.

Merilehto, J. (2024). On Generative Artificial Intelligence: Open-Source is the Way. *SocArXiv, March, 13.*

Mishra, P., & Guru Sant, T. (2021). Role of AI and internet of things in promoting banking and financial services during COVID-19: Pre and post effect. In *Proceedings of the 2021 5th International Conference on Information Systems and Computer Networks (ISCON 2021)*, Mathura, India, 22–23 October 2021; Institute of Electrical and Electronics Engineers Inc., New York, NY, USA.

Mohammad, S. J., Hamad, A. K., Borgi, H., Thu, P. A., Sial, M. S., & Alhadidi, A. A. (2020). How AI changes the future of accounting industry. *International Journal of Economics and Business Administration, 8*(3).

Morgan, M. B., & Mates, J. L. (2021). Applications of artificial intelligence in breast imaging. *Radiologic Clinics, 59*(1), 139–148.

Nemati, D. M., Steiger, L. S., Iyer, L., & Herschel, R. T. (2002). Knowledge warehouse: An architectural integration of knowledge management, decision support, AI and data warehousing. *Decision Support Systems, 33*, 143–161.

Ourdani, N., & Chrayah, M. (2022). Big data and public finance sector. In *Proceedings of the 2022 International Conference on Intelligent Systems and Computer Vision (ISCV 2022)*, Fez, Morocco, 18–20 May 2022; Institute of Electrical and Electronics Engineers Inc., New York, NY, USA.

Patel-Schneider, P. F., & Sebastiani, R. (2003). A new general method to generate random modal formulae for testing decision procedures. *Journal of Artificial Intelligence Research, 18*, 351 389.

Piccarozzi, M., Aquilani, B., & Gatti, C. (2018). Industry 4.0 in management studies: A systematic literature review. *Sustainability, 10*(10), 3821.

PwC. (2016). Global Industry 4.0 Survey. Retrieved September 24, 2020, from http://www.pwc.com/gx/en/industries/industry-4.0.html

Robson, K. (1992). Accounting numbers as "inscription": Action at a distance and the development of accounting. *Accounting, Organizations and Society, 17*(7), 685–708.

Rosenberg, L. (2016, March). Artificial Swarm Intelligence, a Human-in-the-loop approach to AI. In *Proceedings of the AAAI conference on artificial intelligence* (Vol. 30, No. 1).

Shukla Shubhendu, S., & Vijay, J. (2013). Applicability of artificial intelligence in different fields of life. *International Journal of Scientific Engineering and Research, 1*(1), 28–35.

Swain, S., & Gochhait, S. (2022). ABCD technology—AI, blockchain, cloud computing and data security in Islamic banking sector. In *Proceedings of the 2022 International Conference on Sustainable Islamic Business and Finance (SIBF 2022)*, Sakhir, Bahrain, 11–12 October 2022; Institute of Electrical and Electronics Engineers Inc., New York, NY, USA (pp. 58–62).

Zanuttini, B. (2003). New polynomial classes for logic-based abduction. *Journal of Artificial Intelligence Research, 19*, 1-10.

Zehong, L., & Zheng, L. (2018). The impact of AI on accounting. In *Proceedings of the 2018 4th International Conference on Social Science and Higher Education (ICSSHE 2018)*, Sanya, China.

Index

© The Editor(s) (if applicable) and The Author(s), under exclusive licence to Springer Nature Singapore Pte. Ltd 2025
A. S. et al. (eds.), *Trends and Challenges of Electronic Finance*, https://doi.org/10.1007/978-981-96-3304-3

The manufacturer's authorised representative in the EU is Springer Nature Customer Service Centre GmbH, Europaplatz 3, 69115 Heidelberg, Germany. If you have any concerns regarding our products, please contact ProductSafety@springernature.com

Printed and bound by CPI Group (UK) Ltd, Croydon, CR0 4YY

01/10/2026

02225912-0017